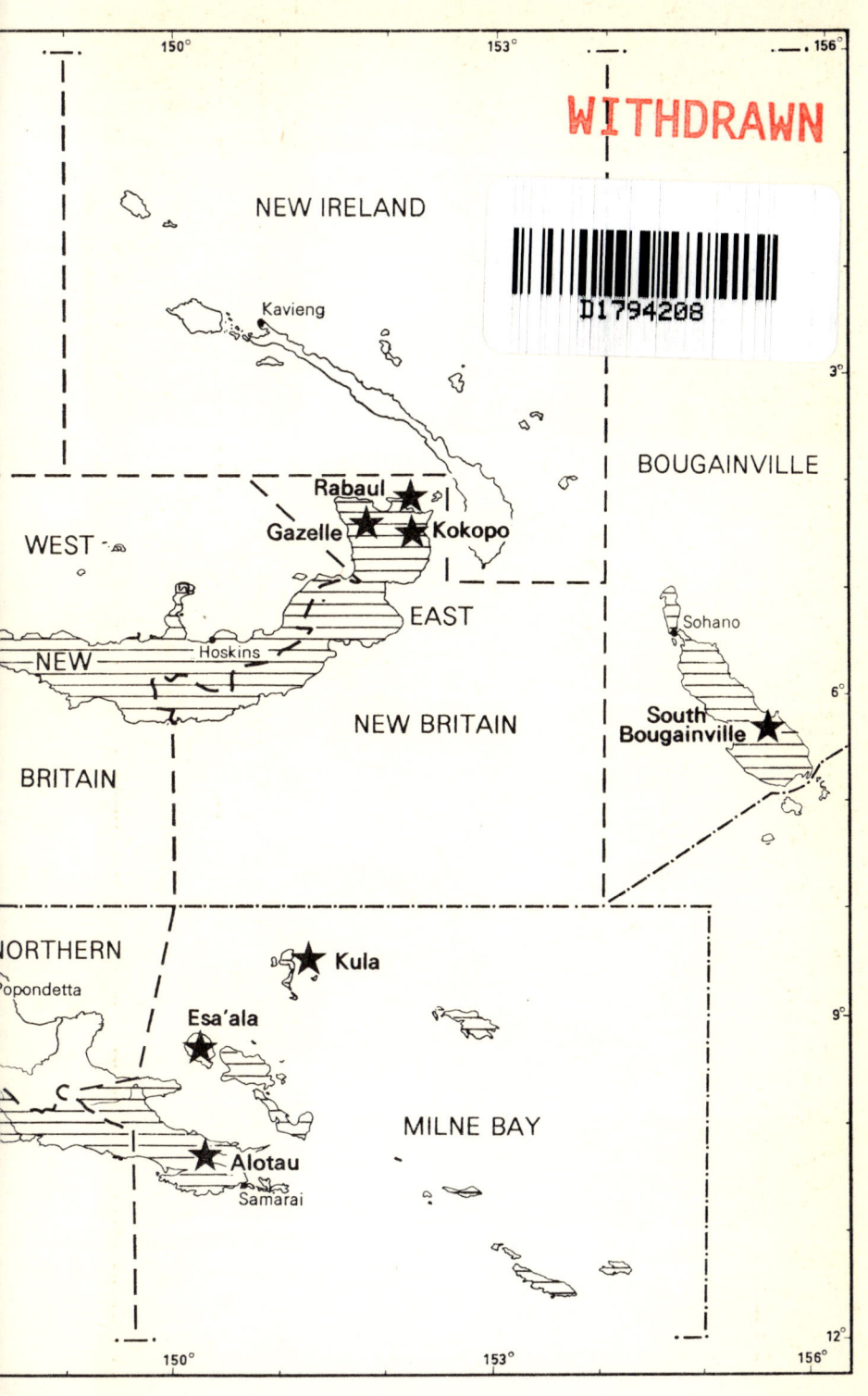

The Politics of Dependence

THE POLITICS OF DEPENDENCE

PAPUA NEW GUINEA 1968

A. L. Epstein
R. S. Parker and Marie Reay
Editors

AUSTRALIAN NATIONAL UNIVERSITY PRESS
CANBERRA 1971

© A. L. Epstein, R. S. Parker and Marie Reay 1971

This book is copyright. Apart from any fair dealing for the purposes of private study, research, criticism, or review, as permitted under the Copyright Act, no part may be reproduced by any process without written permission. Inquiries should be made to the publisher.

Registered in Australia for transmission by post as a book

National Library of Australia Card no. and ISBN 0 7081 0188 7
Library of Congress Catalog Card no. 76-163706

Printed in Australia by Hogbin, Poole (Printers) Pty Ltd, Sydney

CONTENTS

Introduction	page 1
1 THE CONTEXT OF POLITICAL CHANGE R. S. Parker and Edward P. Wolfers	12
2 UNDER THE VOLCANO Ann Chowning, A. L. and T. S. Epstein, Jane Goodale and Ian Grosart	48
3 PERSONALITIES VERSUS POLICIES Olga Gostin, W. Tomasetti, and M. W. Young	91
4 CHARISMA AND RACE Eugene Ogan	132
5 CASH CROPS OR CARGO? T. G. Harding and P. Lawrence	162
6 FREE ELECTIONS IN A GUIDED DEMOCRACY H. K. and Peta Colebatch, Marie Reay, and A. J. Strathern	218
7 A TOWN AND ITS HINTERLAND Murray Groves, R. M. S. Hamilton, and Margaret McArthur	275
8 FROM DEPENDENCE TO AUTONOMY? R. S. Parker	315
I Research teams and planning committee	361
II Briefing document for research workers	364
III Summary of candidates and results	370
IV Political education—sample leaflets	371
References	376
Index	381

TABLES

1	Distribution of preferences in two ballot boxes in Rabaul Open	page 84
2	The election results in New Britain	89
3	The election results in Milne Bay	130
4	The election results in Bougainville	161
5	Candidates: Madang Regional and component Open electorates	174
6	Campaign Teams: Madang Regional and Open Electorates	184
7	Informal voting in Madang electorates	195
8	Distribution of first preference votes by area, Kabwum Open Electorate	210
9	Degree of local support, Kabwum	212
10	The election results on the North-east Coast	216
11	Location of candidates' majorities, Wahgi Open	253
12	Mul-Dei Open candidates	256
13	Percentages of single preferences in each candidate's vote, Western Highlands Regional	262
14	Localisation of candidates' support, Western Highlands Regional	265
15	The election results in the Western Highlands	274
16	Initial returns in Moresby Open Electorate by individual polling booth	307
17	Hiri Open Electorate: first preferences by candidate and location of ballot boxes	308
18	Central Regional Electorate: first preferences by candidate and location of ballot boxes	310
19	The election results in Central District	313
20	Elected members in the Study Areas, 1964 and 1968	319

MAPS

1	Papua and New Guinea—Study Areas	*endpapers*
2	Gazelle Peninsula Open Electorates	*page* 49
3	Milne Bay Electorates	92
4	Bougainville Electorates	134
5(a)	South Bougainville Census Divisions	136
5(b)	South Bougainville Linguistic Divisions	136
6	North-east Coast Electorates, 1968	164
7	North-east Coast Electorates, 1964	165
8	Madang District and Kabwum	166
9	Western Highlands Electorates	220
10	Wahgi Open Electorate	244
11	Central District Electorates	277
12	Moresby Open Electorate	280
13	Hiri Open Electorate	283

Maps drawn by Hans Gunther of the Cartographic Office, Department of Human Geography.

INTRODUCTION

THE study of elections in the less developed countries provides opportunities to increase our understanding of the processes of political change induced by culture contact—often complicated, as in New Guinea's case, by a colonial relationship. In some ways, no doubt, what happens during elections is not typical of the general level of political interest or activity. On the other hand, elections by their very nature involve the whole adult population, however briefly and superficially, in activities peculiarly characteristic of introduced, Western forms of government. There is a search for candidates throughout the community. Once found, these try to whip up public support through propaganda, meetings, and pageantry. Electors are faced with the challenges of appraising the rival claims, making political choices, and (unless they decide to abstain) coping with the mechanics of voting. If there are local or national issues that agitate men's minds, this is a time when they will be made more explicit and discussed more intently. Such events offer valuable clues to the evolution of politics in these countries even if, by themselves, they cannot fully explain it. As W. J. M. Mackenzie (1957: 242) puts it:

> In any country where elections are taken seriously they constitute a sort of bottleneck in the political process, a narrow strait or channel in which political life is for a short period concentrated under the eye of the observer ... A student who sets out shrewdly the main influences that bear on an election thereby gives quite an orderly conspectus of the country's politics. It should be emphasised that he gives a conspectus, not an analysis, and that an electoral survey raises far more questions than it answers; but at least it is as good a way as any in which to start unravelling the skein.

Many studies of Western-style elections in less developed areas have been published in the past twenty years. A number were made in countries still politically dependent, though approaching independence. The problems of administering these elections were often similar to those encountered in Papua and New Guinea, and in many cases the voter population taking part were comparable according to such indices as level of material culture, average real income, literacy rate, and spread of formal education. However, there have been two vital differences: in the role played by political parties, and in the source materials available for study.

Election studies elsewhere have almost invariably dealt with general elections dominated by organisations which, however varied in scope and method, could reasonably be called political parties. The activities of these bodies were crucial in every aspect of the elections: selecting and nominating candidates, 'educating' the voters in policies and polling, defining campaign issues, publicly examining the performance of the government, getting voters to the polls, and of course trying to influence the voting itself. As a result it was natural, though not inevitable, that most of the academic studies should present the elections primarily as contests for power between these organised groups. The focus is squarely upon the distribution of members of the parties in the legislature before the election; the supposed social structure of their electoral support; the parties' machinery and propaganda in the campaign; and the changes in their legislative strength as a result of the election—illustrated by statistical analyses of the blocks of votes received by each party. Further, it has been possible to base the studies in question largely upon a wealth of documentary sources: voluminous official returns and reports, extensive newspaper files, party literature, and histories, memoirs, and biographies in varying degree.

The circumstances of Papua and New Guinea impose a different focus and different methods of study—and thereby, perhaps, offer the opportunity of some different kinds of insight into the politics of change. Papua is a Territory of the Commonwealth of Australia and New Guinea a United Nations Trust Territory, both being administered by Australia as a unit under a single set of governmental institutions. Although the territories have been under colonial rule since the 1880s, and parts of them have known European contacts for even longer, modern political and economic development began to affect most of the population only after World War II. An expatriate population of colonial officials, entrepreneurs, and missionaries, with their dependants, constitutes a dominant influence though a numerically insignificant enclave—about 40,000 in all—among two and a quarter millions of Papuans and New Guineans, the bulk of whom still follow a largely traditional way of life in a subsistence economy modified by a certain amount of cash cropping, minor trading, and wage labour.

Indigenous levels of education and literacy are relatively low and mass communication media, such as they are, reach few of the people.

Non-governmental political organisation—as in political parties, interest associations, and pressure groups—has begun to appear but in 1968 was still rudimentary. The expatriate minority took little interest in formal politics in the Territory, except for the few who had some economic or evangelistic stake in the country. The handful of expatriate politicians in the almost fully elective House of Assembly (for which the first election was held in 1964) maintained a disproportionate influence over its less sophisticated members. But settler politics which, expressing a determined and cohesive interest, so largely shaped political activity in some African colonies, assumed a different pattern in New Guinea where there was scarcely any formal organisation except in the Highlands.

One reason for this lay in the role of the Administration as the dominant expatriate political force. Committed to promoting both expatriate investments in the country and the aims of the Christian missions, it aroused little organised dissent among expatriates. An indigenous political élite was barely beginning to emerge. Thus even elections were almost inarticulate compared with those in countries where substantial interests have been mobilised in a concentrated contest for power. For this reason alone it was not possible to analyse a New Guinea election in terms of political parties, issues, interest groups, platforms, social classes, communal groups, or the personalities and aims of established political leaders. Nor could analysis be based on documentary sources of the conventional kind. In 1968 the three regular Territory newspapers were owned and published by an Australian chain with headquarters in Melbourne; there was no indigenous press, only a number of house-magazines put out by missions and social welfare agencies, and a few fugitive and ephemeral newsletters mimeographed by student groups here and there. Of at most half a dozen journals of opinion showing any interest in New Guinea affairs, only two were published in the Territory. A few of the local politicians had occasionally contributed to these newspapers and journals; at the time of the 1968 election none had published any extended memoirs. Official documentation of political activity scarcely existed except for unpublished reports of District Commissioners and other officers, the reports of the House of Assembly debates, of select committees of the House on constitutional development, and of the Chief Electoral Officer on the administration of the 1964 election. The select committee and electoral reports (in the fashion of official documents on New Guinea) were confined to the barest technical essentials.

Students of New Guinea elections were thus forced into an orientation, and a method, which Mackenzie hinted were desirable complements to the kind of 'electoral survey' he and Robinson had assembled in *Five Elections in Africa* (1960).

In the more common type of election studies (Mackenzie did not mean sample interview surveys), the relations between candidates and voters in the constituencies, and the voters' own perceptions of the whole legislative and electoral process, tended to become merely a vague background to the general struggle between the parties—as indicated by Mackenzie's single remark on the subject in his Conclusions to that volume: 'Just how the purpose and the issues of the election appear to the public is not clear' (p. 466). In the study of the New Guinea elections of 1964 and 1968, by contrast, the political behaviour and perceptions of individual candidates and electors necessarily remained in the foreground because they had not yet been overshadowed by the rise of national political parties. Moreover, the analysis of the elections could be separated from the politics of the legislature, since in the absence of a full party system the election results told little about the ensuing alignment of political forces therein. The orientation, therefore, had to be outward to the constituencies: toward how the candidates and electors viewed the electoral process in which they were involved; how they perceived (if they did so at all) the central institutions to which that process was directed; and how far these perceptions varied from those of the Administration, from each other in different areas, and on the second occasion, from 1964 to 1968.

As Mackenzie pointed out (p. 487), this orientation requires a different method from that of the 'electoral survey':

> Of necessity [the latter] looks at the situation from above, from the national level, and it offers no more than a still photograph at one instant of time. To get any appreciation of the situation in depth it is necessary also to look at the way in which electoral politics fits into the social structure at the level of daily life. One method is that of social anthropology ... Nothing can replace this method for the comprehensive study of politics in a concrete social setting, but of necessity it takes time, and can offer only illustrations, not conclusions, about the politics of a large territory taken as a whole.

There has been more serious writing about the emergent modern politics of Papua and New Guinea in the form of election studies than in all other forms put together. Nearly all these election studies followed the method of direct observation in the field, and most of them have been the work of social anthropologists. Some of this writing is about elections to local government councils, which were established from 1950 on, and to the former Legislative Council, a mainly nominated body which was superseded by the present House of Assembly in 1964. Much the greater part concerns the 1964 general election for that House—the first Territory-wide direct election on a universal franchise—and the two by-elections during the life of the first House (see References).

While these studies covered election activity in many parts of the Territory, and a number of them were undertaken as a joint venture and published together in *The Papua-New Guinea Elections 1964* (Bettison *et al.* 1965), they were all the work of individual scholars collecting and presenting their material in their own way. Largely because of this, they are especially valuable for their vivid and varied eyewitness accounts of New Guinea voters and politicians in action. Many of them also sought to identify underlying political perceptions and aspirations; these too reflected the individual research interests and viewpoints of their authors. When a number of these people, with other scholars from Australian universities, met in November 1966 on the initiative of Dr Marie Reay to discuss a strategy for studying the 1968 House of Assembly election, it was decided to try a different approach, more modest in scope than the 1964 enterprise, but aiming at a more integrated analysis by working through organised field teams to a common research plan. Each 'area' team should include anthropologists familiar with an area and its local vernaculars, and also if possible some political scientists or historians. One would not be an area team, but have a roving commission to study the electoral activities of organisations that transcended area boundaries, such as political parties, missions, and the Administration itself.

Ultimately a group of some thirty-five research workers, from twelve universities in Australia, New Guinea, and abroad, took part in the project, a few of them on the planning committee as consultant members only. Thirty members, including seven research assistants, made up the seven field teams. Each of the six area teams studied a Regional electorate (in one case two) and one or more of its component Open electorates (see chapter 1 for the distinction between 'Regional' and 'Open' electorates). The Regional electorates concerned were: Milne Bay; Bougainville; East and West New Britain; Madang (with one Open electorate from neighbouring Morobe); Western Highlands; and Central. Though their choice was determined mainly by the area expertise of the participating anthropologists, they were in fact fairly representative of the main regional divisions of the Territory, and geographically well spread (see endpaper maps). These seven were from a total of fifteen Regional electorates in the Territory; the Open electorates selected for special study numbered sixteen, the Territory total being sixty-nine.

Some members of the group were in the field by early December 1967; most of them, before beginning intensive fieldwork, attended a final briefing session in Lae early in January 1968, to agree on the detailed interpretation of the common briefing documents already issued; most stayed in the field until about the end of the polling period (mid-February to mid-March 1968), and some stayed longer. Several teams were helped by the reports of selected undergraduates of the University of Papua and New Guinea who spent the long vacation in their home villages within the areas studied, and sometimes acted as interpreters for the teams. (See Appendix I for lists of planning committee and research team members.) All area teams worked from the same briefs, listing detailed empirical questions considered relevant to the main research objectives. (See Appendix II for texts.) Each area team later submitted through its leader a joint report for its area; these form the basis of chapters 2 to 7 below. Chapter 1 sets the scene by describing the political background of the election. It also outlines the constitutional and administrative framework and indicates the main changes since 1964 (cf. Bettison *et al.* 1965).

The aim of the project was to contribute to the understanding of processes of political change in a terminal colonial situation, by trying to gauge the political attitudes and perceptions of election candidates and voters in their own communities. Were different rates or stages of change to be observed in different parts of the Territory, and if so why? Were there any signs of 'national' politics emerging, and if so was it possible to give, in Mackenzie's terms, 'an orderly conspectus' of their nature? How far and in what ways had the imported institutions of elections and the House of Assembly conduced to political change? How far were the Administration's purposes in introducing these institutions being realised? How far were the institutions being operated according to local criteria and for indigenous purposes? How far were they meeting local expectations, and being accepted as vehicles for local aspirations? Putting the last three questions more technically, what were the rate and extent of diffusion, assimilation, and legitimation of the imported institutions? Finally, was it possible to deduce some likely trends of further change, at least for the short run? If so, the future would test in some measure the validity of our observations and analysis. In fact, delays of compilation and publication have allowed the future to forestall in some measure the appearance of these studies, but we have purposely tried to exclude the influence of hindsight. The following texts are based in substance on material assembled to about August 1968, and most of the chapters, including those on

Bougainville and New Britain, have had only editorial revision or re-arrangement since mid-1969.

As indicated, the project sought to explore empirical questions, rather than to test preconceived theoretical hypotheses. For one thing, the novelty of the approach baffled our early attempts to fit it into familiar theoretical categories. For another, a planning group drawn from such diverse backgrounds and different disciplines found it easier to agree upon a list of significant questions than upon a common conceptual framework. As the election approached, more practical problems appeared. For example, in both Bougainville and Milne Bay it turned out that only small research teams with the appropriate experience were available. The former is a relatively compact area on a single large island; the latter covers part of the mainland and many widely dispersed islands, mostly accessible only by boat in favourable weather. Such disparities between the study areas hampered the collection of fully comparable data in equal depth over a predetermined range of issues, and the presentation of area reports on a uniform plan. As another example, the north-east coast team planned, like the rest, to work in a single Regional electorate (Madang). However, the rather late redistribution of electoral boundaries cut their area in two, leaving the part assigned to one member in the Morobe Regional, which seemed likely to be uncontested till late in the nomination period; as it happened, a late nomination produced an important contest (between two European candidates) which could only be marginally covered in this study. On the other hand, as the authors of chapter 7 point out, another contest confined to expatriates failed, for that very reason, to bring out the potential excitement and explosiveness of urban politics in the Territory's capital, Port Moresby.

Recognising these various obstacles to framing or implementing a formal research design, the teams entrusted to the editors, whom they appointed, the responsibility of working out the interpretation attempted in chapter 8. Being an empirical interpretation, it does not embark on systematic comparisons with similar colonial scenes elsewhere; this would properly call for a more elaborate theoretical orientation, and deserves an at least equally extended treatment which might build in part upon the evidence analysed here. It includes occasional comparisons of that kind, and also with aspects of Australian political behaviour. We can make the latter with more confidence; we use them, of course, not as criteria for judging New Guinea politics, nor as pointers to their future development, but simply to indicate more precisely some of the ways in which transplanted institutions are perceived and modified. Here we briefly summarise our approach to interpretation.

Its essential aim is to identify those more or less widespread continuities in the political process which might be projected at least into the short-term future, and might suggest some tentative answers to our empirical questions. The field chapters, following the project brief so far as possible, sought to establish connections between the characteristics of each electorate, the pre-election scene, the roles of candidates, electors, political organisations and the Administration; the working of the electoral machinery, and the election results. From these analyses the concluding chapter tries to derive (because they seem to be the elements of continuing significance) the relations between the relevant institutional structures, the more settled policies of the Administration, and the apparent patterns of perceptions, values, attitudes and expectations that in 1968 seemed to predominate among the electors as a whole.

The process of derivation is sometimes indirect. For example, prevalent political perceptions, attitudes and values are largely inferred from an analysis of the political resources that seemed most conducive to a candidate's success, where 'resources' included his group relationships, political skills and attributes, electors' reactions to his campaign methods, his colour, his reliance on political and other organisations, and his exploitation of specific interests and issues. These inferences about people's beliefs and opinions suggest answers, however tentative, to questions about differential rates of political change, the persistence of indigenous criteria and objectives in operating exotic institutions, and the legitimation of those institutions.

Similarly, the ways in which these institutions were being assimilated or modified are deduced in part by assessing the interaction between indigenous structures, traditions, and experience of culture contact and the first House on the one hand, and Western criteria in such matters as the support sought by different candidates, campaign techniques, and the perceived role of the elected Member on the other.

In other cases conclusions could be drawn more directly from the field chapters. Signs of the emergence of 'national' politics were sought in inter-electorate co-operation among candidates; in the scope, and degree of integration, of political organisations; in the range of electors' political horizons; and in the extent and nature of their expectations from the 'national' election and the House of Assembly. There was some direct evidence also on the diffusion of the Australian institutions, in the form of observations of the electoral procedures in action, statistics of turn-out and informal voting when related to local political history, and the observed impact of political and electoral education.

On such questions as legitimation and political change, the evidence was partly inferential and partly comparative: it was necessary to try to find the underlying meaning of such phenomena as non-voting, cargo activity, and the unpopularity of outgoing Members of the House, and wherever possible to make comparisons with earlier studies in the Territory, particularly of the 1964 election. The interpretation offered is thus in some respects empirically tentative, and we have had to draw it from diverse wells of theory. It reflects a reluctance to rely without question upon mechanistic or organic models of dynamic social phenomena.

The present study is not concerned, except incidentally, with problems of continuity and change in the total structure of indigenous society. In so far as it examines the political behaviour of individual candidates and small groups of voters, it may throw some light on changing attitudes to aspects of indigenous culture. But to have pursued such questions deeply enough into the villages to make reliable generalisations would have required more time and manpower than were available for our particular purposes, and perhaps the use of survey interview techniques, which was impossible. Where participants in their own time were able to study in more depth the implications of the election for indigenous societies as such, their results have been recorded elsewhere, usually in anthropological publications.

Although the aims of the book are modest and its focus limited to parts of a single political system, it is addressed to those interested in comparative political development as well as to people concerned with the future of Papua and New Guinea. It records what was in some ways an unusual, and certainly for those involved a stimulating, experiment in co-operative field research and meta-disciplinary interpretation. From a historical point of view, it raises the question whether Australia's extended opportunity to profit by earlier experiences of 'preparation' and decolonisation can really ensure a slower, smoother or tidier transition to independence than elsewhere.

But it points beyond the temporary phase of decolonisation, if read in conjunction with studies directed to village level politics in the new states of Africa and Asia. To take a striking example, F. G. Bailey's *Politics and Social Change* (1963) shows repeatedly that after ten years of independence in India, voters in rural Orissa perceived their 'own' government and electoral process in much the same way as Papuans and New Guineans saw the Australian Administration and the election in 1968. The government was from their point of view distant, all-powerful, indistinguishable from the administrative apparatus, and could not be unseated by ordinary electors. Candidates were appraised for their individual characteristics, their superior education and their skill in dealing with the administration, and not as representatives of party principles or platforms—though India then had far stronger political parties than New Guinea in 1968. The legislator was to them not even a representative who would watch over their interests when policy was being framed, but merely an intermediary on behalf of individuals in day-to-day administration. The only issues raised in campaigning were purely local ones touching on villagers' parochial worries. Inadequate communication facilities drew a veil between the villager and 'national' politics. The structure of indigenous society remained largely the mould in which representative politics operated at constituency level. Voters followed the instructions of their local leaders but remained politically ignorant and apathetic. The adjustment of interests was difficult because the middle level of associational activity was largely missing.

Every one of Bailey's observations is matched in the pages which follow. We conclude that studies of this kind may help to illumine problems of government and its legitimacy that seem likely to persist in such countries long after colonial dependence is over.

It remains to acknowledge invaluable assistance received by the project as a whole. Officers of the Papua and New Guinea Administration, with the approval of the Minister for Territories and the Administrator, were helpful in many ways, sometimes at personal inconvenience to themselves. We readily acceded to the Minister's only request, that our teams should not press voters for indications of their voting intention, in order to avoid any appearance of influence on voting or risk of confusing the research project with the work of the Administration in electors' minds. Advance copies of informative material were supplied by the departments of Information and Extension Services and of District Administration, and the latter allowed two officers on leave to take part in the research. In particular, the Chief Electoral Officer, Mr Robert Bryant, his Deputy Mr Simon Kaumi, and the Returning Officers and their staff in those Districts we studied, went out of their way to supply us with documentation and explanations of the electoral administration, and with advance voting statistics in a suitable form for our analysis. We are grateful for the help of students of the University of Papua and New Guinea as observers, and to Dr Ruth Latukefu for recruiting and briefing them. We received wise advice from 'non-playing' members of our planning committee, Dr (now Professor) R. G. Crocombe and

Professors C. A. Hughes, K. S. Inglis, and Henry Mayer. We are indebted to Sir John Crawford for, among other things, allocating part of a Ford Foundation grant to meet incidental expenses of the project; to the Australian Research Grants Committee for financial assistance to a number of team members; and to the Institute of Current World Affairs, New York, for permitting Edward Wolfers to devote part of his Fellowship time to the project and to use material from his Newsletters to the Institute. Mr J. Toner, of the Australian National University New Guinea Research Unit, helped with logistics, and Mr H. E. Gunther of the Geography Department in the University's Research School of Pacific Studies has shown his usual skill in preparing the maps. Mary Carter was a model secretary to the project and, with Dorothy Aunela, Kathleen Bourke, and Pamela Fox, cleanly typed version after version of the drafts. Gillian Evans and Yvonne Lonsdale kept up the flow of press clippings. The Australian National University Press have been patient and expert, as always. Finally, of course, those without whose tolerance and interest the study would have been really impossible were the candidates, and other electors in their hundreds, who talked with our teams in Papua and New Guinea and accepted the presence of research workers as an ordinary part of the election scene.

Canberra
17 August 1970

A.L.E.
R.S.P.
M.R.

THE CONTEXT
OF POLITICAL CHANGE

R. S. Parker and Edward P. Wolfers

THE bird-shaped island directly north of Australia is divided into the Indonesian province of West Irian (the former Dutch New Guinea) and a land which, together with a myriad smaller islands in archipelagos to the north and east, comprises the Territory of Papua and New Guinea. This potential new nation is guided towards its destiny by Australia. It is still intersected in law by a boundary set in the 1880s between the British protectorate of Papua (over which Australia acquired control on reaching its own nationhood early this century) and the German colony of Kaiser Wilhelmsland (which became a League of Nations mandate under Australian administration after World War I and a United Nations Trust Territory after World War II). Within the terms of the 1946 Trusteeship Agreement, the unified administration of the two dependencies, which had been established for military purposes during the war, was perpetuated and elaborated by the Australian parliament in the Papua and New Guinea Act 1949, which with amendments remains the constitutional basis for the government of the united Territory and for most of the ordinances and subordinate legislation enacted there. In this book, for brevity, the terms 'New Guinea' and 'the Territory' mean the combined Territory of Papua and New Guinea, except where the context shows that the more precise sense of the Trust Territory alone is intended.

Most of the land area (which is roughly equal to that of Thailand) is densely covered by mountain ranges, usually jungle-clad, which rise to an average of 10,000 feet on the main island and are nearly as high as this on several of the others. Big rivers (including the Sepik) transform some of the coastal lowlands into vast swamps as they spill towards the sea. More than 100 inches of rain fall upon most of the Territory in a year, and torrential streams rage through steep valleys in the mountainous interior. The elections of 1964 and 1968 were both held in February to March, the wet season for most of the Territory, when flooded rivers, brimming swamps, and landslides obstruct movement with more than usual severity. Tropical conditions on the coast and the smaller islands contrast with the more temperate climate of the interior.

A variety of peoples of mixed Papuan, Melanesian, and Negrito stock inhabit the Territory. Before the arrival of Europeans they maintained a relatively affluent subsistence economy based on agriculture and elaborated in various forms of ceremonial exchange. They were affected by the inevitable health hazards of malaria, tuberculosis, dysentery, yaws. Divided by topographical barriers and suspicion of strangers, they spoke over 700 mutually unintelligible languages and waged endemic war. Head-hunting raids were common in some parts, and everywhere fear of sorcery was rampant. The people were effectively isolated from other Pacific populations and from the Malay and Indonesian civilisations to the west until European explorers began to touch their coasts.

By the 1870s European missionaries, labour recruiters, traders, prospectors, and ultimately planters were beginning to be active on the coastal fringes. Between the two world wars they extended their operations over a wider area. But the numerous peoples, amounting to one-third of the total population, who live in the temperate highland valleys above 5000 feet in the central cordillera remained undiscovered until the mid-1930s. Thus European penetration, control, economic enterprise, and developmental policies of any appreciable significance for the Territory as a whole dated mainly from the end of World War II, during which it was a major battle ground for Japanese, American, and Australian armies and navies. The non-indigenous population increased greatly as a corollary of economic development programs but by 1966 constituted only a minute proportion (40,363 persons) of a total population of 2·3 millions. About one-tenth of these non-indigenous persons were Chinese and other Asians; nearly all the rest were Australians, more than half being government employees and their families.

Disparities in the nature, duration, and intensity of European contact in different parts of the Territory meant widely varying involvement of Papuans and New Guineans in activities brought in by the white men. Probably more than half the people—but these overwhelmingly in the hinterland—remained pagan in 1968, though a few indigenous clergy were already reaching high office in some of the Christian denominations that had long been active in Papua and the islands. Thousands of men from all over the country had visited the areas of long contact as labourers on plantations and wharves, as seamen, policemen, interpreters, and domestic servants. Thousands had served as carriers and stretcher-bearers for the armies during World War II; by 1968 the troops and junior officers in the Territory's own army, the two battalions of Australia's Pacific Islands Regiment, were locally recruited. On the Gazelle Peninsula of New Britain and in some other coastal areas, local people had been earning cash incomes from the sale of copra and market produce when more than half of their fellow Papuans and New Guineans were unknown to Europeans; cash cropping was extended to many new areas during the crash development programs of the 1960s. The sharp change in Australian policy from pre-war *laissez-faire* to concern with rapid development was reflected in government spending on the Territory, which multiplied tenfold between 1947 and 1963 and nearly doubled again in the next five years in response to the recommendations of a World Bank mission in 1964.

The pattern of economic growth reflects the dominance of expatriate enterprise and investment from outside the Territory. The money value of income from the subsistence sector grew slowly but income from the monetary sector, which in 1962 represented less than two-thirds of the Territory's total, had doubled by 1968. Over the same period the money value of imports nearly tripled. The great bulk of imports went to feed and clothe the expatriate minority, and to provide equipment and raw materials for creating an economic infrastructure and the beginnings of mining and manufacturing industry. Export earnings from coconut products, cocoa, coffee, rubber, and timber were paying for about half of them, the balance being made up, in effect, from the Australian government grant. The Australian government was hoping that this could be eventually superseded by income from the vast copper deposits about to be exploited in Bougainville, as well as from other suspected mineral and oil resources. The economy would be based indefinitely upon primary industry.

The involvement of indigenous people in these changes was increasing, but again with some unevenness. By 1968 upwards of 12,000 had found salaried employment in government service, though only a handful were yet in positions of any seniority; of about 125,000 in wage employment, at least 15,000 worked for the government. Indigenous cash croppers had nearly as much land as expatriates did under coconut and rubber (mainly in the New Guinea islands and central Papua respectively), and already they were producing most of the coffee (mainly in the Highlands). Apart from some government-promoted co-operatives, indigenous commercial activity was largely confined to trade stores and trucking services. Several individuals who combined such operations with cash cropping on a massive scale had become wealthy even by European standards; as a whole, however, indigenous business enterprises were limited in scale, capital, and expertise. In 1966 as many as 44 per cent of the indigenous population were wholly engaged in the subsistence sector; another 20 per cent were engaged wholly or predominantly in cash cropping; about 37 per cent were involved in varying degrees in both cash and subsistence activities.

The resources for new development came overwhelmingly from outside, so that banking, insurance, commerce, retailing, construction, engineering, shipping, and airlines were concentrated in expatriate hands. But local participation within the new social framework was affected also by differential access to formal education, which still had to surmount language barriers. In 1963 the Christian missions, almost entirely responsible for education before the war, still accommodated 81 per cent of pupils at all levels in schools of varying standard. Provision for tertiary educational and training institutions came late. The first indigenous student to enter a university moved in 1960 from an Australian school to an Australian university, and the University of Papua and New Guinea began to admit students in 1966. In that year rather less than half the indigenous persons who had received full primary education in schools teaching English had proceeded to secondary schools and only a minute proportion of these had any tertiary education; there were still only two university graduates. In 1968 it was expected that about half the indigenous children then reaching school age would actually attend school. Further, less than half of the indigenous population of 10 years and over spoke either Melanesian Pidgin (about one-third) or English (13 per cent); no more than 7 per cent could speak both languages.

The House of Assembly elections of 1964 and 1968 were the only political events in which Papuans and New Guineans from all over the Territory had taken part. Otherwise the involvement of the indigenous public—or publics—with the central government had been localised. They had confronted or obeyed, helped or importuned the government's administrative officers at patrol post, Sub-District and less frequently, District levels. But the Territory Administration had not had to deal with them on a Territory-wide scale except in holding these general elections.

In the House of Assembly itself, and in Australia, the executive government dealt with indigenous politicians from all parts, and with Territory-wide issues. Political activity at these levels generally assumed what appeared to be Western forms, and could be described in Western terms. However, the same activity, issues, and institutions

—whenever they percolated so far—could be interpreted in surprisingly different ways in the urban or rural village. Whether 'traditional' or 'modern' in origin, politics at the local level took forms that were unfamiliar to the outsider—if he managed to observe them at all—and this naturally included the electoral process. Such forms are best explored from the inside looking out, as it were; hence the constituency studies in chapters 2 to 7 which compose the main part of this book.

However, the electoral process in the constituencies was influenced in a number of ways by politics and administration at the centre, and some account of these is a necessary background to the constituency studies. Hence the present chapter briefly reviews the experience of members and constituents with the first House of Assembly, the attempts to create political parties outside the House, and the program of 'political education', and describes changes in the constitution of the House and in some details of the electoral system. Underlying the whole were the relations between introduced institutions and 'traditional' politics, and certain indigenous perceptions of Australian policy towards the Territory—interlacing themes to which we turn first.

'TRADITIONAL' AND 'MODERN' POLITICS

The political entities of the pre-contact world are in a state of flux. Before the imposition of Australian control throughout most of Papua and New Guinea, these entities were both relatively unstable and small. Not many effective political units contained more than a few hundred people, although on occasion thousands might co-operate for a specific battle, or in a trade or ceremonial exchange. Membership of even the smallest primary groups was unstable—as people married in and out, disputes arose between rival leaders, and inter-group warfare forced some members of each group to choose between the claims to their loyalties of, say, their residential or their kin group.

The daily politics of Papuan and New Guinean life, even now, are not unlike those of tradition, without the fighting. Yet gradually, and increasingly often, new political groups and structures are influencing village life, as small, once rival groups are forced to compete, or to co-operate, in local government elections, co-operatives, and other business ventures. It is still too early, however, to decide which groups, or kinds of groups, will claim most people's primary loyalties. A man's loyalty still tends to vary with the social context of a conflict. At home, he may fight for a fellow villager or clansman against a neighbour (as in pre-contact times), or with a fellow member of his language group or trading network in a wider conflict. Occasionally, and especially in town, the same man may fight for his district (as when a group of Sepik fight a group of Tolai in Rabaul), or even for his fellow Pidgin-speaking New Guineans against a Papuan out-group. The political loyalties of most indigenous people are in process of rapid change, and predictable only if the parties to and circumstances of a conflict, or of a co-operative situation, are already closely known.

Political leadership before contact was achieved—by virtue of a person's attributes, wealth, or skills—rather than acquired—through appointment, accession, or election to an office. Leadership was therefore personal, ephemeral, discontinuous, and limited in range. As pacification proceeded the British and Australian administrations appointed village constables to serve the government at the local level in Papua, and New Guinea's *luluai*s and *tultul*s, headmen appointed by the Germans and Australians, were also little more than law-enforcers. It was only accidental when any of these officials was in the traditional sense a leader of his people, and the most powerful of them were often men who misused their offices or claimed more authority than they had legally been granted. So neither the structures of traditional indigenous politics, nor the offices established under the 'native administration' systems in the two territories, constituted a practicable basis on which to erect a system of offices to which men might be elected to represent their people in the making of central government policy.

Such a system, when it came in the form of the House of Assembly, involved a new infusion of entirely exotic institutions, far removed in spirit and content from anything that had gone before, and especially from the accepted modes of traditional politics. Thus, from the point of view of their Australian sponsors, the new institutions could in no way be grafted on, or otherwise related, to indigenous political structures, and the question may be asked: Does this mean that the exotic forms can be transplanted intact into virgin soil, there to grow in the image of their Australian originals? Or will these institutions, their functions, and their daily operation necessarily be modified by the characteristic customs, assumptions, and interests of Papuans and New Guineans? The question is not merely rhetorical, since if the second alternative seems obvious to social scientists, the first is almost inevitably taken for granted by the Australian government, if only for want of convincing answers to the practical supplementary questions: If mutations naturally occur, how and in what parts of the structure do they appear, what forms do they take, in what ways do they reflect traditional structures, and are there any regular patterns in the process? This book is an attempt to assemble some evidence on these questions, taking the introduced, Western-style election as the occasion for a case study.

The mere fact of indigenous elective representation on a Territory-wide basis was perhaps the main change in New Guinea politics signalled by the first House of Assembly. Beyond this, the elected members of the House were hesitantly exploring the implications and possibilities of their new roles and status, while popular knowledge of the structure and functions of the central government, and the sense of involvement in national politics to be found at the village level, increased only a little. The difference was one of degree: among the indigenous people as a whole—so it seemed to the United Nations Visiting Mission to the Trust Territory in 1965—there was

> a deep feeling of inferiority arising from the lack of political education, ignorance of the outside world and ... in the case of certain more evolved elements of the population, who, on the contrary, are aware of the need for and advantages of political advancement, a certain timidity, physical or intellectual .... (Visiting Mission 1965: para. 312)

In all the circumstances of the Territory, a sense of helplessness among indigenous people was natural enough. But there is also a great deal of evidence—for example in the people's testimony to successive Visiting Missions, in the House of Assembly debates, and in political behaviour recorded in later chapters of this book—that this feeling was heightened by their perception of Australian official attitudes to Territory development. From about the time when the House of Assembly was established, the government was manifestly giving priority to an intensive program of economic development, based largely on a World Bank report obtained at the suggestion of earlier U.N. Visiting Missions. This would make the Territory, at least in the short run, dependent on even higher levels of Australian economic aid than previously. A month before the first meeting of the House of Assembly, the Minister for Territories pointed out 'the contradiction between these economic realities and talk of early political independence' (*C.P.D.* 5 May 1965, H. of R. 46, p. 1144).[1] In the same month the 1965 Visiting Mission said in their Report

---

[1] The view summarised in the text was still held by the Minister in September 1969 when he said to a British journalist: 'I cannot say when independence will come. The country would need to be economically viable and I cannot look 15 to 20 years ahead to see when that might be. Perhaps there might be a popular vote for independence sooner, but in that case the Australian Government might have to revise its spending plans there'. *Sunday Times Magazine,* 1 December 1969, p. 61.

(which provides apt texts for all the main issues traversed in this chapter): 'It would be useful to explain that a country which has achieved self-government or independence is not for that reason thrown back upon itself and left without technical and financial assistance' (para. 316). But the Minister repeatedly gave warning that reduction of aid could be the corollary of greater political autonomy in New Guinea—or even of any political demands that seriously diverged from Australian policy, as he indicated during the third year of the first House:

> If this basic harmony between the views of the Government, the House of Assembly and the people of the Territory on aims and strategy and fundamental policies were to disappear, ... the Government's responsibilities to this Parliament and to the taxpayers of Australia would require us to re-examine the position, including the level of Australian aid. (*C.P.D.* 20 October 1966, H. of R. 53, p. 2003)

Statements like this were echoed by Territory officials in the House of Assembly itself, and they reverberated through the Territory. Moreover, they were publicly endorsed by leading expatriate businessmen—including prominent members of the House—who added arguments of their own: orderly economic development, the spread of material prosperity, and even personal security would be threatened by premature insistence upon home rule or independence, which could only be advocated by self-seeking political agitators.

Naturally these pronouncements, taken together, did little to diminish that 'certain timidity' among the indigenous population about political activism; naturally also, they most vividly impressed those numerous groups, such as the Highland peoples, who felt that an untimely end to Australian tutelage would leave them permanently behind their coastal countrymen blessed by longer European contact. Thus in the context of modern politics the recurrent refrain of New Guinea conservatism, figuring frequently in the following chapters, takes the form of a syllogism: The continuance of Australian financial and technical support is endangered by any move towards indigenous political autonomy, especially home rule or independence. Papua and New Guinea need Australian support as long as possible. Hence Papuans and New Guineans must reject those who advocate moves towards home rule or independence, or who otherwise radically oppose Australian policies.

THE FIRST HOUSE OF ASSEMBLY, 1964-7

The events, discussions, and legislation leading to the creation of the House of Assembly are fully set out in Bettison *et al.* (1965: ch. 3); it is sufficient here to outline its main features and composition as it began life in 1964, so far as they bear on the present study.

The Papua and New Guinea Act 1963 (of the Australian parliament) established a House of ten official members, appointed by the Governor-General of Australia on the nomination of the Administrator of the Territory, and fifty-four elected members of whom ten must be non-indigenous. The whole fifty-four would be chosen by an electorate comprising all adult Territory residents as inscribed on a common roll, irrespective of race. The Act provided for a Speaker chosen by the House from its members; it gave the Administrator discretionary authority to dissolve the House at any time within its maximum term of four years.

The House of Assembly was endowed with a general legislative power to make Ordinances 'for the peace, order and good government of the Territory', qualified by governmental veto powers at two levels. First, the Administrator at his discretion could withhold assent to an Ordinance, or reserve it for consideration by the Governor-General of Australia (in effect the Australian government). Ordinances dealing with certain specified subjects (including divorce, defence, land transactions, migration, and the public service) must be so reserved. Second, the Governor-General of Australia could withhold assent to a reserved Ordinance as a whole, and disallow in whole or in part an Ordinance assented to by the Administrator. In addition, before assent an Ordinance could be returned to the House with recommended amendments by the Administrator or, in the case of a reserved Ordinance, by the Governor-General. (Naturally, the veto would in practice be wielded by the Australian Minister or Cabinet, who constitutionally instruct the Administrator and advise the Governor-General.) Where an Ordinance did not receive the assent of the Administrator or Governor-General, or was disallowed in whole or part, the reasons must be laid before both Houses of the Australian parliament.

The 1963 Act made consequential alterations to the constitution of the Administrator's Council, a body which, like the Executive Council in former non-self-governing territories, could be consulted by the Administrator on any policy matter, and must be consulted on a number of matters specified in various Ordinances. Besides the Administrator, the Council had comprised three government members, who were now required to be official members of the House of

Assembly, and three non-official members whose numbers were now raised to seven, all of whom must be elected members of the House.

Within this framework, detailed provisions on the qualifications of voters and candidates, and for the distribution of electorates, enrolment, polling, and counting the votes, were made by the Territory Legislative Council, a Select Committee of whose members had (partly under the spur of the 1962 U.N. Visiting Mission) framed most of the proposals on which the new constitution was based. On the first of these subjects the rules were simple: a voter must be not under 21, not an alien, criminal, or of unsound mind and must have a home in the Territory or twelve months' residence in an electorate at any past time; a candidate must be an elector entitled to enrolment for the electorate he contested, and of course must not be a public official, bankrupt, or in certain categories of convicted persons. The reservation of some seats for European candidates, beyond the ten proposed for official members (who would at this stage inevitably be Europeans) had been recommended with reluctance by the Select Committee on Political Development in their first report (October 1962), in deference to the overwhelming consensus of their indigenous witnesses. In explanation they said [para. 16 (i)]:

> Although opposed in principle to any form of reserved seats and special racial rolls, your committee was forced to take cognizance of three major factors:—
> (a) the universal and very strongly expressed views that there must be non-indigenes on the council;
> (b) the very strong probability that no non-indigenes would be returned from a normal common roll election; and
> (c) the very marked preference for such non-indigenes to be elected by all the people voting together;
> and accepted the fact that in the first elections at least there would have to be special seats reserved for non-indigenous candidates.

The Australian legislation, as already seen, accepted the Committee's view that ten seats for such members should suffice 'to carry out the representative, stabilizing, educative, guiding and informing task for which the people expressly desire to see them elected'. Under the detailed New Guinea legislation the Territory was divided for the purpose into ten 'Special' electorates, so distributed as to contain approximately equal numbers of non-indigenous people (a principle which, incidentally, had not been mentioned by the Select Committee and produced great disparities in their total populations). The remaining forty-four elective constituencies, accessible to both indigenous and expatriate candidates, were called 'Open' electorates and also distributed throughout the Territory, primarily on the criterion of equal population. Thus each elector would have two distinct votes, one for an Open electorate and one for a Special.

Enrolment was made compulsory, but the rolls were compiled by Administration officers in effect interviewing every potential elector in the Territory, which involved house-to-house visiting in the towns, and ubiquitous patrolling outside them. Voting was optional (in contrast to Australia, where voting has long been legally compulsory in federal and state elections) and postal and absent voting were allowed (as in Australia). The law prescribed all possible measures to ensure a secret ballot, but the non-literate voter, composing the vast majority in fact, was allowed to 'whisper' his choices to a literate friend or (as almost invariably happened) a polling official, who would mark the ballot paper for him.

Both Opens and Specials were of course single-member constituencies; the voting method was a variation on the Australian alternative vote system. In essence, the latter is a compromise between the more common 'first-past-the-post' system—under which voters in single-member constituencies mark the one candidate they prefer, the candidate with most votes (i.e. a 'plurality', whether majority or not) being elected—and 'proportional representation', which requires multi-member constituencies, with voters expressing their order of preference among all the candidates and the subordinate as well as first preferences being taken into account in determining the winners. The Australian system combines single-member constituencies with requiring the elector to allot a numerical preference to every candidate if his vote is to be valid. Under this system the elector tends to have fewer candidates to puzzle over, and the counting of votes is less complicated, than under proportional representation. On the other hand, in terms of party politics it gives a better opportunity to smaller parties or groups to secure representation than 'first-past-the-post', and is less likely to result in a party with a national minority of votes gaining a majority of seats—though the latter is not wholly precluded as it is under proportional representation.

In New Guinea, the only important difference from the Australian system was that the expression of preferences beyond the first was optional; subject to this the counting of votes was similar. Thus a vote was valid if the ballot paper showed either a single first preference, or any number of consecutive numerical preferences, beginning with 1, up to the total number of candidates for the electorate. A candidate with an absolute majority of first preferences would be declared elected; if there were no such candidate, the one with the fewest first preferences would be excluded and his first preference ballot papers distributed among the other candidates according to the second preferences marked on them. (Papers showing no further preferences would be regarded as 'exhausted' and eliminated from the computation, thus reducing the total number of votes in it at each successive count—a point on which the Territory legislation was ambiguous until it was corrected after the 1964 election. See Bettison *et al.* 1965: 412-16.) This process would be repeated, if necessary, until one candidate had more of the 'unexhausted' votes than all his remaining opponents combined.

Polling for the first House took place during February and March 1964. The average voter turn-out for the whole Territory was reported to be 72·3 per cent of those enrolled, and average informal voting 3·2 per cent of voters. Just under 300 candidates contested 53 seats, the candidate for North Markham Special (a veteran District Commissioner, Mr H. Niall) being returned unopposed. The assumption that Open electorates were unlikely to return non-indigenous candidates proved mistaken. There were thirty-two European and eight mixed-race candidates in twenty-four of the Open electorates; six of the Europeans and two of the mixed-race candidates were elected, indigenous candidates therefore winning the remaining thirty-six seats. The two Assistant Administrators and heads of the principal Territory departments were nominated to the ten official positions, the senior official member being designated leader of the House. When the House met, Mr Niall was unanimously elected Speaker.

The composition of the elected membership has been fully analysed elsewhere (Bettison *et al.* 1965: 447-9, Tables 1-3; Wolfers 1968b: Tables I, III, IV); only a few significant features need to be recapitulated here.

The outstanding fact was the lack of formal Western education, of familiarity with English and of modern political experience among the thirty-eight local members in general, compared with the European elected and official members as a group. In addition, these disadvantages were substantially more pronounced among the thirty-one local members from the Highlands and the New Guinea Territory islands and coastal areas than among the seven from Papuan coastal areas. While five of the latter had spent some years in European-type white-collar occupations, the great bulk of the indigenous members were subsistence farmers or small traders; six Highland members had been interpreters, and four of the New Guinea members had been teachers or had teacher training. All indigenous members from the Papuan coasts had some formal schooling; nineteen of the others had none, and probably two-thirds of all indigenous members had little or no ability to read. Again, all but one of the Papuan coastal members could understand English, and all had Police Motu, the

Papuan *lingua franca;* most of the Motu-speakers knew something of its New Guinea counterpart, Melanesian Pidgin. By contrast, no more than half of the New Guinea islands members, and hardly any of those from the New Guinea coasts or the Highlands, knew any English at all. Only three indigenous members had served in the old Legislative Council; however, twelve had held office in local government councils, nine of them in the Highlands and New Guinea coastal areas, and five more, from the same areas, had been ordinary council members. However, among local members as a whole there were at least half a dozen shrewd politicians, to varying degrees at home in the expatriate culture, with strong local followings and free from undue deference to the dominant whites.

The six European members from Open electorates were not politically experienced or highly qualified, though three of them were young men in their twenties who had been Patrol Officers in the Department of Native Affairs. On the other hand, the members for Special electorates included two former District Commissioners and four men with substantial experience as members of the previous Legislative Councils. Seven of the ten official members had also served in the Legislative Councils, and the officials' familiarity with policy and administration, combined with their monopoly of real power, gave them a commanding position in the new legislature despite their small numbers. However, unlike most of the elected European members, most of the officials had long been headquarters desk administrators; at first only one, and never more than two or three, had wide contacts with the indigenous people or were fluent in Melanesian Pidgin, the increasingly popular medium of communication throughout the Territory and, as time went on, in the House of Assembly itself.

MOVEMENT IN THE HOUSE

Having established the House of Assembly, with some of the usual formal appurtenances such as a Clerk's office and temporary standing orders, and one unusual one—simultaneous interpretation of debates into its three official languages, English, Pidgin, and Police Motu—the government was faced thenceforth with much harder tasks. After seven months' first-hand study of the House towards the end of its first term, Professor Meller, an expert on the development of legislatures in Pacific dependencies, pointed to a central tension in the government's position when he expressed the view that they had been preoccupied with 'managing' the House at the expense of devising simpler procedures and helping indigenous members to understand them. The standing orders were those of a fully-fledged Western parliament; documents were mainly in English (with a few summaries in Pidgin), and their legalistic verbiage and formalised presentation by official members made no concession to indigenous members' linguistic limitations or to the total novelty of their situation. Non-official members rarely received draft legislation in time for adequate comprehension, and the well-meant but inadequately staffed and trained interpretation service could not do equal justice to the three very different languages.

Meller observed that in detailed debate on Bills and as potential sponsors of private members' Bills, 'indigenous Members were conspicuous by their silence'; they showed little political skill in parliamentary manoeuvre or in framing Questions; he concluded that to most of them 'the processes of government remain alien or incomprehensible' (Meller 1968); and his verdict seemed confirmed by periodic complaints in the House like that of Paliau Maloat, the representative for Manus (Open), who felt moved to observe during the House's eighth meeting that 'Those who do not know English do not understand what is going on' (*H.A.D.* 7 March 1966, 1st House I, p. 1288).

Professor Meller listed a number of possible remedies for this. But the Visiting Mission had inadvertently put a finger on one of the practical difficulties when they wrote (para. 212): 'It would probably be good, too, for the House to meet for longer periods and more frequently in order to carry out its essential duties.' It is true that the first House was never summoned for more than thirty-two days in a year nor met for more than ten sitting days at a time. This meant that sessions were crammed with business, and more leisurely proceedings or 'legislative training' exercises were out of the question. However, it would be fair to say that these facts were due at least as much to the reluctance of many elected members to spend more than a minimal period in Port Moresby, and to their jealous conservation of their private time there during sessions, as to the shortcomings of official tutelage.

There is no doubt that to their elected colleagues, the official members often seemed unduly to dominate the business of the House, to manipulate or exploit its procedures for tactical advantage, and to influence individual members in tough bargaining 'behind the Speaker's chair'. The Visiting Mission reported that 'The influence of the official members weighs rather heavily on the elected members and is exercised rather frequently' (para. 212), and a prominent Highland member, Tei Abal, said in debate:

> We do not know much about what the Official Members think and feel. The Official Members have so much of the power of discussion and debate that they seem to put the elected members down. (*H.A.D.* 26 February 1965, 1st House I, p. 575)

In part at least, the official members' dominance was but one aspect of a wider problem, the greater technical competence of the expatriate members generally in the House, and it may indeed have been somewhat less resented than the dominance of the elected expatriate members. Lepani Watson summed up the feeling of legislative helplessness that not a few indigenous members shared, when he observed:

> I am worried that the Australian Government is trying to make us into a 'rubber stamp' parliament, but I am even more concerned when I see the Papuan and New Guinean elected members being made into 'rubber stamps' by some of the European elected members. This is what is happening here. It is even worse than what the Government is trying to do to us. (*H.A.D.* 7 September 1966, 1st House I, p. 1754)

From one point of view, of course, official dominance was an inevitable concomitant of the House's Westminster model, which reserves the initiative in and control over business to the representatives of the government. It was partly in an attempt to redress this imbalance that during the second meeting of the House, in September 1964, some European elected members persuaded their indigenous colleagues to appoint a Leader, Deputy Leader, and two Whips for the elected members as a whole—a move to which the Administration responded by appointing a government Whip. There was never any intention that elected members should always vote *en bloc,* but it was hoped that an informal caucus might help them to discuss and understand pending business in their own manner and time before the formal sittings, negotiate an acceptable order of speakers and topics with the Administration, and if necessary unite behind acknowledged spokesmen for the interests of elected members and their constituents, as such. Even this modest effort could not survive the conflicting attitudes and commitments of some elected members, the inertia of others, and the reservations of many about the appointed leaders. Halfway through the life of the House the leading positions were quietly abolished and the experiment flickered out.

One suggestion of the 1965 Visiting Mission was that the best way to 'develop the political consciousness of the inhabitants of the Territory' would be 'to associate the New Guineans more closely in the exercise of power'; in particular, they believed it was 'the general desire that Canberra should hand over some of its prerogatives to the House and not make use of its right of veto' (paras. 316, 212).

The association of New Guineans with executive power had already been one of the government's declared objects in providing, by Territory legislation in 1963, for up to fifteen posts of Parliamentary Under-Secretary in the new House. The scheme followed proposals of the Select Committee on Political Development rather than those of the 1962 Visiting Mission on the same subject. A second declared object was to give administrative experience to indigenous politicians. Fears in the Legislative Council that an undeclared object was to facilitate a government majority in the House led to the limit of fifteen being inserted in the Ordinance; in fact no more than eleven (at a time)—all indigenous members—were ever appointed, and the Administration did not exact pledges of voting support. A confused and confusing adjunct to this experiment was the appointment of no more than half of the Under-Secretaries to the Administrator's Council, its remaining places for elected members being filled by European members with no executive appointments. (One of the Under-Secretaries originally appointed to the Council was John Guise, who became Leader of the elected members in September 1964, when he resigned his Under-Secretaryship but remained on the Council.)

In the public utterances of those immediately concerned there is no evidence to show that the Under-Secretary scheme achieved much more than the disillusionment of a number of indigenous members. The mutual obligations of the senior officials and their allotted 'understudies' remained vague; each side had more pressing preoccupations and commitments; the constitutional status of Under-Secretaries was equivocal; in practice they had neither political nor administrative responsibility; at best they became messengers, intermediaries, and spokesmen for their official heads of departments (see van der Veur in Bettison *et al.* 1965: 450-3; Parker 1966, 1967a; and Meller 1968: 3-6). If the experience had any educational value for the incumbents themselves, it was confined to this dozen indigenous members (already comprising, as van der Veur put it, 'the whole educated echelon of Papuans and New Guineans' in the House). Only four of these became Ministerial or Assistant Ministerial Members in the 1968 House. Of the other two re-elected, Paul Lapun declined to submit himself for nomination, and John Guise (who as already seen had only been an Under-Secretary for a few months) became Speaker. Membership of the Administrator's Council during the first House provided only tenuous 'association in the exercise of power'. It was even in law only an advisory body; in practice its proceedings were reported to be almost entirely formal until 1967.

when a new Administrator claimed to be treating it more as a consultative body.

As to the sharing of prerogatives with the House in general, perhaps the main formal steps were the creation of Select Committees of members to examine some specific issues as they arose, and of Standing Committees, notably those on Public Works and Public Accounts, which—as distinct from the usual standing committees for the House's domestic management—were enabled to acquire some critical understanding of proposals and operations of the Administration from inside, through direct access to officials and papers. Nevertheless, critics like Meller considered there could have been more extensive use of standing committees, and pointed out that indigenous members of the House were heavily under-represented on them.

Some members expressed dissatisfaction when the Minister referred important issues that exercised the House (such as control of the public service, the introduction of television, and economic development policy) to committees not answerable to the House though sometimes drawn from its members, or to 'experts' from inside or outside the public service whose reports were not always published. On the other hand, when the Administration's proposals met with strong opposition in the House, it was willing to accept some of its defeats by amending or withdrawing the offending measures. The government's review and veto powers were applied even more sparingly than they had been to the Legislative Council. A small handful of Bills passed by the first House was returned for amendment, mostly on technical points; of its total output of over 200 Ordinances, none was vetoed by the Administrator, and two only, being reserved Bills, were refused assent by the Governor-General.

Reviewing the new legislature after its first year, the Visiting Mission reported in 1965 that there was 'still a long way to go before the House of Assembly can effectively perform the functions which should in principle belong to it' (para. 210). This was still broadly true at the end of its first term, but there were perceptible signs of movement. There had been some increase in the number of private members' bills, and of motions and questions on other than parochial affairs. There was a growing impatience with the difficulty of understanding House functions and procedures, and a growing individuality in members' attitudes to important questions. There was increasing disillusion with the House as an imagined instrument of economic development, and a greater willingness to unite behind some elected member—usually European—in censuring or defeating Administration proposals. The House became a sounding board for some of the more lively political issues of the period.

These began with the government's decision—in the interests of the Territory's future economy and social equality—to reduce the salaries of 'local' (essentially, indigenous) officers of the Territory public service to below half, on average, of the standard salaries (exclusive of special Territory allowances, rental rebates and so on) of expatriate officers in corresponding jobs. These measures, announced in 1964 and early 1965, met with prolonged criticism in the House for their timing and severity, and elected members forced through a protest Bill to remove control of the service from the Public Service Commissioner appointed by the Minister to a Board appointed by the Administrator. After a protracted hearing the Public Service Arbitrator granted local officers increases the modesty of which led many elected members to support public service demands for drastic changes in the arbitration personnel and machinery. Other matters which led to heated debate and sometimes Administration defeats in the House included measures stemming from the proposal to follow the World Bank report in concentrating development effort only on certain selected, 'more promising', regions; the concern of some members about the pace of 'localisation' of the public service; and the respective interests of local landholders and the Papua and New Guinea people as a whole in the terms of an agreement with Conzinc Riotinto of Australia Ltd for the exploration and exploitation of large copper deposits in Bougainville Island.

These examples indicate that elected members in the House had begun to grapple with matters of national import. But they had not been able to convey any sense of these issues to the electorate at large, nor indeed to establish any clear nexus between the House and their constituents. As a member from New Britain told the House:

> When I go back to my electorate all the people ask, 'What have you done in the House [of Assembly]? What laws have you made?' There is only one reply I can make: 'I do not know; I did not understand properly'. (*H.A.D.* 7 March 1966, 1st House I, p. 1290)

One source of frustration was the widespread misconceptions about the functions of the legislature when it was first elected. Many people had seen it as a means of enhancing their power to attract government resources to the development of their areas. As the passage of time exposed the fallacy of this view, electors were inclined to blame their members and sometimes (not without reason) to accuse them of mere self-aggrandisement. Most of the rural villagers saw their member in a more modest role—as transmitter of their views to the government and reporter of government's decisions and doings to the village—and many members disappointed them even in this role. The reasons were various: the burden of duties as Under-Secretaries or committee members; the size of electorates (much larger than the 1962 U.N. Mission had suggested), and difficulties of travel; reluctance, even fear, to visit unfamiliar, 'foreign' parts of one's electorate; pre-occupation with cultivating private businesses; or simple laziness.

In short, by 1967 the general uncertainty about members' roles, their hazy perception of the legislative process, their view of political education as a matter of teaching people about institutions—a job for the Administration rather than of mobilisation for participation—all this had only served to reinforce an already widespread sense of helplessness in, or remoteness from, 'national' politics. Possibly the pre-conditions for 'national' politics were totally wanting. But any attempt to generate them at this stage would have to come, it seemed, from outside the House of Assembly.

THE RISE OF POLITICAL PARTIES

It has already been shown that the Australian government's anxiety about autonomous political change in New Guinea was not confined to the possibilities of self-government or independence. The 1965 U.N. Mission considered that in promoting political consciousness 'another useful step will be the development of political parties' (para. 317). But when the first effective steps to form such parties were taken in 1967, the Minister for Territories told the newspapers:

> At this stage of its development the Territory would be better off without parties. Parties should form naturally [sic]. They should not be force-fed. However it is a free country. (*Canberra Times*, 23 June 1967.)

As though to elucidate this view, Special Branch police (a kind of political security force) were regularly to be observed taking notes of those present and what they said at public meetings of the parties. However, this was only a minor aspect of the hostile environment in which this crop of parties appeared. As there are detailed accounts of them and their predecessors (Wolfers 1967b, 1967c, 1968a, 1968c; Parker 1967b), the following outline gives only the essential background to the area studies in later chapters.

The New Guinea United National Party, which was never much more than a paper organisation in Port Moresby, was formed in

August 1965 and led thereafter by the President of the Port Moresby Workers' Association, Oala Oala-Rarua, an unsuccessful candidate for the House of Assembly in 1964. It held a few public meetings in the town and attempted to recruit some members of the House. Its platform emphasised Territorial unity, the advancement of indigenes in private enterprise, economic planning, and the need for a strong trade union movement. One plank, 'the rapid development of New Guinea to internal Ministerial Government by December 31, 1968', was immediately so controversial that within a few days the date was removed. The party suffered throughout from well-meaning European tutelage, timid leadership, a platform too esoteric for popular appeal, undue attention from the police Special Branch, and lack of organisational skill. In June 1967, after holding no meetings for eighteen months, it was formally dissolved by Oala.

By that time parties were forming in direct preparation for the 1968 elections. Two of these had an even slighter history than the National Party. The only tangible manifestations of the Territory Country Party were a platform announced at Madang in August 1967 advocating various forms of agricultural development, and a list of office-bearers including as Secretary a European journalist of that town, J. D. McCarthy, who was reputed to be the founder. Before the end of the year he declared that the project had been abandoned. The New Guinea Agriculture Reform Party was sponsored at Rabaul by a European cocoa planter, Albert Price, who was a candidate for the Gazelle Open electorate in 1968. Probably a number of other candidates in the Gazelle Peninsula associated themselves with it to some extent; some of them attended meetings; this venture also was moribund by the time of the voting. Its real policy concern seems to have been solely with local economic interests.

Four other political parties appeared during 1967, each of which sponsored a number of candidates at the 1968 elections. The first of these was the United Democratic Party, which had been the subject of rumour and discussion in the Sepik District for over a year before its inaugural meeting was held at Wewak in May 1967. Its members included three indigenous and two European members of the House of Assembly, as well as a number of officials and teachers in Catholic missionary institutions, nearly all being personalities in the Sepik. The word 'Christian' was included in the title at the first meeting, and removed again during the election campaign; the party emphasised Christian principles in its platform, appealing to all denominations. Its other main planks were the encouragement of Pidgin as a national language, the incorporation of the Territory in Australia as a seventh state, the development of primary education, and removal of the Territory's capital to Lae. The seventh state plank was removed after the Minister for Territories, in response to inquiries by party leaders in June, told them he thought it was not feasible, at least for the present. Emissaries were sent to establish branches of the party in other regions of the Territory and some thousands of paid-up members were claimed at various times. For practical purposes it had little impact outside the two Sepik Districts, in which all of its endorsed election candidates stood.

The next party to emerge was Pangu—Papua and New Guinea Union—Pati, so far the most remarkable political organisation in the Territory. Its leadership outside the House of Assembly came mostly from indigenous public servants in their mid-twenties to mid-thirties with at least some secondary education and considerable urban experience. They were directly affected by the policy of differential salaries for local officers, and they were concerned about the lack of definition in Australia's plans for the political future of the Territory. Late in 1966 and early in 1967, a group of thirteen made a series of submissions to the Select Committee on Constitutional Development (see pp. 35, 38), radically criticising the Territory's colonial status and racial inequality, and proposing immediate limited responsible government, a cabinet elected by the House of Assembly, a local Public Service Board, and a High Commissioner to replace the Administrator. Members of the group who figure later in this book included Oala Oala-Rarua; Joseph Kaal Nombri, a Chimbu Patrol Officer, Elliott Elijah from the Trobriands, a training officer in the Department of Trade and Industry, and Cecil Abel, a European ex-missionary born in the Territory. There followed in June the formation of the Pangu Pati, in which most of the original thirteen were shortly joined by some fifteen members of the House. They included John Guise, the veteran politician from Milne Bay who had served in the Legislative Council and been Leader of the elected members' group in the House: Paul Lapun from Bougainville who became parliamentary leader of the Party; James Meangarum, member for Ramu Open, who months earlier had tried to interest local government councillors and others in the Madang District in a political party to offset Administration domination of the House; Eriko Rarupu, the man from the Goilala mountains who was Member for Moresby Open; Stoi Umut, Member for Rai Coast Open; and two young European members, Barry Holloway and Tony Voutas, who had been Patrol Officers and were prominent critics of the Administration. Three of the 'parliamentary wing' were Under-Secretaries. The party executive included Gavera Rea and Oala, who were to contest the Central Regional electorate in 1968 after Oala had been expelled from Pangu; and purported to include two prominent Tolai leaders, Vin ToBaining and Thomas ToBunbun (see p. 57). The party soon produced a platform calling for immediate home rule and eventual independence, Pidgin as a second official language, rapid localisation of the public service, encouragement of overseas investment in the Territory, land reform, better education and housing, and improvements in local wages. This was the only party that proved able to field candidates—officially or informally—in most regions of the Territory at the 1968 elections.

In direct and avowed reaction to the formation of Pangu, and little more than a month later, the All People's Party (*Pati bilong Ol*) was created by a small group of European traders and transport operators, with support mainly in the Angoram Sub-District of the East Sepik, the Ramu area of the Madang District, and in Goroka. The party was strongly opposed to independence or self-government 'at this stage', believed economic development must precede political advancement, and wanted no cuts in the Australian Administration's powers or staff. It was joined by two European and one indigenous member from the House of Assembly, representing the Madang-Sepik Special and the Gulf and Madang Open electorates respectively. A second indigenous member, from the Gulf District, campaigned as a party member in 1968.

Napro, the National Progress Party of Papua and New Guinea, was initiated by a 44-year-old mixed-race employee of the Public Works Department, and launched at a public meeting in Port Moresby in mid-November 1967. Like the other political parties, it was equipped with an elaborate paper organisation, constitution, and platform, and little in the way of grass-roots membership or financial resources. Its political activity was virtually confined to the Papuan coast. It claimed the support of four M.H.A.s, but could not name them. All of its first executive except one were Papuans. Their backgrounds were not unlike those of the Pangu leaders: several had some Australian education, and they were public servants, teachers, journalists, or mechanics. On the other hand, their political program was less like Pangu's than like an indigenous version of that of the All People's Party. It stressed various forms of economic development, called for improved social services (a subject overlooked by other parties), and advocated a form of Ministerial government as a preparation for ultimate self-government. But in public statements its founder and chairman, Bill Dihm, and other leaders made clear their agreement with Australian government policies in the Territory, their disagreement with Pangu's political aims, and their conviction that topics like self-government, independence, and the union of

Papua and New Guinea could be left to the wisdom of Australia and the United Nations in the indefinite future.

Such were, in bare outline, the origins and nature of the political parties that appeared between the 1964 and 1968 House of Assembly elections. Counting in the United National Party, the whole seven originated within four of the eighteen administrative Districts—East Sepik, Central, Madang, and East New Britain, of which the last three are included in this study. None except Pangu gained any appreciable number of adherents or sponsored candidates in areas beyond its District of origin and one or two contiguous Districts. Nearly all activity attributable to the 'parties' as such was the work of a tiny group of leaders, in most cases including European members or unofficial advisers. With one exception all these groups spent a good deal of energy drafting elaborate constitutions, platforms, and organisational structures, though all without exception made decisions *ad hoc,* informally and with little regard for procedural niceties. Despite an elaborate paper constitution, the A.P.P. made no attempt to establish any formal organisation or dues-paying membership. This group alone might possibly have been able to organise and finance such a structure; none of the others could muster the skills or money to sustain it, although Pangu did maintain a fulltime paid secretary, Albert Maori Kiki.

That the Minister's lukewarm comments on the rise of parties in 1967 followed close on the founding of Pangu was hardly a coincidence, considering the prominence its sponsors had given to questions of social, constitutional, and political change. But his concern, like Pangu's enthusiasm for these issues, was soon to appear premature. First, the consternation Pangu encountered among indigenous 'opinion leaders', especially in the Highlands, led the party itself to play down its political objectives. Second, as already shown, new parties sprang up expressly to oppose these objectives. Third, influential voices were raised to discredit political party organisation of any kind.

Pangu's dilemma was dramatically illustrated within a month of its formation when Oala, now one of its four co-chairmen, in the course of a public lecture at Sydney University, said he thought independence for the Territory could in certain circumstances be as close as 1970, and the imposition of the Westminster system there was hard to understand. Pangu's executive hastened to dissociate itself from these views, and after some weeks' hesitation expelled Oala from the party.

Meanwhile, the most prominent elected European M.H.A., Ian Downs, and two other European businessmen in the Highlands publicly warned voters against supporting political party candidates in 1968, calling instead for candidates who would stand for law and order, the security of property, an efficient public service, and co-operation with the Administration. This line was continued in meetings and publications of the Highlands Farmers' and Settlers' Association. In September 1967 an indigenous member from the Highlands initiated a debate in the House in which parties in general and Pangu in particular were criticised by many, mainly on the grounds that they could only be regionally based, would therefore threaten Territory unity, and in any case bewildered the people. These misgivings were soon echoed by the Anglican Bishop of New Guinea, and later by a joint statement from five indigenous businessmen in Goroka including two candidates for the Open electorate (who agreed that Australians in the area had helped to prepare the document).

Thus none of the elements of 1964-7 politics so far discussed seemed propitious for the appearance of 'national' issues or political parties at the 1968 election. As we have seen, the House of Assembly was not fertile soil for either, and they were obviously distasteful to the government and to powerful Territory interests, indigenous as well as expatriate. Parties in general had become suspect, and those that raised national political issues most suspect of all. Yet there remained one other way in which political change might have been purposefully explored. In May 1965 the House of Assembly set up a select Committee on Constitutional Development, 'to consider ways and means of preparing and presenting, and to draft for the consideration of the House, a set of constitutional proposals to serve as a guide for future constitutional development in the Territory' (H. of A. Minutes of Proceedings No. 7, 19 May 1965. Motion by Mr Guise).

THE SELECT COMMITTEE ON CONSTITUTIONAL DEVELOPMENT

John Guise was elected, and remained, chairman of the Committee. It began with a membership of ten, of whom six were Europeans, but by September 1966 had fifteen members, nine indigenous and six European of whom four were officials.

When the Committee was established the U.N. Visiting Mission greeted the idea with enthusiasm, and hoped they would proceed 'as rapidly as possible with the preparation of a draft constitution' (para. 224). The Committee set to work with this in mind, and began collecting written constitutions from abroad, asking the House meantime to put a moratorium on the introduction of any constitutional legislation—a request some members found frustrating. The Committee then asked what limits Australia might put on the possible range of future constitutional, citizenship, migration, and financial arrangements with New Guinea and Papua, jointly or severally. But on taking these questions to senior Ministers in Canberra in April 1966, they were put off with the reply that these were matters for a future government to decide. Even before this setback, the Committee were under official pressure to consider what machinery changes were wanted in the size and composition of the House and in the electoral system, to enable the lengthy processes of redistributing boundaries and preparing new rolls, if necessary, to be completed in time for the 1968 election.

The Committee extensively toured the Territory to consult public opinion before making each of their main reports. Dealing in the Second Interim Report with the structure of the House, they said the principal cause of dissatisfaction was the small number of Open electorates. Their present size prevented the member from visiting all parts of his electorate, and people from some areas said they had not seen their member at all. The Committee recommended that the size of Open electorates be reduced from an average population of roughly 49,000 to about 30,000, and that the increasing identification of the people with their administrative Districts be recognised by no longer allowing Open electorates to straddle District boundaries. On the estimates of population available at the time, they concluded that the number of Open electorates should be raised from forty-four to sixty-nine.

It will be remembered that the Legislative Council's Select Committee on Political Development had recommended that the Special electorates reserved for non-indigenous members should be regarded as a temporary device, to be reviewed before the second House of Assembly election. By 1966 it seemed to be widely accepted in the Territory that the racial qualification would have to go. A minority thought there was no case for retaining Special electorates. The advocates of retention based it on a variety of grounds, mainly the need for some better-educated, if not necessarily white, members to advise the 'less sophisticated' Open electorate members; or the desirability of a special device to ensure representation of the business community; or the justice of providing definite representation for the Territory's most significant group of tax-payers, the expatriate community.

The Committee's recommendation was a compromise. Special electorates, now to be called 'Regional', should be retained, but the racial qualification for candidature should be abolished, and an educational qualification, the Territory Intermediate Certificate 'or its equivalent' (very generously interpreted in practice), established 'to bring broader experience to the House' than might otherwise be secured. (The Territory Intermediate is awarded upon completion of six years of primary and three years of secondary schooling.) The Committee accepted the general view that Special electorates were too large or too populous, and should, like Open electorates, also be aligned on the whole with District boundaries. Hence they recommended that the ten Special electorates should be replaced by fifteen Regional electorates, of which twelve would coincide with the same number of the more substantial Districts, while the remaining three would comprise pairs of the smaller or more sparsely populated Districts, namely Gulf and Western, East and West New Britain, and Manus and New Ireland respectively. (Of course, population is not proportional to area, so that this still left Western and Gulf, one of the less populous Regionals, an electorate that sprawled over 54,219 square miles of mountains, beaches, and especially swamps.) The Open electorates were thus grouped within the proposed Regionals, between which there remained considerable disparity: they ranged from the Western Highlands Regional, which on the Committee's figures would contain 296,861 people in nine Open electorates, down to the Northern Regional, with an estimated population of 56,631 in two Open electorates.

The Committee did not recommend any changes in the maximum term of the House, the number of official members, the minimum voting ages, the preferential voting system, or the qualifications of electors. On the last point, they accepted a continuance of the rules under which an elector at any time could switch his enrolment to any electorate for which he was qualified by previous residence, and register an absentee vote there no matter how long he had been in his current place of residence. As the Committee wrote, these rules were based on the assumption (para. 62) that 'large numbers of people who are working in areas other than their home area maintain their ties with their home, and fully intend to return upon completion of their contract or period of employment'. The Committee agreed with some witnesses (para. 65) that 'the tendency to think on a local or village level, rather than a national level, may have the effect of hindering the development of a sense of national unity', and apparently accepted the inference that 'the development of a national identity' would be more effectively promoted by requiring people to vote in the electorate where they currently lived and worked. However, they thought the time had not yet come to enforce a strict residential qualification, though it would have to be thought about in future. They did propose an addition to the qualifications for candidates, intended to ensure adequate acquaintance with and concern for the country's problems and needs: to be eligible to nominate, a person not born there should have lived in the Territory for a continuous period of five years.

This report was readily accepted by the House of Assembly, after a brief debate, by 59 votes to nil. Only two amendments were proposed, and both were defeated. In due course, all its proposals were embodied without change in the necessary legislation in Canberra and Port Moresby. There was one afterthought when it was realised that the five-year residence rule for candidates would disqualify Tony Voutas, Member for Kaindi Open since he won the by-election there in 1966, from contesting the next election. Without demur the Electoral Ordinance was further amended to exempt from this rule sitting and former elected members of the House or Legislative Council, and to provide that temporary absences not longer than two years would not affect continuity of residence under the rule.

In the time left to them the Select Committee on Constitutional Development produced only one more report. In the course of their deliberations they had resolved that the present system of Under-Secretaries was 'not workable' and that 'some system must be instituted which involved members in departmental decision making' (Select Committee 1967: 38). They devoted their Final Report to the problem of enabling 'greater local participation in ... the executive arm of the government' (para. 3). Noting that 'one large sector of the community was against any change ... at least until 1972', and that, on the other hand, the proposals of 'one small group' (the thirteen progenitors of Pangu) amounted to 'limited self government', the Committee adopted the 'intermediate position' maintained by the majority of their witnesses (para. 5). They recommended a mild enlargement of the size and functions of the Administrator's Council, and its rational integration with a system of semi-responsible Ministers and Assistant Ministers, to be chosen from elected members after consultation with the House. These recommendations also were endorsed by the House, without a word of debate, and enacted by parliament with no other change than to replace the title 'Ministers' by 'Ministerial Members' (and similarly for 'Assistant Ministers') because, as the Minister for Territories said, these officers 'would not be exercising the full executive responsibility and authority' (Ministerial Statement in the House of Representatives, *C.P.D.* 26 October 1967, H. of R. 57, p. 2310).

As they were to come into force only in the next House, the

THE CONTEXT OF POLITICAL CHANGE   39

alterations to the executive structure do not concern this book except as a further reminder of the lack of radical political issues at a national level when the second general election was held in 1968. The House of Assembly was beginning to give expression to broad conflicts of interest in the Territory. But it had not been able to generate a nationally-conscious public opinion, and had shown little interest itself in constitutional advance, except to resolve enthusiastically that Papuans and New Guineans would not be stampeded in this matter by bodies like the United Nations, and that 'the road to self-government can best be travelled with one guide— ... the Administering Authority' (*H.A.D.* 2 September 1964, 1st House I, p. 158). The Select Committee on Constitutional Development, far from producing anything like 'a draft constitution', was content with proposing a bigger legislature which through its Ministerial Members could take more part in the work of the executive, but rejected even 'limited self-government'. In short the House and its Committee were still imbued, by and large, with the same attitudes of political dependence as the electorate in general.

THE DISTRIBUTION COMMITTEE

Under the Electoral Ordinance, redistribution of electorates was entrusted to a Distribution Committee of five members, including the Chief Electoral Officer (who was made chairman), Surveyor-General and Commissioner for Local Government *ex officio,* and two indigenous private members chosen by the Administrator. Their main problems arose from technical deficiencies or gaps in the Report of the Select Committee and in the legislation.

For a start, the Select Committee had been given out-of-date figures for the Territory's population. This had risen by 95,022 (the equivalent of three electorates) since the figures they used had been compiled. As a result, the Distribution Committee were bound by a prescribed number of electorates (69) that would not allow the distribution to observe the proposed average population of 30,000. The average would actually be 31,638, which, for example, would have the effect of depriving the Eastern and Western Highlands Districts of one seat each compared with their entitlement under a 30,000 average.

Next, the requirement that all Open electorates be wholly contained within District boundaries was found to be ambiguous, since fifteen of the eighteen District Commissioners, for the sake of convenience, administered some areas outside the gazetted boundaries of their Districts. Physical accessibility, rather than the lines drawn upon a map in Port Moresby, often determines which patrols go where. The Distribution Committee, therefore, gained the informal approval of the Select Committee, with the advice of the relevant District Commissioners, to relate electoral boundaries to the actual administrative areas rather than to the strictly legal entities.

The Committee finally discovered that they had no statutory authority at the requisite time to draw up Regional electorate boundaries. They decided nonetheless to make recommendations, and leave it to the House of Assembly to authorise the boundaries by resolution.

Apart from the criterion of more or less equal population, the Committee, in close conformity with the Ordinance, kept a number of other factors in mind when drawing up the Open electorate boundaries. As stated in their report they were:

(a) community or diversity of interests;
(b) local government council boundaries;
(c) proposed future movement of people into existing local government councils;
(d) means of communication;
(e) physical features;
(f) census divisions; and
(g) existing electoral boundaries.

(Distribution Committee 1967: para. 7. Cf. *Electoral Ordinance* 1963-7, s. 18, which does not mention items (c) and (f), but does refer, additionally, to 'the distribution of the population'.)

The proposed electoral boundaries were gazetted early in May 1967, after which three months were allowed for the public to lodge objections. In all, twenty objections were formally received by the Committee and nine were accepted. Very little information about the objections is available, but one of them is of particular interest here. In the case of the boundaries between Alotau and Kula, Open electorates in eastern Papua, the Committee clearly began with the prescribed criterion of roughly equal population. To take cognisance of those traditional ties which would place Samarai in the Alotau electorate would have created two very unequally populated units: Alotau with a population of 41,235, and Kula with 25,802. So they set up two roughly equal electorates, and waited for appeals to indicate whether traditional or democratic considerations would be preferred. They finally accepted a tradition-based proposal presented in person by the presidents of the four main local government councils in the Milne Bay area.

When the Committee's report came before the House of Assembly, many members complained about particular aspects of individual boundaries, but no-one cavilled at the somewhat dramatic ways in which the peculiar problems of the Central District had been resolved, particularly in regard to Moresby Open Electorate. Outside Moresby, the gathering into one electorate of the coastal sophisticates, especially the Motu and the people of the Kairuku Sub-District, freeing the Motu from their previous numerical domination by the inland Goilala, was so welcome that there were no complaints at the coastal Hiri Electorate containing some 44,066 people to Goilala's 23,456. The principles of ethnic and cultural homogeneity were, apparently, equally acceptable in the case of Moresby Open Electorate, whose boundaries enclosed a population of 36,347, most of whom were transients—indigenes who wanted to vote in their natal areas and short-term European contract public servants not yet entitled to vote in Territory elections. The Committee had included the eleven Motuan villages within this area in the Hiri Electorate, thus leaving Moresby to the 'foreigners'.

Having outlined the political context and constitutional framework in which the 1968 election was held, we now turn briefly to two administrative aspects of the electoral process, the programs of political and electoral 'education'.

POLITICAL EDUCATION

One of the recommendations of the 1965 U.N. Mission was that 'political education should be vigorously pursued' (para. 313). As the experience of 1964 showed, some quantum of political education was an inevitable concomitant of conducting so novel an operation as a general election. In the first place, it was hardly possible to acquaint people with the essential mechanics of voting and their rights and obligations as electors, without telling them something about the objects of popular elections and the functions of the House that was to be elected. In the second place, the elaborate preparations for the election produced the usual spate of wild surmise about its underlying implications, which had to be countered by still fuller explanations.

To some extent these minimal needs for political education were anticipated in 1962-3. Between the two elections the Administration continued to provide what it called political education to members and potential members of the House of Assembly, mostly in the form of conducted tours to public institutions in Australia and abroad. But it still did not pursue continuous political education at the grass-roots, nor, as Bettison said of the previous period, 'any coherent program to educate the people to an awareness of the political opportunities presented by an indigenous majority in the House of Assembly' (Bettison et al. 1965: 69; and see generally chapter 4 therein). Instead, another *ad hoc* campaign was devised to cope with the specific needs of the 1968 election.

This included one formal change. In 1963-4 the Department of Native Affairs (called District Administration after 1964), which conducted the field program before both elections, used the terms 'political education' and 'election education' interchangeably. In 1967, 'political education' was seen as a program 'to give the people the necessary facts about politics and government so that they can assess issues from a basis of understanding and so make the best use of their vote' (D.D.A. 1967c: Attachment on 'The 1967 Political Education Programme', para. 2). 'Electoral education' comprised instruction on the formal procedures of nomination, voting, the count, and so on. An administrative implication of the distinction was that the political education program was supposed to cease when writs were issued and nominations for the election opened on 27 November, to avoid official involvement in the discussion of 'political' questions once the campaign period had opened. Though they necessarily overlapped in time and content, the two programs are separated here in an outline sketched mainly from the headquarters viewpoint, to enable comparison with the glimpses of their grass-roots application given in the constituency studies.

The political education program was planned during 1965 and 1966, as in 1962-3, by a committee including representatives of the Department of District Administration (which provided the chairman and executive officer), the Department of Education, and the Department of Information and Extension Services. District Administration would again be primarily responsible for formulating the message, and its field staff for carrying the story to townsmen and villagers. The other departments would advise on content and on technical methods of communication, and co-operate in dissemination. It was realised that most people could be effectively reached, if at all, only by word of mouth, and hence that, as before, every Administration official in contact with the people would be helping to explain the impending election, beginning with the patrols compiling the common roll. But this time it was desired to secure more consistency and authority in the expositions of individual officers, and to avoid the embarrassments of 1964, when a radio campaign on 'The Role of the House of Assembly' had to be mounted within a month or so of the election, to counter some of the alarming rumours that were circulating. The device relied on in 1966, which assumed a central place in the formal program, was to lay down an authorised version of the facts about politics and government in a number of printed publications.

The main products of this decision were a 28-page booklet entitled *Government in Papua and New Guinea* and another of 32 pages, with illustrations, on *Local Government in the Territory of Papua and New Guinea*; six school-level booklets of stories giving practical examples of government in action, collectively entitled *Sowai Finds his Country*; and a numbered series of twenty single-sheet leaflets, of which seventeen discussed some of the elements of democratic government, while the final three belonged rather to 'electoral education', summarising the essential facts about the conduct of the elections. The booklet on *Government* began with some historical paragraphs (such as 'How Courts and Judges Started'; 'How the big council of the people took over the work of the Kings'; 'Even in a Democracy the people must be alert'; and 'The Big Council of all Papua and New Guinea') and proceeded to outline 'The Three Parts of Government' in the Territory, adding a longish section on finance ('A good citizen pays his tax'). The *Local Government* booklet, after briefly asking 'Why do we need local government councils?', maintained a severely practical emphasis, describing how councils are started, and summarising their powers, functions, procedures, financing, elections, staffing and relations with various Administration departments. Examples of the topics discussed in the 'green leaflets' (this colour—though not all were green—identifies them in the constituency accounts below) are 'Majority Rule', 'The Rule of Law', 'The Representatives' Responsibilities', 'Interest Group' [*sic*], 'Industrial Organizations', and 'Political Parties'.

The general level and tone of these publications can be gauged from the extracts reproduced in Appendix IV. Of the *Government* booklet, some 15,000 copies were printed, in English only; of that on *Local Government*, a distribution of about 5000 in English was envisaged—though, according to the Secretary of the Administrator's Department (*H.A.D.* 20 November 1969, 2nd House II, p. 2120), 10,000 copies in English and 20,000 in Pidgin had been circulated before the election. Of the green leaflets, 35,000 in English and 70,000 in Pidgin were sent out, and of the *Sowai* stories, some 3000 copies in English and 7000 in Pidgin.

Most of these materials had been prepared during 1965 and 1966, but they were not ready for distribution in February 1967, when the Director of District Administration sent a circular to field staff describing them in general terms, but saying there had been 'many unavoidable delays both in drafting and printing'. Officers were instructed to discuss and explain the processes of government with as many of the people as possible whenever opportunity could be made. The printed materials, which would be distributed through District Commissioners to field staff of all departments and to 'Council libraries, ... local officers, ... schools, clubs and sufficiently literate people', were meant 'to ensure accuracy and consistency as well as provide handouts, which the people may retain and re-study at their leisure'. It had been intended to distribute the *Sowai* booklets throughout 1966 as a preliminary to the more formal approach in 1967, but here too, 'printing was delayed' (D.D.A. 1967a).

These delays were bound to dislocate the program. The two main booklets were produced in May and June 1967 respectively (judging by their imprints) and then in English only. By July, these, together with the *Sowai* stories and the first ten leaflets, in English and Pidgin, had been despatched to District offices. The other ten leaflets were still in various stages of preparation; a promised Pidgin version of the *Local Government* booklet, and a further booklet called *Our Government—Why?* (which never appeared), were still with the printer. The last of the leaflets (according to imprints) were not completed till October, and this study's Madang team observed some still reaching the District Office there in the following January.

It was not until the middle of August 1967, when the main distribution had been managed, that field staff were given a detailed written briefing on the use of the printed material. Assistant District Commissioners were to arrange 'short informal seminars' at Sub-District level for the various officers to familiarise themselves with the materials. Officers going into a 'contact situation' were to carry a copy of *Government in Papua and New Guinea* and sets of the leaflets to hand out 'if necessary'. District Administration officers in their extension work and teachers in their civics classes were expected to introduce the new concepts, sticking closely to the printed matter and referring back to headquarters for the 'correct' information for replies to questions they could not answer themselves (D.D.A. 1967b, 1967c).

It appears from this evidence that those who originally planned the political education program saw the printed materials mainly as instruction manuals for the field officers, and envisaged the latter, after absorbing their meaning through study and local seminars, transmitting the contents to the voters as they went about their duties in the countryside. The delay in producing the materials and associated instructions, and the further time needed to get them to the field, evidently prevented the operation from working in this way, except on a comparatively limited scale. In many areas the common roll patrolling was largely over by the time most of the printed material was available. A normal patrol into many of the rural areas might take several weeks and might not be carried out more than once in two years. In practice, therefore, especially in the rural areas, the exercise often took the form of physically distributing the printed papers to whatever focal points could be reached in the available time, in the hope that indigenous officers, local government councillors, or even election candidates would expound their contents to the villagers or simply hand them on further. Harassed District officials gave additional reasons for this mode of distribution besides the delay in receiving the 'literature'. They were short of trained staff, even for routine administration; they did not want to be accused of manipulating the election; it was better for the people to learn about government for themselves, or from their own compatriots, than from white men.

There were supplementary measures in the program. About mid-1967, Administration radio stations, controlled by the Department of Information and Extension Services, were asked to compile short sessions based on the printed papers, especially the booklet on *Government,* and to try to stimulate listener response through letters and questions, which would be referred to the District Administration office for guidance on replies. Some stations reported success with these programs; others did not run them. In any case, their impact would be limited by the small number of receiving sets in the villages, especially inland. Finally, three copies of a film made by the Commonwealth Film Unit covering all stages of the 1964 election were circulated through the Territory.

ELECTORAL EDUCATION

Information about the electoral process was given in the field by much the same people—officials and others—as purveyed political education, and often on the same occasions. On the official side, District Administration field staff, who organised the political education campaign, also had to administer the election in such positions as Returning Officer and Presiding Officer, and to inform would-be candidates and voters about the necessary procedures. In these capacities they were finally answerable to the Chief Electoral Officer in Port Moresby.

Of course, instruction on the administration of the election was as important for polling officials as for citizens generally, especially as it was deliberate policy on this occasion to use indigenous officials wherever possible; for example, most poll clerks in rural areas were indigenes. At a different level so also was the Deputy Chief Electoral Officer, who conducted training courses of a day or two in various Districts for electoral officials, explaining in detail the Electoral Ordinance and their duties on polling day. According to their zeal, Returning Officers held one or more further briefing sessions with their subordinates, whose retentiveness and skill in such novel tasks inevitably remained uneven, irrespective of race.

It was not thought necessary to conduct so intensive an electoral education campaign as in 1963-4. This was partly because older electors could remember that occasion, but mainly because a majority of them were now used to elections conducted on similar lines for local government councils, which since 1963 had nearly doubled in number and in people covered, who now composed about two-thirds of the Territory's population. Throughout the later pre-election months field staff were answering questions about nomination and voting, the difference between Open and Regional electorates and the names and boundaries of those in the area, and polling procedures.

The main program was kept till late January and February 1968, so that the details would be fresh in people's minds during the polling. In addition to the last three of the green leaflets, a four-page pamphlet, *Talk about the 1968 Elections,* outlining the essential points in English, Police Motu, and Pidgin versions, was distributed during January in much the same way as the political education leaflets. The Chief Electoral Officer and his Deputy gave radio talks in the same three languages. For three weeks before the beginning of polling the various radio stations throughout the Territory made repeated spot broadcasts on polling rules and procedures. In these later stages, Returning Officers and their staffs were able to give additional local items such as the names and identities of the candidates in each electorate and the exact dates, times, and places for polling. Throughout the period, flip-charts and posters were available to illustrate informative talks.

Again, however, as with political education, field observation suggested that communications became the more attenuated the nearer they approached village level. Here, according to several of our constituency teams, much of the job was left to local government councillors and the candidates themselves. In Lawrence's area 'the only authoritative information which systematically reached the councils was the stencilled schedule with dates and places for polling'. This may be one reason why candidates frequently began their campaign speeches by reminding their audience of the voting routine, and even by identifying the other candidates in their area. The double role of instructor and participant could be invidious, even for councillors who were not candidates, when they were known to be committed, for example, to one candidate rather than another. However, the Chief Electoral Officer felt able to report, six months later, that by and large the program had forestalled the wilder misconceptions that had attended the previous election. 'These fears, misunderstandings, and cargo-cultism', he wrote, 'did not assume anywhere near the proportions that they did in 1964' (C.E.O. 1968: 20). He appeared to ignore the contribution of political (as distinct from electoral) education in achieving this result.

In addition to dates in the election timetable already mentioned, it may be useful to note the following: nominations of candidates closed on 5 January 1968; polling began on 17 February and ceased on 16 March; primary votes were counted on 16 March and preferences were counted on 30 March. Writs with final results were returned on 26 April 1968. Voting and counting procedures remained as already described for the 1964 election. There was one innovation: in 1964 the votes for the Open and Regional electorates were cast on a single ballot paper; in 1968 two separate ballot papers, differently coloured, were used. The following constituency chapters record some of the problems observed in the actual conduct of polling in the areas studied; some of their implications for the voting system now in force, and for the understanding of New Guinea politics at this time, are drawn together in the concluding chapter.

UNDER THE VOLCANO

Ann Chowning, A. L. and T. S. Epstein
Jane Goodale and Ian Grosart

CHANGES in the electoral system since 1964 affected the elections on New Britain in a number of ways. With the abolition of the Special electorates, the East and West New Britain Districts were included within a single Regional electorate, with the two sitting Members now opposing each other. Secondly, whereas in 1964 there were only three Open electorates, the whole island was now divided into five Open electorates: Rabaul, Gazelle, Kokopo, basically all on the Gazelle Peninsula, and Kandrian-Pomio and Talasea. The last two stemmed from a decision to split the island west of the Gazelle 'horizontally' rather than 'vertically' as in 1964. This resulted in more homogeneity within each electorate as regards culture and history of contact, but as the members for the former East and West New Britain seats were both from the south coast they too became rivals in the same constituency.

Whatever considerations guided the drawing of the new Regional electorates homogeneity could not have been one of them. From whatever angle one views it, New Britain, some 13,000 square miles in area, is as varied in composition and character as any part of the country one might care to mention: in terms of heterogeneity it could indeed serve as a microcosm of New Guinea as a whole. There are marked variations in ecological and topographical conditions, ranging from the fertile and densely populated areas of the Gazelle Peninsula in the north-eastern corner to the mountainous and thinly inhabited parts of the interior. Where physical conditions are so often extremely difficult, movement between groups is restricted, and it is not surprising to discover that the linguistic situation is both varied and complex (see Chowning 1969). Differences in social and economic organisation also occur, though in most groups variants of cultural forms widespread throughout Melanesia can be readily recognised. More important in the present context are the striking disparities between different groups in the nature of their contact

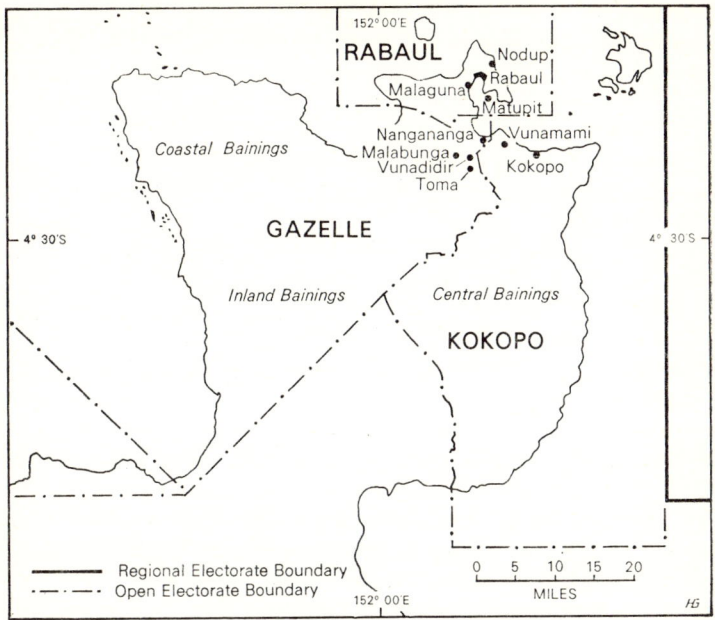

2 Gazelle Peninsula Open Electorates

experience and degree of acculturation. The Tolai of the Gazelle Peninsula have had close and continuing contact with Europeans for almost a century, and are frequently referred to as one of the most advanced, and certainly the wealthiest, of the indigenous peoples of Papua and New Guinea. Other groups, such as the Kombe of the Talasea Sub-District, have also had a lengthy history of contact, but their relationship with the wider society created by the coming of Europeans has been less intense and immediate, and the marks of the impact on their social system and culture accordingly much less evident. Finally, various small groups in the interior, although long officially listed as controlled, have experienced only very recent and cursory contact with missions and the Administration; while even on the thoroughly pacified coast outside the Gazelle Peninsula, the effects of contact diminish sharply as soon as one leaves the vicinity of long-established plantations, mission stations, and government posts.

Inevitably then there are differences in the degree of economic and political development, even within groups. For example, while the majority of the Tolai have had local government councils since the early 1950s, there are still parts of the Gazelle Peninsula, as well as elsewhere on New Britain, where councils have not yet been introduced. In some places indeed attempts to do so have met with a signal lack of enthusiasm, if not actual resistance. It is interesting to record that in Kombe, the Passismanua, the Tolai non-council areas, and notably in the Duke of Yorks, word of the arrangements for the elections to the House of Assembly quickly came to be associated in people's minds with the question of the possible or likely formation of local government councils. Reluctance to enter the council system appears in many instances to be compounded of a rational assessment of the local situation as the people or their leaders see it, combined with a variety of fears of the consequences of incorporation into such a system. The frequent confusion of the two issues reflects their unfamiliarity with the working of the governmental system where it touches on issues that lie beyond their parochial horizons, the general failure of sitting members to visit the whole of their electorates, and the poverty and ineffectiveness of the Administration's attempts to implement the extremely difficult task of mass political education which it set itself.

At Kombe, for instance, outside the village of the single Kombe candidate (a government boat captain who usually lived at government stations), nothing was known of the House of Assembly and nobody was found who even understood the expression. The name of the sitting Member was not recognised, and no one could say who he was or what he did. Again, in the bush west of Kandrian on the south coast, while the people knew the names of both sitting Members and many had seen them at Kandrian, they showed no more understanding of their member's duties, the House of Assembly, or the purpose of the elections. The sitting members, both of them from offshore islands, were thought to identify themselves with the interests of coastal people only: neither had ever visited these interior villages, nor did any other candidate do so.

Both Barrett and Ashton, the sitting Members for the former Special electorates, now contesting the Regional, campaigned extensively throughout the island, but Ashton was the only candidate for any electorate to campaign in the villages being studied in Kombe. Although he undoubtedly gained votes by coming he did little to straighten out the confusion about the elections themselves. It is fair to say that many people in West New Britain were just as ignorant of the House of Assembly and the elections as they had been in 1964; if they knew they had a member, they felt that he had done nothing for them and held few if any expectations of gaining anything by voting again. The single exception seems to have been those areas in which the elections were tied in with one of the local cargo cults. Otherwise, only near European settlements, and often as a result of European activity, does there seem to have been somewhat more knowledge and interest.

In the circumstances the fact that the elections in these parts sparked off little public discussion or activity can hardly be surprising, and the material fieldworkers had to elicit by direct questioning was accordingly thin and often negative in character. We have therefore concentrated here on the elections in the politically more advanced Gazelle Peninsula.

THE GAZELLE PENINSULA

The Gazelle Peninsula, and its north-eastern corner in particular, occupies a position of prominence in the affairs of the Territory out of all proportion to its size. In this development the facts of geography, topography, and ecology have all had an important part to play. By the 1870s there was a considerable expansion of trading and other activities in the Western Pacific, and within a short time a movement westwards of traders, planters, and missionaries had begun to converge on New Britain. When shortly afterwards the area was annexed to form part of the colony of Friedrich-Wilhelmsland, the Germans found the Gazelle, with its extremely fertile soils and favourable location in regard to trade routes, admirably suited to the establishment of a plantation economy. The town of Rabaul, set within the magnificent natural haven of Simpson Harbour and ringed around by volcanic craters, was founded in 1910, and quickly developed as an important administrative centre and port. The area has experienced many fluctuations of fortune since then, but the factors which helped to shape its early development under the German régime are still at work, accounting for the considerable measure of continuity in its basic social character in what has otherwise been a period of notable and rapid change.

From the outset then, as already noted, the Tolai have had a closer and more sustained experience of alien groups than almost any other people in New Guinea. From the beginning too they have shared in the growing prosperity of their district, initially through the sales of unprocessed coconuts and then of copra, but also by producing foodstuffs to meet the demands of a newly expanded market. They have also been well placed to take advantage of the other opportunities that go with living close to a major seat of administration. In particular, they benefited from the presence of government and mission schools and other training institutions that were established in or around Rabaul. In the main the early headstart that the Tolai gained over other indigenous groups has been maintained: indeed, it put them in a position to go further ahead when, in the period following World War II, Australian policy came to be marked by an increasing emphasis on development. Thus one of the first major ventures of the new policy, aimed at stimulating and diversifying indigenous economic activities, was the setting up of the Tolai Cocoa Project in the early 1950s. The industry is now firmly established and cocoa has gradually come to rival copra as a source of Tolai income.[1] Simultaneously, the first official steps towards political development in the Territory were being taken with the introduction on the Gazelle Peninsula of a system of Native local government councils. Initially, five councils were established there; and although in several areas local groups refused to participate in the new administrative arrangements, the amalgamation of the existing councils in 1963 to form the Gazelle Local Government Council was a clear expression of increasing Tolai awareness of their area as a single community and their heightening sense of group identity. Educationally, too, the area has been favoured, and with young men moving out to fill more or less skilled posts throughout Papua and New Guinea there was a marked tendency for the Tolai to emerge as a kind of indigenous occupational élite.

The marks of the present relative affluence of this part of New Britain are evident to the most casual visitor: in the confidence with which the Tolai saunter the streets of Rabaul; in the way they throng the town's stores, offices, and banks; and in the large number of Tolai-owned cars and trucks to be seen moving everywhere in the district.[2] However, closer familiarity with the local scene also reveals a number of disquieting features which current prosperity tends to mask from the fleeting visitor, but of which local officials and the more percipient Tolai are often acutely conscious. Currently, the Gazelle is experiencing a population explosion of quite staggering proportions, rising from 40,000 to 60,000 in the past eight years. This increase, it should be noted, goes on in an area of little more than 300 to 400 square miles, about 40 per cent of which since German times has comprised alienated land, most of it taken up

---

[1] In 1964-5 the total sum paid out to growers by the Project amounted to $216,292. Income fell heavily in the following year as a result of losses from 'dieback', but rose again sharply in 1966-7 when the figure was $523,000. In 1967-8 the sum paid out to growers who had sold cocoa to the Project amounted to $658,000. In addition, variable amounts are sold to fermentaries outside the Project (see Epstein, T.S. 1968: ch. 6). Estimated Tolai cash income from copra for 1967 was $947,000.

[2] In March 1968 there were 497 such vehicles registered at the Rabaul Sub-District Police Station, giving a vehicle ratio roughly of the order 1:80 of total Tolai population in the Sub-District.

by plantations now in the hands of European companies, missions, or individual planters, an increasing number of whom in recent years have been local-born Chinese. In these circumstances, population increase in itself would suffice to raise the spectre of land shortage. But the enthusiasm with which the Tolai have taken to cash cropping, particularly in the post-war period, further aggravates the situation, for the successful growing of cocoa has set off a clamour for more land while at the same time making considerable inroads into the supply of land that was formerly available for subsistence crops. There is here a major source of strain, and it can hardly occasion surprise when the tensions erupt into incidents of the kind that occurred shortly before the election at the Raniola plantation.

The plantation consisted of several 'sections', all except one of which had been found after court hearings to vest in Coconut Products Ltd. The remaining section had been, quite legally, vested in the company by the Custodian of Lost (wartime) Titles. Nevertheless, there had been no open hearing concerning this section and the local Tolai had continued to claim it as their own. Early in October 1967 a well organised group of villagers (men, women, and children, each with an allotted task) descended on this section, warned off the company immigrant labourers working there, and planted the area with their own crops, which shortly afterwards they were compelled to uproot when an armed detachment of police was sent to the spot.

Thus far such outbursts have been rare, though not completely unknown, among the Tolai, but the immediate relevance of the land issue to the contemporary politics of the Gazelle is suggested by two facts: firstly, that a leading part in the Raniola affair was played by a young man called Oscar Tammur who a little later was to nominate as a candidate for, and ultimately to win easily, the Kokopo Open. Secondly, that Matthias ToLiman, the sitting Member for Rabaul Open and Under-Secretary for Education, although worried by suggestions that he had only one policy—land—had nevertheless strongly associated himself with the redress of 'just claims'. Without achieving Tammur's plurality, ToLiman also won comfortably.

Rising population and increasing pressure on land are already posing serious problems for the Gazelle: they also draw attention to a related issue which is beginning to concern many Tolai: the question of openings for paid employment. In recent years, larger and larger numbers have been going through primary and secondary schooling, and many are not able to find suitable employment. In particular, a high proportion of students drop out at Standard VI because they have failed their examinations, and, because of the rising educational standards in recent years, are unable to find jobs for which a little earlier their level of schooling would have been considered adequate.

The major remedial measures being canvassed before the election included making more land available, by 'unlocking' undeveloped land on the Gazelle and by opening up the Bainings; making more jobs available through the encouragement of light industry; restricting population growth by birth control; and improving the range of educational opportunities available, particularly for Standard VI dropouts. Some initiatives had been taken in each of these areas by the Administration, which was encouraging intra-Tolai negotiations through Lands Demarcation Committees to establish ownership and effect the transfer of land rights to the landless under mutually acceptable and binding conditions. Further, a Special Lands Commissioner had recently been posted to the Gazelle to assist in the resolution of disputes involving alienated land: the District Commissioner in his Christmas 1967 radio message had endorsed the notion of road building to open up the Bainings for agricultural development: legislation to attract 'pioneer' industries had been passed by the House of Assembly: birth control information and plastic 'loops' were available at the Base Hospital: and the Education Department had endeavoured, yet again, to provide a vocational type of post-primary education for the Tolai. The churches also had associated themselves with several of these activities, which in general had made an impact on village thinking: a desirable future was seen as involving some or all of them.

Nevertheless, there was some uneasiness since the promise to date had been greater than the fulfilment. The Administration had not encouraged private Tolai initiatives in the Bainings, on the grounds that it had a duty to protect the Bainings people from exploitation: it had used unusually large numbers of police—armed, according to rumour, with at least one machine gun[3]—to remove squatters in the Raniola dispute: the new factory at Ulapia was recruiting Sepik labourers, not Tolai: and the Education Department seemed disposed to restrict further expansion of schools in the interests of the more underdeveloped areas, elsewhere in the Territory. Too often indeed policies conceived in a context wider than that of the Gazelle Peninsula appeared to take scant account of local needs. For the Tolai therefore important questions were also raised about the whole future development of the Territory, and of the position of their

---

[3] In raising the matter in the House (heatedly and at some length) ToLiman referred only to 'rifles'. *H.A.D.* 21 November 1967, 1st House I, p. 3049.

own area within it. Thus despite the prosperity and apparent surface calm, many Tolai approached the election in a state of uncertainty, anxiety, and confusion.

THE EMERGENCE OF THE CANDIDATES

Given the changes in the electoral system, one of the first questions of interest to arise was whether any Tolai would nominate for the Regional. It appears that at one point Matthias ToLiman had briefly contemplated the possibility. In the 1950s and early 1960s ToLiman had taught in many of the non-Tolai areas and expected to be remembered favourably. In the end, however, he decided against, calculating perhaps that with the prospect of re-election, particularly now that he would not have to confront Epineri Titimur, his closest rival in 1964, and the virtual certainty of ministerial office once elected, it would have been foolhardy to undertake the more risky task. Nason ToKiala from Nangananga, a former paramount *luluai* (the highest of government-appointed headmen) and first President of the Gazelle Council, was also mentioned. Although some felt that his lack of English had been the main reason for his failure to win Rabaul Open in 1964, some Europeans argued that his present position as a Deputy Lands Commissioner would entitle him to qualify for the Regional. Perhaps because he was now 59 and because as a Methodist he was less confident than ToLiman in grasping the potential of the many Catholic mission stations throughout New Britain as staging posts, he did not nominate. Had he done so, the Price-ToKiala alliance of 1964 would have recurred in an intriguing form with the European contesting an Open seat (Gazelle) and the Tolai, a Regional. There were other younger Tolai who did possess the required educational qualifications. The general view that they were too young and inexperienced obviously needs some qualification in view of Tammur's victory, but clearly they lacked his will to win and ToLiman's experience in the rest of New Britain which had enabled him, however briefly, to contemplate standing. The field was therefore left open to the Europeans, thus making it impossible to refute those pundits who had variously declared that the first New Guinean to stand would sweep the poll or that no Tolai could hope for a single vote anywhere in New Britain save the Gazelle Peninsula.

Don Barrett's nomination was a foregone conclusion. The successful candidate in the West Gazelle Special in 1964, Barrett was by this time an established political figure and a dedicated parliamentarian who enjoyed a wide range of contacts among New Guineans (Polansky 1965). Given too his active interest in the welfare of ex-servicemen, his efforts to encourage indigenous athletics, and his record in attending to the problems of individual constituents, Barrett felt assured of strong support and approached the election with breezy optimism. The other successful candidate for a Special electorate in New Britain in 1964 was Roy Ashton. Visiting New Guinea for the first time in 1945, while serving with the Australian Navy, Ashton returned to the Territory in 1950, and for the next ten years managed a number of plantations in different parts of New Britain—Garua Island near Talasea, Lingalinga in the Kombe area, and Notremal in the Northern Bainings—before taking up a soldier settler block in the Warangoi area in 1960. These activities gave him the opportunity to become well known to indigenes in some of the more remote parts of the island: more important here are the reports of anthropologists who had worked in these areas that he was also well liked. Nor was he entirely out of favour with the expatriate community, as seen in his continued membership of the Executive Committee of the New Guinea Planters' Association. None of the other Europeans who had been candidates for Special electorates in 1964 decided to stand again, except Albert Price, who was the only European to contest an Open electorate within the Gazelle Peninsula.

The situation in regard to the Open electorates was much more complex. Although a good deal of discussion about political issues went on amongst individuals and in small groups, there had been as yet little development of any vigorous associational life, political or otherwise, among the Tolai. Recognising its own political role, if only by implication, the Administration had largely confined its political education program to the mechanics of voting. The churches, notably the Catholics and Methodists, had attempted to fill the gap in various ways, in particular by holding 'leadership courses' of about ten days each. Strong endeavours were made to secure some representation from all the educated groups and strata, while speakers were invited from the Administration and from other denominations. After four years of these, speakers could expect to be politely but persistently grilled on at least some of the controversial issues which fell within their ambit. By this time, too, the number of secondary and post-secondary educational institutions on the Gazelle was approaching double figures. Many Tolai students were thus in a position to interact frequently with each other, with students from other parts of the Territory and the British Solomons, as well as with their parents and other village folk. The students' role in the preliminary meetings which preceded the public hearings of the Select Committee on Constitutional Development was particularly noticeable and early in 1967 ToLiman flew from Port Moresby specially to attend one of the meetings which they had organised at Kokopo. Nevertheless, the main political forum remained the Gazelle Local Government Council. Senior councillors were often well-known throughout the area, but since they were after all representatives of small localities, their position on the council provided no reliable guide to the degree of popular support they enjoyed within their electorate as a whole. In these circumstances there was the distinct likelihood that a large number of candidates might come forward and in the pre-nomination period there was indeed much discussion of this possibility around Rabaul, where rumour had it that at least ten candidates would nominate.

Pre-selection of candidates, and attempts at regulating the numbers who stand, are of course important functions of political parties where these exist, and it is interesting to note that in the attempts to form a party on the Gazelle Peninsula prior to the election some saw this aspect as crucial. Previous attempts to form parties had ended in failure (Polansky 1965; Wolfers 1967b) and were not pursued, but during 1967 developments elsewhere in the Territory inevitably led to some discussion of the issue among the Tolai. Early in that year a conference of councils of the New Guinea Islands Region had recommended the formation of a Local Government Council Party, a suggestion apparently originated by Tony Voutas (see also p. 328). When the matter came before the Gazelle Council in April, the members promptly decided to ask the Regional Local Government officer to address them on the subject and make clear to them just what a party was. Some time later representatives of the United Christian Democratic Party visited Rabaul in the hope of forming a branch there, and when the Pangu Pati was founded in Port Moresby it was quickly announced that Thomas ToBunbun and Vin ToBaining, two prominent figures in Gazelle politics, had become office-bearers in it. Towards the end of 1967 steps were taken to launch a New Guinea Agriculture Reform Party on the Gazelle Peninsula.

The new party never really got off the ground (see below p. 58). However, the point of immediate relevance is the way a number of people clearly saw the party as providing a means of guiding the course of the election. After the inaugural meeting, another was called at Nangananga in mid-December, the main purpose of which was to select candidates in the various Open electorates who would stand with party support. Much to the disappointment of the convenors, it was poorly attended and, after some desultory discussion, it was decided to reconvene a few days later at the Council Chamber in Rabaul. On this occasion about half-a-dozen councillors, who had stayed on after the conclusion of a council meeting earlier in the day, were standing around, expressing their annoyance that nobody else, not even any of the likely candidates, had turned up. One observed angrily that if the party did not select candidates, a lot of people would want to stand. 'Then there will be those from this part and those from another part, and the votes of each will be small, with the result that a Chinese or a half-caste may win, and that is the last thing we [Tolai] want.' Others agreed, observing that time was running out, for they had only until 5 January (when nominations closed); if something was not done quickly, the party would have lost the opportunity to ensure that they got in the men they really wanted.

But by this time it was clear that such party organisation as existed had collapsed utterly, and there was no further effort from this quarter to influence nominations. The names of various likely candidates continued to circulate and, since some appeared anxious not to declare themselves too soon, it remained uncertain right up to the moment nominations closed just who would stand. In the event, the numbers were not as large as had seemed likely: some of those whose names had been freely bandied about had either been the victims of false rumours or had decided to reconsider the matter. The final line-up in the three Open electorates was therefore as follows:

Gazelle	William Tawanga Mualat
	Bolton Tamean
	Stanley ToMarita
	Albert G. Price
	Matthias ToLiman
Kokopo	Beniona ToKarai
	Oscar Tammur
	ToKau ToLogo
	Vin ToBaining
Rabaul	Thomas ToBunbun
	Isimel ToWalaka
	Samson ToPatiliu
	Lawrence ToLavutul
	Epineri Titimur
	Tiut Turmarum

In the Gazelle Open, Mualat (aged 45) came from Yalem, one of the Bainings settlements. Without formal education, he had been a government interpreter and succeeded his father as *luluai* before he was elected to the Bainings Local Government Council in 1964. 'A bit brainy, but he doesn't speak English' was the comment of one informed Tolai. At the time, he was a member of the Bainings Local Government Council Finance Committee and Chairman of the Bainings Land Demarcation Committee. It was widely believed that he had been encouraged to nominate by Administration officers, not because he stood much chance of affecting the outcome, but as a means of promoting Bainings participation and interest in the election, and giving one of their number some experience of modern political processes.[4] Nevertheless the effect was to jeopardise the 800 odd Bainings votes which had been cast for ToLiman in 1964 and while these might have gone elsewhere in any case, the affair serves as a reminder of the delicate position occupied by the Administration and its field officers.

Bolton Tamean (aged about 42) from Nangananga was the son of a Methodist *misionari* (Tolai pastor) and a younger brother of Nason ToKiala. He had completed the government primary curriculum (interrupted by the war) and had taught in government schools for more than ten years around the Gazelle, before resigning to become an official of the Cocoa Project and a cash cropper. Although derided by most Tolai for his eccentricities he was perhaps closer to them in spirit than they cared to admit. Eager for a new and better life, he saw lack of political education, fragmented land holdings, and lack of credit as the main impediments. He had no solutions to offer, however, and having made his gesture and invested his own money in his candidacy he had little notion of what to do next.[5] He campaigned little and then, by his own report, only after vigorous prodding from his fellow villagers.

Stanley ToMarita (aged about 48) was another *misionari* son, from Raluana; he had attended the government school at Malaguna and was a government teacher briefly before the war. Subsequently he had taught in various schools on the Gazelle before finally being posted in the late 1950s to Malabunga Primary T, where he was currently Head Teacher. Since the war, he had developed a keen interest in politics, reading what he could and attending meetings. Speaking English with confidence, he had been twice officially

---

[4] He did not campaign amongst the Tolai and was not interviewed at any stage.

[5] 'Everyone was saying who? so I thought I would go in. I asked if they would accept my money and came back with it the next day.'

sponsored to discuss educational policies with U.N. Visiting Missions. Although he claimed to have been 'upset' by Titimur's famous outburst (see below p. 66) in 1961, the proposal to establish a House of Assembly had excited him and only his lack of experience in public speaking, he said, had deterred him from standing in 1964. Two years later he secured election to the Gazelle Local Government Council with a 332-44 victory over the sitting councillor and was currently confident of beating ToLiman and Price, whom he regarded as the only other serious contenders. As a councillor and 'portfolio member' for Education ('You can hear me in the Council') he felt free to gibe: 'Matthias is a good man, I like him, but it's a big jump from small children to the House of Assembly'. Nevertheless his own political perceptions were still more those of a scholar than of a vote-seeking politician. 'Worry about the future' was his goad. To avoid the mistakes of Africa he felt a continued European, and even Chinese, presence to be necessary until the young could talk to the old and above all the educated could talk with the more backward peoples. Recognising that 'people don't want to hear' about this and that Tammur 'might' (i.e. probably would) win Kokopo, he nevertheless persisted with education as his sole policy plank and in reply to questions on land stressed the sanctity of title and the need for due process. In addition to owning some cocoa and coconut trees he was one of the leading subscribers in the society formed by Raluanas to buy back Kuradui plantation, as a result of which he expected to be allotted 12 acres.[6] His 'natural' bases of support lay around his school and in his 'home' area, although much of this lay in the Kokopo electorate. For the rest, he thought he would be well remembered where he had started schools after the war, but above all he emphasised that lots of Tolai leaders were helping him. Thus while recognising the situation which existed he adopted an essentially conservative position: there would be a time for the young men—'Later, not now'.

Albert Price (aged 52) had polled well for the West Gazelle Special in 1964 (Polansky 1965: 262) and had often campaigned on that occasion with Nason ToKiala, who had secured 1200 odd votes in what was now the Gazelle Open. They had continued to work together in various projects and in 1968 Nason performed many of the functions of campaign manager and advance agent for Price. It is possible, as many claimed, that they hoped to use the New Guinea Agriculture Reform Party as a vehicle or at least a

---

[6] They raised the deposit and with official assistance secured a loan to cover the remainder of the purchase price. This loan had just been completely repaid.

means of launching Price's candidacy. If so, these hopes were largely unfulfilled. At the initial meeting, the question of Open seats for Tolai and Regionals for Europeans was raised and it remained an issue throughout the campaign. Price put forward no policies and promises of his own, but offered himself as an intermediary between the people and central government; although in common with the other serious contenders in Gazelle and Kokopo he emphasised that their words would be strengthened if he first persuaded or bargained with other members. He hoped that his activities on behalf of the multi-racial Cocoa Growers Association and North Coast Development Association would stand to his credit. Both of these appealed principally to the better off Tolai and like ToMarita he overemphasised the electoral significance of 'traditional' leaders. On the question of independence, he was discouraging: 'Independence', he said, 'is like a car in a shop window. When you have the right money in your pocket you can have it; but to get the money, you must work hard!'

ToLiman could be forgiven for suspecting a conspiracy: a Baining, three Methodists, a Catholic (Price), and a European were amongst the roles assumed by his opponents. He did not forbear comment ('The Europeans have put up Price because of my attempts to straighten out land disputes'), but he did not alter his basic strategy (see p. 67). He had been aware as early as 1966 that he was being criticised for neglecting his constituents and in 1968 his alleged failures had become a cliché of political discussion in all three Open electorates. Nevertheless his critics would often spontaneously note, elsewhere, that Matthias had also looked after 'the Kokopo side', where the Tolai had seen little of their elected member from the South Coast.[7] Despite the conservative tinge of his principal opponents he did not adopt an overtly radical approach, but emphasised the more positive prospects offered by the existing framework of institutions. Instead of deadening enthusiasm by emphasising their lack of readiness, he focused attention on what could be done tomorrow and the next day. Above all he sought to secure his home base, the well populated Toma area, where his father had been paramount *luluai,* a prominent Catholic layman, and a pioneer businessman.

In Kokopo the contest seemed more clear cut. Beniona ToKarai (aged about 46) was a village elder in Vunamami, which was also the home of Vin ToBaining. Educated in a Methodist village school,

[7] Admittedly this was not entirely Koriam's fault. On the one occasion when he had visited this part of his constituency he had been badly received.

he was literate in the Tolai vernacular and had been a successful cash cropper during the 1950s, active on the Vunamami Council and in the Vunamami Co-operative Society. In the mid 1960s his selection as Chairman of a land demarcation committee had apparently re-awakened his interest in politics and in 1966 he had contested ToBaining's seat on the Gazelle Local Government Council, being decisively beaten 94-15 in a low poll. Nevertheless he stood in 1968, and campaigned actively, on a relatively conservative platform which featured 'No Independence before Unity'. He had kinsfolk on the Duke of Yorks, but could hope for little support on the mainland beyond that accruing from the internal divisions within his own village. Apart from the heavy calibre of his two principal opponents, his recent domestic difficulties were mercilessly raised at the public meetings he addressed: if he could not control his own affairs, it was asked, how could he aspire to control those of others?

ToKau ToLogo (aged 36) was born in Raluana, where his uncle, a Methodist lay preacher, was *luluai* for over 24 years. ToKau himself had six years of post-primary education and a certificate for marine engineering from the Port Moresby Nautical School. Unmarried, he had resigned from the Marine Department in 1965 to care for his mother. He had little land, like most Raluana, and had invested in several societies including the one formed to buy back Kuradui. He was also a Sunday School Teacher; Steward for the Raluana Circuit; and a Captain in the Boys' Brigade. With little organised backing he campaigned where he could find an audience: yesterday, there was a funeral, tonight Roi (Ashton) will have a meeting. Like Price he offered no policies of his own. ToBaining could not win, he thought, because he had made too many mistakes and enemies.[8] Tammur was, he argued, the best candidate, but people might not vote for him because he was so young and in that case, he (ToKau) should have a good chance. Naturally, if there was any sectarian voting he could also hope for the votes of the more radical Methodists who could not bring themselves to vote for Tammur: he did not say this, but could scarcely have been blind to the possibility.

Vin ToBaining, M.B.E. (aged 52) was not the sitting Member, but was clearly the man to beat. Born in Gaulim on the other side of the Gazelle to a Methodist *misionari*, he had lived in the Vunamami area since the war. As a *tultul* (minor headman) and the protégé of ToEnos, the grand old man of the area, he had become involved in council affairs in the early 1950s, and was

[8] Those distressed by Tolai drinking habits emphasised that he had voted for the right to drink during his term in the Legislative Council. (See also below p. 78).

eventually elected on a restricted franchise to the Legislative Council in 1961 (Epstein, A.L. 1969). One of the architects of the Gazelle Local Government Council, he was currently its President. Understanding the most colloquial English without speaking it, he was also a member of a large number of committees and bodies, mainly by appointment; while his extensive travels inside and outside the Territory included two visits to the United States. On one of these, a stopover in Hawaii had impressed him with the money in tourism. In 1964 he had stood for East New Britain and gained more Tolai votes than his Tolai rival Stanis Boramilat (a brother of ToLiman), although their combined vote was swamped by Koriam's south coast supporters. In the largely Tolai electorate of 1968 and with no rival of Stanis's stature, his prospects seemed excellent. His handicap, however, was epitomised by his M.B.E., awarded in 1965: he had held public office for so long, and was so often reported in the press and on the radio, that it was difficult not to think of him as a figure of the Establishment. In these circumstances, his endorsement of Pangu's objectives and acceptance of office in the party might have seemed an aberration; but this could be explained as a tactical move. However, Pangu's inability to provide assistance to its candidates was a blow; for although he saw well enough the desirability of party organisation, he was not himself a party builder or even a very successful builder of bridges and coalitions amongst the Tolai. For much of his life he had worked through, with, or on the Administration and its officers in a largely personal manner.

Oscar Tammur (aged 26) was aware that by traditional standards he was too young to count and presented himself as 'about 30'. The son of a prosperous cash cropper and former *luluai*, he lived at Ulagunan within easy walking distance of the other three candidates. A good student, he had preferred teaching to the priesthood and between various teaching stints had acquired a 'B' certificate, before deciding to join the Pacific Islands Regiment. After a year training as a motor mechanic in Australia, he had reluctantly sought discharge on compassionate grounds, despite prospects of a technical commission. Returning home in 1967, he had several months later assumed leadership in the Raniola land dispute and impressed all parties with his organising abilities. Discovering that he was eligible to stand for the House, he approached the election in an equally methodical way: as a young man, newly returned and scarcely known—despite Raniola —he engaged in careful 'consumer-research' and on the basis of this drew up a ten point program. Although regarded by some as radical, this amounted to little more than explicit proposals that certain of the Administration's own declared policies be implemented less vaguely and with more speed. On the question of immediate independence he was specific and unyielding: not yet—when the number two and three men in every department, the police, and the army, are New Guineans, he declared, then will be the time; but of course he was opposed to any procedures or courses of action which did nothing to hasten that day.

The contest in Rabaul, at least at the outset, appeared the most open: the electorate included the different ethnic groups within the town itself, the more sophisticated and to some extent more 'urbanised' Tolai of the coastal settlements around Rabaul, and the more numerous Tolai of the hinterland. Six candidates presented themselves, of whom three and possibly four were entitled to feel reasonably confident about their chances. Lawrence ToLavutul was a primary schoolteacher working for the Catholic mission in one of the more remote inland villages of the constituency. A candidate in 1964, he had been eliminated then on the first count (Polansky 1965: 251, 261). Little had happened in the meantime to suggest any upsurge in his popularity, but Lavutul himself thought that his move from Malaguna, just outside Rabaul, to Ratongor had considerably improved his chances. His calculation was that with four candidates from coastal settlements, the urban segment of the constituency, they would split the 'town' vote amongst themselves, while he and Turmarum would share the much larger rural vote. But as things turned out, he enjoyed little support even within his own area, and he would have finished bottom of the poll again if Isimel ToWalaka had not deprived him of that doubtful distinction.

ToWalaka came from one of the group of Nodup villages just outside Rabaul. A man in his mid-forties, he was a product of the pre-war government primary school (now known as the Waterhouse Memorial School) at Nodup. He had served with the Administration for many years, in particular being associated with the work of the native local government councils almost from their inception. With his excellent command of English he was frequently called upon to act as interpreter when visiting missions came to Rabaul and on other similar occasions. Yet in spite of all his experience, ToWalaka gave the appearance of being curiously lost in the world of politics, and it was something of a mystery why he elected to stand at all. Indeed, having nominated, he seemed at once to resign himself to the fact that his chances of winning were remote. Thereafter he did little or no campaigning, giving up the race in a sense almost before it had started. This was all the more surprising in that ToWalaka was clearly a highly intelligent man with a very acute insight into some of the most pressing of the Gazelle's contemporary problems. But it came as no surprise to anybody when he polled only 87 votes and lost his deposit.

The other four were made of sterner stuff. Tiut Turmarum was the second rural candidate. A man of about 40, his formal education had stopped at Standard V, though he worked for a number of years as a teacher for the Catholic mission until he saw that he was getting nowhere. He returned to his village, established a trade store, and began growing cash crops, gradually building up a position for himself as a local entrepreneur. Eventually, he was elected as local government councillor. Very much the self-made man, Turmarum was a complete individualist who had in the past expressed opposition to such developments as the Tolai Cocoa Project, which for him smacked of socialist enterprise. In a constituency like Rabaul, his lack of formal education and inability to speak English (see Polansky 1965: 261) might have seemed a handicap, but he was a powerful orator in the vernacular, and he invariably made a good impression among the Tolai with his forthright and down-to-earth manner.

Samson ToPatiliu contrasted with Tiut in almost every respect. Where Tiut was bluff and hearty, Patiliu, a huge, shambling figure, was quiet-spoken and retiring. Another product of the Waterhouse School at Nodup, Patiliu had served as a wireless operator during the war. After the war he went to secondary school at Sogeri, near Port Moresby, completing his Queensland Junior in 1951. He became a teacher, and then in 1959 he joined the broadcasting service, spending a number of years in Port Moresby before returning to Rabaul as an Assistant Broadcasting Officer. In Rabaul he became Vice-President of the Public Service Association. Patiliu was in many ways fairly representative of a new class of 'Westernised' Tolai gradually emerging on the Gazelle Peninsula, yet he also avowed a strong attachment to traditional Tolai culture, one of his hobbies being to record, and so preserve, the ancient songs associated with the *tubuan* and other ceremonies now disappearing. By temperament and conviction Patiliu was a moderate; keenly aware of the many problems confronting the area, and of the need for change, he also believed in the need to hasten slowly.

Thomas ToBunbun, from the island of Matupit, had also attended the Waterhouse School. In time he became a senior Tolai schoolteacher, but for the past year had been engaged in administration in the Education Department rather than teaching. Now in his forties, ToBunbun appeared in some ways the compleat politician, a man of ambition who measured carefully each step on what he hoped would be the road to power. In 1964 he had been content to gain experience by assisting in the electoral education program. In the meantime he had been building up for himself what seemed to be a position of very considerable political influence, becoming a central figure in all the 'command posts' available to him. President of Rabaul Workers' Association from its inception, he was also at this time Senior Vice-President of the Gazelle Local Government Council. He also served on the Town Advisory Council, the Tourist Board, and many other bodies and committees. Over the years he had travelled quite widely to attend meetings and conferences outside New Guinea. As mentioned already, he was an early supporter of Pangu Pati. However, by the time the election got under way, ToBunbun (like ToBaining) had had second thoughts on the matter, and his links with the party were quietly dropped.

Finally, there was Epineri Titimur (aged 36), also from the island of Matupit. Epineri had run ToLiman a close race in 1964, and with ToLiman now standing in the Gazelle Open, Epineri felt quite confident of success. He had achieved some notoriety in 1961 when he asked Sir Donald Cleland, the Administrator of the day, then on a visit to Rabaul, a question touching on the future independence of the Territory (see Epstein, A.L. 1969). Since then Epineri had been a consistent spokesman for the Tolai, voicing local dissatisfaction with the slow rate of development and change, whenever United Nations Visiting Missions, Australian politicians or other notables came to Rabaul. With less formal education that the other Matupi-Nodup candidates, and markedly less proficient in English, he also lacked much of the surface polish and self-assurance of his 'urban' rivals, and amongst Europeans and in the Chinese community in particular he was widely regarded not simply as a radical, but as a 'wild' man or man of the bush (*man bilong bus*).[9] A sensitive and highly strung individual, Epineri's is a complex personality in which elements of the dreamer are compounded with those of the pragmatist, and a lyrical idealism goes with a certain calculating cunning. There is indeed in his psychic make-up more than a suggestion of emotional disturbance, so that amongst Europeans and Tolai alike there were not a few who frankly regarded him as mentally ill. On the other hand, his inner conflicts—whatever their nature—seem to have generated in him an intensity of feeling that undoubtedly contributed a major source of his appeal to many Tolai.

[9] A suggestion of radicalism is also conveyed in Polansky's remark (1965: 251) that Titimur was the only Tolai candidate to drop the usual prefix 'To' from his name. But Polansky is clearly in error on this point. It is true that 'To' is the usual male prefix, somewhat akin to our own use of Mr, but it is not employed when the name itself begins with a 't' followed by a vowel other than an 'o'. It may also be noted that Titimur occurs here as a patronym; Epineri was the name by which the candidate was most commonly known by his fellow Tolai.

CAMPAIGNING: THE CANDIDATES' PERSPECTIVE

Budding Tolai politicians approached the elections for the first House of Assembly with little in their background to provide a model for the conduct of an electoral campaign, and their inexperience is clearly reflected in Polansky's account. Few Tolai candidates campaigned rigorously and a number indeed appeared to concentrate on their own local areas, where support might have been assumed, ignoring more remote parts where they were largely, if not completely, unknown. By 1968, however, there had been ample time to ponder the lessons of the earlier experience, though it soon became clear that not all had drawn the same conclusions.

ToLiman, who had conducted the most extensive campaign on the Gazelle Peninsula in 1964 (Polansky 1965: 254), did not follow the same course on this occasion. With perhaps uncomfortable memories of a similar gathering in 1964 (Polansky 1965: 257), he joined the majority of Gazelle and Kokopo candidates, together with Ashton of the Regional, in boycotting the Discussion Group's Forum in Rabaul (see below p. 69) and in fact to many observers ToLiman did not seem to campaign at all. If to the observer this appeared to be a risk, it was nonetheless a calculated one. Although some of his detractors were quick to attribute this to laziness and even incompetence in that ToLiman no longer had the services of his former Chinese campaign manager whose interests now lay in Rabaul, it can also be regarded as a shrewd move. New Guineans, ToLiman remarked during one interview, require a different campaigning approach from Australians. Whatever the truth of this, he had as sitting Member been in a position to campaign since 1964, and deliberately to stimulate interest in an election contest now was not necessarily to his advantage. Obviously, since he won comfortably and increased his 1964 vote despite substantial losses in the Bainings, his alleged failure to visit the villages was not the millstone which so many had anticipated.

The Toma area was unquestionably his vote-bank, a fact which he modestly attributed to being his father's son, but he had over the years given considerable thought to the question of leadership. Neither the traditional style nor the current Catholic notions separately met the bill, he felt. What the times required was in his view a bridge-builder, a broker or arranger of compromises. Thus he sought to deal with groups and their leaders rather than to appeal directly to the masses. In the House he had said little more on 'national' issues than the average indigenous member, but he had raised matters of Tolai interest notably concerning land and the local government system;

although he failed to support Ashton's initiative to improve mission teachers' salaries. On the Gazelle, he habitually took a place of honour on public occasions, whether these were sponsored by the Administration, Catholics, Methodists, or students; maintained careful relations with the Gazelle Council, despite at least one near confrontation;[10] and sought to cultivate the younger more educated Tolai on whose behalf he had endeavoured (unsuccessfully) to secure special transit accommodation in Rabaul. Even his position on land fitted this pattern. He was only interested, he said, in rectifying 'just grievances': unless these were cleared up now it would be difficult to maintain such a distinction after independence. As indicated earlier, however, he recognised that calm confidence had its limits as an electoral approach and he let it be known that as a Minister he would be able to do more than had been in his power as an Under-Secretary . . . (pause) . . . 'if I am re-elected.'

But the options open to ToLiman were not available to other candidates, most of whom had come to recognise the need to go to the people if they were to win their votes. In general therefore the election was marked by hard, sustained, and extensive campaigning. With this there appeared to be a heightened awareness of the electorates as having their own internal structure, of being made up of a variety of groups and categories each of which had to be reached, however marginal it might be in terms of voting power. Ashton and Barrett were of course the more practised politicians, but among the Tolai candidates too quite a few displayed an embryonic professional touch in their approach to the campaign.

Epineri, for example, had been preparing the ground long before the date of the election was officially proclaimed. Over the years he had taken every opportunity to maintain a position of prominence as a spokesman for the Tolai. He had also travelled widely within the constituency simply talking to people, listening sympathetically to what they had to say, and making himself and his own views known. Epineri was one of several who studied carefully the official literature on the arrangements for the election, eager to seize on anything that might be used to advantage, and he worked through his copy of the electoral register meticulously, counting the numbers in each village and voting category, clearly using the register as a means of checking on the progress of his campaign. Epineri's campaign was essentially an individual one, but he employed his grass-roots approach

[10] Early in his career he had been attacked in the council for using the word *kanaka* in a Pidgin broadcast from Port Moresby. Some of his supporters felt that he behaved weakly by appearing before the council and apologising. Recognising that the attack was politically motivated, he himself felt that his response had been the politically appropriate one.

skilfully and discomfited his rivals by disseminating a number of canards. As Epineri himself remarked on one occasion, 'there are a lot of "tricks" in winning an election'.

ToBunbun too gave the appearance of having given careful thought to planning his course of action and itinerary. But he saw the problem mainly in organisational terms. At the time he was busy preparing his 'platform', he spoke of the need to appoint a campaign manager and committee whose task it would be to help him map out his program, prepare the way for him wherever he was to appear, and keep him informed of the doings of his opponents. Confident of the support he enjoyed among his fellow councillors, he counted on a number of them, together with other contacts, to act as his agents in the villages, quietly canvassing on his behalf and countering at the same time the propaganda of the other candidates. Events were soon to show that many of his hopes were misplaced, and that his organising skills did not always measure up to the promise of his ideas, but, as we shall see shortly, there were other considerations which played a more important part in bringing about his downfall.

A number of Tolai candidates went to considerable expense printing and distributing thousands of pamphlets, in which they set out their policies and views in English, Pidgin, and the vernacular. A few also had expensive advertisements in the Territorial press. But for nearly all candidates the royal road to success was seen to lie in direct verbal appeal to the voters. A few meetings were held in Rabaul for the benefit of the townsfolk of all races; the most successful of these was one organised by the recently formed Gazelle Discussion Group, the highlight of which was the attempt by a Catholic priest to 'rubbish' Epineri.[11] But most of the campaigning of course was done in the villages. Sunday morning after church was a popular time for meetings, but candidates also had to campaign throughout the week if they were to cover the whole of their electorate. In an area where so many are in paid employment many meetings had to be held at night, some candidates visiting two or three villages in the course of a single evening.

Village meetings were for the most part quietly conducted affairs,

[11] There seems little doubt that from the point of view of most of the Europeans present the priest succeeded splendidly. Epineri in his nervousness generally found difficulty in coping with hostile questions, and on this occasion he was quickly reduced to mumbling incoherence. But so far as the Tolai were concerned his interlocutor appears to have misjudged their views of right conduct on such occasions, and the attempt completely backfired. Far from losing ground by his public discomfiture, Epineri in fact gained a good deal of sympathy, including that of at least one of the rival candidates.

usually free of incident or controversy. Tolai candidates spoke in the vernacular, often working through the main points of their address in a speech that was repeated with little variation from one meeting to another. Afterwards there was an opportunity for questions; if few questions were asked, as was often the case, candidates tended to interpret this as an expression of support. Polansky reports that in 1964 there was little to choose between the Tolai candidates on their platforms. On this occasion, while many of them tended to cover the same ground, there were also pronounced differences of viewpoint. In the Kokopo Open, these were exacerbated by Tammur's situation, which suggested that a strong attacking stance would serve both to make himself better known and to undermine ToBaining, who for his part quickly recognised the seriousness of this challenge. A relaxed, unemotional speaker, ToBaining had never been a great vote catcher, and he did not share with his wellwishers the view that the 30 per cent poll in his ward for the 1966 council elections was due to the confidence of his supporters. He knew that in other wards supporters had affirmed their solidarity with retiring councillors by turn-outs exceeding 90 per cent. Tammur, it quickly emerged, was an orator, capable of adjusting his set speech as the occasion required, while continually developing his major themes, even acting them out occasionally. Tourism he ignored, while ToBaining struggled to spell out its potential to those for whom it was scarcely comprehensible. On land, the issue was squarely joined between the sanctity of title and due process on the one hand and the immediate righting of just grievances on the other.[12] Second to land for Tammur (where were the councillors at Raniola?) was the council and taxation; the council and its tacit endorsement of birth control; the council ... Even in this contest, direct public attacks by name were avoided; but everyone knew that to attack 'the council' was to attack its President, while to attack 'some young men' was to attack Tammur. In opposing the cautious official and Methodist approach to contraception ('if you are worried, see the doctors at the government hospital'), Tammur bestirred some of the women into vocal dissent, but he was not to be deterred. He did not rest his case solely on Catholic teaching. There was, he urged, no land shortage on New Britain or in New Guinea at large; the country could support a population of 40 millions: more people meant more wealth and more taxes.

In Rabaul the ideological differences between candidates were less apparent, yet here too the fact that there were differences was highlighted on occasion when by chance a number of candidates

[12] It is important to note that some benefits were being secured by this means.

happened to arrive together at the same village, and found themselves having to share the platform. Once, for example, a clash developed in this way between Epineri and Patiliu. Epineri had been advocating an increase in wages for labourers. Patiliu, who had not included the question of wages in his platform, countered by asking Epineri if it were not the case that he owned a block of land on the Warangoi, and employed a number of labourers there. Would he be able to pay them at the higher rate he suggested?

Although Patiliu felt that he had come out the winner in this encounter, he was plainly unhappy about the incident, and said he thought it was better for each candidate to appear before the people on his own. This indeed seemed to be the general view, for such confrontations were rare, and Rabaul candidates at least appeared anxious to avoid them. It was as though the campaign speeches were seen as providing an opportunity for a solo performance, the effect of which would be destroyed by any debate of the issues which the speech itself raised. As at Kokopo, candidates rarely referred directly in their speeches to their rivals by name, and they were generally silent on the policies and stated views of their opponents, sometimes claiming, when questioned by one of the research team, that they did not know what they were. But of course there are other ways of damaging an opponent besides attacking his platform or blackening his character. Epineri, for example, was especially adroit in suggesting to his audience why others were less fitted to be their Member than he was, playing skilfully on the general dissatisfaction over the recent sharp increase in council tax, an increase for which ToBunbun was widely held to be responsible.

Eventually ToBunbun learned of the stories circulating about him and he sought to defend himself. 'I know my name has become bad because of the tax', he would say, and would then go on to explain that the decision to increase the council tax was not that of one man, but of the council as a whole. The explanation cut little ice in a constituency where at that very moment considerable numbers were being taken to court for tax default.

Epineri, a self-employed contractor with extensive plantings of coconuts at Matupit and a block of land on the Warangoi, also used the argument that those who were employees of the Administration could never be good representatives. They were 'bought' men who would never fight for the people. ToPatiliu tried to meet this charge in his various speeches:

> For 22 years I have worked with the Administration, and I have seen the work that it does to help the people ... Of course it is true that in all those years it was as though I had sat within a fence,

and they had sealed my lips, for the Government then was as my father, giving me work and paying my wages. It would be the same as though you were employed by somebody like ToWartovo [the councillor] here to look after and run his store. I don't think you would talk strongly to him then, for he would be your father who cared for you in everything. But now I have left the Administration, I have resigned, and I am on the other side of the hill [a reference to the fact that he was no longer living amongst Europeans on Namanula Hill, one of the select parts of Rabaul, but was back in his village] ... If you elect me I will be standing on that side of the hill, and I will be your spearhead against our father the Government. But this does not mean one has to fight aggressively [he used here the English word], and threaten to throw all the Europeans and other foreigners out of the country. In the House of Assembly one fights not with one's fists but with one's mouth and brain and with the help of the wisdom given you by God.

It was noticeable that the few meetings held in Rabaul that were attended by Europeans generated more heat than was usually the case at village gatherings. Similarly, overt charges, refutations, and counter-charges were far more common between the two Regional than amongst Tolai Open candidates; there were also reports of innuendoes, canards, and henchmen whose activities provoked cries of 'foul play'. To some locals (European and Tolai alike) such behaviour seemed in bad taste and out of place in New Guinea, although in fact nothing alleged against either candidate was particularly shocking to those with experience of elections in Australia or elsewhere. At the same time, as we have seen, the conduct of some Tolai candidates was less 'gentlemanly' than appears to have been the case in 1964.

But if there were changes in the character of the campaign as between 1964 and 1968, it should also be plain that there was no uniform pattern throughout the Gazelle. The dynamism which all the surrounding circumstances might have been expected to promote, while certainly present at Kokopo, was largely lacking at Rabaul. There the candidates displayed little of the spontaneity and flexibility of Tammur, and the campaign remained curiously static. No alliances were formed, and while there were rumours from time to time of deals between candidates, and arrangements to exchange preferences, evidence to substantiate these was difficult to obtain, and the parties themselves invariably denied them. For the most part, indeed, Rabaul candidates, despite the seriousness with which they approached the election, went about their task rather like figures in a tableau, each concerned mainly with his own performance, and acting out his part with little reference to the others on the stage.

THE RESPONSE OF THE ELECTORATE

Once campaigning got under way fieldworkers found that they were quickly able to gauge which candidates appeared to be forging ahead, which lagging behind. In Kokopo, for example, Tammur was attracting large and enthusiastic meetings, while at Rabaul, despite the fact that Tolai were often highly circumspect in expressing their views (even amongst themselves),[13] the evidence soon suggested mounting support for Epineri. But 'spotting winners' was one thing; it was quite another, particularly without the advantage of properly conducted sample surveys, to judge the degree of general interest in the election and to assess what voters saw as the central issues, if any, in it. The low level of interest displayed by the majority of Europeans and Chinese was not unexpected, for their numbers were too small to affect the outcome, but at least around Rabaul there were few indications that the election had generated a great deal of enthusiasm among the Tolai either; the public mood remained elusive. Conversations with those one knew best suggested at times a somewhat tired scepticism.

> Yes, we heard so-and-so speak. A very good speech. But who knows, perhaps he will be like ToLiman. See, at the last election the candidates said all sorts of fine things, made all sorts of promises, but they forgot all about them when they got to the House. They were concerned only with their own salaries, and the style of life this made possible, and they ceased to think about the people who sent them there.

Similar views were once expressed by an elder from an inland group who concluded with the comment: 'They [the Members of the House] do a good job, but we don't know ...'. His sentence finished in mid-air, conveying perfectly his doubts about the whole matter.

Disenchantment with the performance of members was accompanied by anxieties at a deeper level. Over the years there had been increasing discussion of the political future of the Territory, and the issue had become a source of uncertainty and confusion. An immediate difficulty was the lack of understanding of the terms being used in the debate, for in the Tolai vernacular the one term *a tibuna varkurai* was commonly used to cover the notion of self-government as well as of independence, so that the difference between the two concepts was rarely seen as clear and unambiguous. The issue was further obscured by a widespread tendency to interpret independence

[13] Robin Kumaina, Patiliu's campaign manager, once commented that he was finding it so difficult to know how people would vote that he intended after it was all over to conduct his own survey to try and discover just how they did vote.

as meaning not only the end of the Australian Administration, but also the departure of all Europeans from the Territory. For many the prospect was frightening. The following was a fairly typical comment:

> There are some people who are in a hurry. But see, there are not enough people who are sufficiently educated to govern the country properly. Perhaps in the years to come young people will have acquired a proper education, but for the moment there are few. Everything we have at the moment, everything that is provided, is the work of the government. If the government were to leave there would be great conflict and confusion. Who would govern us properly? See how often we Tolai start businesses. We work through the *turguvai* [a form of joint enterprise], but no sooner does it start than the parties to it are quarrelling amongst themselves, and then the whole thing collapses.

In all this the Administration was seen as playing the benevolent role of guardian. Yet at times a strong undercurrent of ambivalence was also revealed. One ward committee-man from a rural settlement referred to the many different régimes they had had in New Guinea, and then recalled bitterly how when the last war came the Australians had run away, leaving the people to die like sheep. He spoke as though the Administration was now planning another act of betrayal, leaving the people defenceless against external aggression.

As indicated earlier, even Tammur did not contest the reality behind such pessimistic assessments, although he adopted a more positive and inspirational approach. In general, most candidates expressed similar views on the question of independence though there were differences between them in regard to timing and tactics. For many Europeans and Chinese, and some Tolai, Epineri alone stood out as an advocate of early independence. Apart from the incident at the Gazelle Discussion Group when Epineri was attacked for statements he was alleged to have made in 1964, there was an occasion at the Kuomintang Club when a European charged Epineri with having told a village meeting that they would have independence in five years. Although Epineri denied this, other candidates repeated the charge in their efforts to discredit him. One of them, asked to account for Epineri's apparent grip on the Matupi, replied without hesitation that the people of Matupit wanted independence tomorrow. Epineri had raised the matter long ago, and they still followed him. Yet by this time it had become apparent that Epineri was enjoying widespread support throughout the area; it would have been extremely odd if, given the anxiety that the issue appeared to arouse, particularly in the remoter villages, the people had flocked to him as an apostle of independence. And indeed to supporters of Epineri the matter appeared in quite a different light. As one man from Matupit once expressed it:

> Epineri claims he was the first man to raise the question of self-government with the Administrator and then Mr Hasluck. And that is so. At that time it was a completely new idea. On so many things he has spoken, and gradually the people have come to see his words fulfilled, as though he spoke with the words of a prophet. Not long ago Ephraim Jubilee went to New York. What did he say? From the moment he left Port Moresby his mouth was closed. He behaved, Epineri says, like a mute. 'Had I been there, I would have talked about the problems of our country.' This is why people support him. It is not a question of independence tomorrow but a proper preparation for it now, so that if in five years' time it should come, we shall be ready for it.

Quite early on in the campaign an educated Tolai had remarked to one of the research team that we should not expect issues to play a central role in the election, which would quickly resolve itself into a simple clash of personalities. Nonetheless, questions put to the candidates at village meetings suggested that there were a number of matters which were the subject of deep concern throughout the community. A great deal of anxiety was expressed about the numbers of teachers who were leaving employment with the missions because of low wages, and all candidates were asked to give an assurance that they would fight for increased subsidies to the missions so that their teachers' salaries could be brought into line with those of teachers employed by the Administration. Another question, of more direct political import, that was raised repeatedly at meetings in the Rabaul area concerned relationships between Papua and New Guinea. What prompted the immediate concern was that whereas on the Gazelle Peninsula council tax had recently been raised to meet the cost of building new schools, elsewhere these charges were still being met by grants from the Administration. But the concern also went much further and there was no mistaking the strong feeling that existed that the Tolai were being 'soaked' to subsidise development in Papua. Despite the many references that were made to the need for unity between different groups and regions within Papua and New Guinea, Tolai attitudes in the matter revealed a marked element of ambiguity, well conveyed in a few paragraphs from Patiliu's policy statement:

> Unless people of every language group are able to come together for the advancement of the country we will not have here Government of the People by the People, but government by some group. And

what group will that be? It will certainly not be government by the Tolais.
But we Tolais are the most wealthy group in the country.
It must be government by a less wealthy group, and I fear they may want to spread our wealth around.

Questions covered a wide range of other issues, but two in particular came up at meeting after meeting with almost unfailing regularity: (1) would the candidate, if elected, visit his constituents regularly to hear their views and complaints and to advise them what was going on in the House; and (2) would he accept a Ministerial Membership if one were offered to him. The second question was little more than a variant of the first; together both drew attention to Tolai perceptions of the duties of a Member as well as to certain attributes that served to delineate an acceptable representative. How important such considerations could be, as distinct from the views expressed by candidates on such issues as independence, education etc., emerged with peculiar clarity as the campaign unfolded at Rabaul.

There the contest from the beginning was seen to lie principally between Patiliu, ToBunbun, and Epineri. But it is the position of ToBunbun which holds most interest in the present context. As between ToBunbun and Epineri few Tolai could point to many basic differences in their social philosophies. A number, indeed, accepted ToBunbun as the best candidate in terms of his experience, his clarity of thought and expression, and his general ability. But they were still not prepared to vote for him. From the outset one heard many adverse comments on his personality and temperament, and a variety of incidents was related to show that he was unfitted to serve as a representative of the people. What was of interest to the observer in so many of these comments was that they related to alleged attributes or events of his past which must have been common knowledge at Matupit, but which the Matupi had evidently ignored when they elected him as their councillor some years before. The fact seems to be that ToBunbun was held in quite high regard until the increased council tax was introduced, a measure for which he, as the dominant personality in the council, was widely held to be personally responsible.[14] While there were strong objections to the

[14] The tax increased from $10 to $16 a year, the additional amount representing an educational levy. The move to increase the tax seems to have been initiated by the Education Department, apparently on the understanding that there had been a change in policy whereby the government would no longer undertake financial responsibility for putting up new schools in council areas. Officers in the Department of District Administra-

tax as such, people were if anything even more incensed by the manner of its introduction, ToBunbun, it was claimed, having pushed it through without first consulting the electorate. In the context of the election the implication was that such a man could not be trusted to 'represent' his constituents; far from heeding their wishes, he would follow his own line and impose harsh measures which would 'destroy' the people. Even some 'strong' councillors had commented on his unwillingness to compromise with them: 'he wants it all his own way, all the time'.

In contrast to ToBunbun, Epineri was able to create, as the remarks of one of his supporters quoted earlier indicate, a view of himself as a man of the people. Although Patiliu and ToBunbun generally wore shorts and stockings, Epineri retained the *laplap*, the standard garment among Tolai older men. But this was only part of his image.[15] More important, in his speeches he successfully projected himself as an ordinary villager who knew the difficulties and worries that confronted people in their daily lives. The remark constantly heard with reference to Epineri was that *i tata ure ra balana gunan*, an expression difficult to translate literally, but indicating one who talks out about the problems facing the community as a whole, and not simply his own.

In Gazelle and Kokopo land was pre-eminently what many people had on their minds. Europeans and some Tolai had tended to dismiss ToLiman lightly in 1964 as a 'mission stooge'. However, by 1968 both he and Tammur were considered to be serious candidates by most Tolai, and were regarded with considerable unease by many Europeans. ToLiman claimed some credit for the successful establishment of land demarcation committees and in the House had shown both general and specific concern for the land problems of the Gazelle.[16] Most recently, he had bitterly criticised the official

---

tion advised us that this was not the case, and that the action of the Education Department had been based on a misunderstanding of the position. Whether this is so or not, it is apparent that ToBunbun, himself an employee of the Education Department, was caught up in a conflict of roles of the kind to which Epineri had drawn attention, and wittingly or not had to pay the penalty.

[15] Of other successful candidates it is worth noting that although ToLiman was occasionally seen in a *laplap*, frequently, and always on formal occasions, he wore a suit and tie, while Tammur habitually wore long trousers.

[16] This is most clearly reflected perhaps in the Land Bill (No. 2) of 1967. Technically speaking, this was an Administration Bill, but it was generally acknowledged to be a direct consequence of ToLiman's petition in 1965 against undeveloped freehold. The Bill was taken to a second reading (*H.A.D.* 16 November 1967, 1st House I, pp. 2926-9) and then held over for the new House to take up if it so wished.

handling of the Raniola affair, implicitly supporting Tammur despite his own position as Under-Secretary. ToBaining was no less seriously concerned about land matters than other Tolai, but he was handicapped by a political style developed in an earlier period, and less skilful in dissociating himself publicly from official policies and actions. Hence his opponents had considerable scope for ringing the changes on a single theme, that he had ceased to be 'a voice of the people' and was neglecting them, even siding with the Europeans against them when they most needed his support.[17] Some of the more virulent went further: he has to, they said. He has no wealth of his own. Without these jobs the Europeans give him, he would be nothing.

Thus, despite their differences in education, temperament, and political style, the successful Tolai candidates all appeared to offer the promise of men who would truly voice the aspirations of their people. ToLiman was one of the small group of Under-Secretaries to be re-elected and although he made no secret of his Ministerial ambitions,[18] he did succeed in increasing his vote. Tammur also was no more than becomingly modest when asked about his willingness to accept a Ministerial position. All three in their own way had on at least one occasion 'stood up on their own two legs' and perhaps this 'irresponsible' behaviour had marked them in Tolai eyes as worthy candidates.

THE REGIONAL

We have seen earlier that many Tolai appeared to adopt quickly the view that the Open electorates should be the preserve of indigenous candidates, and that the Regional should provide the appropriate arena for expatriate politicians. This at once suggested the possibility of a different kind of public interest being displayed as between Regional and Open contests; it also raised the questions whether voters would hold the same expectations in regard to both sets of candidates and whether they would apply the same criteria in

[17] To mention but one example: many Tolai were convinced that when trouble broke out at Raniola plantation, it was ToBaining who was responsible for the appearance of the police riot squad. It was also alleged that he made no attempt himself to visit Ulagunan and learn at first hand the facts of the case.
[18] It probably did him no harm, that he occasionally spoke of conditional acceptance: 'I will only accept Education, on the understanding that something is done for mission teachers'.

selecting between Regional candidates as for Open ones. Following the Open campaigns within the Gazelle Peninsula, fieldworkers were able to gain some direct impression of public response to the election and, as polling day approached, they could feel a fair degree of confidence in their ability to predict the likely outcome in each electorate. This was not so in the case of the Regional. For reasons stated at the outset, over much of New Britain we simply did not have the information to assess public reactions to the election, and we could not know therefore what weight to attach to the observations made on the Gazelle. Our analysis of the Regional therefore has had to be built up on inferences from other kinds of evidence, and to that extent is more tentative.

A point of immediate relevance is that the recommendation of the Select Committee to consolidate the Special electorates into a single Regional one affected Barrett and Ashton in different ways. Barrett indeed suffered from a genuine disability. The electorate which he had tended—or as some of his detractors claimed, failed to tend—included only one-third of the voters in the new electorate. The remainder had been in Ashton's care for the previous four years and there seems little doubt that Barrett was placed at a disadvantage in being a 'new boy' to more voters than his opponent. Since both had made some impression on their former constituencies and had been willing to take up the grievances of individuals and groups, this was important. It was also important that Barrett's 'national' reputation, as a parliamentarian and as a tireless worker on behalf of amateur athletics, for example, was more likely to impress his own constituents of West Gazelle (i.e. the Rabaul Sub-District) than those of Ashton's New Britain Special who had far less access to radio or the press and far less opportunity in general to comprehend the significance of these activities.

Associated with such 'structural' factors, there can perhaps be discerned another major difference between the two candidates. While there appeared to be little to choose between them in terms of ideological orientation and basic attitudes towards the future development of the Territory, there were fundamental differences in political style. Neither favoured early independence. Both felt that too much money was being spent on Port Moresby and the higher bureaucracy at the expense of grass-roots development. Both felt that the House would be more workable and overall political development facilitated by the existence of parties and neither was openly unsympathetic to the basic aims of Pangu. Nevertheless, both recognised that parties, and Pangu in particular, appeared to have acquired an unfavourable public image and they were therefore very cautious in their public comments on them. The difference lay in the images which they projected for indigenous voters and the nature of their interactions with them.[19]

Given the compact nature of and good communications in his constituency, it was sensible of Barrett to maintain an office in Rabaul, where constituents could visit him and receive advice or other assistance concerning new crops, small businesses, loans, income tax returns, jobs for school leavers, land disputes, community projects, and new or proposed legislation. There is little doubt that he was of great assistance to many of those who came to him. It was perhaps unfortunate and yet significant that he accepted the Administration's offer of an office in the new air-conditioned District Headquarters for this purpose. For the Tolai, life in Rabaul does not centre around this building, but around the market, the Gazelle Council Offices, and the Chinese stores several blocks away. It is relevant to note that the Administration's own Welfare Officers were located in the Council Office complex. Similarly, although Barrett was actively involved in official attempts to clear up long-standing land disputes, including the Raniola case, in the most satisfactory manner, this was not generally known.

Ashton, too, discussed these disputes with officials and made representations to the Administrator concerning them, but was more disposed in addition to discuss them with the aggrieved Tolai, seeking to induce their participation in some creative solution. For some Europeans, Ashton was a mere opportunist, 'irresponsible' on land matters and 'always sticking his nose in'. The fact remained, however, that Ashton had clearly associated himself with several schemes to 'buy back' freehold plantation land, in which groups of Tolai raised a cash deposit between them and then sought a loan to pay off the balance owing. Similarly, while Barrett recognised that finding jobs for the sixth grade school leavers was a growing problem he gave scant consideration to light industry on the grounds that there was no land available. Ashton did not deny that formally this was true.

---

[19] It seems worth mentioning here that although no formal alliances were forged between Regional and Open candidates in the Gazelle, elsewhere in New Britain the position may have been rather different. In the Kandrian-Pomio Open, for example, both Ashton and Barrett recognised the vote-winning capacity of the cargo cult leader Koriam (who was to secure 7,913 first preferences of the 11,430 votes cast) and both managed to campaign in his presence. But Ashton appeared to have the closer links with Koriam: he sat next to him and often helped him in the House, and their voting records were very similar. In his electoral handbill Ashton also associated himself closely with Koriam (*'Bipo mi Memba belong yupela wantaim Koriam'*—formerly I was your Member together with Koriam).

He believed, however, that by reassessing priorities and the exercise of a little imagination suitable land could be secured for industrial complexes at Vulcan and Kurakakaul. Nor were his interests confined to the Tolai. He had, for example, encouraged the Bainings people to co-operate with copper and other mineral prospecting surveys; advocated a road from Vudal to Pondo to open up the Bainings to agricultural development; and had excited interest along the north coast of New Britain in a proposal to send frozen fish to the abattoirs at Lae for processing and sale in the Highlands.

Undoubtedly Ashton's credibility was enhanced by a variety of extraneous factors. He had not initiated the oil palm project at Cape Hoskins and he was not responsible for the increasing willingness on the part of the Administration to discuss land problems or to think in developmental terms. What he had done was to associate himself with existing and projected developments; to radiate optimism; while he alone had stood up in the House on behalf of 'wage justice' for mission teachers. Altogether he amounted to a formidable opponent and Barrett, whose virtues were far less apparent to the average voter, did well to poll 11,882 votes to Ashton's 26,501.

VOTING BEHAVIOUR

Once polling began it soon became evident that the percentage vote was going to be lower than in 1964. At Rabaul the figure dropped by 10 per cent to 63 per cent; in the Kokopo Open it was 53 per cent and in the Gazelle Open 60 per cent. These figures of course tell us little about the response in different parts of the electorate. That there could be considerable differences in this regard is shown in some figures available for the Gazelle Open. In the Baining villages the poll was 48 per cent, in Tolai non-council villages 27 per cent, and in other Tolai groups 65 per cent. However, in the absence of an adequate breakdown of all the figures, it is difficult to draw firm conclusions. It should be remembered that the voluntary nature of voting was more widely grasped on this occasion than in 1964. Further, it may provide some useful perspective if we recall that even in the famous 'independence' election of 1956 on the Gold Coast (Ghana), only about 50 per cent of the total electorate voted (Apter 1968). What does emerge clearly is that voters in the non-council villages in Gazelle and Kokopo came close to boycotting the elections and in some cases did so with complete unanimity. Often they had publicly stated their intention to do this on the grounds that voting for the House would make them more vulnerable to incorporation within the council (some had in fact already been 'gazetted-in' and the desirability of general incorporation was being freely canvassed). Considerable efforts were made by some Administration officers and missionaries to explain to their immediate areas that there was no connection between this election and the council; further, non-council villages were not all situated in the least developed areas; far from it.

Since anti-council sentiments were invariably (to Europeans) accompanied by fervent protestations of loyalty to the Administration, these facts suggest at the very least that in these villages no advantageous connection was seen between participation in House of Assembly or council elections and their own problems as they diagnosed them. Obviously the attempts made by most candidates to engage in some political education of their electorates met with only limited success here,[20] although the value of a block of non-council votes was generally recognised.[21] Why was this? Was it some inadequacy in their ability to explain the advantage of the system or their own policies; were their policies less relevant to these areas; were they themselves regarded as 'outsiders'? Several reported that the politeness of their reception was at best forced and strained. While such questions cannot be answered with any degree of confidence, they are perhaps a reminder that it is also necessary to ask why people did vote.

A second area characterised by low turn-out was the Raluana census division. Here land shortage was particularly acute, while the population was large and by local standards well educated. If circuit finances are any guide, it was also fervently Methodist. Since it had been represented by the non-Tolai Koriam since 1964 this too must be considered. Two possible explanations suggest themselves. Again, that even for these people no advantageous connection between their problems and voting was discernible. Alternatively, that they resolved a situation in which they were acutely 'cross-pressured' in the classical manner, by not voting. Tammur's program according to this hypothesis should have appealed to them but they could not bring themselves to vote for a candidate who, unlike ToLiman, had had little time to demonstrate that he was more Tolai than Catholic. ToKau, it will be recalled, had suspected that Tammur's policies might be more acceptable than his person, but had obviously been unable to establish himself as a viable alternative. Finally, we may note

---

[20] 'Will the government give us all European style houses?' one candidate was asked on the Duke of Yorks.
[21] There were about 2500 votes to be had on the Duke of Yorks. Less than 700 votes were cast, a decline of about 100 on 1964.

the acute disappointment expressed by some Rabaul candidates at the poor turn-out in some of the inland villages where they had campaigned hard. On one occasion a few of them and their helpers were sitting together at one of the polling stations when someone remarked on the small number of voters who had turned up at one village booth the previous day. ToLavutul observed that there had been a death there, adding that people were too busy distributing shell money, which they regarded as more important than an election. This remark was greeted with general laughter, as if to say 'Bushies! What can you expect of them?' However, the correlation this implies does not appear to be supported by the voting figures in the Regional, for which the overall poll was 63 per cent.

Given the greater awareness on this occasion that voting was not compulsory, a lower poll than in 1964 was not altogether surprising. A more curious feature was the situation revealed by the figures on informal voting. The considerably higher rate of informal voting in the Regional (9·8 per cent) than in the Open electorates (2·8 per cent) might be attributed to the greater interest in the latter and therefore the greater care in filling in the ballot paper, but there remains the puzzling difference between a figure of 3·4 per cent for the three Open electorates of the Gazelle and 1·4 per cent in Kandrian-Pomio and Talasea.[22]

One other aspect of voting behaviour that deserves mention is the use electors made of their preference votes. As noted earlier, candidates did not enter into arrangements to exchange preferences, and most simply asked voters for their second preference if another candidate was preferred as their first choice. Later on, after all the electoral formalities had been completed, we had the opportunity to sample a couple of ballot boxes, one containing votes cast in villages near Rabaul, the other Rabaul 'rural' votes. That the system was not employed as its designers intended is abundantly clear from table 1.

The table shows that in the 'rural' sample 52 per cent of voters cast only their first preference, while in the coastal villages the figure was 70 per cent. Undoubtedly, the method of preferential voting is still widely misunderstood on the Gazelle, but the results could also

---

[22] Unfortunately, we do not have information on the extent to which use was made in different parts of the 'whispering vote'. Some observers suggest that in more remote parts voters are more prepared to accept the 'whispering ballot'; in areas of greater sophistication there is less readiness to do so, with a consequent increase in the numbers of spoiled papers. But even if there were evidence of greater use of the 'whispering vote' in the more outlying places this would still not account for the higher degree of informal voting in the Regional.

TABLE 1—DISTRIBUTION OF PREFERENCES IN TWO BALLOT BOXES IN RABAUL OPEN

No. of preferences exercised	Rural No.	Rural %	Urban No.	Urban %
6	151	16·8	58	8·1
5	9	1·0	7	0·9
4	13	1·5	7	0·9
3	66	7·3	19	2·6
2	191	21·3	118	16·4
1	468	52·1	508	70·8
Total votes cast	898	100·0	717	99·7

be read as supporting the view that some at least deliberately rejected the system. Before polling began a number of comments were heard at places like Matupit to the effect that the best way of ensuring that an unpopular candidate would not win on a second or later count was for voters to abstain from making any use of their preferences.

In the absence of a finer breakdown of the results than was available to us no detailed examination of the factors determining voting behaviour is possible here. Nevertheless, there is sufficient evidence to enable us to draw a few conclusions. When interviewed before polling began, some of the candidates gave as a reason for expecting support in certain villages that their clan, or sometimes their father's clan was strongly entrenched there. While in a few instances this view seems to have been justified, most candidates also recognised that such backing could only be of marginal significance. Local support was a more important factor and, save for ToBunbun whose case illustrates the fate of any politician who fails to secure his home base, candidates appeared to score well in their home districts. But even so, the evidence of our two sample ballot boxes makes it clear that local communities did not vote as blocs. We have noted earlier how in planning his campaign ToLavutul hoped to exploit the rural-urban cleavage within the Rabaul constituency. It is true that Tiut Turmarum gained most of his votes in the inland parishes, but ToLavutul's calculation that he and Tiut would sweep the rural vote was not borne out by events. Even in ToLavutul's and Turmarum's home areas candidates like Epineri and Patiliu were able to secure a respectable number of first preferences.

Early in the piece some Tolai would refer from time to time to the important part played by religious divisions within the community in the 1964 election, and after the incident at the Rabaul meeting described earlier (p. 69) there were suggestions that this might be the case again. However, as the campaign proceeded such comments were heard less frequently, although no one denied that it might be 'unfortunate' if all three Open seats were won by Catholic candidates. In their official pronouncements and parish magazines the missions maintained a scrupulous neutrality; where pastoral guidance was sought it is clear in a number of instances that advice was given on non-sectarian lines. If Epineri was attacked by a Catholic priest, it is important to record that he also received material assistance and support from other priests. But it also appears to be the case that within the Tolai community there has been a recent tendency for religious differences to be subordinated to the interests of secular ends. In the Rabaul Open, for example, ToBunbun might have expected to receive a good deal of Catholic support. This did not materialise. As one Matupi commented wryly: 'Catholics have to pay the increased tax too'. Although mission 'spheres of influence' no longer have the importance they had in the past, it is still possible to map out roughly what areas are predominantly Catholic, and what Methodist. Clearly a convention did operate to keep overt sectarianism to a minimum. Individual outbursts against Tammur, for example, provoked immediate apologies. Nevertheless, the candidates' religious affiliations and the intensity of these were public knowledge. It is possible, as suggested earlier, that the wrong religion of a candidate otherwise to their liking may have induced some people not to vote; but other things were also known about the candidates (at least to many voters) such as their families, clans, and villages, drinking habits and so on. Thus although there is some evidence that interested Catholics sought, without complete success, to deter strong Catholic candidates from opposing one another, it is unlikely that religion alone was the decisive factor which determined voting behaviour.

CONCLUSION

What meaning then is to be attached to the elections on the Gazelle? The account provides evidence of a greater degree of forethought and application on the part of candidates than was the case in 1964. Yet, despite the commendable zeal that marked much of the campaigning, it remains an important question how far the Tolai had assimilated and absorbed the full implications embraced in the concept of election. There were, for example, a number of candidates whose motives in standing baffled observers and Tolai alike; having nominated, they took no further serious part in the contest; as some informants put it, they simply offered their money as a gift to the government. Then there was the striking inability of so many candidates to make any realistic assessment of their chances in different parts of the electorate. Of course chronic optimism about the outcome of elections is not a trait peculiar to Tolai politicians, but something more than this seemed to be involved. For some of the actors it was as though they had learned that certain kinds of behaviour were necessary to the proper conduct of an election; if only the prescribed 'techniques' were followed the voters could not help but be impressed, and victory would go to the one who commanded the most 'ritual' knowledge. This was seen very clearly in the importance that the more educated attached to having a 'platform'.[23] The speaker at a village meeting who did not work systematically through the various headings of his platform was likely to be interrupted by a hostile schoolteacher calling out: 'What are your points (*Ava kaum "point"*)?' For the majority of the villagers present, however, the effect of such a speech was frequently soporific.

The fact that the elections had this 'ritual' aspect is not to imply that they were therefore without political significance. In his account of the 1964 election Polansky regarded the results in the Rabaul Open as an index of certain important changes taking place within Tolai society; in particular he pointed to the eclipse of more traditional-type leaders at the hands of younger and more educated men. By 1968 the direction and pace of change had become more pronounced, and we can perhaps carry Polansky's analysis a little further. Looking at the candidates on this occasion, for example, it is at once striking that four of the Rabaul contestants were products of the pre-war Waterhouse school at Nodup: they represented in a sense the first generation of Tolai English-speaking leadership. Even more significant was the emergence of the youthful Tammur, the first to appear of the second, post-war generation. While such a development presages of course quite a different style and approach to politics, it is also important to note that it does not necessarily imply a radical estrangement of the younger leaders from their elders. The three successful Tolai candidates were all sons of influential men who, taking advantage of the means available to them in their day, had achieved prominence in the economic sphere, in village politics, and as lay leaders in the church. Such men were the products of a society already experiencing change, but they still retained many of the characteristics of the

---

[23] Albert Price's speech at the Rabaul Discussion Group's meeting drew an immediate protest from ToBunbun, who complained that it was shameful to the other candidates who had gone to the trouble of preparing policy statements that Mr Price had offered no 'platform'.

traditional 'big man', and what was particularly striking was the way in which the sons were at pains to identify themselves with their fathers. From another point of view, of course, this is simply to emphasise that the new leaders were not themselves 'big men' in any traditional sense. Further removed from that tradition, they had established their position by their participation in modern political activities and institutions, and their concerns were with the problems of their people in a new rapidly changing society, increasingly marked by strain and conflict.

For over a decade Tolai society has been characterised by mounting tensions in the shaping of which population growth, land pressure, and education have all played an important part. Associated with these developments, there has been a growing estrangement between the 'haves' and 'have nots', categories which in material terms are closely related to those of age and youth. For the 1968 elections youth had the numbers: a conservative interpretation of the 1966 census data indicates that some 55 per cent of enrolled Tolai voters were under 35. It is not surprising therefore that those candidates who appealed rather exclusively to the older generation (notably Price, ToMarita, and ToBaining) should have fared so badly. What is of greater interest is that, given the evidence of a generation cleavage (see Epstein, A.L. 1969), none of the younger candidates sought to exploit it. On the contrary, among the Rabaul candidates, while Epineri and ToBunbun kept quiet in the matter, Patiliu repeatedly appealed to the traditionalists by speaking in favour of preserving what was best in Tolai culture. Even more strikingly, at Kokopo and in the Gazelle, Tammur and ToLiman won very easily after presenting themselves as brokers between the generations: fully versed in modern ways, they also claimed to be more knowledgeable in and respectful of things traditional than their peers. Stressing the desirability of intra-Tolai harmony, they directed attention to the prospects for relief from pressing problems outside that society: the remainder of New Britain, largely undeveloped, was put forward as a frontier for Tolai enterprise and (in a complex mixture of symbolism and special interests) the title to certain European-held plantations was disputed.

The fact that Tammur and ToLiman were successful in promoting contentious social issues, while at the same time appealing to all Tolai, might be taken as an indication that Tolai society has not yet become consciously polarised. Further evidence in support of this contention can readily be adduced. Thus it is apparent that, in spite of an increasing involvement in the wage economy, Tolai 'have nots' are not yet mere 'hands': the majority are still dependent on their clan 'haves' and are able to levy some reciprocal claims on them. Moreover, it is not uncommon to find instances of partnership arising between the generations where the older contribute the material resources in the form of land and wealth and the younger and more educated their more recently acquired modern skills.

At the same time, as the reference to expansionism and the questioning of title in various European-held lands make clear, the way in which intra-Tolai cleavages are given expression in a political context has also to be seen in terms of the position of the Tolai in the wider colonial society. Here too change has been proceeding in complex and sometimes contradictory ways. Perhaps one of the most striking features of recent economic and social development in Papua-New Guinea has been its unevenness.[24] As we noted at the outset, large numbers of young Tolai are to be found today in relatively skilled posts throughout the Territory; from their position of advantage it might be expected that many of them would see their futures set in this broader national context. But from that same position they also become keenly aware of the relative affluence and the other advantages their home area enjoys over other parts of the country; they are quick to perceive too the disproportionate contribution that the Gazelle makes to the Territorial revenue while observing at the same time how centres like Port Moresby and Lae rise in importance as Rabaul stagnates.

Some of the ambiguities in this situation have already been illustrated in the citation from Patiliu's published platform. They emerge too in many of the discussions we had throughout the election about the development and role of political parties. The formation of Pangu in 1967, even though it included two Tolai, ToBaining and ToBunbun, as members of the executive, was received in Rabaul with considerable reserve and suspicion, not so much perhaps because of its declared aims, but simply because it originated in Port Moresby, and was seen by many as a device whereby Papuans would come to dominate New Guinea. Following the emergence of other parties on the mainland, the attempt to found a local party on the Gazelle was perhaps a predictable response, but this group too made little headway and quickly petered out. Individual Tolai offered a variety

[24] By way of illustration we cite here some figures, for which we are indebted to Mrs Ruth Finney, showing numbers of indigenous primary schoolteachers employed throughout the Territory and classified in terms of their Districts of origin. According to this index (calculated for the purpose on the basis of teachers per 100,000 head of population), the figure for East New Britain (Tolai) is 472, for Madang 43, and for Chimbu and the Eastern Highlands 8. Further details are given in Mrs Finney's New Guinea Research Unit Bulletin, *Would-be Enterpreneurs?: A Study of Motivation* (1971).

of reasons for this negative reaction. It was something new, some said, and for those unfamiliar with the set-up in the House of Assembly, the purpose behind parties was not entirely clear, and the way they worked difficult to grasp. For others the idea of parties offended their notions of how the game of politics should be played. One candidate was quite explicit in his opposition to the development of parties, saying they were a device by which a man without strong popular support could gain power through the support of a party when this should come direct from the people.[25] Another comment that was made repeatedly by some older people was that parties were a source of division within the country. Parties, they said, destroyed the unity of the people under the government; progress lay in working in co-operation with the Administration. These views are of course an expression of the paternalism that is still so strong a component in the Tolai outlook. Yet not all Tolai expressed such negative attitudes towards parties, and in private conversation a number showed keen interest in the concept. Indeed, experience elsewhere suggests how in critical periods these attitudes may change with quite remarkable rapidity (see, e.g., Epstein, A.L. 1958: 76-7). The 1968 elections coincided with such a critical period in the development of the Gazelle Peninsula. The victories of such men as Epineri and Oscar Tammur offer some evidence that the Tolai may now be emerging from the paternalist phase in their colonial history. The conflicts inherent in this transitional stage would seem to go far in accounting for much of the confusion and uncertainty that surrounded these elections.

TABLE 2—THE ELECTION RESULTS IN NEW BRITAIN

East and West New Britain Regional	1st and final count	
Don Barrett	11,882	
Roi Ashton	26,501	
Informal	4513	
Gazelle Open	1st count	2nd and final count
Mualat Tawanga	774	795
Bolton Tamean	549	Excl.
Stanley ToMarita	996	1264
Albert Price	575	700
Matthias ToLiman	2707	2771
Informal	184	—
Exhausted	—	71

[25] Such a view is consistent with traditional notions of 'big man' leadership, and it is perhaps worth noting that of all the Tolai candidates the speaker was the one who conformed most closely to the stereotypical character of a 'big man'.

TABLE 2—continued

Kandrian-Pomio Open	1st and final count
Julius Ayong	1547
Paul Manlel	521
Koriam Michael Urekit	7913
Anton Bos	1141
Pele Taol	308
Informal	1160

Kokopo Open	1st and final count
Oscar Tammur	3783
Vin ToBaining	1065
Beniona ToKarai	468
ToKau ToLogo	218
Informal	218

Rabaul Open	1st count	2nd count	3rd count	4th count	5th and final count
Thomas ToBunbun	1099	1121	1215	Excl.	—
Isimel ToWalaka	87	Excl.	—	—	—
Samson ToPatiliu	1335	1350	1387	1817	2114
Lawrence ToLavutul	648	653	Excl.	—	—
Epineri Titimur	2984	2992	3048	3220	3601
Tiut Turmarum	1261	1266	1445	1600	Excl.
Informal	501	—	—	—	—
Exhausted	—	32	319	777	1699

Talasea Open	1st count	2nd count	3rd count	4th count	5th and final count
Maus Bala	1642	1658	1691	1789	1879
Lima Yohanis	1467	1515	1623	1645	Excl.
Akai	1888	2050	2220	2255	2383
Theodore Kaiwa	710	775	Excl.	—	—
Otto Rerio	1103	1117	1133	Excl.	—
John Maneke	3307	3359	3538	4358	4548
Alois Baki	394	Excl.	—	—	—
Informal	130	—	—	—	—
Exhausted	—	37	306	464	1701

PERSONALITIES VERSUS POLICIES

Olga Gostin, W. Tomasetti, and M. W. Young

THE Milne Bay Administrative District, to which the Milne Bay Regional Electorate corresponds, is the most easterly in Papua. Scattered over a total area of some 97,000 square miles (of which only about 10 per cent is land), it has a population of just over 100,000. In 1964 the District contained two Open electorates: Milne Bay, which included the mainland tip and the Louisiade Archipelago, and Esa'ala-Losuia, which included the D'Entrecasteaux Islands, the Trobriands, Woodlark and a number of smaller island clusters.

The Open electorate boundaries were adjusted in 1968 to form three electorates with a population of approximately 33,000 each. These are: Alotau, comprising the mainland sector and the adjoining islands as far as the Engineers; Esa'ala, consisting of the D'Entrecasteaux Group; and Kula, embracing the residual scatter of peripheral islands. These revisions gave clear definition to the compact culture-area of the D'Entrecasteaux, but failed to do so for Alotau and, most notably, for Kula, which must be the most far-flung Open electorate in the Territory. Even its title is a misnomer for its boundaries exclude some of the main centres (Fergusson, the Amphletts, and the Engineers) involved in the traditional *kula* trading expeditions, and include other islands (Sudest, Rossel) which were never associated with it at all (see Malinowski 1922). However, this was at least partly in accord with local wishes, as some of the Kula islands were transferred to Alotau at the request of the presidents of the four main local government councils in the area (Distribution Committee 1967: 4).

The majority of the peoples of the Milne Bay District share a

Among numerous individuals and organisations that helped the team in the course of the study, thanks are due specially to: the students from the University of Papua and New Guinea, Benjamin Toyola and John Noel, who kept extensive diaries and acted as interpreters in the Kula Open Electorate, and John Kadiba for his work in Milne Bay; the Catholic Mission at Sideia; and Selina Esau and her family, for unparalleled help and hospitality to Olga Gostin during her stay in Kiriwina.

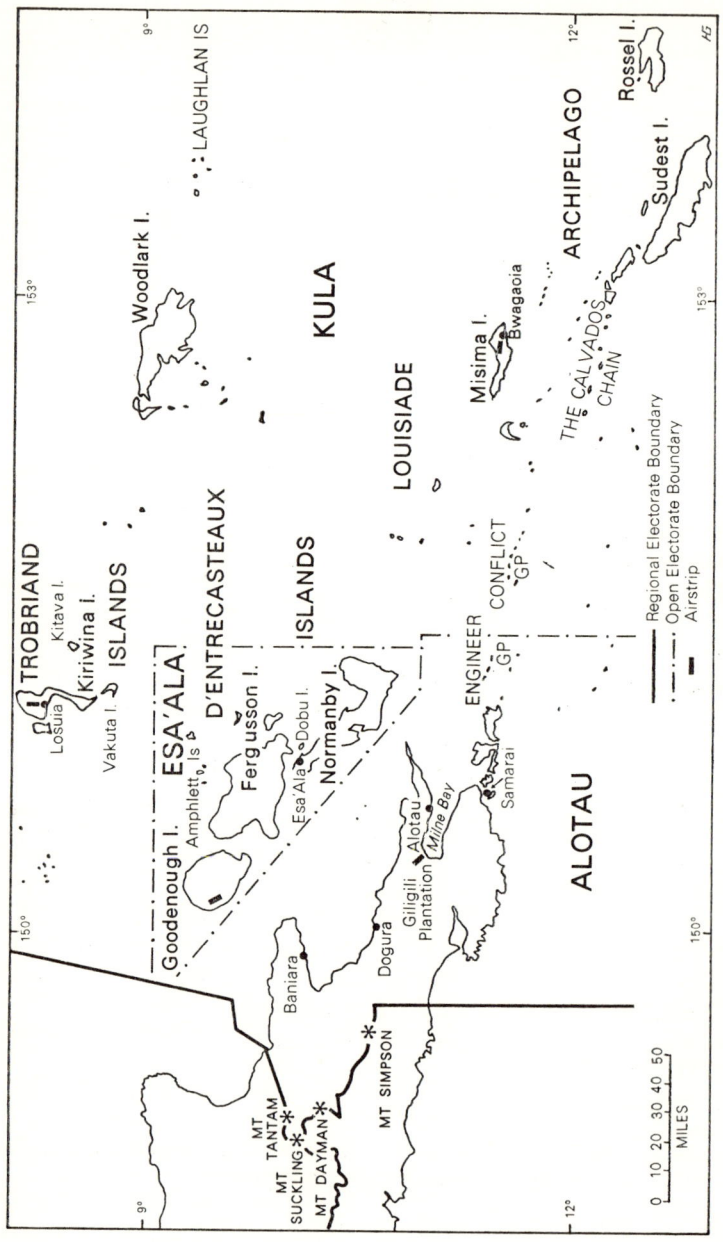

3 Milne Bay Electorates

relatively uniform ethnic type and culture: Seligman's Eastern Papuo-Melanesian and Massim respectively (Seligman 1910). The peoples in the north of the mainland sector, those of the northern D'Entrecasteaux and, most distinctively, the Rossel Islanders, possess traits which exclude them from the conventional Massim category. The most notable of these, perhaps, is the patrilineal reckoning of descent in contrast to the matriliny of the true Massim. Everywhere, however, people live in hamlets grouped into small villages and have subsistence economies based on the cultivation of root crops and bananas. Fishing is important coastally and pig-husbandry probably universal. There is some variety in the extent to which rank complicates indigenous political leadership. There is variety too, for instance, in the extent to which local resources or craft specialisation formed the basis of inter-community and inter-island trade. Traditional modes of life remain the norm rather than the exception: Amphlett Islanders continue to produce pottery without the aid of wheel or kiln; Goodenough Island women continue to wear leaf skirts and shell necklaces; and Trobriand men continue to undertake long *kula* voyages and pay annual harvest gifts to their chiefs.

Alongside the local diversity found within broad cultural similarities are diversities resulting from different degrees and types of acculturation. Traditional cultures have absorbed, or have in varying degrees themselves been modified by, traits and influences from outside: Amphlett Islanders sell their pots for cash; Goodenough women play netball and take their children to mission welfare clinics; Trobriand chiefs are in conflict with the local government council. The history of European contact in the Milne Bay District spans almost a century. Its unevenness and complexity reflect both the geographical fragmentation of the area and the variety of interests which agents of acculturation have represented and pursued. Excluding the major set-back caused by World War II, the history of administration and mission activity in the area is one of progressive expansion. There are today over a dozen centres of administration and six Christian missions, which between them claim at least the nominal allegiance of a majority of the population. The history of commercial enterprise has been more erratic, and needless to say, the exploitation of local resources has not always been to the advantage of the indigenous peoples. Sudest and Woodlark, for instance, were among the first goldfields to be worked in the Territory, though neither has anything to show for the wealth they once produced.

European settlement has tended to favour the southern portion of the District, though it has never been intensive and land alienation has been minimal. Less than 1 per cent of the present population is European, and the greatest number of these dwell in relative social encapsulation either in the commercial centre of Samarai or on government or mission stations. Most European enterprise is concerned with trading or copra production and frequently a combination of both. Minor commercial empires have been built during the eighty years of Samarai's existence.

Since World War II, indigenous commercial enterprise has been a feature of the Samarai region, and to a lesser extent the whole of the southern Massim. In this respect, the previous Open electorate boundaries separated a marginally more 'developed' region from a less 'developed' one. The old Esa'ala-Losuia Electorate is conspicuous for its relative absence of entrepreneurs, minimal European settlement, greater administrative neglect, and a history of poorer educational facilities. The D'Entrecasteaux have been further stultified by inertia from within, by sorcery fears which generate inhibition rather than ambition, and by migrant wage-labour patterns which have become integral to the way of life. Trobrianders, while showing a disdain for work abroad, have also been indifferent to European-type enterprises. The recent blooming of a commercial wood-carving industry in Kiriwina is therefore to be seen as a happy compromise.

Copra is the main export of the District, an estimated half of it produced by indigenous growers. Other cash crops, such as coffee, cocoa, and rubber, are grown on a far smaller scale and, like the majority of the coconut plantations, are to be found in the southern portion of the District. In this area the role of Samarai as a ready market and direct stimulus to local enterprise is obvious. More remarkable—indeed unique—is the stimulus provided by the Kwato Extension Association (an offshoot of the London Missionary Society), which over the years has created a local élite of tradesmen and boatbuilders (Belshaw 1955). Developments such as these have stimulated the growth of co-operatives and led to the early establishment (1951) of the District's first local government council.

During the last decade, the whole of the District came under local government—the first in Papua to achieve this distinction. Some of the councils have clearly been imposed prematurely or too suddenly, and the success of the fourteen councils, in terms of efficiency and substantive achievements, varies considerably. More than any other single influence, however, the councils appear to have created a general awareness of public issues wider than the village. This has probably been accomplished through individual councillors acting as transmitters of information to isolated communities, rather than by the institutionalised efforts of councils acting as corporate bodies in sponsoring adult education courses or distributing pamphlets. For the majority of the District elections are regular events reasonably well understood.

It is to be expected, however, that in an electorate of such spread and such tenuous communications, a wide spectrum of political awareness or 'literacy' will be found. This shades horizontally from that of the élite educated workers in the townships and government stations to that of the non-literate subsistence gardeners dwelling in mountain fastnesses or on isolated islands guarded by treacherous reefs. The latter are beyond the reach of most effective information media and, also because of their isolation, are passed over by rushed candidates and neglected by busy sitting members. There is also a vertical shading of political literacy to be found within any area. The young tend to be better educated and more receptive to change than their fathers, and in the Kula Electorate at least a cleavage was apparent between the young sophisticates with progressive political views and the old conservatives, tradition-conscious and suspicious of what might prove to be a threat to their position. Perhaps everywhere, however, the wind of change, heralded by political parties and talk of independence, had been felt.

ALOTAU OPEN

There were three nominations for the Alotau seat: Osineru Dickson, Bondai Pita, and John Guise. Dickson, a brother of Merari Dickson, who represented the area in the Legislative Council from 1951 to 1957, was born on Kwato in 1909, and grew up as a member of a family highly respected and well known throughout Milne Bay. Educated to Standard V, he came in the post-war years to serve with distinction as a public servant in various positions, including the role of Papuan adviser to Colonel J. K. Murray when he was Administrator. Dickson had been living in Port Moresby since 1948. Bondai Pita, a somewhat younger man, was also born at Kwato, and he too had been educated to Standard V. Pita was vice-president of the Cameron Club and treasurer of the Rabe Cricket Club immediately before the election. However, his major experience in public affairs has been in the Milne Bay Local Government Council, of which he has been secretary since its inception in 1952. Finally, there was John Guise, the sitting Member, of all indigenous politicians perhaps the most widely known to local and overseas people throughout New Guinea.

Campaigning in Alotau, as indeed throughout the entire District, required extensive travelling and made heavy demands on the candidates' time and resources. In the circumstances it is surprising how few found that co-operation was to their mutual advantage. Dickson flew from Port Moresby to Alotau on 5 January 1968 to begin campaigning. After several days at his home village, he went to Kwato, which he used as a base for covering the islands near Samarai. The trip to Kwato was made on a vessel chartered by Dennis Young, a candidate for the Regional: Bondai Pita was also on board. Thereafter the trio spent much of the rest of the month travelling together, and holding joint meetings at various places. At Rabe they were the only candidates to attend a meeting arranged by the Milne Bay Local Government Council to which all Open and Regional candidates had been invited. Towards the end of January Dickson began independent campaigning in the coastal villages on the north shore of Milne Bay.

Dickson's association with the National Progress Party (Napro) led it to supply him, at the cost of $3.50, with 5000 leaflets printed in English with a few vague phrases on Napro's 'policy'. These he distributed as he moved from village to village. He did not attempt to set up any organisation that could be used both to spread his policy, and get out his voters on polling day. His campaigning depended mainly on the technique of village meetings, held for preference in the evening. Apart from the gift of leaflets from Napro, Dickson financed his own campaign, which covered the electorate fairly extensively, though excluding the villages inland from the north coast, where a large number of voters live, and where Guise's support was known to be strong. Had time and finance permitted, it is likely that some of the time spent in Milne Bay area could have been profitably spent in these inland villages.

Dickson made tentative approaches to Pita on a preference deal, but no arrangements resulted from it. The main points of his program were drawn from Napro's published policy, though he also included some additional items of his own such as encouragement of co-operative societies and local government councils and an adult literacy campaign. However, as his campaign progressed, Dickson steadily played down his membership of Napro when he found a general suspicion of parties on the south coast, the Islands, and the Bay, and on the north coast, a general inclination towards Pangu. But he kept to the original elements in his policy.

Pita's campaigning was more limited. As clerk of the Milne Bay Local Government Council he could conveniently canvass in the villages of the Bay, and this he did in late December and early

January. Thereafter, at Young's invitation, he joined him and Dickson on a tour of villages in the Samarai Islands. These collective endeavours were extended to include the south coast, and the inland villages to the south-west of Milne Bay.

Pita did not campaign on the north coast. His campaign thus was not planned to reach more than half the voters. Pita made no preference deals and did not make open affirmation of any party affiliation. His platform was a simple one, concerned generally with local issues. He undertook, if elected, to foster economic development in the villages by assisting local government councils and co-operatives.

Like the other candidates, his main campaign technique was the evening village meeting, at which he made a speech and invited questions. No posters supporting his candidacy were seen. He does not seem to have sought or received assistance from any of the modern institutions in the electorate and it seems likely that his support was derived largely through clan connections.

John Guise's position always seemed secure, and he could perhaps safely have rested on his laurels and depended on the support he enjoyed in the electorate. In fact he took no chances, and made a most comprehensive tour of the area, renewing contacts, friendship and support everywhere.

Guise made it clear during his campaign that he would make no formal preference deals with any other candidates. He also had no overt arrangements for mutual support with any of the Regional candidates (though it is worth noting that some of these did claim that they had received promises of support from Guise). He believed that his membership of Pangu was well known in the electorate, but did not campaign as a Pangu member: he did not make a point of publicising his membership, but neither did he seek to deny it. His platform, moreover, was essentially that of Pangu: its main points were (i) immediate home rule and ultimate independence; (ii) unification of Papua and New Guinea; (iii) economic development with continuing expatriate investment and local participation, and expansion of co-operatives; (iv) localisation of the Public Service; (v) greater subsidies to missions and local government councils for social development projects; (vi) provision of urban housing; (vii) increased wage rates; (viii) rapid expansion of communications; (ix) steps to safeguard human rights.

Guise has an inimitable capacity to illustrate points by the use of analogies that make an immediate and striking impression on village audiences. This capacity served him well in the evening meetings he held in all the villages he visited. People in this area usually return to their houses in the village in the late afternoon.

It is during this period that community discussions traditionally take place. An evening village meeting thus has the advantages of reaching a large proportion of the village people, and reaching them at the time and in a way that accords with their own usages.

Most of the villages in the electorate had one or two persons who looked after Guise's political interests. It may perhaps be premature to describe these arrangements as a machine, but they helped in getting out his voters on polling day.

Guise considered that he enjoyed widespread support from local government councillors, women's clubs, co-operative societies and churches. He believed some members of Kwato (adherents of the London Missionary Society mission based on that island) supported him; and he was confident of Anglican and Catholic support. There was some evidence that the local government councils on the north coast informally agreed among themselves to support Guise exclusively. But whether this was so or not, Guise's expectations were abundantly fulfilled by the results. His victory in 1968 was as complete as it had been in 1964 when he received 84 per cent of the votes cast. His four years as sitting Member both kept him in the public eye and gave him the opportunity to advance the interests of his constituency. The new electoral boundaries were at worst neutral to his cause. Osineru Dickson had been easily beaten in 1964, and though in his second effort he considerably improved his position, even in his best performance in the Milne Bay Sub-District he could still only obtain about a quarter of the votes cast for Guise. Bondai Pita was not seen as a national figure nor was he well known throughout the electorate, and he could only muster less than 4 per cent of the total votes cast. Guise's victory was overwhelming; given his reputation, the thoroughness of his campaigning, and the skill of his 'politicking', it was perhaps inevitable.

ESA'ALA OPEN

The boundary revision which separated the D'Entrecasteaux from the Trobriands was regarded by informed voters in the Esa'ala Open Electorate as a stroke of fortune for Lepani Watson. The opinion was frequently expressed that he could not have carried the D'Entrecasteaux vote a second time (Fink 1965). Disappointment in his performance as representative was general, and some of the less informed voters even appeared to believe that the reason for the elections at this time was the government's own dissatisfaction with

Watson. Specific criticisms against him had as their common denominators neglect and failure to fulfil election promises made in 1964. In terms of its influence on the 1968 elections in this area, the legacy of Lepani Watson's representation was twofold. Firstly, a substantial majority rejected the idea of putting another Papuan representative into the House, and secondly, electors were as wary of accepting election promises as candidates were of offering them. It can be argued, however, that the widespread disappointment in him had the salutary effect of deflating overblown expectations regarding the role performance of a member. By injecting a dash of healthy cynicism into public attitudes, Watson did the D'Entrecasteaux Islanders a service they would not at this stage be prepared to thank him for. But it can also be argued that for some sectors of the electorate (Goodenough and West Fergusson particularly) high expectations of performance of members may not have been substantially lowered but merely shifted onto Europeans. It is perhaps ironical, therefore, that despite the attitude which in 1968 favoured almost any European candidate over any Papuan, no European stood for the Esa'ala Open. Two Europeans, both locally well-known plantation owners, considered standing specifically against Watson before it was known that the realignment of boundaries would make this unnecessary. If Watson gave the electors reason for wanting to try a European, he also diminished their chances of getting one by not being available to stand for re-election himself.

The candidates and their campaigns

All six candidates could rightfully claim to be Papuan and four of them had been born in the Dobu area of the D'Entrecasteaux. All stood on their own initiative, financed their own campaigns, and canvassed fairly extensively. In other respects they had few things in common.

Enosi Baloiloi, aged 34, belongs to the locally eminent and influential Baloiloi family of Dobu, another member of which had sought election in 1964. Urbane in appearance, manner, and outlook, Baloiloi clearly felt it would be advantageous to project the image of one thoroughly at home in the European dominated milieu of Port Moresby, where he lived and worked. He could enumerate an impressive list of church and urban community activities in which he had been, and in some cases still was, energetically involved. He was currently a hostel manager. In 1967 a body calling itself the Pre-Electoral Ballot Committee was formed in Port Moresby by D'Entrecasteaux men interested in choosing a candidate to contest the 1968 elections in their home area. For a variety of reasons all those men initially considered by the Committee proved unwilling or unable to stand, so it encouraged one of its members, Baloiloi, to nominate. The Committee pledged him as much voting support as it could muster,[1] though it gave him no financial aid. The Committee appears to have had no particular platform and Baloiloi admitted that from the time of his nomination in November 1967 to the commencement of his campaigning in January, he had been 'trying to work out a policy'. He had no personal interest in political parties and thought they were pointless until there was more political understanding at the village level. The canvassing point for which he was best remembered by his audiences was his plan to stimulate the production of root crops by marketing them in Samarai and Moresby, thereby drawing a trickle of much needed cash into the villages of the electorate. This was one of the most striking and original ideas offered by any candidate, but it did not noticeably fire the electors' imaginations, probably because they regard their food surpluses as political rather than economic assets, essential to the regulation of traditional community life. Unlike most other candidates, Baloiloi neither overrated his chances of winning nor set great store by victory. In the overall polling he did tolerably well, coming second to the winner with 16 per cent of the first preferences. Had so many electors not been so determined to return a European rather than a Papuan, they might well have decided that Enosi Baloiloi, with so many European attributes, was a better compromise. As it is, his popularity over the other losers strengthens the impression that what the voters were seeking in their representative was a European image.

Joseph Nimagore's campaign was the least extensive of any candidate's and he remained for most voters a rather shadowy figure. Aged 38, and also from the Dobu area, he had worked with A.N.G.A.U. during the war and subsequently taught at a Catholic mission school. More recently he had become a trade-store manager in the Esa'ala area, and he was reported to have saturated his speeches with references to business enterprise. By all reports his platform was not very clear. In order to make the electorate 'strong' he believed it was necessary to discourage men from leaving it in search of work, and advocated the creation of 'markets' throughout the area. How they were to be established, and what commodities they were to sell and to whom, informants could not remember—if indeed they were ever told. A European who heard Nimagore's campaign speech described it as 'a mixture of gobbledygook and cargoism'. Although,

[1] Baloiloi polled 37 per cent of absentee first preference votes, most of which may be assumed to have been cast in Port Moresby. The winner of the seat, Norman Evennett, gained 31 per cent of absentee votes.

like Baloiloi, he polled better in sectors where he was previously unknown than in his home area, it was plain everywhere that he would win little numerical support. His was the name that villagers found most difficulty in recalling.

At 37, Poate Henry Andrew had spent most of his working life teaching schoolchildren. Currently, he was headmaster of an Administration school at Rigo, 'too far out' as he put it, 'to hear much of the talk about political parties'. With the manner of a humble schoolmaster, he campaigned persistently and thoroughly, in bare feet and with meagre resources. He felt strongly about the poor educational attainments of D'Entrecasteaux Islanders, and he made education his main platform. He also wanted Esa'ala to be declared a township to give it more scope for growth and to 'attract business people'. In addition he wanted plantation workers to receive higher wages—a valuable campaigning point in an electorate which had for so long been a pool of migrant labourers—and he believed that a dominant need of the area was for a rural school of agricultural training. Andrew saw the contest as between himself and Norman Evennett. He assumed that his closest support would come from the Dobu area where he was known, even though this was also Evennett's (not to mention three of the other candidates') home ground. He was aware of what he termed 'a racial issue', and in his campaign tried to counter the bias that had developed against Papuan candidates as a result of disillusionment with Lepani Watson. 'We natives have to show our people that we can do better than he did', Andrew maintained. In the poll, however, Andrew's belief that he had the support of his home area was shown to be based on false hopes.

Norman (Nomani) Evennett was born in Samarai in 1929, the son of an Australian planter-trader and a Wari Islander. His grandfather had come to the District as early as 1902. Evennett, therefore, had every justification for telling his campaign audiences that he was a Papuan like themselves and that this was his country too. Moreover, he was by choice a D'Entrecasteaux settler, having lived in the Dobu Passage for twenty-one years with every intention of staying there. Evennett realised that it was important for him to impress on people the permanence of his business interests in the area. He was fully aware of the climate of opinion which favoured a European candidate, and he did not hesitate to exploit it; but at the same time he was careful to anticipate the objections of those who mistrusted Australians. Being of mixed descent Evennett knew he could have it both ways, and this was the way he played it in his skilful campaign speeches. In projecting his image as 'the right man for the job' he also found it helpful to provoke apprehensions about self-government in his audiences. He warned them about Pangu, making it clear that he belonged to no party himself. He also warned that he had no promises to make, that the road ahead would be hard no matter who was elected. In his reiteration of the poverty of Papua-New Guinea, the extent of its dependence upon Australia and the difficult prospect which would face the country when it became independent, he played on the fears of his listeners to a greater extent than any other candidate. In an appeal for votes he presented a list of essential qualifications which he believed the elected member should possess: education, knowledge of political processes in the capital and the electorate, ability to understand and talk to Europeans (the 'real governors'), and a permanent home in the electorate with a knowledge of local people and their needs. Evennett then demonstrated how well he met these criteria. It is significant that the list is almost identical with the voters' own appreciation of the necessary qualifications of their ideal representative. If Methodist Christian virtues were a notable feature of the criteria applied to candidates in the last election (Fink 1965, 310-11), they were much less evident than the pragmatic qualities sought in 1968. The feeling was that while the last member might have been a good Methodist he was a bad representative; now it was time to choose a good representative whatever his religion.[2] In refusing to make promises to the voters, Evennett also sidestepped the need to offer them any concrete policy for the development of the electorate. It was said by some of his opponents that he had no policy because 'he wants to keep things the way they are'. There was naturally some resentment and envy among the other candidates of Evennett's evident popularity; he possessed advantages of wealth, education, and 'status' over most of them. Yet to their credit there was little public mud-slinging (in contrast to the Regional campaign), though some of the candidates, with ears cocked for rumours about themselves, were probably apt to exaggerate the endemicity of those there were and overestimate their influence on the voters. Evennett himself had no need to criticise the other candidates. He was the only one not to feel that he had a serious rival, and he was confident— or 'scared' as he put it—that he was going to win as early as a whole month before the ballot.

The only woman to nominate for election in 1968 was Jo Wilkinson, 43, the wife of an Australian planter-trader who himself had been an unsuccessful rival of Lepani Watson's in 1964. Of mixed race, Mrs Wilkinson identified with D'Entrecasteaux women without difficulty. She saw, in the appeal she could make to female voters,

[2] Evennett and Wilkinson were Anglican, Nimagore and Kalade Catholic, and Baloiloi and Andrew Methodist.

an opportunity denied to the other candidates. She perceived her mission, in seeking election, in quasi-religious terms. Her task was to 'uplift' the people and to help them outgrow the 'neglected children' role they had been cast in for so long by Administration and missions alike. Her candidature was, in her husband's term, 'a family venture', and one assumes that had she won it would have been a family seat. Jack Wilkinson had been approached to stand a second time but decided that he was too old and irascible. It is likely that the extent of his personal unpopularity was brought home to him by his poor showing in the 1964 results. He reasoned that his wife would stand a better chance than himself, and throughout the campaign seemed fairly confident of her winning, acknowledging only Norman Evennett as a serious rival. Just as the electors wanted to try a European or a person of mixed race 'for a change', the Wilkinsons argued, so they might also be prepared to try a female representative instead of a man. Despite this optimism, the general feeling in the villages seemed to be that whatever it was Jo Wilkinson had to offer, it was offset by the fact of her sex. Very few people indeed—including women— were sympathetic to the idea of a female representative in the House of Assembly. Despite the comparatively high status of women in the D'Entrecasteaux it not only went against the grain of traditional culture for a woman to stand and talk as an equal in the councils of men, but it was almost unthinkable that she would be able to achieve anything that a man could not. It is not surprising, therefore, that Mrs Wilkinson polled weakly in those areas where she was previously unknown. In Normanby, where she was known to the majority by name if not by sight, she did reasonably well (29 per cent) and in her home sector she defeated all other candidates by capturing 48 per cent of total first preferences. In contrast to some of the other candidates, Jo Wilkinson's popularity decreased in proportion to the distance from her home. Her overall voting support was a mere 10 per cent.

Francisco Kalade, 34, was the only Pangu Pati supporter to contest the Esa'ala Open. While not its official nominee, he defended Pangu policies and did his utmost to correct the lopsided and damaging views put forward to the electors by some of the other candidates, notably the two Independents contesting the Regional seat. It was clearly a losing battle, however, and by the time polling began Pangu policies, or the simple distortions of them that were bandied about, were thoroughly discredited and Pangu's name was anathema to most villagers. If Enosi Baloiloi presented an image of the urbane committee man, and Henry Andrew that of the gentle schoolmaster, Francisco Kalade, a fellow Dobuan, appeared as the sombre intellectual

—an image enhanced by his black shirt and sunglasses. He had been a Catholic mission schoolteacher, a plantation overseer, a councillor on Dobu Local Government Council, and was currently secretary of the Milne Bay Workers' Association in Samarai.

Kalade saw himself as a member of the emergent Papuan intelligentsia. More than any other candidate he concerned himself with broader, country-wide issues on which he allied himself with Pangu policies. On his own local platform, Kalade was lucid and forthcoming. He had definite views to which he had obviously given some thought. What the electorate needed most, he believed, was education and economic development. Without the former there could be only a limited amount of the latter, and until there were more well-educated people in the area, it would remain politically stagnant and continue to reject, through fear and suspicion, parties like Pangu which are a good and necessary thing for the whole country's development. It was to argue in a circle, he maintained, to say as other candidates did, that this area was too backward to support Pangu demands for speedy political development, when political ignorance and apathy were the root causes of its backwardness. Kalade saw little hope for improvement until there were some operational changes in what he termed the 'political systems' of the electorate. At present there were three such systems: the Administration, the missions, and the councils. All were working broadly towards the same ends, but they were motivated by different interests and there was frequently conflict between them and far less than full co-operation. Even worse, each of these systems was internally divided: the Administration into departments, the missions into denominations, and the councils into parochial areas. This fragmentation was detrimental to the orderly and rapid development of the electorate (or Sub-District) as a whole. Kalade perceived the elected member's role as one of co-ordinator of these systems. If he were elected he would initiate regular conferences at which the representatives of these bodies could discuss ends and means and how to avoid getting in each other's way.

If Kalade had the most purely political platform of all, he also had most difficulty in getting it across to the voters, and it is ironical that his most articulate concern—the political ignorance of the electors—was their greatest obstacle to understanding him. He was forced to simplify his ideas to a general level of comprehension where they were robbed of significance. Some listeners assumed his criticism of the political cleavages in the area to mean that he wanted to stand the Sub-District on its head. D'Entrecasteaux Islanders are nothing if not conservative and the prospect of 'revolution' was terrifying.

For the most part, however, Kalade appeared to have failed to impress any idea at all on his audiences. His self-styled allegiance to Pangu may have handicapped him marginally, but far more unfortunate was the omission of his photograph from the official polling poster. By the time polling began Francisco Kalade was the 'faceless man' in more ways than one. He captured a mere 2 per cent of total first preferences.

Voting behaviour

The level of general interest shown in the elections did not appear to be high in the D'Entrecasteaux. While the candidates were not necessarily in the best position to gauge interest, some of them commented on the general lack of response to their campaigning. John Stuntz, a Regional candidate with some experience of public response elsewhere, was 'struck by the apathy and lack of interest' in the Esa'ala Sub-District compared with the Misima and Milne Bay areas. Of the 18,753 voters enrolled in Esa'ala 10,066 (or 53 per cent) exercised their right to vote. Although this may serve as a rough 'apathy index', the figure of 53 per cent is probably too high. Voting percentages are a doubtful guide to electoral interest in areas where people believe officials expect them to vote.

There was a perceptible correlation between the interest and knowledge of villagers on the one hand, and the amount of canvassing they had received on the other. Even so, very few people indeed were able to name all the candidates in the Open, explain the difference between the Regional and Open electorates, or even describe the extent of electoral boundaries. (Not all the candidates had grasped the mechanism of preferential voting, so it is needless to state that the voters had not.) Political parties were universally misunderstood, and while it is probable that virtually all the electors had heard the word 'party', it was regarded as synonymous with Pangu. The speeches of the candidates were the most important source of political education for villagers. The pre-electoral patrols by Administration officers had little impact, being primarily census checks which, owing to staff shortages and other contingencies, slowed them down to the extent that they were unable to reach even a majority of the villagers. Government pamphlets were ineffective, being aimed at a far higher level of political comprehension than is general in the D'Entrecasteaux, and they were not, in contrast to the candidates' ubiquitous screeds, in evidence in the villages. If the candidates themselves, then, were the main source of political information, the local government councillors were the main channels for diffusing this information to the large section of the electorate unable to hear the candidates for itself. Generally better educated than the average villager, having a modicum of literacy and being much more mobile and in touch with island or Sub-District events, the councillors were more influential than probably either they or the candidates realised. Once a candidate had seized upon the councillors as a means of conveying his platform and personality to villagers he had neither time nor resources to visit in person, he put himself at the mercy of the councillors' impression of him. It was a worthwhile gamble to take. If a councillor reported to his village negatively or not at all, the candidate would have gained nothing, but if a councillor reported favourably he could hope to win a bloc vote. It is likely that councillors, more than any other category of local leader, had much to do with the bloc votes which were a feature of polling in this electorate.

Perhaps the most significant aspect of voting behaviour was the extent to which it was dominated by the use of the official posters featuring the photographs of the candidates. The posters, situated outside the polling tent and also inside each polling booth, were more than merely *aides-mémoire* for the electors. Far more importantly, they were frequently the only medium used by the voter in recording his votes. In this predominantly non-literate electorate, the ballot was less a 'whispering' than a 'pointing' one. As a distinct form of voting behaviour it might be termed a 'picture identification ballot'. It was a feature of the polling in all six sectors of the electorate, though some teams reported greater use of it than others. There was no prior intention to conduct the polling in this manner; as it became apparent to each polling team that the posters were simplifying its work by speeding up the process of vote recording, it naturally encouraged their use.

Norman Evennett's confidence was justified. He polled consistently high in all sectors except one and emerged from the contest with a clear majority of 53 per cent. Despite his somewhat reserved and uncordial manner, his overlong speeches and apparent lack of a constructive policy platform, Evennett's advantages over the other candidates were apparently decisive in the eyes of most voters, who in 1968 were disillusioned with a Papuan representative, frustrated by their ignorance, and increasingly self-conscious with regard to their meagre entrepreneurial achievements. Moreover, his wealth gave him a month's start on the other candidates and his campaigning took him twice round the islands and into inland villages on Fergusson which no other candidate reached. Finally, his ability to communicate with the rulers of the area—Administration officers—was not in question. It did not go unnoticed on Goodenough that he was the only candidate to stay at the Patrol Officer's house, or on Fergusson that his boat was hired by the Administration to transport a polling team during the elections. It was then, above all, his European background that spoke most convincingly for him, of his unmistakable identification with Europeans, his European mode of life and his European business success. In fact, by those people who knew him only slightly, the question asked was not 'Is he really a European?' but 'Is he really a mixed-race man?'

KULA OPEN

The candidates

Of the three candidates in this electorate, Lepani Watson was by far the best known. Born at Vakuta in the Trobriands in 1927, Watson had completed Standard V when the Japanese invasion interrupted his schooling. Subsequently he had a varied career, holding different positions in the Trobriand Islands or Port Moresby until 1954 when he became a Welfare Assistant in the Department of Native Affairs at Port Moresby. Nearly ten years later he resigned this position to contest the 1964 general election for the Esa'ala-Losuia Open Electorate (see Fink 1964, 1965).

Elected to the House of Assembly by a decisive plurality, Watson came to terms with the new political institutions fairly quickly, and was subsequently appointed Under-Secretary for Trade and Industry. During his period in office, he remained an active member of many bodies, societies, and institutions, amongst them the Interim Council of the University of Papua and New Guinea, the Trobriand Islands Saving and Loan Society, and the Volunteer Service Association. He also remained associated with the Methodist Welfare Society which had given him strong organisational backing during the 1964 elections, though it did not actively support or finance his campaign in 1968.

Goweli Taurega had unsuccessfully contested the Esa'ala-Losuia seat in 1964, polling 15 per cent of the votes as against Watson's 49 per cent. Born at Losuia government station on Kiriwina in 1923, Taurega completed Standard V at the nearby Oiabia Methodist Mission. When he was employed in the Military Administration, he improved his English and became an interpreter. In 1947 he left Losuia and was an interpreter at Samarai, and then a general foreman. In 1960 he returned to Losuia as government interpreter, a post he held at the time of both elections.

Both Taurega's parents had been Methodist lay-preachers, and Taurega himself was for some time actively engaged in Methodist church work. From 1957 to 1960 he had been vice-chairman of the Bromilow-Chalmers Society at Samarai, and on returning to Losuia became its leading lay-preacher and chairman of the Losuia Club. In 1966, however, Taurega terminated his activities as a lay-preacher because his church associates objected to his drinking habits. His drinking attracted general disapproval and almost certainly undermined his reputation among a people for whom the moral uprightness of a candidate (judged according to their standards) is at least as important as the political platform for which he stands.

In 1964, Taurega had contested the elections largely from a sense of frustration. In the course of his patrols as government interpreter throughout the Trobriands, he had often been drawn into local issues; his advice had been sought, and villagers had often solicited his assistance or intervention before that of field officers. Though he had at first sought to meet these requests, Taurega soon realised that he was in no position to achieve anything and that, indeed, he might well jeopardise his post if he carried his interest too far. By nominating for the elections, Taurega had hoped to find an acceptable channel to express the needs of his people. After his defeat in 1964, he returned to his position as government interpreter at Losuia and did not seriously consider nominating for the 1968 elections until as late as November 1967.

What brought his decision to a head was an exchange of letters between Watson and himself in which the former implied that Taurega had taken advantage of his position as government interpreter to publicise himself as a potential candidate during the program of electoral and political education preceding nomination. Taurega denied doing this and on the spur of the moment decided to contest the election, if for no better reason than that he did not want to see Watson re-elected. This estrangement coloured the tone and manner of campaigning in the Kula Open Electorate and made it an unpleasantly personal and bitter contest.

The third candidate was Jack Patterson. Of Finnish ancestry on the paternal side, Patterson was born at Mulosaida village on Kiriwina in 1929. Educated at the London Missionary Society school at Losuia, Sogeri High School, and the Administrative College in Port Moresby, he obtained the Intermediate Certificate and Teacher's 'B' Certificate. At the time of the elections he was stationed at Losuia as Education Officer Grade IV. Previous to his appointment at Losuia (in 1963) Patterson had spent four years teaching on Misima Island, between 1952-4 and 1958-60. This background of experience in the southern section of Kula was a potential asset, as neither Watson nor Taurega was known in those parts. In fact, Patterson's decision to nominate for the 1968 elections was in response to the invitation of the Louisiade Local Government Council. (This was established in 1958 and covers the islands of the Louisiade Archipelago, including Sudest and Rossel, although the latter have been represented by councillors only since 1966.) In June 1967, Patterson received a letter from the President of the Louisiade Local Government Council asking him to stand for Kula Open since he (Patterson) knew the people of Misima and their needs. Patterson pondered this proposition for some time before making up his mind. He did not underestimate the strong position held by Watson as the sitting Member, and realised that he would be sacrificing seniority and a considerable income if he resigned from the Education Department. This was no mean consideration for a man with a young family and no alternative source of income. Nevertheless, after weighing up his advantage in Misima (whose vote in his favour he took for granted, mistakenly), and after considering the dissatisfaction with Watson in the Trobriands, he decided that it was worth taking up the challenge.

Patterson's decision to stand was thus calculated, and taken only after a long estimation of his chances. This was in marked contrast to Taurega's spontaneous nomination. The difference in temperament between the two men, and their common background of personal antagonism to Watson was subsequently reflected in their campaigns. At the time of nomination, however, Patterson and Taurega were merely nodding acquaintances, and each nominated independently.

The campaign

Perhaps because of his wider political experience Watson's campaign appears to have been organised more systematically and carried out with much more verve than that of either of his rivals. Certainly his past record carried much weight with the electors, if only in evoking their curiosity 'to hear and see Lepani, of whom we have heard so much on the radio'; and he attracted larger numbers than his opponents. Watson also showed a keener sense of campaign tactics, and appeared to have learned a number of lessons from his experience in 1964. Then he had concentrated his canvassing on local government council areas outside the Trobriands, notably in Esa'ala. Although this had paid off, he had polled unexpectedly poorly in the Trobriands. Now it appeared that he wanted to consolidate his position in the Trobriands first, since he was aware not only of his low polling there in 1964 but also of the personal attacks being made upon him by his opponents. Accordingly he remained on the scene as long as possible to refute charges being made against him and to consolidate his position. He must have been confident of progress by the end of January when he left to attend a meeting of the Summer School of the Australian Institute of Political Science in Canberra. He returned a week later, and went to Misima where he hoped to undermine Patterson's influence, since the latter had not returned to the area for eight years. Many informants remarked on the astuteness of Watson's approach, and thought that his visit to Misima just before polling could swing the vote there in his favour and so clinch the election.

Watson's campaign was almost identical in style and content to that which he conducted in 1964 (see Fink 1965). His meetings were invariably conducted within a formal framework which included a chairman and provided for a minister or the candidate himself to begin and end the meeting with a prayer. This was well advised in a community which was predominantly Methodist, and where being 'a good Christian' was considered a basic requirement in a candidate. Prayer for guidance had been suggested to the people by the (expatriate) head of the local Methodist mission in a letter written while he was on leave in Australia. The letter was read out at the Central Mission Church on Kiriwina early in December and was understood by the people to endorse their widespread view that they should base their choice on the various candidates' respective adherence to Christian principles. This approach could have had an important bearing on the election, since neither of Watson's rivals was a churchgoer. Patterson, indeed, considered religious affiliation to be irrelevant and professed none.

Watson's policy on the future political development of the Territory appears to have been ambiguous. Some informants reported that he opposed any policy advocating speedy self-government as short-sighted because it disregarded the wishes of the majority of the Territory's people; while others reported that he had suggested that the people of Papua-New Guinea should set a target date for independence. Some informants spoke of him as the true spokesman of (conservative) village opinion, while others suspected him of Pangu Pati affiliations, though at no time did Lepani openly identify himself with any political party.

He also stressed the need to give more opportunities to educated Papuans and New Guineans in the Public Service; to train youth in leadership; to advance rural economic development and to preserve the traditional cultural heritage of the country. Speaking in the Trobriand Islands in particular, Watson regretted 'the deterioration of the authority of traditional leaders'. This was a touchy point in the Trobriands where the traditional leadership was currently being challenged by the younger generation in general, and by local government councils in particular. Traditional chiefs there still wield enough authority, however, for Watson's observations to have solicited favourable support from them—and presumably, therefore, from their following.

Questions of platform aside, there were a number of ways in which Watson appeared to enjoy a clear advantage over his rivals. There was, for example, his reputation for being *tolilalasi*—hospitable and generous—for abstaining from drink, and his active membership of the Methodist Church. Informants contrasted the 'open-house' hospitality of Watson and his wife who welcomed 'everybody' to their home, and whose verandah was always crowded with visitors in the evening, with the restricted gatherings at Patterson's place which included 'only close relatives and persons from leading clans'. Watson's alleged adherence to Methodist norms of behaviour and his association with Methodist preachers with whom he kept in close contact throughout his campaign, also reinforced his image among the people as a 'sound, experienced and Christian man'.

Watson's exuberance in his campaign did not detract from its substance. On the contrary, informants reported how, in villages where he knew himself to be unpopular, Watson would deliberately set out to woo his audiences with jokes, oratory, and irrelevancies until 'people were just shaking their heads and sighing "ah Lepani!".' At this stage he would abruptly change his style and launch into his marathon campaign speech. Although younger informants in particular were highly critical of this approach and referred to it as 'pulling wool over our eyes', there is no doubt that Watson's personal impact was much greater than that of either of his rivals.

Nevertheless, although from a number of points of view Watson's position seemed secure, he had not escaped criticism during his term of office. One major source of complaint was that he had concentrated too much of his attention on his home area (Vakuta) and neglected the rest of the Trobriands. Another point, of which his opponents made much play, was that he was engaged in retail trading on Kiriwina. The widespread resentment this aroused was intimately related to the almost fanatical obsession of the Trobrianders with establishing co-operative stores.

Watson replied to these criticisms by reminding the people that it was while he was their Member that co-operatives came to Kiriwina, and that he had always advocated their establishment in the area. As for his own private store, he pointed out that he had opened it before co-operatives were introduced, and suggested that his initiative should be an incentive to the people and an assurance that they too could have businesses like Europeans. If they had to vent their anger, it would be better directed against European storekeepers who owned no less than six private stores on Kiriwina, with a far greater revenue than his own.

The other candidates did their best to dislodge the widespread notion that Watson had been personally responsible for the establishment of co-operatives on Kiriwina, but the argument about departmental responsibilities appeared too complex for most people. A complicating factor in the situation was the official opening of the Luba Co-operative early in January 1968 by the Administrator, Mr D. O. Hay, at which Watson acted as official interpreter. In his speech the Administrator lauded the co-operative movement in the customary terms. In the circumstances it is not surprising that Patterson and Taurega were very much embittered by this event, which they took as yet another demonstration of Administration backing for the sitting Member. They saw no reason why the official opening of the Luba Co-operative should have been delayed after September 1967, when the building was completed.

But although his opponents made a big issue of this, and of his alleged lapses between 1964 and 1968, Watson himself was confident of re-election. He made the most of his experience and achievements in the House as the sitting Member by appealing to the people to vote for the man they knew and could trust, not for newcomers. This was also the inscription (in Kiriwinian) below the large poster photograph of himself which he distributed during his campaign. The logic of this argument appealed to many Trobrianders to whom Port Moresby and the affairs of the House seemed very far removed and complicated. There was thus a feeling that Watson should be given another chance in the House, despite criticisms.

In contrast to Watson's forceful and colourful campaigning, that of Taurega and Patterson was rather dull. Neither of the men distributed any campaign literature, and both had to struggle to muster an audience. The approach of the two men was roughly similar, being primarily concerned with local issues, and criticisms aimed at Watson.

Taurega had discussed his campaign with an expatriate friend prior to setting out on his canvassing. He was advised to refrain from making any promises since these would count against him in the long run if he was unable to fulfil them, and he was also admonished, should he be elected, to voice all the people's requests in the House even if he thought nothing would come of them, as this would assure his electors that their wishes were being taken seriously. Apart from this advice he worked out his platform on his own.

Before leaving for Misima in mid-December, Taurega agreed with Patterson that they would support each other in their campaigns though they did not make any explicit preference deal. This was only clinched and put into effect after Cecil Abel's arrival in Kiriwina early in February (p. 126). Taurega was not very satisfied with his campaign in the Misima Sub-District. Apart from language barriers he found that his campaigning was hampered by the awkward schedule of the Administration launch on which he travelled during a brief tour of Sudest and Rossel Islands. The launch was on a routine round to pick up local government councillors for their regular council meeting at Misima, and Taurega was able to arrange only one gathering, attended by thirty persons, on Rossel Island. Most people were unaware that he had passed through the area, and had never heard of his name. This was also the situation at Misima where he spent a whole week but held one meeting only, as his visit coincided with Christmas and New Year festivities.

In the Trobriands, to which he returned soon after the New Year, Taurega's impact as a candidate was only slightly greater. Most informants saw the contest as being between Watson and Patterson. Taurega was considered almost as an outsider and people referred to him as young, inexperienced, too poorly educated, estranged from the church because of drink, and lacking status in the traditional hierarchy. Despite these criticisms and drawbacks, which were known to him, Taurega's manner during his campaign was disarmingly straightforward. He acknowledged the objections raised against him and countered them by referring to his record as a government interpreter, to the help which he had rendered to the people over the years, and to the fact that, as a person without traditional status or obligations, he would be able to render assistance more equitably to everybody. This point was sometimes elaborated into a criticism of Watson's alleged favouritism for the Vakuta, and an enumeration of Watson's shortcomings. This defence was well taken by Taurega's audiences; almost too well, for a recurring argument was that he had been such a good interpreter that the people did not want to lose him to the House of Assembly.

Taurega conducted his meetings without the pomp and formality which characterised Watson's campaign. He would usually open his meeting with a prayer, after which he introduced himself as coming 'simply to tell you about myself, without money and without tobacco'. This was clearly an allusion to Watson's campaigning, but was also said partly in self-defence as Taurega could not have afforded gifts even had he desired to give them. He would then proceed to a rather elaborate exposition of political education (the meaning of democracy, elections, the free vote, etc.). This usually lasted some ten minutes, after which he would spend a little longer explaining electoral procedure—half of his campaigning time thus being given over to political and electoral education.

Taurega's platform was distinctly and exclusively 'Trobriand'-oriented for he had nominated specifically with a view 'to help the Kiriwinian people'. There was no attempt to grapple with national issues in the way that Watson, for example, discussed the public service, and spoke of the five-year development plan, or about the political future of Papua and New Guinea. Taurega was concerned with the improvement of socio-economic conditions in the Trobriands, and Kiriwina in particular. Thus he advocated the introduction of a fishing industry and the promotion of copra cultivation. He also discussed the possibilities of expanding tourism as a means of providing a market for the local carving industry, and raised the possibility of building a new wharf on the west coast of Kiriwina. He was particularly careful to present these points as projects which he would back in the House but whose fulfilment he could not guarantee.

Although Taurega's manner was easy enough, and although he mixed with the people freely, the reaction to his campaigning was somewhat guarded. In contrast to the open declarations of support which usually followed on Watson's speeches, statements at the conclusion of Taurega's speeches were usually to the effect that 'we like you but can't promise anything; each one must decide for himself'. Taurega had moderate hope that this decision might be in his favour as he had polled relatively well in the Trobriands during the 1964 elections.

Although Patterson's platform was almost identical with Taurega's, his method of campaigning was somewhat different. Patterson felt himself constrained by the prevailing social system in the Trobriand Islands which attributed so much influence to traditional chiefs, local government councillors, and ministers of religion. He considered the influence of these persons to be so pervasive and dominant as virtually to preclude a dialogue with the masses during campaigning. For this reason, although Patterson held meetings like his opponents, he persistently sought contact with leaders.

The most important part of Patterson's campaigning could not therefore be studied by observers. He spent much time dropping in on families, chatting with prominent persons of this or that village, and, in one instance at least, presenting gifts of food and tobacco to an influential chief. Nor was he contented with a single visit to any locality: as long as he had some doubts about the affiliations of a particular village he would return there persistently to chat, invite questions, criticise his opponents. This method of campaigning clearly restricted him to the northern half of Kiriwina, which he could conveniently cover on foot or by bicycle. Even so, he could not hope to keep up with the changes in sentiment throughout the area. To bridge this gap Patterson had hired two local men to sound village opinions in selected parts of the island and to report to him regularly. Where these reports were unfavourable he would return to the area and in his unobtrusive manner, try to win over the leaders of the community.

There was thus something almost conspiratorial about Patterson's campaigning—a tendency of which the candidate himself was ruefully aware: 'politics is a dirty game mind you, filthy crook it is'. Even in his public addresses, Patterson retained some of this quality. In contrast to Watson's declamatory style, and Taurega's quietly forceful manner, Patterson's tone was conversational, almost confidential. Whereas his rivals campaigned standing, facing their audiences some ten feet away or more, Patterson invariably spoke sitting down: 'standing puts your listeners at a disadvantage—you must speak as equal to equal'. Whenever possible he would sit among his listeners, joking with them or speaking in earnest according to how he felt their mood.

In his public meetings Patterson rarely spoke for longer than fifteen minutes. Unless the meeting was formally opened with a prayer by a minister, he never started proceedings with prayer of his own accord. Like Taurega, he campaigned exclusively on the basis of local issues. His platform included all the points raised by Taurega, and in addition to these several others. The most important of these was his interest in the establishment of a high school in the Trobriand Islands, which produced a high proportion of the secondary school-goers in the Milne Bay District. Patterson was also concerned about the state of primary education on Kiriwina, and was equally interested to see something done about adult education and establishing a training school for school drop-outs.

Despite his platform, and however effective his method of campaigning may have been, Patterson's position was undermined by several factors. Chief amongst these were his reputation for drinking, his open scepticism about religion, and his alleged Don Juanesque disposition. These traits were matters of widespread discussion among the people and were sometimes openly brought up at his own meetings and those of his opponents. Another criticism levelled against him was his relative aloofness and so-called lack of generosity compared to Watson's open hospitality. Many interpreted this less as a personal trait than as a reflection of Patterson's status as a member of the high-ranking Tabalu sub-clan which cut him off from the masses of the people in the still highly rank-conscious Trobriand society.

Many informants, indeed, viewed Patterson's Tabalu background as a factor against him. There was a general fear that he might seek to reinstate the traditional authority and supremacy of the Tabalu if he were elected to the House. The feeling was reinforced after the unexpected death of a prominent Tabalu chief in 1966, when it was rumoured that the Tabalu were still jostling for power amongst themselves as of old. Suspicion of foul play was widespread and some people expressly referred to Patterson in this context. On the other hand, Patterson's Tabalu connections were not altogether negative. One chief was heard remarking to another after a speech by Patterson that it would be a pleasant change to have a Tabalu instead of 'a nobody' coming to give them orders as their Member of the House of Assembly.

Other factors which counted against Patterson were apparent tactical mistakes in his campaigning. Several informants expressed disappointment that a man with his education should have allowed himself to be drawn into a personal mud-slinging contest against Watson and that he should have campaigned so negatively whereas he had every reason to thrust forward his own views. This reaction was particularly widespread among younger informants who admired Patterson's vitality and independent stand when it came to criticising Administration policy. The same category of informants thought that Patterson's criticism of Watson's 'gift-giving' as 'buying the vote' was a foolish move, since it could only alienate him (Patterson) from the persons who had accepted these gifts and whose support he also sought. Some informants thought that Patterson would have done much better to keep quiet about the whole issue and try to out-give Watson.

Indeed, the attitude of the electors towards gift-giving by candidates was rather ambiguous. Some (especially older villagers) did not see anything untoward in the practice, and clearly expected 'something' in return for their vote, while others (particularly younger voters) regarded such behaviour in the context of the election as tantamount to bribery. Recipients of gifts varied similarly in their reaction: some took it as their due, others were embarrassed and sought to hide the fact that they had received anything. Candidates too showed some ambivalence towards the practice: the same candidate might give openly in one situation and make a secret gift in another, whereas some (e.g. Taurega) rejected gift-giving as totally improper in an electoral campaign. The confusion appears to stem from a clash between the acceptable traditional practice of prestation on the one hand, and the alien (electoral) context in which it is currently finding uncertain expression and reception on the other.

Another possible tactical mistake in Patterson's campaigning, though it did not seem to be one at the time, was his open association with the Regional candidate, Cecil Abel, during the latter's campaigning in the Trobriands. In a sense Patterson had almost no choice in the matter as Abel resided at his house and took the initiative of linking their names in his (Abel's) own campaign. This association was profitable as long as Abel's impact was favourable. When, however, as we shall discuss shortly, public opinion swayed against Abel in favour of Elliott Elijah, it was almost certain that Patterson's fortunes would also be affected. This was all the more likely because Elijah himself expressly favoured Watson for the Kula Open Electorate.

On the credit side, Patterson had the almost unequivocal support of the teachers on Kiriwina, many of whom openly promoted his campaign. This was particularly true of the Catholic sector of the population, which although not numerous (estimated at some 500 converts) was allegedly strongly behind him. There seems little reason to doubt that the local Catholic mission also favoured Patterson's candidature though it is difficult to gauge how far this was translated into active support.

There was a 70 per cent poll in Kula. Watson had an absolute majority on the first count, obtaining 62 per cent of the votes. Yet his dominance was not everywhere as secure as these figures might suggest. All things considered, Patterson did extremely well in the Trobriands, taking 34 per cent of the votes against Watson's 51 per cent; his fatal mistake was to assume that because he had been invited to nominate by the Louisiade Local Government Council he could count on the large Misima vote without having to campaign there. Lepani's shrewder campaign tactics paid a handsome dividend: his late visit to Misima brought him 3097 votes (69 per cent) as against the 710 (16 per cent) cast for Patterson.

MILNE BAY REGIONAL

In the three Open electorates observers following the campaigns had little difficulty in forecasting the outcome. In the Regional the issue was in doubt until the counting of third preferences had been completed. But not only was the Regional more closely contested than the Open electorates, it also produced much more 'movement' and interaction between the candidates themselves and the electors. This situation owed much to the personalities of the candidates and their motives in standing, but no less to the policies they espoused.

The candidates

As the sitting Member for the East Papua Special Electorate (1964-8) John Stuntz, 39, was the only nominee for the Regional with any previous experience of campaigning. His familiarity with the District dated back to the early 1950s when he was stationed at Losuia as a field officer in the (then) Department of Native Affairs. Subsequently he was elected as a Member of the Legislative Council (1961-4), and then in 1964 to the House of Assembly. Most of Stuntz's twenty years in the Territory were thus spent in east Papua, where he currently owns a copra plantation at Mullins Harbour.

During his period in office Stuntz was an active member of various bodies, committees, and associations: the Administrator's Council, Select Committee on Constitutional Development, Standing Orders Committee, and the Milne Bay District Advisory Council. In addition, he was a one-time Deputy Chairman of the Public Works Committee and the Chairman of the Committee on the Public Service. During his 1968 campaign Stuntz was to refer to his activities in these bodies to rebut charges that he had not devoted sufficient time to visiting his sprawling electorate. He made these points in printed testimonials, in Motu and English, signed by Dirona Abe, a former Under-Secretary and candidate in the neighbouring Open electorate of Rigo-Abau, and Robert Tabua, an affinal relative of Elliott Elijah.

Stuntz was not affiliated to any political party. On the contrary he regarded the establishment of political parties in Papua and New Guinea as premature, if not irresponsible, and based his campaign largely on denouncing them, Pangu Pati in particular. In seeking re-election Stuntz saw himself as a representative and protector of the 'true' interests of the majority of Papuans and New Guineans, most of whom he considered to be fundamentally opposed to rapid change and political evolution. By implication, therefore, his policy was to uphold the political *status quo* in the face of a wish for change by so-called hotheads.

The other candidates were Cecil Abel, Elliott Elijah, and Dennis Young. Young was born in England in 1936. His political views had been influenced by his experiences in Irian Barat (then Dutch New Guinea) where he had been employed by an electrical firm for fifteen years up to the time of the transition to the Indonesian Administration.

During this time, and particularly during the four years immediately preceding the commencement of Indonesian government, Young formed a very poor opinion of United Nations activity, particularly of its intervention in the affairs of so-called colonial countries. This view formed the basis of his campaign platform.

Arriving in the Territory in 1962, Young went to east Papua where he leased Giligili Plantation at the head of Milne Bay and where, in due course, he resettled about a hundred West Irianese Papuan refugees. In the years that followed, his activities in the area and the interest he showed in local affairs gave him a reputation among local Papuans and expatriates for being 'a good man with the problems and needs of the people at heart'. His popularity in the Milne Bay area was clearly attested when he accepted the invitation by indigenous supporters to stand for the newly organised multi-racial local government council and polled more than 90 per cent of the votes, to win from his Papuan opponent. This overwhelming success convinced Young that he should contest the national elections. Even so, he did not rate his chance of success as very high, since he was opposing candidates who were more widely known, and who had been in the area, or associated with it, for at least twenty years.

Like John Stuntz, Young felt that he had a contribution to offer to the Territory's future by swelling the ranks of those who would oppose radical or hasty political evolution. Viewing Papua-New Guinea essentially as a guided democracy, he thought that the interests of the country would best be served by supporting the existing political arrangements and by concentrating on economic development. For this reason he had little time for political parties, which he considered a threat to the stability of the country, and a wasteful diversion of energy and funds which could more profitably be used in other spheres.

Cecil (Seselo) Abel, 65, was a research fellow at the University of Papua and New Guinea at the time of the elections. Born in Samarai of a well-known missionary family, Abel had headed the Kwato Mission for twenty-five years. The mission had been founded in the 1890s by his father, the Reverend C. W. Abel, and its influence was particularly marked in the Suau area on the southern coast of the mainland, and round the shores of Milne Bay proper. As will be seen, Cecil Abel relied heavily on his association with Kwato in his campaign, though the mission itself did not actively support him. Abel was closely involved in politics in the Territory and liked to refer to himself as one of 'the 13 angry men' whose demands for limited executive responsibility in government by mid-1968 created a stir in 1967 (*South Pacific Post* 20 March 1967. See also pp. 31, 38).

Abel's reasons for nominating were fairly clear-cut. Although friends had asked him to contest the 1964 elections he had declined to do so on the grounds that he was not adequately prepared to engage in political activity on the national level. By 1967, however, after doing research and lecturing on politics and government at the Administrative College in Port Moresby, Abel considered himself better qualified to stand for election. More importantly, as an active and dedicated member of Pangu Pati, he was eager to swell the number of party members in the House of Assembly by standing in an area where he was well known and where he rated his chances of election very high indeed—at least until Elijah's surprise nomination.

Elliott Elijah was born in 1924 at Vakuta village on the island of that name in the Trobriands. He attended Sogeri High School near Port Moresby and the Administrative College, where he studied under Cecil Abel in 1966. For ten years between 1958 and 1967 he had been a training officer at the Co-operative Education Centre in Port Moresby, a post that enabled him to establish widespread connections with co-operative staff. These contacts proved to be invaluable in the planning and running of his campaign.

Elijah's membership of numerous societies (e.g. Methodist Welfare Society), associations (e.g. Executive Member of the Public Service Association 1960-3, and Member of the one-time Mixed Race Club in Port Moresby), and administrative bodies (e.g. Member of the Native Loans Board, Papua-New Guinea Decimal Currency Conversion Commission, and P.N.G. Superannuation Board) attest his wide-ranging interests and prominence in local affairs. He was also a foundation member of the Pangu Pati. All these activities, however, were centred almost exclusively in Port Moresby, and Elijah's marriage to a member of the prominent Tabua family from Daru in the Western District did not help to strengthen his links with his home area—a fact which some of his rivals were quick to exploit in their campaigns.

Elijah's interest in national politics was not new. In 1964 he had considered standing for the Esa'ala-Losuia Open Electorate but had decided against it in favour of his co-villager Lepani Watson. But his political interests remained, and in 1967 he helped to found Pangu Pati. Disillusioned with conditions in the Public Service and frustrated by the lack of avenues through which dissatisfaction with the *status quo* might be expressed, Elijah decided to nominate in 1968 since he felt that 'in the House of Assembly at least, one may speak freely and obtain a public hearing'.

Thus, when leading members of Pangu (including Cecil Abel)

held informal meetings in Port Moresby towards the latter end of 1967 to discuss nominations for the forthcoming elections, Elijah announced his intention to stand for the Kula Open. This decision was endorsed by Pangu since none of the persons expected to nominate in this area, including the sitting Member, Lepani Watson, was a member of the party. Elijah was confident of winning Kula, since it included his home, and he was well known (through his co-operative links) in Misima as well.

Up to within a month of nomination, then, the 'official' Pangu Pati position was that Cecil Abel and Elliott Elijah should stand for the Milne Bay Regional and Kula Open Electorates respectively. If elected, this would mean that two-thirds at least of the Milne Bay district would be represented by Pangu men, since John Guise was also a member, and an overwhelming majority for him was anticipated in Alotau. In this event, they hoped that the winner in Esa'ala would join the party as a matter of solidarity.

For a couple of months preceding nomination Abel and Elijah several times informally discussed their plans for campaigning. It was understood between them that they would promote each other's interests whenever the occasion arose. This would be particularly beneficial to Abel who had never been to the Trobriands and who counted on Elijah to familiarise the people with his name, and to pave the ground for his own campaign. In the meantime, both men began to organise their campaign literature, and Elijah had several thousand posters printed outlining his platform as a candidate for the Kula Open.

However, with scarcely three weeks left before nominations opened, Elijah changed his mind, and decided to stand instead for the Regional. A number of reasons underlay the switch. According to Elijah, who claimed to have wrestled with the matter for four or five weeks before making up his mind, the main point was his suspicion, allegedly confirmed by rumours from the Milne Bay area, that Abel had grossly overestimated his chances of success. In that case, Elijah held it more important to ensure a Pangu victory in the Regional than in the Kula Open, since the former embraced the latter. It was also important to ensure the defeat of Stuntz who was considered to be conservative and to represent the opposite of what Pangu stood for. In these views Elijah was strongly supported by a circle of influential friends in Port Moresby who were undoubtedly instrumental in his final decision to switch electorates.

As Elijah saw it, his move was not directed against Abel personally. Indeed, when the two met in Port Moresby about a week later, Elijah asked Abel to exchange second preferences with him so that Pangu interests would be doubly secure. Elijah of course could hardly explain his course of action to Abel in the terms stated above. Instead he said that he had decided to stand for the Regional because he had the necessary educational qualifications, and because he did not want to oppose Lepani Watson, the sitting Member for Esa'ala-Losuia, since they were both from the same village. Abel interpreted this as an admission that Elijah had overestimated his chances of defeating Watson, who was well-known and popular at least in the northern half of the Kula Electorate. Though Elijah denies that he ever doubted his chances of defeating Watson, this possibility cannot be dismissed, particularly as he (Elijah) had only infrequently visited the Trobriands in the last twenty years.

In fact, the position of Lepani Watson may have been the determining factor in Elijah's decision to stand for Milne Bay Regional. Not only was Watson one of the more prominent members of the House of Assembly, but his 'enlightened conservatism' made him more acceptable to Elijah and his Port Moresby advisers than any of the candidates (Abel excepted) who might stand for Milne Bay Regional. In addition, there was some anticipation that Watson might join Pangu if he were re-elected to the House of Assembly. Under these circumstances, and given Watson's renown in the Trobriands, it would have been hazardous to challenge him.

To Abel, Elijah's change of plans came as a shock. For several weeks he had heard rumours to that effect, but had dismissed them as preposterous. Thus when Elijah announced his decision, and asked for an exchange of preferences, Abel was caught unawares, and refused any co-operation. Hitherto Abel had been confident of his chances of being elected, but after Elijah's nomination he openly expressed his doubts of success. Abel was particularly disappointed by the effect that Elijah's nomination would have on Pangu's image in the area and, indeed, throughout the Territory. More importantly, Abel feared that opposition between two party candidates would play into their opponents' hands by splitting the vote. Nevertheless he refused to envisage a partnership with Elijah. Ironically, therefore, the two Pangu candidates entered the elections in a spirit of rivalry, each accusing the other of being an individualist and of placing personal interests above party ones. Even more ironically, each candidate was convinced that he was championing the cause of Pangu Pati.

The campaign

Campaigning was hard, and marked by a diversity of styles and approaches. Stuntz's resources enabled him to charter a vessel in which he made a comprehensive coverage of the islands in the electorate. The loan of a small aircraft enabled him to campaign further afield than any of his rivals. Stuntz considered it important to influence both individual voters and organisations. He used printed hand-outs and arranged village meetings as often as possible. He included in his campaign party the President of the Suau Local Government Council and other Papuan associates who assisted him as interpreters and general campaign aides. At meetings his formal and aloof bearing contrasted with Abel's lighter, easier manner, but it probably impressed many electors.

In campaigning, Stuntz invariably began with an explanation of his failure to visit his constituents over the last four years, and having done this, he launched into attacks on Cecil Abel and Elliott Elijah, both of whom he identified as members of Pangu Pati. He opposed the party's policy of 'self-government by 1968' and denounced it as the dream of urban bigheads who had neither care nor interest for the needs of village people. 'Self-government would lead to independence and the latter reduce Australian influence in the Territory to negligible dimensions. Did village people think that they could run their own country?'

The doubts thus sown during his meetings grew to disproportionate dimensions when the voters were left to ponder his message. Fear became the dominant sentiment and the rumour became widespread that independence would be followed by a big battle between Papuans and New Guineans in which the odds would be overwhelmingly against Papuans. This dread was particularly entrenched in the D'Entrecasteaux Islands, where Stuntz did most of his campaigning. Hence Elijah's hostile reception in this area when he arrived to campaign. In some areas the two men were in fact campaigning two or three hours' walk from each other, and it was during this period, as we shall see, that Elijah adopted his more forceful stand which, reduced to its simplest expression, amounted to a racial platform.

As the youngest and least experienced of the candidates, and a relative newcomer to the Milne Bay District, Young entered the contest well aware of the odds against him. Accordingly he planned his campaign with particular care. 'You've got to do this type of thing properly or not at all.' Young believed that leaders could effectively manage the vote in the village and so, whilst his campaign did not ignore individual electors, he was primarily concerned with ensuring that he had the support of leaders, both traditional and modern. Young took the view that a candidate's policy was more important than his personality. His platform had two aspects: local and national. Like Stuntz he campaigned on local development, but presenting his successful commercial background as especially fitting him for the task. It was in his views on the development of the Territory, however, that he squarely confronted voters with the issues that in his view the election raised:

> Now there are two very important points to this election. The first one is: do you want quick Home Rule and Independence? or are you afraid of this and do you want to go slowly? If you want it quickly then you should vote for Cecil or for Elliott. And if you are frightened, and you want to go slowly, vote for John Stuntz or for myself. And the second question is: do you want United Nations or do you want Australia to look after you? If you want United Nations to look after you, you should vote for Cecil and Elliott. If you, like myself, prefer to trust Australia, you should vote for me.

Opposed to Young in matters of policy, Abel also followed a different mode of approach to the electorate. His campaign was planned around the central assumption that the electors had a high level of political shrewdness: not that they had large stores of factual knowledge, but that many of them were capable of astute judgments, if given relevant facts. He therefore campaigned slowly, and while he was careful not to neglect organisations, the main thrust of his effort was directed at impressing as many individual voters as possible.

Abel considered electors would give their vote according to their judgment of a candidate's personality rather than the policy advocated. His campaign techniques therefore included the use of visual aids and photographs of himself (his photograph, which was distributed widely, was the same as that used in the polling booths), to promote his personality. He preferred evening meetings in the villages and tried to make these as informal as possible, although the Papuan flair for ceremony often made this difficult. He strove for and achieved a light and friendly atmosphere at his meetings and it is safe to say he impressed as a good personality.

Policywise two points were always stressed: first, that it was time that Papuans assumed increasing responsibility in the running of their own affairs; and secondly, that achievement of this, or of any desired end in the House would depend on the concerted and co-ordinated action of its members. Both these points were forcefully made through colourful comparisons with examples drawn from every day village life. There is no doubt that the electors appreciated Abel's meaning.

Initially, he campaigned as a member of Pangu, without any preference deals. However, he soon realised that association with

Pangu was not as favourably viewed by the people as he had hoped; indeed sometimes it evoked outspoken reaction against him, particularly in those areas where his expatriate rivals were influential, or where they had preceded him. Accordingly, he shifted his stance somewhat, stressing the importance of concerted political action, assuring the people that the framework for such action already existed in Port Moresby, but refraining from mentioning Pangu Pati by name. If the occasion arose, however, Abel did not hesitate to acknowledge his membership of the Party or to defend its platform. In fact, he had devised a subtle means of letting his Pangu membership be known without having to explain the complexities of party machinery to the people. This was by wearing a Pangu Pati T-shirt under his native design shirt, and unbuttoning the latter in the course of his speeches to reveal as he put it, 'my noble chest' with the Pangu Pati crest. If the design was meaningful to the people, Abel was prepared to meet any queries; if not, he saw no point in pursuing the matter.

Had it not been for Elijah's challenge, Abel was confident that he could win the Milne Bay Regional Electorate easily. He ruled Stuntz and Young out of the contest almost automatically; the former because of his reputed unpopularity, and the latter as a newcomer to the scene, although a promising one. Abel thought Young would have done better to spend four years on the Milne Bay Local Government Council before launching into national politics.

Abel considered Elijah to be his main rival, and in fact had serious doubts whether he could defeat him. This was not only because he considered Elijah to be an impressive candidate in his own right, but because he was acutely aware that he could not actively campaign against Elijah without damaging the Pangu Pati image, or indeed without undermining his own basic tenet that it was time that local people should run their own affairs. This apparent contradiction between Abel's platform and his challenging a local candidate played into Elijah's hands and became a central issue in the campaigning in the Trobriands.

The Trobriand campaign saw an interesting confrontation of Regional and Open candidates. Before Elliott Elijah's switch to the Regional, Abel had counted on Elijah to make his name known to Trobriand voters. When Elijah became his rival, Abel turned for help to Patterson, taking the initiative in openly and explicitly linking his name with Patterson. He promised to support the latter in the House should they both be elected, and indeed gave the impression that voting for either candidate implied support for the other. This tactic was not without apparent initial acceptance. Abel himself created a very favourable impression as the first Regional candidate to campaign in the Trobriands, and since the others were then virtually unknown and Watson's popularity was sufficiently in the balance in this sector of the Kula Electorate, people were prepared to give Patterson a chance. Abel was also instrumental in crystallising an exchange of preferences between Taurega and Patterson, both of whom had personal reasons for opposing Watson. Abel's arrival in the Trobriands thus stimulated several alliances both within and across electoral boundaries and made for a particularly interesting campaign.

If Abel's was the most striking campaign, Elijah's was perhaps the most interesting, not only because of the complications posed by his last minute change from the Kula Open to the Regional, but also because of the change in campaign technique over the canvassing period. Apart from the cost and bother of reprinting his campaign literature, Elijah's decision came too late for him to seek the financial support which he felt he needed for campaigning in the considerably larger Regional electorate and which he was confident he could have obtained from Methodist organisations.

Elijah's assessment of the state of public political awareness was rather different from Abel's: he did not rate it so highly. Therefore, while he aimed at individual electors, he also concentrated on influencing leaders favourably; he worked with the leaders of modern organisations such as church congregations and local government councils and particularly co-operative societies. But he was also careful not to neglect traditional leaders.

Like Abel he believed voters would respond more to personality than to policy. He distributed posters and arranged evening meetings but also, perhaps more than Abel, used informal discussions with individuals and small informal gatherings as a major technique.

Elijah's early campaigning rested heavily on John Guise's reputation. This was a safe line to take since Guise's popularity in the Milne Bay District could scarcely be doubted. Briefly, Elijah argued that recent socio-economic development in the Milne Bay area had been largely due to the efforts of Guise, whom the people had elected as their member to the House of Assembly, and that the pace of this advancement would be increased if Guise were backed by Elijah, since the two men had similar ideas.

Elijah's initial line was thus simply to ask people to trust him and to vote for him on the assurance that he would do his best for them if elected to the House. However, as time passed and reports of other candidates' campaigning began to reach him, Elijah changed his tactics, and adopted an increasingly forceful and individual approach. Responding to Stuntz's and Young's attacks on Pangu, and himself as a member, he proclaimed himself as the only Papuan standing in the electorate, opposing three 'white men'. He argued that he was the best candidate for reasons of good communication if for no other. 'The white man is always "too busy" to speak to us, or if he does, makes us feel small so that we do not speak our real thoughts.' This new tactic, with racial overtones, elicited many favourable responses from electors. If villagers were disillusioned with the apparent failure of Watson as their sitting Open Member, and thought that a European might serve them better, they were not blind or indifferent to the justice of Elijah's remarks. But Elijah went even further, arguing that Stuntz's failure as the sitting Special Member showed conclusively that Europeans were not interested in representing local interests, and that Watson could hardly be blamed for inefficiency under such poor tutelage. The argument was especially convincing in the Trobriands, and Elijah's forceful campaign on his home ground soon began to undermine the impression made by the Abel-Patterson team. Intentionally or not, the voters came to view the contest as one between two opposed Regional-Open coalitions: Abel-Patterson v. Elijah-Watson.

Elijah was confident that he could defeat his opponents. He discounted Abel for the very reason which had prompted him to stand for the Regional in the first place—Abel's alleged unpopularity in the Milne Bay area. For similar reasons he thought that Stuntz would be no opposition. This left Young as the only contestant Elijah thought might effectively challenge him—not because Young was well known but because Elijah was wary of the latter's tactics. Young's approach was in fact almost identical to Elijah's, both men stressing the importance of personal contacts with prominent persons throughout the District. Elijah was also keenly aware that Young was in a better bargaining position than himself, because as a prosperous businessman and member of the Milne Bay Local Government Council, Young could promise assistance in local projects, where Elijah could only express goodwill. As matters turned out, this assessment was wide of the mark in a number of respects. While it was true that Elijah was no match for Young in Milne Bay proper, Young was still inadequately known in other parts of the electorate, and came bottom of the poll. More important perhaps, Elijah had completely misjudged Abel's standing within the electorate as a whole: in the end Abel had a comfortable victory, but what is of particular interest is that in the Milne Bay Sub-District Abel secured 1470 votes (16 per cent), and Elijah himself a mere 276 (3 per cent).

CONCLUSION

Firm generalisations about the 1968 election in Milne Bay are not easy to make. The area is neither a geographical, nor a cultural or socio-economic entity, and its unity as a Regional constituency rests entirely upon its existence as a superimposed administrative entity. So far as the three Open electorates are concerned, they could have been many hundreds of miles apart for all the interaction and mutual influence there were between them. Perhaps remarkably in view of the acute problems of transportation that campaigning posed, few candidates fully exploited the possibility of alliances across the Regional-Open division. What promised to be one, the Abel-Elijah 'team', was transformed from the start into a rivalry for the same seat. What was particularly interesting about this situation was the way a potentially strong and helpful alliance between Abel and Patterson turned to their individual and mutual disadvantage when it was challenged by the Elijah-Watson coalition. Had Abel alone challenged Elijah, his position might have been stronger, since voters retained their admiration for him even after Elijah's campaigning. But villagers felt they could not in justice vote for Patterson (and therefore not for Abel either) when Elijah had helped to restore Watson's public image. Stated in different terms, the electorate grasped the implication of a coalition so well as to feel bound to vote for the partnership or reject it *in toto*. The misunderstanding here was as much due to poor electoral education as to shortsightedness on the part of candidates initiating such alliances. Elsewhere there were other sources of confusion about the Regional/Open dichotomy, epitomised in the remark of a Goodenough Islander to the effect that Evennett (Open) was preferable to Young (Regional) because he lived in Esa'ala.

It would be surprising, then, if striking and detailed uniformities in electoral behaviour were to be found. Just as economic development and political sophistication differed in degree from one Open electorate to another, so also did administrative and representational history and the kinds of expectation held by constituents. If the candidates had anything in common, it was that they were, in the last resort and in spite of what they may have set out to do, independents fighting for support of their individual personalities rather than for their policies. If the electors had anything in common, it was that they were at best suspicious of political parties in general, and at worst downright fearful of Pangu Pati in particular. The electors called the tune, and Pangu, after promising to be *the* great issue, proved to be a damp squib as candidates who were members or sympathisers found it safer not to mention the party at all.

There was no single formula for success, though there were certain minimal conditions: education (sophistication in non-indigenous matters in the voters' eyes) was one and conscientious campaigning was another. But there appears to have been considerable variation, for instance, in the extent to which individual candidates sought to exploit their connections with influential groups, such as missions, councils and even clans, though as some learned to their cost, support from these quarters was not automatically forthcoming. It is probably true to observe that opposition to a candidate by organisations such as churches and councils meant defeat. A wiser course was to treat these bodies as collections of individual voters, and many candidates found it useful to seek out meetings convened for other, non-electoral purposes (tax-payers' meetings, mission services, local government council meetings, and so on). The aim was to seek the support of organisations and also to reach as many people as possible with a single speech, and hope that ripples would spread from this point of impact.

A most striking illustration of the role of councils was John Stuntz's address to a full general meeting of the Goodenough Local Government Council, which not only delivered the biggest blow that Pangu Pati was to receive in this area, but also gained him a higher percentage of votes there than he was to receive anywhere else in Milne Bay.[3] But the councillors on this occasion were influenced collectively, not corporately, and at the same meeting the President of the council told them that they must 'think for themselves whom to vote for', and did not call for debate or motion on the matter nor even make his own preferences public. The lesson can be told in reverse: the fact that Patterson was persuaded by the Louisiade Local Government Council into nominating for the Kula Open lulled him into the belief that support from the quarter that this body represented was secure. In fact, its corporate pledge gained him only 16 per cent of the votes in Misima Sub-District. It is important to stress, then, that councillors acted as individuals in favourable positions of influence, and not as members of corporate bodies. This is likely to be misunderstood whenever the role of councils in the elections is discussed. As channels of political information the councillors were acting in their perceived role of messengers for their communities. Isolated and politically ignorant villagers seemed willing to allow their councillors to do their election thinking for them because they regard this as part of the councillors' job. It is their

[3] Stuntz polled 36 per cent of the votes on Goodenough and 21 per cent in the Regional as a whole.

acknowledged task to mediate between the people they represent and all aspects of 'the world outside'—particularly anything to do with the government—which impinge on the communities. Probably as many as half the villages in the District—and certainly well over half the voters—are politically insulated in this way. Currently, the key to this bank of votes is held by the most mobile, the most informed and in touch man in any community, and he is likely to be the local government councillor.

In sum, the 1968 elections in Milne Bay were fought by independent candidates on individual lines, by individual means and through largely individual agencies. The Opens were handsomely won: in Alotau by a proven leader with entrenched support, in Esa'ala by the most professional of the team of polite amateurs, and in Kula by a seasoned politician with winning ways. The Regional, finally, was narrowly won by a shrewd man who wisely preferred charm to vituperation, and who, like the other winners, could rightfully claim to be a local-born Papuan. The use of national issues by some candidates was not matched by the significant appearance in campaigning of national organisation.

TABLE 3—THE ELECTION RESULTS IN MILNE BAY

Regional	1st count	2nd count	3rd count
Cecil Abel	9248	10,400	11,845
Elliott Elijah	8116	9217	11,635
Dennis Young	6167	Excl.	—
John Stuntz	6813	8128	Excl.
Informal	1724	—	—
Exhausted	—	2599	6864

Alotau Open	1st and final count
Osineru Dickson	1528
John Guise	9912
Bondai Pita	480
Informal	461

Esa'ala Open	1st and final count
Enosi Baloiloi	1606
Joseph Nimagore	737
Poate Henry Andrew	1091
Norman Evennett	5356
Jo Wilkinson	945
Francisco Kalade	212
Informal	119

TABLE 3—continued

Kula Open	1st and final count
Lepani Watson	5918
Goweli Taurega	2238
Jack Patterson	1111
Informal	299

CHARISMA AND RACE

Eugene Ogan

BOUGAINVILLE DISTRICT was transformed by the 1967 apportionment from a single Open electorate and a component of the New Guinea Islands Special Electorate into two Open and one Regional electorates (map 4). While the District no longer constitutes the largest single Open electorate in the Territory, in terms of average population represented by a member, the island remains much 'less equal than others' (Meller 1968: 42-50).

The present chapter discusses the Open and Regional elections in the South Bougainville Open Electorate. (Unless otherwise indicated, the terms 'south' and 'southerners' refer to the area and population covered by the South Bougainville Open Electorate.) Since the author is most familiar with the Nasioi-speaking peoples of the Kieta Sub-District, in what follows he occasionally takes a 'Nasioi-eye view' to point up comparisons and contrasts.

In ethnological terms, the population of Bougainville is sharply set off from the rest of New Guinea; rather, the islanders' connections are with the nearby islands of the British Solomons. Within the Southern Electorate, however, the ethnic-linguistic situation is less complex than, for example, in some Highland areas. An estimated 92 per cent of South Bougainville inhabitants are speakers of one of four languages—Nasioi, Nagovisi, Siwai, and Buin—which together form a geographically continuous non-Austronesian linguistic stock. The first of these languages is spoken in the Kieta Sub-District, the others in the Buin Sub-District. The remaining villagers speak another non-Austronesian language, Eivo, or Austronesian languages, of which Banoni, on the

---

Field work was supported by grants from the University of Minnesota (Office of International Programs) and from the Penrose Fund of the American Philosophical Society. All elements of Bougainville society co-operated generously, but special acknowledgment must be made to Fr F. Miltrup, S.M. and staff of Tubiana Mission, Kieta; Mr and Mrs M. Martin and Mr and Mrs G. D. Straughen of Kieta; and Mr and Mrs K. Cochrane of Buin. Discussions with M. A. Rynkiewich aided greatly in preparation of the chapter; W. L. Rowe provided helpful comments on an earlier version. Maps were prepared by G. Lothson. The author alone is responsible for any deficiencies in the final version.

west, and Torau, on the east, are the most prominent (Allen and Hurd, n.d.: map 5).

Siwai culture in the 1930s has been described in detail by Oliver (1955) and that of the other southern non-Austronesians was certainly similar: an economy based on taro cultivation and pig husbandry, and political atomism in which a 'big man' exercised influence based on prestige feasts. The four major linguistic groups did vary in such matters as the use of shell valuables in exchange, the degree of power exercised by a 'big man', and the frequency of armed combat. Some of this cultural variation is connected with ecology, but perhaps more important was the influence of relatively sophisticated Austronesian speakers from the south, who raided and traded along the Bougainville coasts. On this basis, it seems reasonable to rank the Buin people as the most sophisticated by the time European rule was established, the Nagovisi most 'aboriginal', with the Siwai and Nasioi occupying intermediate cultural positions.

The chronologically first and, at least until World War II, most intensive European influence in South Bougainville was the Christian missions. All three missions moved into the island from the British Solomon Islands Protectorate (B.S.I.P.). The Catholic Marists—originally French and German but with increasing numbers of English-speaking personnel—established the first station in Kieta in 1901. Methodist missionaries began work in Siwai in 1916.[1] The Seventh-Day Adventist mission moved into Buin in 1924. Adequate figures on mission adherence are not readily available; what seems certain is that Catholics are today the most numerous sect in the south and for Bougainville as a whole. Extrapolating from data kindly provided by the Most Reverend Leo L. Lemay, S.M., and the Reverend Brian Sides, one may suggest as approximate proportions in the electorate: Roman Catholic 75 per cent, Methodist 20 per cent, Seventh-Day Adventist 5 per cent or less. Methodists are more numerous in Buin than in the Kieta Sub-District; the reverse is true for Seventh-Day Adventists.

Generally, missions have not taken an active political role since European rule was established in Bougainville. The reasons for this are too numerous to detail here. Suffice it to say that, until recently, only the Catholic mission has exerted any significant political pressure, and then only in reaction to government activities the mission felt infringed upon its prerogatives. Education has been the major issue: education in south Bougainville was entirely in the hands of missions

---

[1] In January 1968, the Methodist mission entered into the United Church of Papua, New Guinea and the Solomons. Since, at the time of the election, villagers still spoke of themselves as Methodists, this usage has been retained here.

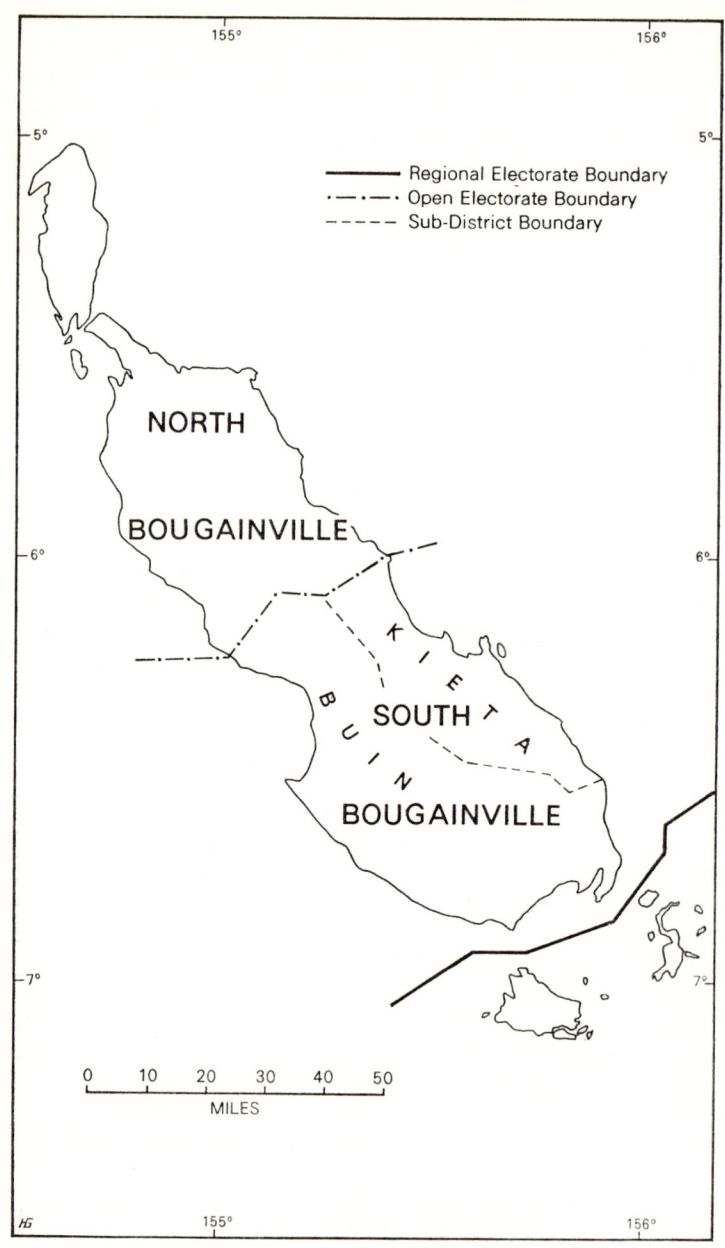

4 Bougainville Electorates

until the last decade, and most children still receive primary training at mission schools. The Catholic mission has been jealous of its educational role and, predictably, has pressed for larger subsidies to mission schools rather than establishment of government institutions. However, not only has the Catholic mission taken some strong political stands in the last few years (see below), but mission activity has more subtle political effects which the present paper will attempt to make clear.

German administration followed the missionaries into southern Bougainville and, as elsewhere in Melanesia, was initially concerned with pacifying pugnacious islanders (see White 1965: 87). Despite their efforts and those of the Australians who continued their policies (Rowley 1958: 10-11, 21, 192), many Bougainville villagers—especially the less accessible Nasioi and Nagovisi—seem to have succeeded in avoiding much contact with European administration till the 1930s. Whatever political changes might have been instituted had the Administration been able to apply more resources over a longer period, in fact the Japanese invasion overturned the entire situation. By the middle of March 1942, Japanese troops had occupied key points on Buka and Bougainville (White 1965: 124), and most Europeans—with the exception of some Catholic mission personnel—fled just before or during this occupation.

As Mair (1948: 198-9) points out: 'Cases are cited to prove the loyalty of the New Guinea native, or his treachery, according to the interest of the speaker. In fact it merely obscures the issue to interpret actions in either category as though one were judging a nation of persons aware of the war as presenting a choice which could not be avoided.' Most southerners appear to have followed a pragmatic course: if the Japanese were now in power, the Japanese were to be obeyed when they could not be avoided.

When the tide of battle began to turn, villagers maintained their pragmatic emphasis on survival. Allied bombing of the island did not, apparently, kill many villagers but it thoroughly demoralised them. At least some drifted over to the west coast after the Allies established a base at Torokina in late 1943 (Long 1963: 90), and even those who remained near home heard about the vast supply of material goods deposited, and the generous servicemen—primarily but not exclusively American—who were stationed there. White's general remark (1965: 134) can be applied to south Bougainville: 'The deep and abiding effect of the Second World War on the minority of New Guineans who experienced it at first hand stemmed less from the tremendous material destruction, loss of life and physical suffering . . . than from profound psychological and social trauma.' Not the least significant

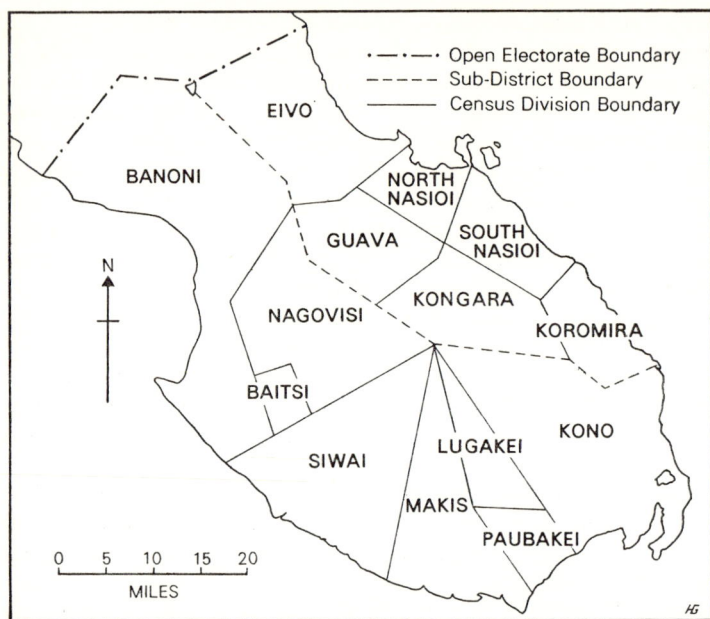

5 (a) South Bougainville Census Divisions

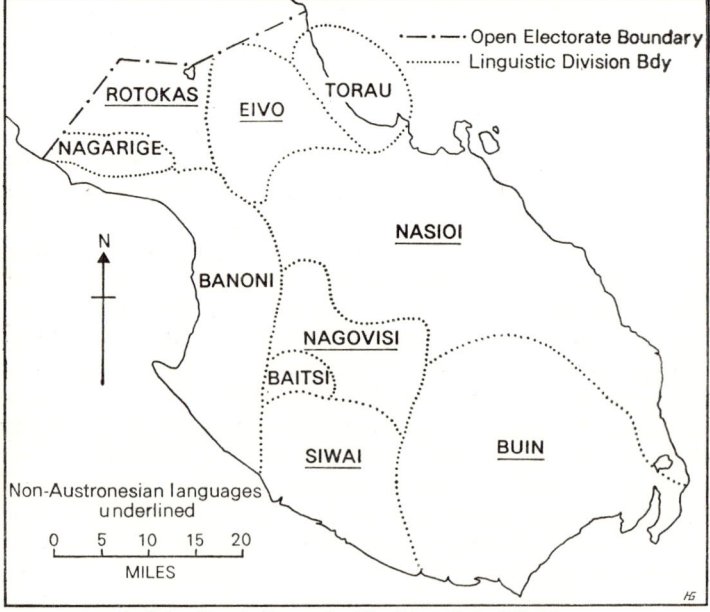

5 (b) South Bougainville Linguistic Divisions

aspect of this trauma was the sight of Australians 'abandoning' the island and its people.

After the war, Bougainville District headquarters was moved to Sohano in the north. Since the 1950s, Bougainville has shared in the accelerated efforts by Australia to develop the Territory, but it must be emphasised that the District's share has been a disproportionately small one. The island, farthest removed from Territorial headquarters, has until the present decade suffered a relative disregard by higher authority. 'Out of sight, out of mind' has clearly affected the governing of Bougainville as much as any more grandiose theory of colonial rule.

The most significant post-war administrative project in south Bougainville, up to 1962, was the District Malaria Eradication Programme, which has effectively eliminated the disease as a major killer. Administrative efforts in education and economic development have not been so successful, being particularly hampered by lack of personnel and financial resources. However, government primary schools were established at Kieta and Buin, and co-operative societies, initially stressing copra marketing, began to be established in the late 1950s. Roads and other means of communication remained generally poor; good harbours are non-existent on the west coast.

South Bougainville villagers were slow to adopt local government councils, despite strong pressure from the Administration. Not until four years after the first Bougainville council was established at Teop-Tinputz in the north did the Buin people undertake this new political activity. Siwai, Nasioi, and Nagovisi-Banoni followed in order, but in 1967 the villages governing themselves through the Kieta (Nasioi) Local Government Council amounted to no more than an estimated 68 per cent of the population of the Kieta administrative area. Whether in terms of general enthusiasm, projects completed, or revenues raised (the whole issue of taxation has been a major obstacle in the adoption of councils), the south Bougainville local government councils compare unfavourably with those reported from areas in Highland New Guinea.

Commercial interests followed closely on the heels of government in south Bougainville. Aided by good harbours and early settlement by missionaries and German officials at Kieta, planters developed large, flourishing holdings by World War I. These enterprises suffered through the vicissitudes of the copra market between the wars, and all planters left during the Japanese occupation. However, since World War II, plantation enterprise in the Kieta Sub-District has prospered, aided by the thriving cocoa market which foresighted Bougainville planters entered early.

Planter influence in the Buin Sub-District has been indirect only. Although even today one European-owned plantation operates in Buin, the social situation contrasts sharply with Kieta, where planters set the tone for the Sub-District until 1964. European references to one of the planters as 'Mayor of Kieta', or to 'The Big Three [planters]' only partially concealed in jest the truth that these interests wielded a more unified political influence than did any other element of the population. As elsewhere in New Guinea, the Kieta planters approximated a 'stronghold of racial discrimination, an attitude that tends to spread to all European residents' (Hogbin 1958: 176; see also Rowley 1965: 74). While at their best, planters provided paternalistic assistance to villagers as well as developing the resources of the Sub-District, their attitudes toward indigenous residents created considerable anti-European resentment.

Between the wars, Bougainville men left their villages to work on plantations elsewhere in the District and beyond. Thus Buin, Siwai, and Nagovisi had experience with the variably authoritarian or paternalistic system, although they did not have before them at all times the sight of planters occupying land which tradition claimed as the villagers' own. One of the symptoms of World War II trauma is the disinclination of south Bougainville men to undertake plantation work, so that in the last fifteen years, more and more Kieta plantations have operated with contract labourers drawn primarily from Chimbu and Sepik regions.

Chinese entrepreneurs handled the bulk of retail trade in both Kieta and Buin Sub-Districts, and have at different times owned small plantations, although these were generally managed by European or mixed-race personnel. Perhaps since there are so few European planters in the Buin area, one has the impression that villagers in that Sub-District feel considerably more resentment toward the Chinese than do those around Kieta.

If one were to try to sum up the social and psychological situation of villagers in south Bougainville as of 1962 in a single word, that word might well be 'dissatisfaction'. Rowley's contrast (1965: 72) between the New Guinea Highlands and coastal areas is thus perfectly applicable to the electorate:

> Where the people have rapidly become involved in making new decisions, in new economic activities, in new experiences in a wider world, there is every chance that attitudes change, and early traditions of tyrannical interference fade away with the old men. But where the government has maintained over long periods what seems pointless interference in the affairs of villagers; and its officers seem to have pointlessly exercised power at their expense, the initial resentment will remain, often under a facade of what the white man sees as 'apathy'.

This general observation was made even more relevant to south

Bougainville by the relative administrative neglect, admitted by most Europeans outside Konedobu, of the entire District and by the unsatisfactory experiences—direct or indirect—of the villagers *vis-à-vis* plantations and their management.

Evidence of this dissatisfaction includes not only villagers' resistance to such innovations as local government councils, but more explicit behaviour. For example, in 1962, several Nasioi requested of a visiting United Nations Mission in Kieta that Australia be forced to relinquish the administration of Bougainville to the United States (see *Pacific Islands Monthly* May 1962, p. 138). Equally disturbing to administrators are periodic outbreaks of 'cargoism'.[2] While evidence of 'cargoist' thinking has appeared throughout the electorate since World War II, such attitudes have been endemic among Nasioi and, reportedly, Nagovisi speakers. In the former area, 'cargoism' until recently took an essentially supernatural form—sometimes called in Pidgin *longlong lotu* (a senseless equivalent to church)—in which specifically political overtones were muted, if present at all.

THE 1964 ELECTION AND AFTER

The author has elsewhere (Ogan 1965) described the conduct and outcome of the first House of Assembly election among some Nasioi villagers of the Aropa Valley. To summarise briefly: this notably dissatisfied group rejected a Catholic Nasioi candidate, Severinus Ampaoi, in favour of the Banoni, Paul Lapun. (Lapun, because of the geographic proximity of Banoni and Nagovisi, is often identified by Nasioi and others as being ethnically Nagovisi.) On the one hand, Ampaoi was justifiably regarded by Nasioi as the protégé of the incumbent Assistant District Officer; on the other, Lapun had in this area a reputation for essentially supernatural power to improve the villagers' lot. He was described by Aropa Valley Nasioi—themselves adherents of the Catholic mission but highly susceptible to 'cargoist' thinking— as having left the seminary to bring the supernatural knowledge acquired there to help indigenous residents of Bougainville. While the casual use of Weber's term 'charisma' to denote any sort of personalised leadership has been justifiably criticised (e.g., Friedrich 1961; Worsley 1968: ix-liii), the author suggests that this word provides an economic and adequate description of Paul Lapun's 1964 victory among the Nasioi. These people, distressed by their situation *vis-à-vis* Europeans

[2] 'Cargoism' is used here to refer to a general philosophy or world view, in contrast to a specific social movement, or 'cult'. Cf. Harding 1967b.

and European culture, voted for Lapun because they believed he possessed 'specific gifts of the body and spirit; and these gifts . . . believed to be supernatural, not accessible to everybody' (Gerth and Mills 1958: 245).

(On the other hand, the enigmatic nature of Lapun's own personality—to be explored in greater detail below—precludes the possibility of stating with assurance that he, himself, believes that he has received a transcendent call (Friedrich 1961: 14).)

The author made no attempt at the time or subsequently to examine intensively the 1964 election outside the Nasioi region. Consequently, what follows immediately is impressionistic, and the points raised are no more than suggestions. There were two other candidates from South Bougainville in the 1964 election: a Siwai Methodist, Nelson Laisi Laru, and a Buin Catholic, Andrew Komoro. Apparently, they suffered the same fate as Severinus Ampaoi, although not necessarily for the same reasons; that is, they received considerable support from their own ethnic and/or local group, but nevertheless were unable either to extend their support beyond those groups or to deny Paul Lapun votes from their home areas. To put the matter another way, of all the candidates in the 1964 election, only Paul Lapun was able to obtain a significant number of votes outside his local and/or ethnic base. However, he does not seem to have received much support in the northern half of the island. Since somewhat more than half of the District's population is in what is now the South Bougainville Open Electorate, Lapun's victory in 1964 suggested that an island-wide election could be won by carrying the south alone, foreshadowing results in 1968.

There is little one can say at this date about the conduct of the 1964 Special election in south Bougainville. Certainly Jim Grose was the only campaigner in the area and certainly most of those villagers who voted in the Special contest gave their votes to him. However, the Nasioi directly observed by the author simply refused to vote for any European, and it seems that many villagers elsewhere followed the same course. (Thus, the total votes cast in the New Guinea Islands Special Electorate amounted to less than 58 per cent of those cast in the Open electorates—Bougainville, Manus, and New Ireland—of which the Special electorate was composed.) Informants' comments in 1968 suggest that more Buin villagers voted in the 1964 Special (i.e. voted for Jim Grose) than did those of the other southern ethnic groups, which point, if correct, is consistent with the 1968 Regional results.

At approximately the same time as the 1964 election, an Australian geologist began the most decisive social change in Bougainville's recorded history. This is not the place to trace the complete story of Conzinc Riotinto mining operations (see *Pacific Islands Monthly* July 1968: 81-3; U.P.N.G. News No. 9, May 1968). One need only stress the following:

(1) A copper deposit worth estimated billions of dollars has been discovered centring in the Guava Census Division (map 5a), a relatively backward part of the Nasioi-speaking area.

(2) Led by certain Administration personnel, Conzinc Riotinto of Australia (C.R.A.) began its operations with totally inadequate knowledge of the local social situation and, therefore, with totally inadequate efforts to ensure co-operation of villagers. (The author's first-hand observations on this point have been corroborated by unofficial admission by C.R.A. executives and, indirectly, by extensive C.R.A. efforts to remedy the tense situation with the help of outside consultants, public relations programs, etc.)

(3) The potential financial benefits to the Territory (where, until the Mining Ordinance was amended as noted below, all subsurface mineral rights belonged to the government) have forced the highest officials in Port Moresby and Canberra to direct some attention to a District heretofore largely ignored.

(4) Strong opposition to the presence and activities of the mining company expressed by the great majority of adult Nasioi must be seen in terms of previous deep-seated dissatisfaction with Europeans and their behaviour toward villagers. In other words, for many Nasioi, C.R.A. is merely 'the last straw', the most recent and dramatic example of a long record of Australian exploitation in the island.[3]

In connection with the last point, many Nasioi informants have stated that a European mining company (perhaps even C.R.A. itself) would be welcome—provided that such operations would be carried out for the villagers' benefit, in contrast to plantation and other European-managed activities in the past. However, such statements cannot obscure the magnitude of villagers' distress over the present situation. Indeed, beginning in 1965, threats of violence have resulted in imprisonment of some villagers and the establishment of an armed police detachment in the Guava area.

The political repercussions of C.R.A. activity were several, varied, and not easily understood in terms of Anglo-Saxon political experience. One notable effect was the stand taken by the Catholic mission. Sparked by some younger priests (whose individual attitudes about mining operations and social change were themselves varied), a meeting at mission headquarters produced official mission statements protesting

[3] It should not be, but probably is, necessary to state that this does not accurately represent the author's personal opinion.

the current Mining Ordinance, and supporting any legislative change which would ensure some form of royalty payment to Nasioi landowners.

A number of non-missionary Europeans expressed outrage at what was perceived as missionary 'meddling'. The accusation was frequently made that two American priests, in particular, were stirring up the otherwise contented Nasioi. Enough evidence has already been presented here and elsewhere to show the inaccuracy of such accusations: whatever may have been the role of individual priests in the C.R.A. case, Nasioi resentment long antedated the arrival of C.R.A. and hardly needed any stirring up, especially after that company began exploring village territory.

European consternation mounted at the appearance in 1966 of an issue of *Dialogue,* the mimeographed organ of student expression at the Holy Spirit Regional Seminary in Madang. An editorial by a seminarian from Nissan Island (North Bougainville) and an article by a Buin seminarian specifically mentioned the Bougainville mining situation as examples of Australian (and, more especially, Administration) disregard of villagers' rights. The latter article (*New Guinea* I, 8: 33-5) also sharply criticised a lease arranged in 1964 for timber rights at Tonolei in Buin, for the same reasons.[4] Two other articles by Buin and Nasioi seminarians, respectively—while not citing specific examples from the Bougainville scene—emphasised the authors' feelings of dissatisfaction with the Australian presence and record in the Territory. The articles in question thus provided more evidence of discontent —in this case, among educated Bougainville people—extending beyond the narrow range of the villages immediately affected. Further, the distressed reaction of the Catholic church—at least three of the above authors are no longer in the seminary—indicated that Bougainville resentment is beyond the control of any missionary.

Mining and timber rights, then, constituted issues which could be treated as political in European terms and, indeed, Paul Lapun directed a major effort in the House of Assembly toward a legislative solution of the disputes. In 1966, he introduced an amendment to the Mining Ordinance which would have provided royalties to land owners, but the measure was defeated. Although, under the rules of the House, the measure should not have been reintroduced during the same session, tension in Guava—at one point C.R.A. personnel had to flee their base of operations—caused the Administration to abandon protocol, and the re-introduced amendment was passed in November 1966. A number of European members indicated that their support

[4] Some of the 'facts' cited about Tonolei appear to have been inaccurate. Such errors do not negate the article's sociological significance.

was purely pragmatic; that is, they voted for the measure in the hope that promise of a royalty amounting to 5 per cent of the government's share would persuade Nasioi villagers to give up their opposition.

By European standards, the Mining Ordinance amendment represented a major political triumph for Paul Lapun, but he had distinguished himself in the House of Assembly in other ways. His superior education and articulateness enabled him to take a much greater role than less sophisticated members from the Highlands (Bettison *et al.* 1965: 501, 503). He was chosen Under-Secretary for Forests. By the end of the first session, many observers marked him as one of the most outstanding members (see for example Wolfers 1967a: 25, 27; 1967b: 27-9).

Yet one must emphasise that these distinctions were largely meaningless to Lapun's constituents in South Bougainville, and the point is worth further examination. First, like most villagers in the Territory, those in South Bougainville have never had any clear idea of the organisation and functions of the House, or the role of the member. Many simply felt that Paul Lapun was going to *givim mipela gutpela lo* (give us good laws), but any details of these projected benefits were liable to be phrased in quasi-supernatural terms. Second, 'political education' in South Bougainville never consisted of more than local government council activity on the one hand, and the 'crash course' immediately preceding the 1964 election on the other. There was no consistent follow-up effort to expand villagers' extremely limited understanding of the House. The 1964 election had been carried out successfully, and the Administration seemed content to let the matter rest there.[5] Third, no channels of communication existed whereby reasonably accurate reports of Paul Lapun's achievements or any other House activity could be disseminated to villagers. Few people over 25 years of age in South Bougainville can read even simple Pidgin and the only local 'newspapers' are mimeographed sheets variously prepared by missionaries or an occasional A.D.O. These seldom deal with political activity and, given the unsophistication of the few readers, are easily misunderstood. Pidgin leaflets about government prepared in Port Moresby arrived in insufficient numbers and never seemed to be distributed beyond local government council chambers or a mission station. While by 1966, a radio might be found in many of those villages closest to European settlements, reception

[5] Any criticism of deficiencies in political education must, of course, take into consideration both the inherent problems in the Bougainville situation and the Administration's responsibilities for a multitude of other programs, to be carried out despite limited financial and personnel resources.

of the most popular station in Rabaul was likely to be erratic, and the Pidgin news broadcasts so little concerned with Bougainville as to be largely ignored. Finally, Paul Lapun himself made no noticeable effort to report back to his constituents about his work on their behalf.

The failure of Lapun to mend his political fences in the Western fashion provided a small element of truth in the reports circulating widely among Europeans in Bougainville in 1966-7 that the indigenous residents of the District were disgusted with their representative. Some administrators and planters maintained that Lapun was afraid to show his face in the District for fear of violence to his person; others stated that he was simply discouraged by his various failures and intended to withdraw from politics. Reports of villager dissatisfaction may have been accurate in the north—where, as noted, Paul Lapun had never enjoyed any considerable support—but, for most southerners, these stories were as incorrect as most planters' pronouncements about 'what the natives think'.

It is not surprising that Europeans misjudged indigenous opinion about Paul Lapun in the south since these attitudes, indeed, 'don't make sense' in terms of Anglo-Saxon politics. The most dramatic issue, the mining controversy, provides a notable example. Immediately before, during, and shortly after the passage of Lapun's bill, the author, then living in Kongara Census Division, was able to interview a number of visitors from Guava villages. Their responses made clear that they and their neighbours were able simultaneously to reject Lapun's political accomplishments while remaining steadfastly loyal to the man himself. These Guava villagers dismissed the Mining Ordinance amendment and Lapun's face-to-face speeches advising their co-operation with C.R.A.; they insisted that Paul must have a better plan which he would reveal in his own good time. In other words, the belief of these (and many other) Nasioi in Paul Lapun's special 'gifts of body and spirit' was so strong that they could ignore his own statements when these words failed to agree with their expectations of him. Lapun was their man and circumstances of importance to the Western political process were simply irrelevant to their choice of representative.

Paul Lapun's reluctance to appear outside Port Moresby on the one hand, or his Nagovisi-Banoni home area on the other, was remarkable. During 1964-7, there were many young Bougainville men in the seminary at Madang, some of whom were clearly politically conscious and sympathetic with Lapun's apparent aims. One of them stated that at least a score of letters were written to Lapun, asking him to speak to the seminarians, but he never responded nor did he even visit the seminary during a stay in Madang. Unlike many other members, he seemed to have no European confidants; rumours of a certain priest serving as *éminence grise* were effectively dispelled by the priest's own complaint that Paul neither answered his letters nor came to see him. While some villagers purported to 'talk for Paul', the author was able to discover only one in the Kieta Sub-District whom Lapun acknowledged as a representative (see below). But the disappointment expressed by southern villagers over Lapun's failure to visit them was not generally stated in terms of disapproval of the man himself. His charismatic appeal was too strong for that.

While misinformed Europeans were thus looking forward to the political demise of Paul Lapun,[6] other observers were debating the possibility that he would choose to contest the Regional election. One cannot know what prompted his decision to remain in the South Bougainville Open, but there is no doubt that his choice made sense in terms of a 'bird in the hand' caution. In 1967, he made some of his infrequent Bougainville appearances outside his home area to discuss the new electoral divisions, and to announce the formation of Pangu Pati and his association with it. Among the Nasioi, the latter statement became thoroughly confused with the area's endemic cargoism.

By 1967, one became aware of different forms of cargoist thinking among different groups of Nasioi speakers. The Koromira, North Nasioi, and South Nasioi Census Divisions had earlier emphasised supernaturalism or *longlong lotu* in their efforts to attain a European standard of living. Now more politically-oriented behaviour appeared, with Koromira as 'headquarters'. An 'army' of young men trained in secluded Koromira villages. Sexual promiscuity was reported; whether as a recruiting device, a means of obtaining funds via prostitution, or a kind of ritual cannot be clearly determined. In short, the 'new cargoism' resembles reports on the Hahalis Welfare Society in Buka (see Rynkiewich 1968; *Pacific Islands Monthly* July 1962, 27-9); however, it is more likely that both movements are parallel responses to similar discontent than that the Koromira movement is a direct offshoot of Hahalis.

In Guava Census Division, cargoism is further complicated by opposition to C.R.A. The two young men most outspoken in denouncing the mining company and the Administration had both been associated with the Catholic mission. 'Simon',[7] who had been a mission teacher,

---

[6] In 28 months in Bougainville (most of the time, admittedly, in villages removed from Europeans) the author heard no European—whether connected with mission, Administration, or business enterprise—speak of Lapun in terms of unqualified approval.

[7] 'Simon', 'Bartholomew', and 'Matthew' are pseudonyms.

gave speeches throughout the Sub-District to rally anti-C.R.A. sentiment; the speech recorded by the author in January 1967 advocated a rational (in Western terms) approach to the problem. His associate 'Bartholomew', on the other hand, betrayed his confusion of religion and politics by costuming himself after the fashion of a Catholic priest, talking about the 'secret knowledge' which must be wrested from Europeans, and predicting millennial events.

Simon and Bartholomew managed to associate themselves in villagers' minds with Paul Lapun and Pangu Pati; the resulting confusion which beset even their followers may well seem incredible to a European unfamiliar with the Nasioi scene. A few facts emerge from conflicting Nasioi, mission, and Administration testimony:

(1) Paul Lapun read from, and left behind in Nasioi villages, copies of a Pidgin statement 'Platform and Policy of the Pangu Pati. *Ol Rot Na Tingting Bilong Pangu Pati*'. *Inter alia,* this statement listed a membership fee of 20 cents but indicated that a *'Donar Memba'* might contribute *sampela moni moa sapos wanpela man i laik givim* (some more money if any man wished to give it).

(2) Simon and Bartholomew, with the help of other men, made collections of money throughout the Kieta Sub-District. (Some informants stated these collections extended into the Buin Sub-District as well.) Estimates of the amount collected ranged from $8000 to $16,000 or more.

(3) The purpose of this collection was variously described as: the support of Pangu and Paul Lapun as Pangu leader; hiring of legal assistance and/or representation to the United Nations in order to oust C.R.A.; formation of a 'development fund' to be used on behalf of villagers under the general direction of Paul Lapun. It must be emphasised that even many of the contributors were unsure as to which of these alternatives was most important; they were only sure that they would benefit in some mysterious way.

Administration pressure forced Simon to return at least some of this money, and Paul Lapun revisited the Sub-District, ostensibly to clarify Pangu and to expedite refunds. It is clear that Paul Lapun, cargoism with varying degrees of supernatural emphasis, opposition to C.R.A., politics in general and Pangu in particular were all thoroughly mixed in Nasioi minds before nominations opened for the 1968 election.

Nothing quite so bizarre was reported from the Buin Sub-District during the same period. However, similar discontent was evidenced by a resolution, passed by the Siwai Local Government Council and unsuccessfully put forth by them at a meeting of the Bougainville District Councils, forbidding any European or Chinese to establish new businesses in the area. While the Siwai approach was less supernatural in tone, the underlying feeling was not unlike that of the Nasioi.

The nominating period, 27 November 1967—5 January 1968, was also the period of electoral education in south Bougainville; such efforts were unsuccessful among Nasioi and hardly noteworthy for Buin speakers.[8] For example, as of 30 January, four patrols had been carried out in the Kieta Sub-District and four more were scheduled, yet neither the author nor his Nasioi assistant could find more than a few villagers who knew the new electoral boundaries and understood the difference between the Open and Regional electorates. Even Kieta local government councillors remained in the dark through December. The Administration apparently expected Buin speakers to learn through local government councillors; officers made no special patrols. Several patrols were reportedly undertaken from the Boku Patrol Post serving Nagovisi-Banoni. Generally, however, the candidates themselves seem to have provided the most effective electoral education during their campaigns (see below).

For most of the nominating period, it seemed that Paul Lapun would run unopposed. Europeans in the Kieta Sub-District spoke of a number of potential Nasioi candidates but none filed. Severinus Ampaoi, now employed by C.R.A., simply replied 'I don't want to' (Nasioi: *Piamoa*) when asked about his plans. He and other potential Nasioi candidates—mostly councillors—probably made a realistic appraisal of Lapun's strength in the area, although some advanced other reasons for declining to run ('I'm too old'; 'I'm not a big man'). There was no report of Nelson Laru's interest in running again, nor of any potential rival to Paul Lapun in his home area. Finally, reportedly in response to strong hints dropped by an Administration spokesman, Andrew Komoro filed on the last day of nomination.

THE CANDIDATES AND THEIR CAMPAIGNS

Much has been written here and elsewhere about Paul Lapun; one need note only a few additional points. He had, of course, the advantages and disadvantages of incumbency. Even the least sophisticated villagers

---

[8] The author was in the electorate 29 December 1967-28 February 1968, mostly in the Kieta Sub-District. His own observations were supplemented by those of Messrs Leo J. Laita (Buin) and James Rutana (Nasioi) of the U.P.N.G. for the period 1 December 1967-30 January 1968. Since transportation problems precluded personal visits to Siwai and Nagovisi-Banoni areas, the author has depended on reports from several individual informants, European and indigenous, as to developments in these parts of the electorate.

were likely to know his name. On the other hand, he ran the risk, albeit small, that anti-government resentment might focus on him.

More remarkable, however, is the fact that he did no real campaigning at all. During most of the three months before actual voting, he was outside the District, attending the Summer School of the Australian Institute of Political Science in Canberra and visiting Port Moresby. At least three suggestions—not mutually exclusive—have been advanced for his failure to campaign: he realised that his victory was assured and campaigning unnecessary; he consciously avoided personal appearances to enhance the awe with which he was regarded; he was discouraged from campaigning by European ill-wishers who, indeed, regularly arranged for special trips to get him out of the way. The first of these possibilities seems by far the most likely.

Andrew Komoro, Lapun's last-minute opponent, shared with him a good command of English and an extensive—by New Guinea standards—Catholic education. In Komoro's case, this included training at the Marist Fathers' Novitiate in Sydney. The two men are of the same generation: Komoro 42, Lapun 45. Both received special political education from the Administration before the establishment of the House of Assembly.

But there are important differences between the two. Lapun is a Banoni, with strong Nagovisi connections; Komoro is a Buin speaker. Whereas Lapun, even before his election, was cool toward the Administration, Komoro's association with local government councils—he is clerk of the Buin Local Government Council—marked him as something of a 'government man' in the Bougainville context. Lapun's relations with the Catholic mission, like so much of his activity, were ambiguous; Komoro had the reputation among missionaries of being an outspoken opponent. Komoro himself stated to the author that 'some missionaries' had told their parishioners not to vote for him in 1964.

Komoro's campaign was limited in scope and as lacklustre as one might have expected from his belated entry into the contest. He gave one speech in Buin town to an audience of about twenty-five men, in which he simply promised to improve the villagers' lot. He made no mention of political parties (although he subsequently told the author he knew that Paul Lapun was a member of Pangu and that he had heard of the Christian Democratic Party in New Guinea). While his position as council clerk made him known in Buin, and thus removed some incentive to campaign in that area, he was thereby tarred with the brush of higher council tax, and he mentioned this point apologetically in his Buin speech.

During the week before balloting, Komoro made speeches along the Kieta coast, sometimes on Catholic mission grounds. No eyewitness reports of his appearances are available, but stories were widespread among Catholic missionaries that Komoro was promising to expel the missions if elected. (Outside Buin, of course, Komoro spoke in Pidgin, increasing the ambiguity of his statements.) His mimeographed Pidgin leaflets, on the other hand, outlined promises to improve local agriculture and marketing, to strengthen the voice of the villagers in government, to increase the number of schools in Bougainville, and to visit all local government council chambers to learn the wishes of the people. These leaflets resembled those of Regional candidate John (Jock) Lee.

In short, Komoro's speeches reached relatively few people outside his home area (and Kieta and environs where a number of Buin migrants might be found), nor was there any evidence that he had representatives speaking on his behalf in remoter parts of the electorate. Although nominally a Catholic and identified as Catholic-educated on his leaflets, he certainly did not enjoy support in mission stations or schools.

On 1 February 1968, the Catholic Bishop of Bougainville spoke on the mission radio network to all mission stations, explaining the official mission policy: the mission did *not* back any candidate; any candidate was to be offered the hospitality of mission stations, regardless of race or creed; priests might answer parishioners' questions as to candidates' qualifications, on the same basis for all candidates.

However, the situation was not so simple in practice. Individual priests enjoyed considerable independence on their respective stations and could make their attitudes known in a number of subtle ways. At least one European candidate was denied mission hospitality on the grounds that strongly anti-European parishioners would resent his presence on the station. But more importantly, in an atomistic social and political situation, a common religious bond could attract a voter's allegiance to one of a field of otherwise unknown candidates. The communication network provided by mission stations and schools loomed large in this electorate, where other channels were so inadequate. The point is elaborated below.

In contrast to the Open candidates, those in the Regional filed relatively early, and two of them conducted vigorous campaigns.

John Cairns (Jock) Lee might be described as an 'old school' Bougainville planter, except that he was clearly more concerned with villager welfare than were many of his peers. Lee was 43 years old and had operated a plantation off the west coast of Buka since 1953. He had been active in the Bougainville Planters' Association, a member of the District Advisory Council, and a councillor in the (multi-racial) Buka Local Government Council since 1966. He was a Presbyterian, though he did not make a point of this affiliation in campaigning.

Lee campaigned throughout the Buin Sub-District, but had to cancel appearances in the Kieta Sub-District because of illness. Unlike either of his opponents, he offered in speeches and Pidgin leaflets a specific platform: improved marketing facilities for Bougainville produce, to include additional Copra Marketing Board depots and produce inspectors; improved education to include more secondary schools and increased government subsidies to mission teachers; improved agricultural extension and education.

During his campaign, Lee—not himself a member of any political party—saw no evidence of party activity. Before voting began, he told the author that he felt the anti-European bias he encountered in the south would hamper his chances, but admitted that Administration failure to develop this area made such resentment understandable.

Gayne F. Cooke represented a 'new breed' of European, a type which has recently been politically active elsewhere in the Territory. He originally came to New Guinea as a Patrol Officer, was stationed for a time in the Highlands, and was subsequently transferred to Bougainville. He left the public service to operate a plantation in Tinputz and became active in the Teop-Tinputz Local Government Council, of which he was currently president.

Cooke, a man of 34, addressed meetings in all southern Census Divisions except the most remote areas of Nagovisi and Nasioi speakers. Furthermore, he added a unique touch to the Bougainville campaign by dropping leaflets—bearing his picture and the legend 'How to Vote/ Vot Olosem/1—G. F. Cooke'—from an airplane over most of the south in early February. He put forth no specific program but briefly explained the new electoral divisions, detailed his personal background (emphasising his experience in government), and promised to return to every census division if elected, in order to learn the people's wishes.

Judging from the speech recorded by the author in the South Nasioi Census Division and from reports by Buin and North Nasioi informants, Cooke's approach was like that of the *kiap* (administration officer). He stressed villagers' responsibilities: *Nau taim yupela sindaun na kaikai buai, em i pinis. Nau em i taim bilong hatwok na tingting* (Now the time when you idly chew betelnut is over. Now is the time for effort (literally 'hard work') and thought). He did not mention his Catholic background nor did he discuss political parties (he was not a party member). In contrast to Lee, he felt that his chances were appreciably better in Siwai and Nasioi areas than in Buin, although he was aware of general anti-European feeling in the south. Like Lee, he noted that he was often asked to explain the new electoral divisions, indicating some shortcomings in the Administration's electoral education program.

Joseph Adrian (Joe) Lue, the third candidate, differed from his opponents in almost every respect. A Siwai man of 34, he had been closely associated with the Catholic mission for most of his life. He received all his formal education in Catholic schools, culminating in two years' work at the Marist Brothers' College in Australia. As a Marist Brother, he taught for seven years at St Joseph's School in Kieta, a Marist secondary institution for boys specially chosen from the entire district (as well as a few from the British Solomon Islands). Although he left the teaching order in 1965 to become an insurance agent, he did *not* break with the church, and in 1967, represented Papua-New Guinea and the Solomons at the Third World Congress of the Lay Apostolate in Rome.

Joe Lue campaigned only briefly in his home area, and was otherwise almost as elusive as Paul Lapun for most of the election. However, he did use leaflets and letters to local government councils. The former, in Pidgin, were almost identical to those of Cooke (who, indeed, said that Lue had simply copied his format), briefly explaining the three electorates and describing his personal background. Lue's letter to the Buin Council was written in English and contained a specific endorsement of Paul Lapun: 'But I would like to just mention that it would be a pity to drop out Mr Paul Lapun, our own present Member—he has done well and has acquired good experience so we should re-vote him for the South Bougainville [sic].'

There was other evidence for this association, unique in the election, of Paul Lapun and Joseph Lue. A Siwai friend of the latter, himself a Marist Brother, told the author that Lue had asked Paul Lapun about campaigning in the Nagovisi-Banoni area. He was told not to bother, since Lapun had already instructed all those people to vote for Lue. Paul Lapun's own representative in the North Nasioi (see below) stated that he was telling people to vote for Lue as a 'Lapun ally'.

Lue's candidacy was also advanced by a kind of 'old boy' network of indigenous Catholic mission teachers. The few Bougainville men who have attained the status of priest or brother are known and respected by Catholics throughout the District. Furthermore, the best educated Catholic men have attended St Joseph's School where Lue taught, and they feel a strong bond with the school and its teachers. Evidence for this network was provided by a discussion of the elections led by the author among upperclassmen at the school. The one candidate in the three Bougainville electorates whom all these students supported was Lue. (One should note in passing that the name of Francis Hagai, the Hahalis candidate in the North Bougainville Open, brought forth hoots of laughter.) Despite official mission neutrality, Lue could fairly be described as the Catholic candidate.

GENERAL CAMPAIGN OBSERVATIONS

No direct observations were made in Nagovisi-Banoni or Siwai portions of the electorate. Comments by individual informants before voting began strongly indicated that Paul Lapun remained all-powerful in the former area, but the degree to which his influence would help Joseph Lue was open to question. Reports from Siwai suggested that Lue could depend on support in his own backyard, and that Lapun's strength was undiminished. There was no indication that political parties would be a factor in voting; Pangu was rarely mentioned and then as no more than another attribute of Lapun.

In Buin villages (where some Siwai visited to discuss the election), some small degree of sophistication was apparent. Partial credit for explaining the difference between Open and Regional electorates must be given to candidates Cooke and Lee. Perhaps more important was the influence of indigenous mission teachers, and of secondary and university students home for the holidays. This is not to say that villagers had a Westerner's view of the political process; for example, few if any knew much about political parties. Further, some traditional attitudes persisted, as when older men voiced continuing support for Paul Lapun by comparing him to traditional 'chiefs' who held office for life.

Yet Buin people also talked among themselves about the duties of a member, the qualities required for office, and the relative weight he should give to his own and his constituents' views. They expressed their strong anti-European sentiment in terms which a Western observer could understand; Europeans had no roots in the island and, in a crisis, might return to Australia; if Australian priests were criticised by other Europeans for 'meddling' in questions of timber rights, then clearly an indigenous person must be elected to remove any ambiguity over loyalties; European campaign promises could be specifically and devastatingly contrasted with European performance. Led by younger, more educated men, these discussions produced an early commitment to Joseph Lue, and mixed support for Paul Lapun against his Buin opponent.

The Nasioi, on the other hand, had much less understanding of the election. Only Cooke made campaign speeches in the Kieta Sub-District; Paul Lapun's 1967 appearances had tended to create confusion. Administration electoral education had proved inadequate, particularly in more remote areas like the Kongara Census Division. Catholics in these villages had no appreciation of the new electoral divisions; they were only certain they would vote for Paul Lapun and no one else. Some Seventh-Day Adventists had reservations about Lapun, and expressed interest in Cooke's speeches, but such opinions constituted a very small minority.

For most Nasioi, the combination of anti-Europeanism and absolute loyalty to Paul Lapun could be expressed in alternative ways. Inland villagers stated they would not vote in the Regional, any more than they had voted in the 1964 Special electorate. A major cargoist leader on the coast, however, said he and his followers would vote for Paul Lapun in *both* contests. (The result, of course, would be the same: an informal vote in the Regional.)

Only one Nasioi informant demonstrated considerable knowledge of the elections, and his case is worth examining in detail. 'Matthew' is an ex-seminarian, slightly younger than Paul Lapun; it is not known whether they attended school together. After leaving the seminary, Matthew attempted to set up a large-scale co-operative business enterprise, including copra marketing and trade stores, in his North Nasioi home. Like many such ventures, it foundered on insufficient knowledge and the conflicting demands of traditional socio-economic organisation; equally predictable, the demise of the business was associated with an outbreak of cargoism. Matthew was finally imprisoned for 'spreading false reports'.

However, since his release, he has regained prestige and influence among Nasioi dissidents. He moves behind the scenes in new co-operative ventures, he counsels anti-C.R.A. agitators from Guava, and he maintains a flow of typewritten correspondence—in Nasioi, Pidgin, and English—to further his political and economic ends. Most important, his claim to be Paul Lapun's 'man in Kieta' has been validated by Lapun himself, who refers villager and European visitor alike to him.

Matthew was able to name, more or less accurately, five political parties in the Territory, and contrasted Pangu's plan for swift progress toward self-government (as distinct from independence) with the Country Party's stand on continued Australian rule. Unlike any other villager interviewed, he identified Joseph Lue as a member of Pangu, and stated that Nasioi speakers north of Kieta would vote for both Lue and Lapun. He claimed that the Nasioi collection of $16,000 would be given to Lapun to be used solely by Pangu, whose president he identified as Albert Maori Kiki. Matthew further indicated that Pangu's plan for New Guinea's future would unite New Guinea proper and all the islands, including Bougainville, as a unit in contrast to Papua. (This view further contrasts with the idea, widespread among Bougainville villagers and mentioned in the House by Paul Lapun, that Bougainville's political future lies with the islands of the present British Solomons Protectorate.)

Matthew thus showed an unusual grasp of the election and political processes, while his personal history indicated that his sophistication was combined with cargoist thinking and anti-European sentiment in general. He might reasonably be regarded as a kind of 'new cargoist', very roughly similar to certain Hahalis leaders. (That the older, more supernatural forms of cargoism were still active was demonstrated by reports from Guava at this time; Bartholomew and a former Nasioi teaching brother, described as psychotic by European missionaries, were rallying followers in preparation for the end of the world.)

What, then, was the political picture in the electorate on the eve of voting? On the basis of all observations through the campaign period, the following predictions appeared reasonable:

(1) Paul Lapun would be easily re-elected; his greatest strength would be among Nagovisi, Banoni, and Nasioi speakers.

(2) Informal voting would be appreciably higher in the Regional than in the Open contest.

(3) (a) Strong support for Paul Lapun would be negatively associated with support of a European candidate in the Regional electorate.

(b) Whether Lapun support would be positively associated with votes for Joseph Lue or with informal Regional voting was problematical; the latter outcome seemed most likely in the Nasioi area.

VOTING

The author observed balloting only in Kieta town; he did not scrutinise ballot papers after the official count. Consequently, this section is based on informants' reports, voting figures kindly provided by the Returning Officer, and the author's general knowledge of the electorate. Because of the small number of candidates, a reasonably thorough analysis is possible without certain data which might be necessary to understand a more complex electorate (e.g., in Highland New Guinea). The interesting and important question which cannot be answered here concerns the extent to which the high number of informal Regional ballots represents simple refusal to vote versus the attempt to vote for Paul Lapun (or any other individual) not running in that contest.

Voter turn-out at polling places represented 68·5 per cent of those enrolled, and according to the Returning Officer was essentially uniform throughout the electorate. (The difference in voting totals between Kieta and Buin Sub-Districts is in accord with the differences in respective total populations.) This is approximately the same as the 1964 turn-out.

Voting figures were made available by ballot box. Geographic areas represented by each box (twenty in all) vary markedly in size, as do numbers of votes cast and, for the Regional contest, percentages of informal ballots. Therefore, it has seemed appropriate to examine each ballot box as constituting a distinct analytical unit, and to speak of 'ballot box areas'.

Paul Lapun received 82·1 per cent of the total vote, to Andrew Komoro's 17·6; informal ballots constituted a surprisingly low percentage (table 4). The overwhelming nature of Lapun's victory was to be expected, but a more detailed examination of those 'ballot box areas' in which he received relatively high (90 per cent +) or relatively low (less than 80 per cent) support provides additional significant data.

Four of the areas of greatest support are in the Buin Sub-District, six in the Kieta Sub-District. The former represent Lapun's 'home base', ethnically Banoni, Baitsi, and Nagovisi, and need no further explanation. Four of the Kieta areas which gave Lapun high support are particularly anti-European; one, the Guava, has been described earlier as a centre both for anti-C.R.A. sentiment and a belief in the imminent end of the world. A fifth Kieta area, in North Nasioi, is one in which Lapun is actively represented by Matthew. The sixth ballot box, located at the C.R.A. base, contained only 59 votes; little can be said about its significance.

Lapun received less than 80 per cent of the votes in six of the twenty ballot box areas. He actually lost—with 43 per cent of the vote—in only one of these areas, in Kono Census Division, which is Komoro's 'home base'. The significant point here is that Komoro's margin was so small. The other areas of low support break down as follows:

(1) Buin town—Lapun 54 per cent, Komoro 43 per cent. Lapun's relatively poor showing is due in large part to the 'foreign' (European, Chinese, and non-indigenous New Guinean) vote, and, to a lesser degree, to Komoro's prestige as Buin Local Government Council clerk.

(2) Kieta town—Lapun 60 per cent, Komoro 40 per cent. Total votes number only 59, so it would be unwise to draw conclusions, though one can speculate about the 'foreign' vote.

(3) Lugakei Census Division—Lapun 60 per cent, Komoro 40 per cent. This is a Buin ethnic area, closest to Komoro's 'home base' and, additionally, may be influenced by the presence or proximity of Seventh-Day Adventist and Methodist missions.

(4) Siwai area closest to Buin—Lapun 65 per cent, Komoro 35 per cent. Ethnic factors and the strength of the Protestant mission appear to have operated to reduce Lapun's victory margin.

(5) Buin area closest to Siwai—Lapun 70 per cent, Komoro 30

per cent. Figures demonstrate Lapun's ability to surmount ethnic boundaries.

Paul Lapun's victory should refute, for the southern part of the District, all the European rumours that the villagers were dissatisfied with him. His victory was convincing not only in terms of the margin over his opponent, but because of the relatively high turn-out and low percentage of informal ballots—the reverse of these factors might have indicated disillusionment even if totals had made Lapun the winner.

It should also be clear that Paul Lapun has great strength in the most supernaturally cargoist, anti-European segments of the electorate, though his strength is by no means confined to those areas. (On the other hand, there is some, albeit inadequate, evidence in the voting figures that non-indigenous voters are just as firmly against Lapun.) Guava villagers, rejecting the amended Mining Ordinance which represents Paul Lapun's great legislative triumph and awaiting the end of the world, nonetheless turned out to give him all but two of their 735 votes (while failing to vote in the Regional by almost the same margin). Results in this and other parts of the electorate demonstrate that this man may be properly described as having charisma.

Joseph Lue's margin of victory in the Regional voting was much lower, and the percentage of informal ballots much higher (table 4: the Returning Officer did not explain the small discrepancy between Regional and Open totals). Lue received low—less than 50 per cent—support in twelve of twenty ballot box areas, which can be broken down thus:

(1) In two of the twelve areas, informal balloting amounted to 97·9 per cent and 99·5 per cent of the respective totals; that is, villagers rejected and/or failed to understand the Regional ballot. Both of these areas are Nasioi-speaking, both are cargoist and anti-European, and both gave strong support to Paul Lapun.

(2) In five of the twelve areas, although Lue received less than 50 per cent of the total, he nonetheless achieved percentages higher than the combined figures for his two European opponents. All of these are ethnically Nasioi; percentages of informal voting ran from 30·3 per cent to 66·7 per cent of the total. In all five, it seems clear that anti-European and/or pro-Paul Lapun sentiments were expressed in alternative ways: refusal to vote for anyone but Lapun (he received 80 per cent or more of the Open votes in all five) *or* preference for the indigenous candidate. Thus Matthew delivered 48·6 per cent of his 'home base' vote to Joe Lue but could not prevent a 30·3 per cent informal vote.

(3) In four of the twelve areas, Lue received a higher percentage

of the vote than either of his European rivals separately, but not more than their combined figures. A further breakdown shows:

(a) A Nasioi-Torau area with only 76 total votes, of which 47 or 61·8 per cent were informal—thus little can be determined;

(b) Kieta town, with a low total vote and probable effect of 'foreign' voters;

(c) Two Buin areas which provided the highest support for Andrew Komoro. Even though Lue was linked with Paul Lapun, the same areas which tended toward Lapun's rival gave the Siwai candidate 40·8 per cent and 46·6 per cent of their Regional ballots. (Respective figures for the Europeans are Lee 34·9 per cent, Cooke 21·3 per cent; Lee 28·4 per cent, Cooke 24·9 per cent.)

(4) In only one ballot box area in south Bougainville did Jock Lee beat Joseph Lue, 47·5 per cent to 38·7 per cent; Cooke received 13·3 per cent. This was the area centred on Buin town, and the presence of many 'foreign' voters undoubtedly constituted the key factor, as with Paul Lapun's relatively poor showing in the same area.

The areas giving relatively high (60 per cent +) support to Lue were, in all but one case, geographically continuous with his 'home town'. However, it is worth noting that he received his highest percentages, not in his ethnic area of Siwai, but in Nagovisi land. While the differences are not notable, the greater Nagovisi strength suggests influence by both Paul Lapun and the Catholic mission; the lower Siwai figures may reflect a 'Methodist vote'. On the other hand, in Lapun's two 'home town' areas, Lue's percentages were somewhat lower, while informal balloting rose to 22·9 per cent and 25·7 per cent, suggesting once again that some of Lapun's staunchest followers could not bear to vote for anyone but their hero—even in a different race.

One Nasioi area gave Lue 80·1 per cent of its votes, and is of special interest. This ballot box served Koromira—where the new movement reminiscent of Hahalis Welfare flourishes—and the site of the Methodist mission as well. The suggestion in this case is that Lue attracted support from two quite different groups: the less supernaturally-oriented cargoists, on the one hand, and the pro-local government council villagers, on the other.

As for more general points about the Regional contest, one must note the failure of voters in the Kieta Sub-District to utilise the Regional ballot, as demonstrated by the much higher percentages of informal voting. At least part of this failure must be laid to inadequate instruction by Administration, mission, and other interested and informed parties. Nasioi felt that either the Regional ballot continued to be *'samting bilong ol masta'* (a matter (exclusively) for expatriates) and anathema because of their general anti-European feelings, or that Joseph Lue was in competition with their hero, Paul Lapun. Even after the election, a young Nasioi man writes that 'Joe Lue *em i numbatu long* Paul' (Joe Lue is second to Paul).

Joseph Lue's victory in the south, which effectively won the whole election for him, represents a combination of Paul Lapun's influence, together with racial and religious identification. He won without extensive campaigning, because south Bougainville villagers knew that Paul Lapun looked favourably on him, because he was 'one of us' in contrast to his rivals, and/or because of efforts by indigenous mission personnel.

Lue's support was essentially that of Lapun, less the most extreme Nasioi cargoists. Only in one of his own ethnic regions did Lue gain a higher percentage of votes than Lapun, and even here the difference was not great. It seems possible that Lue also received votes from Protestant pro-local government council villagers who rejected Lapun, but the facts are not clear.

Jock Lee ran consistently ahead of G. F. Cooke wherever both had made campaign speeches. It is conceivable, given the narrow margin of Lue's win, that, had illness not prevented Lee from campaigning in the Kieta Sub-District, he might have been able to pick up enough votes to carry the election. But here one enters a speculative realm (what if Joseph Lue had decided to campaign in Lee's 'home base' in the north?) in which it is not profitable to dwell. As one with considerable experience among Nasioi villagers, the author doubts that speeches by Lee would have tipped the balance; any votes he might have picked up would more likely have come from Cooke's support, than from Lue's or from the informal ballots. (One should also note that, in the distribution of Cooke's preferences, 54·2 per cent went to Joseph Lue, only 25 per cent to Jock Lee, the remainder exhausted.)

Two final points must be made for the entire electorate.

First, specific issues were not significant in voting. The only 'issue', if indeed it can be so described, was a generalised dissatisfaction with their lot on the part of the villagers, especially in connection with the European presence in the area. The two candidates—Lee and Komoro—who offered specific programs were defeated; the two victors did not, for all practical purposes, campaign at all. The burning issues to a Western observer—European utilisation of mining and timber resources—only affected the election as two of many examples of perceived European 'oppression'.

Second, the political role of the missions remains problematical. Certainly knowledge of Joseph Lue was spread by a kind of Catholic 'old boy' network in areas where he would have otherwise been unknown, but the colour of his skin was at least as potent a factor in his victory. Similarly, Andrew Komoro's anti-Catholic mission reputation undoubtedly caused some mission personnel to counsel parishioners against him, but this was hardly the cause of his defeat.

While it seems fair to say that Catholic villagers were generally anti-European in their voting, it *cannot* be said that Protestants voted a *pro*-European ticket. For example, one ballot box in the Kieta Sub-District covered a relatively large number of Seventh-Day Adventist Nasioi. A European observer at this 'mixed' village, Daratui, reported that Seventh-Day Adventist villagers voted in both contests while Catholics voted only in the Open. Lue took 22·5 per cent of the votes, while 66·7 per cent were informal. The results strongly suggest that Lue received Seventh-Day Adventist support here.

Rynkiewich (1968) has provided a provocative analysis of voting in the North Bougainville Open Electorate, and only two points need be emphasised here. First, the clearcut differences between voting patterns in the Regional contest should give some satisfaction to those who drew the electoral boundaries. The voting turn-out in the southern Open electorate was 7 per cent higher than in North Bougainville. Informal voting was very low in both Opens, but was five times smaller in South than in North Bougainville; on the other hand, while it ran at about the same modest rate in the northern part of the Regional as in the corresponding Open, it was over seven times as high (more than 20 per cent) in the southern part. Similarly, while Lue gained three-quarters of his first preference votes in the south, his European opponents got the great bulk of theirs in the north. On Bougainville, the boundary does, indeed, represent a division of sociological significance.

Second, and more specifically, while there are broad similarities between cargoist thinking in the south and the Hahalis Welfare Society in Buka, differences in voting patterns (Buka villagers voted both for Francis Hagai and Jock Lee, Nasioi cargoists either voted for Joseph Lue or not at all) suggest that administrators and others dealing with such sentiment and behaviour should be alert to subtle but significant distinctions in separate cases. (Cf. Davenport and Coker 1967: 174: 'the rule for specifying the most salient aspects of cults and movements shall be, "To each his own".')

THE FUTURE

This examination of the election in south Bougainville has argued that victory was not achieved on the basis of issues or programs. Rather, racial attitudes and belief in supernatural qualities (charisma) of a candidate constituted the most potent factors. If this analysis is, to any significant degree, correct, what are the implications for future political developments and, particularly, for the next election?

Wolfers (1967d: 69) has succinctly made an important point in this connection:

> Once local prestige is assured, the member will be relatively free to adopt any ideological position he may choose, or to join a party, for the issues that are at stake in the House of Assembly exist on quite a different plane to those that will ensure the return of most (especially the non-Papuan coastal) candidates.

Obviously, Paul Lapun has been in this position since 1964. One cannot predict when—or even if—his supporters will begin to examine his specific legislative accomplishments (or failures) in making future voting decisions. Similarly, if his racial extraction elected Joseph Lue in 1968, how can the observer guess what might happen if he runs against one or more black men in 1972?

The situation is further complicated by the inescapable circumstance that social change in Bougainville will continue to accelerate in a manner undreamed of by villagers. The Territory cannot afford to allow Bougainville copper to remain unexploited. One can speculate, with some confidence, that Administration expenditures in the District for the period 1968-72 will surpass those for the preceding twenty years. To what extent will Paul Lapun and Joseph Lue receive credit for the new roads, the new radio station, the new schools, the new copra marketing facilities? To what extent will they be blamed for the inevitable and imminent destruction of village life as it has existed in the post-war period?

One point seems clear. The people of south Bougainville are going to be aware as never before of what their representatives are doing. The opening of Radio Bougainville in 1968 marks a new era for a District which was impoverished, even by Territorial standards, of communication channels. At the very least, Radio Bougainville may divest Paul Lapun of some of his aura of mystery.

Finally, what will be the effect of the generation gap between the very few educated Bougainville men who grew to maturity before and during World War II, and the much larger group of men in their 20s now receiving tertiary education? There are obvious contrasts in personality, background, and outlook between Paul Lapun and Joseph Lue. (Lue, despite earlier reports, has not proved to be a 'Pangu man' either in terms of formal membership or in his general political viewpoint.) But there are much more significant differences between Lue and those now in the seminary and at the university who have already expressed strong, radical political views. A young Nasioi seminarian wrote the author that Administration officials 'fear our educated Bougainville boys'. More generally, one could argue that these younger men represent a threat to anyone wishing to avoid or postpone radical social and political change in the Territory. Whether the winners of the 1968 election will find allies or enemies among 'our educated Bougainville boys' constitutes one of the most important questions in the District's political future.

TABLE 4—THE ELECTION RESULTS IN BOUGAINVILLE

a. *Bougainville Regional*

	1st count	2nd and final count
Jock Lee	7394	8795
Joseph Lue	8361	9561
G. F. Cooke	3905	Excl.
Informal	2829	—
Exhausted	—	1304

b. *Bougainville South Open*

	1st and final count
Paul Lapun	9990
Andrew Komo Komoro	2174
Informal	43

c. *Voting in south Bougainville, by Sub-District*

	Kieta Sub-District		Buin Sub-District		Total	
	No.	%	No.	%	No.	%
*Bougainville South part of Regional**						
Jock Lee	140	3·3	1287	16·8	1427	12·1
Joseph Lue	1386	33·2	5243	68·6	6629	56·0
G. F. Cooke	414	9·9	827	10·8	1241	10·5
Informal	2242	53·6	289	3·8	2531	21·3
Bougainville South Open†						
Paul Lapun	3869	92·4	5866	76·4	9735	82·1
Andrew Komoro	300	7·2	1792	23·3	2092	17·6
Informal	20	0·5	17	0·2	37	0·3

* Excluding 302 postal and absentee ballots.
† Excluding 343 postal and absentee ballots.

CASH CROPS OR CARGO?

T. G. Harding and P. Lawrence

THE Madang-Sio team studied the 1968 campaigns in the southern Madang and northern Morobe Regional Electorates: on Karkar Island, and along the mainland coast and sub-coast between Sarang and Finschhafen (see map 6). From the point of view of the whole area, the interest of the election centred ultimately on the way in which the revision of electoral boundaries affected the development of a hitherto consistent political tradition. At the outset, we assumed that we should be able to present our findings as an integrated report, for geographical, socio-cultural, and historical reasons. The area was self-contained. Since contact with Europeans, its inhabitants had had substantially similar political experiences. Although belonging to separate Districts (Madang and Morobe), they responded fairly uniformly to colonial rule because of the stereotyped pressures on their homogeneous socio-cultural systems and trade network. Their emerging common political outlook was apparent during the 1964 campaign for the House of Assembly, the electoral boundaries for which are marked on map 7. Much of the Sio area was included in the first Rai Coast Open Electorate, which had close ties with the adjacent Madang Open. One local candidate campaigned in both these electorates and the people reacted consistently to generally similar political ideas (Harding 1965; Hughes and van der Veur 1965: 403). After 1967, however, the pattern changed. As a result of electoral redistribution, as can be seen

Material on the Kabwum Open and Morobe Regional electorates was collected and prepared by Professor Harding. Material on the southern Madang Regional was prepared by Professor Lawrence from reports on different parts of it by the remaining members of the team as listed in Appendix II. Team members worked independently and not as research assistants under specific direction. Hence they should share credit for this published account. The main fieldwork was carried out by the team during January-March 1968; Professor and Mrs Lawrence re-visited the Madang area for three weeks in August 1968. We are grateful for helpful comments from Mr M. Stevenson (University of Sydney) and Miss L. Hogg (London School of Economics), who worked in and near Madang during and after the election respectively.

by comparing maps 6 and 7, the old association between Madang and the western Rai Coast, on the one hand, and the eastern Rai Coast, on the other, was lost. The Madang District and the Morobe District (to which the eastern Rai Coast belonged) became discrete political regions—Regional electorates with their own component Open electorates, dynamics, and problems. Except marginally, the campaigns in those parts of the two Regional electorates studied, while endorsing the continuation of the common political outlook mentioned, developed along different lines.

We have, therefore, abandoned an integrated approach and present our material in four sections. First, we sketch the background to the 1968 election in the total area covered, giving data on population, geography, traditional socio-cultural systems, the trade network, and contact history until 1964, and stressing the broad similarity of indigenous political reactions until that date. Next, we describe separately the 1968 campaigns in those parts of the two Regional electorates covered: the southern Madang Regional and Kabwum Open, which was part of Morobe Regional. We conclude by summarising the similarities and differences between the two campaigns, and by showing how the 1967 electoral redistribution influenced them.

BACKGROUND TO THE ELECTION

The people of the total area number about 144,000, of whom some 94,000 inhabit what we have called the southern Madang Regional Electorate (consisting of Mabuso, Sumkar, and the Rai Coast Open Electorates) and some 50,000 Kabwum Open. In the past, partly because of their natural environment, they never achieved general political unity, but the similarity of their socio-cultural systems and the network of their trade ties always facilitated contact and, after the establishment of colonial rule, a gradually awakening sense of common interest expressed in cargo cult.

The mainland north-east coast is very rugged. It contains several mountain ranges bounded, to the south-west, by the Ramu River and, to the north-east, by the sea: the Adelberts, the Bagasin and Hansemann ranges, the Finisterres, the Saruwageds, and the Cromwells. West of the Ramu are the Bismarcks. The only flat land is on the coastal plain and in the Ramu Valley. Karkar has similar features: a coastal plain encircling a mountainous interior (see map 8). There are two seasons: the dry from about March to November and the wet from about November to March.

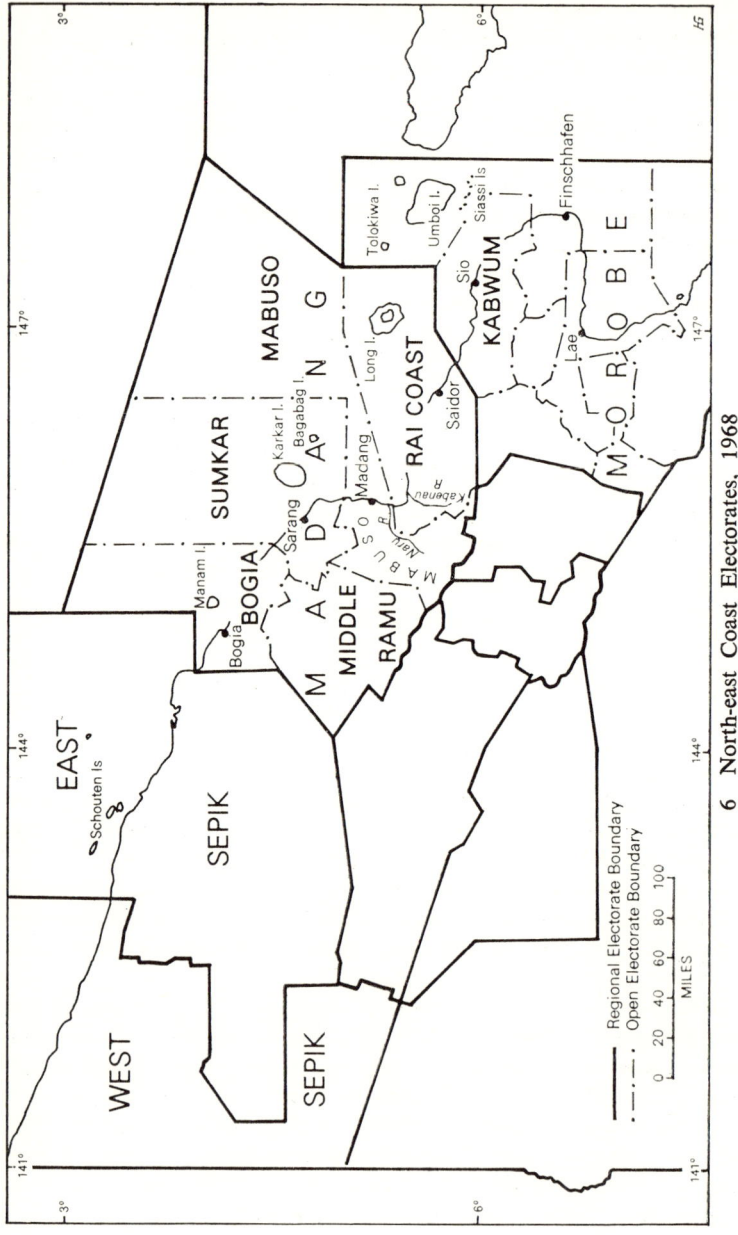

6 North-east Coast Electorates, 1968

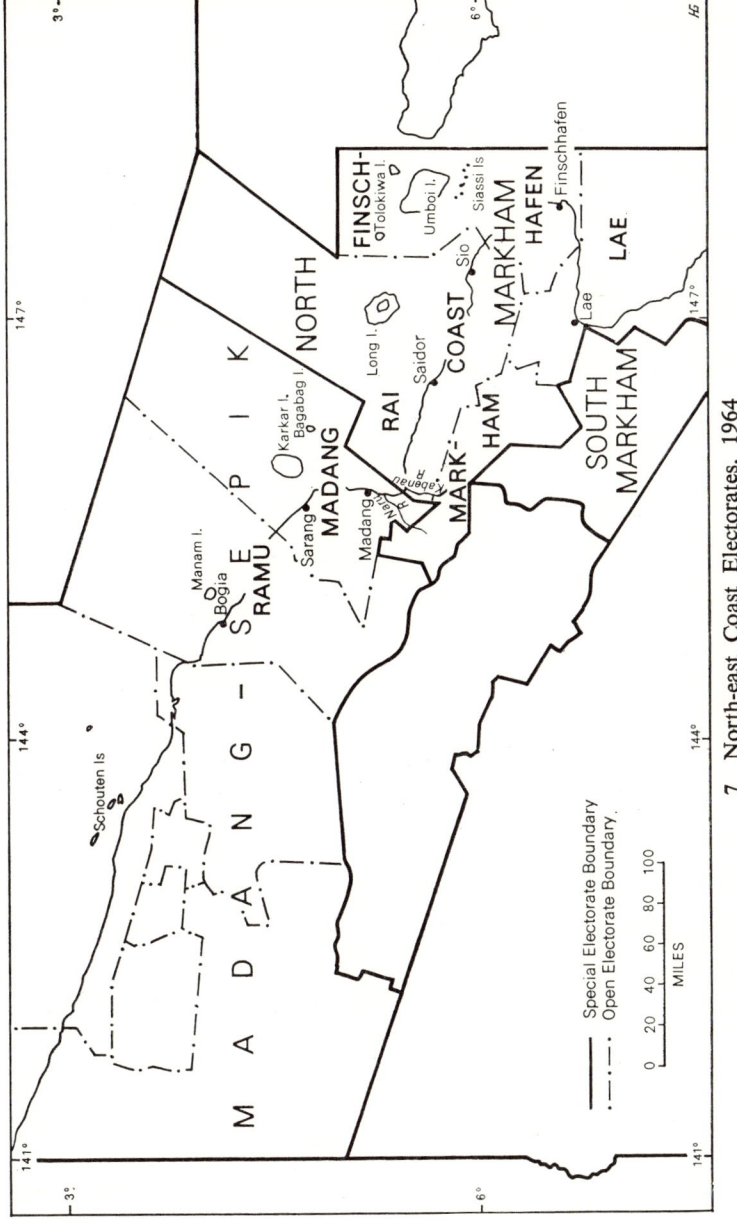

7 North-east Coast Electorates, 1964

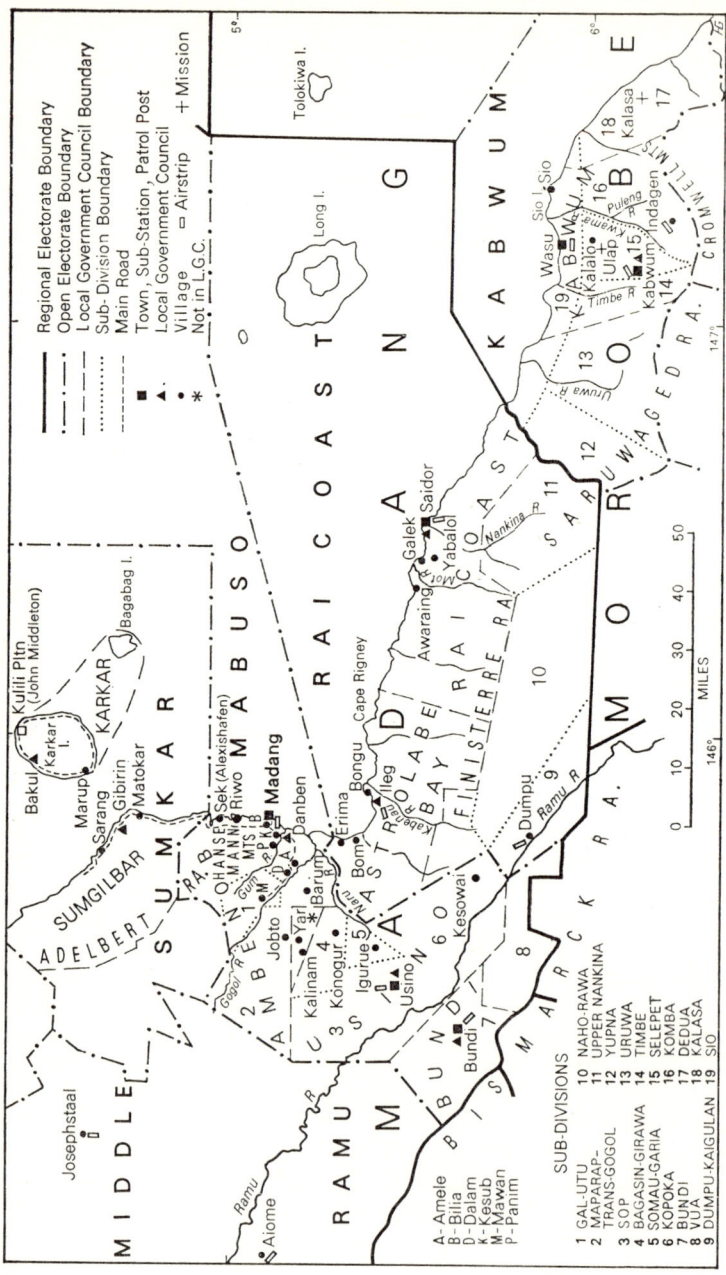

8 Madang District and Kabwum

The population can be divided initially into coastal dwellers and inland bushmen, who have always been mutually suspicious. The relatively sophisticated beachmen patronise bushmen but fear their sorcery. There is an unknown number of language groups ranging from 150 to over 11,000 speakers. Even in the case of the largest groups, traditional political horizons have always been, for most purposes, far narrower than those implied by today's national electorates, although trade relationships, as indicated, cut across linguistic borders and evoked wider interests. Yet, whatever their range, political groups, associations, and relationships invariably emphasised consensus of interest and outlook, and discouraged controversy. The ideal was always unanimity.

Except in the Bagasin Area, traditional societies are unilineal. Each language group consists of a number of major political and military units (phratries, bush or island groups, village confederacies, or tribes), divided into several named, exogamous patriclans and patrilineages. A man's allegiance is primarily to his major political group but can be extended beyond it by marriage, kinship, and trade ties. There are variants in the pattern. On the Rai Coast, inland from Saidor, there are systems of double unilineal descent (Lawrence 1965). There are differences in size, as already indicated: the language groups on Karkar, in the Sio hinterland, and inland at Bundi are bigger than elsewhere. The Bundi groups probably represent an extension of the eastern Highlands peoples (Read 1955; Berndt 1962; Salisbury 1962). They appear to be more aggressive than beachmen, with strong rivalry between patriclans and major political groups as a constant feature of their political life.

In the Bagasin Area, between the Gogol and Ramu, societies are cognatic. Descent is traced through all possible male and female links, so that the individual's politically most important group is a circle of close bilateral kin, affines, and exchange partners randomly dispersed throughout his locality and augmented by trade friends outside it. Periodic migration between settlements is necessitated by the haphazard distribution of people's land holdings resulting from a flexible system of acquisition from both patrilineal and matrilineal kin.

A coastal trade network reaches from the Huon Peninsula to west New Britain, Saidor, Madang, and Karkar, and is linked to ancillary routes running inland from the beach villages as far as the Bismarck Range. It knits the people into trade leagues, which ideally enjoin mutual protection, although too frequent contact can lead to bickering. The trade network has never had an automatic political role but, under certain conditions, despite occasional ruptures, it has provided a framework for wider association and communication. Especially, by fostering a sense of interdependence, it has helped to offset the distrust between beachmen and bushmen (Harding 1967a; Lawrence 1964/67: 26-8).

It is necessary to outline also the nature of traditional social values and religion. Social values are materialistic and egalitarian. Economic considerations dominate political life. Without fixed ranks, people see themselves as equal in status and access to basic resources: possessions are a prerequisite of social relationships, which exist only through the exchange of equivalent goods and services. Withdrawal of goods and services creates hostility and warfare. Religion, too, stresses materialism. The people believe that, in the beginning, local gods created the earth, human beings, and everything of socio-economic importance (food plants, animals, and artefacts). Spirits of the dead are not seen as creators but as guardians of their living descendants' interests (by protecting crops, providing help in hunting and war, and bringing gifts). To ensure economic success, man must harness the power of gods and spirits by means of ritual.

A century of contact on the north-east mainland coast has seen the growth of two distinct institutions: on the one hand, Western modernisation, the complex of economic, political, and educational development introduced by Europeans, and, on the other, the cargo movement, the people's own response to colonial rule.

The first European visitor was the Russian scientist Miklouho-Maclay, who settled at Bongu, and explored the coast from Madang to Sio, between 1871 and 1883. The area has been administered by Germany between 1884 and 1914, Australia between 1914 and 1942, Japan between 1942 and 1944, and Australia since 1944. In the southern Madang Regional, Madang is the administrative centre and there are stations at Bogia, Saidor, Josephstaal, Aiome, and Usino. In Kabwum Open, the administrative centre is Kabwum Station. There are four main Christian missions: Roman Catholics north of Madang, at Bundi, and in pockets on Karkar and inland from Saidor; Anglicans around Aiome; Seventh-Day Adventists in pockets around Madang; and Lutherans on Karkar and most of the mainland south and east of Madang to Finschhafen and Lae.

There are two main areas of economic development: the coast and the Ramu Valley. European economic development along the coast began in the 1880s with the plantation industry. Especially between Sarang and Cape Rigney, although far less from there towards Sio, much land was alienated to Europeans as freehold. Europeans and Chinese control the plantations, the trading and stevedoring concerns, and industries such as the tobacco factory, in Madang. Since the 1950s, the native economy has begun to progress. Along the coast, there are cash crops (copra, cocoa, and coffee), co-operative societies, village industries and trade stores, and launch and trucking services. There are native markets in Madang and other centres. One important venture is Namasu, the Lutheran-backed trading co-operative operating from Lae. Demarcation of native lands sponsored by the Administration and local government councils has enabled the owners to get bank loans for agricultural projects. Development has come to the Ramu Valley only since 1962 with the creation of the beef-cattle industry but already some indigenes, especially around Bundi, are keeping their own beasts. Coffee is planted in a few villages.

Along the whole Rai Coast, development is independent of the economic conditions of the towns. (We give details for Kabwum in a later section.) But between Astrolabe Bay and the Ramu, both European and native business enterprise is affected by the decline of Madang as a commercial centre. Before 1960, the town prospered as the airport for the Highlands, where there was rapid expansion, but since then has lost much of its trade to Lae, which has been linked to Goroka by a highway promoting relatively cheap motor transport. European and Chinese businessmen in Madang are seeking either their own road link with the Highlands or openings elsewhere. They cannot provide work for the increasing numbers of indigenes now being forced into the town by the population explosion in many parts of the Territory. In 1968, Madang's indigenous population was 7422, of whom about 6400 came from other Districts (the Sepik, the Highlands, and even Papua) or distant parts of the Madang District, and about 1,000 from villages near the town itself.

In the political field, virtually the whole area was under administration by 1942. After 1956, village headmen were gradually replaced by local government councils. In the southern Madang Regional, the only groups still under village headmen in 1968 were the people of Long Island, the upper Nankina villages on the Rai Coast, the Naho-Rawas and Dumpu-Kaigulans in the Ramu Valley, and five villages around Yar in the Bagasin Area. In Kabwum, some 5000 inland people were still under village headmen. In the first House of Assembly, after 1964, the area was represented as follows: the Madang-Sepik Special Electorate by Frank Martin of Wewak, the North Markham Special by H. R. ('Horrie') Niall of Lae, the Madang Open by Suguman Matibri of Karkar, the Rai Coast Open by Stoi Umut of the inland Sio region, and the South Markham Open by Gaudi Mirau of Lae, an immigrant Papuan (see also map 7).

Education aims to complement economic and political development. There are Administration and mission primary and secondary schools through the whole area, an Administration Teachers' College at Madang, and an Administration Technical School in the Gogol Valley, but few people have progressed to tertiary education, especially at the University in Port Moresby. Even so, those prominent in economic and political affairs are beginning to form a distinct indigenous élite. Karkar is noteworthy: before 1942 Lutheran education, and since 1945 Administration education, have had great success on the island, and its population is the most literate in the southern Madang Regional. Members of the élite speak English, while others speak only Pidgin and their own languages.

The cargo movement (Lawrence 1964/67; Harding 1967b) is based on traditional social values and religion. The people wanted cargo, first, because it was superior to its indigenous counterpart and, second, because it symbolised European-native relationships, which were based on the principle of superiority-inferiority and ignored the native ideal of equivalence. The acquisition of cargo would give them parity with Europeans or, in extreme cases, make it possible to drive them out with military weapons. They assumed that cargo was made by a deity who, in response to ritual honour, would send it to human beings via the spirits of the dead.

There have been many expressions of cargo cult between Karkar and Finschhafen. It was most elaborate in the southern Madang District, where it went through five stages of belief. The first two stages (1871-1914) were based on the belief that pagan deities made cargo. The third (1914-33) was based on Christianity: God was the cargo deity and conversion the avenue to the new wealth. After the 'failure' of Christianity, the fourth stage (1933-45) was based on pagan-Christian syncretism: indigenous gods were equated with God and Jesus Christ as cargo deities. The fifth stage began in 1948: it involved the rejection of Christianity and the belief that all pagan gods were cargo deities. The leader was Yali Singina of the Rai Coast, to whom the cargo deities were thought to have given special powers. By 1950, his influence (but not full control) reached from Bogia to Sio and into the sub-coast. By 1968, it had shrunk considerably. His career is traced later. Karkar had its own Christian-revisionist cult, the Kukuaik, after 1940. In the Sio region, cargo cult has taken Christian, Christian-revisionist, and pagan forms. The Sios came under Yali's influence after 1947 and experimented with a pagan cargo cult in 1959.

The spread of these beliefs between Madang and Finschhafen was facilitated by the trade network augmented by friendships made in the labour compounds, which provided means of communication, and by the similarity of religious belief and ritual, which made for ready understanding. Cargoism represented common popular attitudes towards, and interpretation of, colonial rule, especially in the politically crucial field of economic life. It enabled indigenous politicians to get a ready hearing throughout the whole area, as happened in the 1964 election. Yali, who stood in the first Rai Coast Open, campaigned around both Sio and Madang, and was associated with a cargoist program in both places. Although he won few first preferences at Sio because of local loyalties, he was greatly respected for his reputed religious powers (Harding 1965:204-5). In the Madang Open, although not a candidate, he received some 3000 informal votes from local cultists (Hughes and van der Veur 1965:403).[1] Again, Stoi Umut succeeded in the first Rai Coast Open by persuading the electors that his flourishing trade stores proved that he had unravelled the cargo secret (Harding 1965; see below on Kabwum). But in 1968, when the area had been cut in two, the western Rai Coast becoming part of the southern Madang Regional, and the eastern Rai Coast part of Kabwum Open and the Morobe Regional, there was far less correspondence between the campaigns in the two areas.

SOUTHERN MADANG

The Madang Regional Electorate contains five Open electorates. Of these, we studied only three, which, as already indicated, we have designated collectively the southern Madang Regional: Mabuso (population 35,477); Sumkar (population 29,690); and Rai Coast (population 29,133). We could not cover the other two Open electorates: Bogia (population 28,268) and Middle Ramu (population 28,993).

Before polling day, the Administration initiated two campaigns to inform the people about the election: the Political Education Campaign, and the Electoral Education and Polling Information Campaign. But, as far as possible, it encouraged the indigenous élite and even the candidates to implement both campaigns, so as to avoid accusations of manipulating the election and to teach the people to run their own political affairs.

The aim of the Political Education Campaign was to get people on the Electoral Roll and help them understand democratic processes, the meaning of voting, and the structure and powers of the House of Assembly. The campaign began in June and ended on 27 November 1967, the opening date for accepting nominations, so that it would not be confused with the candidates' election campaigns. Its management varied from the pattern of 1963-4, when Administration patrols

---

[1] The published total of informal votes was 3220, but of these some were cast in favour of Kaum of Kalinam, leader of the Bagasin Rebellion in 1944 (Lawrence 1964/67: 110-15). Kaum did not stand in the 1964 election.

carried oral instructions to the electors. Most reliance was placed on a series of twenty printed leaflets on government, prepared in English and Pidgin early in 1967 by the Department of District Administration, and on broadcasts from Radio Wewak based largely on these leaflets.

In the Madang District, 7000 leaflets were said to have been given to local government councillors to discuss in their wards, and to schools for pupils to read to their parents. In fact, numbers of leaflets did not reach councillors or schools, or remained unopened in council chambers. Some were in English and could not be understood. Some European officers explained them to councillors, while others handed them over without comment. Some leaflets were received and handed out only after 27 November. How much of their contents reached the non-literate villager in any form cannot be estimated: the level of awareness among even the most enlightened persons interviewed was elementary. Some councillors claimed to have read the leaflets consistently to their villagers, while others did not. Many leaflets were used for rolling cigarettes. Few villages away from the coast had radio sets. Although Administration patrols were supposed to take oral instruction to non-council areas, not all such places were visited, and those that were showed little evidence of it afterwards.

The aim of the Electoral Education and Polling Information Campaign was to tell voters the names and boundaries of the Regional and Open electorates, the names of the candidates in each electorate, and the dates, times, places, and procedures for polling. The Administration gave the job to the councillors and candidates, but did not always make it easy for them, certainly the councillors. Often the only authoritative information systematically reaching the councils was the stencilled schedule of polling dates and places. There must also have been some temptation, not only for candidates but also for councillors politically committed to one candidate or another, to hide or slant the truth. As will appear, although they had no *locus standi* for national electoral purposes, individual councillors, groups of councillors, and even whole councils often gave strong support to or endorsed the nominations of specific candidates. In fact, however, many candidates and councillors stifled partisanship and presented the information with impeccable neutrality.

No fewer than four political parties appeared in the Madang District in 1967 but only two put up candidates. The Territory Country Party, founded in Madang in July or August 1967, had faded away by the end of the year. A representative of the Christian (later United) Democratic Party visited a village north of Madang during 1967 but got little response. Only Pangu Pati and the All Peoples' Party (A.P.P.) got candidates to the polls: Pangu was represented by James Meangarum in Bogia Open, and the A.P.P. by Bruce Jephcott in Madang Regional, Jim McKinnon (its founder) in Middle Ramu Open, and Saramuri Sinamaiba in Mabuso Open. As we could not study Bogia and Middle Ramu, we cannot comment on Meangarum's and McKinnon's politics, but party allegiance influenced Jephcott and Saramuri so little that we present them in virtually the same way as the other candidates—as independents.

The dislike of most candidates for political parties was due mainly to shrewd assessment of the people's attitude. Many candidates asserted that the Territory could not yet cope with party sectionalism, but they were nearly all aware that most people were strongly opposed to a party system, partly because they did not know what parties were, partly because they wished to avoid the political conflict they imagined parties would promote, and partly because, after the stir caused by Pangu in 1967, they associated parties with immediate self-government or independence, which only the cargoists advocated, and which they assumed would bring an end to Australian administration, protection, and financial aid. Nevertheless, although parties played no part in the campaign, there was a set of formal, personal political alliances between different candidates in the Madang Regional and its component Open electorates. We describe these later on.

The candidates

We introduce the candidates in the four electorates studied in the order of their success at the polls. (For a full list, see table 5).

In Madang Regional the three candidates were all Europeans and stood for different aspects of modern economic development: Jason Garrett, large-scale urban and hinterland commercial interests; Bruce Jephcott, inland pastoral interests; and Edward Whitaker, small-scale urban and village commercial interests. During the campaign, Whitaker also became involved with the cargo movement.

Jason James Garrett (Pidgin, Garet), a Tasmanian aged 30 with four children, came to New Guinea in 1960 after an Anglican and Quaker education, obtained his surveyor's certificate, and built a substantial surveying business, becoming a member of the Madang Chamber of Commerce and various professional bodies. Enthusiastic and forceful, he rejected A.P.P. approaches in 1967 on the grounds that he opposed political parties at the present juncture. In his speeches, he favoured the development of indigenous as well as expatriate commercial enterprise and stressed the need for a road from Madang to the Highlands, not only to restore Madang's declining economy but also to open up timber lands between the Gogol and Ramu, which would help native business. He hoped to advance native enterprise also by subdividing land that was ownerless or which the owners were willing to sell into 50-acre blocks for farming and market gardening. To underpin this program, he advocated sending more native children to Australian schools, and establishing agricultural, forestry, and trade schools around Madang, which would also help relieve the problem of the unemployment of native youths in town. He favoured eventual independence after a period of limited home rule, and opposed measures likely to discourage Europeans from remaining in the Territory, such as pegging expatriate public servants' salaries or requiring expatriate business profits to be wholly reinvested in the Territory.

Bruce (Pidgin, Brus) Jephcott, 39, born in Melbourne and with a science degree from Adelaide, was married with three children. After working in the Eastern Highlands, he took up a 19,000-acre cattle station near Dumpu in the Ramu Valley in 1962. He failed in the South Markham Open Electorate in 1964 despite an energetic campaign in

TABLE 5—CANDIDATES: MADANG REGIONAL AND COMPONENT OPEN ELECTORATES

Electorate	Candidate
Madang Regional	J. J. Garrett
	B. Jephcott
	E. J. Whitaker
Bogia Open	J. Meangarum (P.P.)*
	R. Saretofa*
	L. Mondolau*
	J. Sakiap*
	J. Bareng*
	F. Nabura*
Middle Ramu Open	J. McKinnon (A.P.P.)*
	Walai Toba*
	Taptap*
Mabuso Open	Angmai Bilas
	Saramuri Sinamaiba (A.P.P.)
	Bato Bultin
	Togop Siburia
Sumkar Open	J. Middleton
	Kaki P. Angi
	Wadau Marun
Rai Coast Open	J. B. Poe
	Yali Singina
	Iaga Bakuk

P.P. = Pangu Pati
A.P.P. = All Peoples Party
* = Candidate not studied

which he visited many mountain villages on foot. In 1967, under McKinnon's influence, he allowed his name and candidature to be associated with the A.P.P. While endorsing its policies, he sensed the electorate's hostility to political parties and, like other candidates, stood virtually as an Independent. He was severely handicapped for at least two months by an injury in a riding accident. Viewing Madang mainly as an outlet for cattle exports rather than a commercial centre, he supported a road link to the Lae-Goroka Highway via the Naru River, Usino, and Dumpu, rather than a rival scheme for a developmental road to Mt Hagen via a route further north. Paternalistic but by no means unfriendly or unsympathetic, he held views on home rule (to begin about 1976) and independence similar to those of Garrett. He, too, hoped that Europeans—including his own descendants—would be wanted in New Guinea after independence.

Edward John Whitaker (Pidgin, Witika), a South Australian, a bachelor, born in 1929, held the Leaving Certificate and, at the age of 30, joined the Papua and New Guinea Administration as a Cadet Patrol Officer. In 1967, while in charge of Bion Corrective Institution near Madang, he resigned, criticising official policy towards prisoners. With the proceeds of a lottery win and with a native friend from the Sepik, Raphael Boivan, as partner, he operated a small business near Panim: two tourist buses, two trade stores, and various agencies. At one time he was prominent in several Madang public bodies, and he claimed to have close ties with local people through his trade stores. Cheerful and friendly, he regularly mixed with indigenes at the hotel in town where they drank.

In 1968, Whitaker stood without any party connections, Boivan acting as his campaign manager. His election leaflet emphasised five needs: a network of roads between Madang, administrative and mission stations, and villages; jetties in major coastal villages; schools to improve subsistence agriculture; greater Administration support for mission schools; and better liaison between local government councils and the House of Assembly. On other matters, in keeping with his closer business and leisure time association with the people, his stance was radical in comparison with those of Garrett and Jephcott. He advocated pegging expatriate public servants' salaries and compulsory reinvestment of overseas company profits in the Territory. Unlike Garrett, he saw no problem in the high unemployment rate among urban immigrants. Although he did not stress it in his speeches, so as not to alarm native opinion, he favoured home rule in 1970 and independence in 1972. He promised, if elected, to visit councils and mission stations every three months to hear complaints, which he would relay to the House of Assembly.

In Mabuso Open all four candidates were indigenes and supported Western modernisation, but stood for different regional interests: Angmai Bilas and Bato Bultin, the Madang coast and sub-coast; and Saramuri Sinamaiba and Togop Siburia, the Ramu-Bagasin area and Erima coast.

Angmai Bilas, 30, forceful, a Catholic married to a Lutheran, born near Madang, with three children in Catholic schools, was both a subsistence and a cash crop (copra and cocoa) farmer. He left secondary school after Standard VI, speaking English as well as Pidgin. After a year's training in Port Moresby in 1958-9, he worked for four years as a Co-operatives Inspector around Madang. From 1963, he represented his birthplace, Riwo, on Ambenob Council, of which he became vice-president in 1967, when he defeated Bato Bultin. Also in 1967, he became Chairman of the Stevedoring Committee of the Madang Workers' Association and, by 1968, was serving on the Madang District Business Advisory Council. Politically, he took the same line, although not always for the same reasons, as his running-mate Garrett: on the Madang-Highlands road, because it would bring business to Madang's new wharf; on land subdivision, and the work of the councils and Administration on land demarcation, which he thought would keep people in economically useless areas instead of encouraging them to look for more profitable holdings elsewhere; on opposition to early self-government; on the need to retain Europeans in the Territory; and on vocational schools for Madang. He urged strong measures against cargo cult, which he regarded as more dangerous than talk of self-government, and the establishment of more businesses to combat unemployment, which exacerbated the cult. Direct action would have to be taken by indigenes rather than Europeans, who would only be accused once again of trying to hide the cargo secret.

Saramuri Sinamaiba, about 50, from Usino, spoke Kopoka, Garia, and Pidgin, but no English. He was non-literate, despite a few years in mission school, a subsistence farmer just beginning to plant coffee, and a pagan, although he was a baptised and practising Lutheran until he saw the loose conduct of native mission helpers with local women. He had five children by four wives, two of whom were still living with him. As first president of the Usino Council in 1967, he was persuaded to stand by McKinnon of the A.P.P., which paid his nomination fee. Although respected in his own area (as shown by the voting figures), his horizons were narrower than those of the coastal candidates: he had no idea of Mabuso boundaries and thought in terms of the Usino Council Area; and, barely understanding A.P.P. policy, he concentrated on urging a road from the Ramu to Madang to help the marketing of locally grown coffee.

Bato Bultin, 37, slow-spoken, thoughtful, a Seventh-Day Adventist from Panim near Madang, attended and taught in the mission's school but no longer went to church as he rejected the Adventist ban on alcohol. He had six children, was a subsistence and cash crop (cocoa) farmer, knew English but preferred Pidgin or his own language, had visited Australia in 1963, and had served on Ambenob Council from 1959, as vice-president between 1964 and 1967. He was chairman of the Land Demarcation Committee in 1966 and 1967 and deputy commissioner of the Land Titles Commission after 1967. In the 1964 campaign for the House of Assembly, he ran Suguman Matibri very close. He considered joining Pangu, but refrained because of local feelings against parties and Pangu in particular. Politically, he stressed economic development but, like his political associate Whitaker, with concern for the village rather than for the modern District economy. He wanted higher prices for cash crops, higher wages, better local roads, better education, and more Australian aid. He called for localisation of the public service, and for training to fit New Guineans for self-government and independence, which he thought possible in 1978. He did not want the Territory to be Australia's Seventh State because its people would be treated as second class citizens. He was oppressed by the remoteness of Europeans and their world. Although he hoped Australians would stay behind as partners and tutors in modernisation, he believed that close personal association would be possible with only a few.

Togop Siburia was born in the Garia village Igurue near the Ramu about 1918.[2] He learnt to read and write Pidgin and Amele in the Lutheran village school. Although never baptised, he was a monogamist with four children. About 1945, he took a small Garia colony to Erima to start a modest copra and trading business, and become a labour supervisor on Erima Plantation. He was persuaded to nominate by the councillor of Igurue, who was concerned for Garia prestige, and ignored the warning of the officer in charge of Usino station that he might split the Ramu-Bagasin vote. He barely campaigned, although he was known to advocate economic development and the building of motor roads. We did not learn his views on self-government.

Of the three candidates in Sumkar Open, one European and one indigene (Middleton and Kaki Angi) stood for Western modernisation, and one indigene (Wadau Marun) was associated with the cargo movement.

John (Pidgin, Jon) Middleton was born in Sydney in 1938 but,

[2] Togop Siburia could not be interviewed. This profile is based on material gathered by Lawrence between 1949 and 1953, and Lawrence and Taylor in 1968.

apart from his years at school in Australia, had spent all his life on one of the five plantations owned by his family. Friendly and forthright, married with two children, he always had close ties with the island people, offering them casual work, and buying their copra and cocoa, whenever they needed cash. In 1964, he was defeated in the Madang-Sepik Special Electorate. In 1967, he brought his willingness to stand to the notice of Karkar Council, which agreed to support his nomination. He campaigned with the simple program of economic development, personal identification with New Guinea, and opposition to early self-government and independence. His candidature partly explained why the sitting Member, Suguman Matibri, did not seek re-election. Suguman knew and liked Middleton, and believed that he could not compete with him. He let it be known that, having served four years, he wanted time to develop his business interests. In any case, he probably would have had little success at the polls: during the first House, he did not travel widely in his electorate and the people regarded him as an unsatisfactory member.

Kaki Paul Angi, 36, with two children, easy-going and open, had a Catholic education interrupted by the war, was a catechist at Aronis, his natal village north of Madang, between 1954 and 1958, and thereafter became a subsistence and cash crop (copra and cocoa) farmer employing five workers. He was president of the local Legion of Mary between 1958 and 1961, president of Sumgilbar Council (except for a two-year break) since its proclamation in 1961, president of the local branch of the Savings and Loans Society, and a deputy commissioner of the Land Titles Commission. His decision to stand was personal. He nominated after Karkar Council had endorsed Middleton and Sumgilbar Council had failed to agree on a candidate. He did not campaign actively, relying on his reputation as council president, businessman, and kinsman. His 'roads and bridges' policy had some unusual elements: a railway system to open up the interior; stabilised prices for cash crops; land tenure conversion to individual titles; and the reversion of plantation and mission holdings, especially north of Madang, where alienation had been heavy, to original native owners.

Wadau Marun, about 50 with eight children, was also born north of Madang, in Matokar village, of a Catholic mother and Lutheran father. In 1963, he retired from the police as a Sergeant-Major after twenty-seven years' service, broken only by three years in the Australian Army during the Pacific War. He became a subsistence farmer. Dour and slow, he was much under the influence of Yali of the Rai Coast, his true sister's husband, who had prompted his wish to return to paganism. Wadau asserted that the District Commissioner had instructed him to stand. This was certainly untrue. It is probable that Yali persuaded him to do so. He gleaned his political views from Yali, whom he promised to support in the House of Assembly in a drive to have native lands restored to their original owners. He wanted early self-government lest New Guinea lag too far behind liberated British colonies. He did not discuss these matters with voters at large.

All candidates for Rai Coast Open were indigenes. John Poe and Iaga Bakuk stood for Western modernisation. Yali Singina had been leader of the cargo movement since the 1940s.

John (Pidgin, Jon) Baptist Poe, quick thinking, competent, was a rare phenomenon, a Papuan standing in a New Guinea electorate. Born in 1931 at Kairuku, he reached Standard VII at Yule Island Catholic School and entered the Public Service. After clerical duties at Aiome, he came to Saidor in 1963 as storeman-clerk, postal assistant, and radio operator. He organised air charters and the Native Club and, after 1966, represented Saidor Station on the council when it became multi-racial. He was married with three children. He nominated with the support of twenty-nine of thirty-two Rai Coast councillors, who regarded him as the best available politician to achieve their aim of defeating Yali, the cargo leader. He spoke good English, Pidgin, and Police Motu, and thus would be able to understand immediately all business in the house. As a former public servant, he understood the machinery of the Administration and could deal with Europeans with a measure of equality. He was a good safeguard against splitting the anti-cargoist vote. As a Papuan, he stood above possible regional or sectional rivalries. He advocated cash crops (European vegetables and coffee) and building roads, especially to villages which had renounced cargo cult for business enterprise, as proof that the Administration would help those who supported it. He also hoped to operate a launch with which to transport cash crops to Madang. Encouraged by responses at his meetings, he opposed the formation of political parties and immediate self-government which would mean a return to ancestral warfare.

Yali Singina was well known for his leadership of the cargo movement (Lawrence 1964/67), the resurgence of which was the most dramatic feature of the 1968 campaign in the southern Madang Regional. Born at Sor village, inland from Saidor, about 1912, pagan, non-literate, a member of no party, but a charismatic figure despite his age, at the time of the election he had four wives: three from the Rai Coast and one (the most important in this context) from Matokar, true sister of Wadau Marun. He belonged to the Saidor Native Club and represented the Yabalol (Sor-Paramus) ward on the Rai Coast Council since its proclamation in 1964, serving as President between 1964 and 1966.

To explain Yali's role in the 1968 campaign, it is necessary to refer to his earlier career. After long and loyal service to Europeans, as *tultul* (1931), policeman (1936), and soldier (1943), he came home as a Sergeant-Major in 1945. His wartime and post-war career has been documented elsewhere (Lawrence 1964/67): his military training in Queensland; his support of the Administration after the war; and his entanglement with the cargo movement in 1948. Three incidents must be recapitulated. First, he escaped from the raid on Hollandia in 1944. Madang indigenes believed that the Japanese had killed him and that he had returned as a spirit of the dead with superhuman powers from God or the local deities. Second, he believed that, when he joined the Australian Army in Brisbane in 1943, an Administration officer had promised to reward loyal natives with a higher standard of living—bulk supplies of cargo. After the war, he relayed this message to his people and was responsible for a great change in their attitude towards Europeans. When he was summoned to Port Moresby in 1947, he assumed that he would be given this reward. Inevitably, he was disillusioned and became bitter, especially towards the missionaries, whom he accused of having hidden the cargo secret. Third, back on the Rai Coast in 1948, he called for a return to paganism and unwittingly inspired a new cargo belief.

It was held by many that a Madang deity, Manup, had invented cargo, failed to give it to New Guineans, and had journeyed to Sydney, where he had given it to Europeans. Wanting to benefit his own people, Manup was reborn as Jesus Christ, intending to return with the missionaries. But, to keep the cargo secret in Australia, he was crucified and kept prisoner in Heaven (near or above Sydney). Before the war, the Catholic mission had sent native artefacts, including statues of the pagan gods, to the Lateran Museum in Rome. In 1944-5, Yali visited the Queensland Museum in Brisbane, where he saw statues of New Guinea deities. It was claimed that he had found 'Rome' in Australia, where the missionaries had hidden the pagan gods, whom they had stolen and whom now Jesus-Manup had taught to make cargo. As noted in an earlier context, the old gods had given Yali special powers and, if he could reintroduce traditional religion, they would send cargo.

This led to a violently anti-Christian cult. Yali spent five years in gaol after 1950 for deprivation of liberty and incitement to rape. After his release, his cargo activities seemed to wane (Lawrence 1964/67: 267-8; 1967: 274-5) but, in retrospect, this view has proved naive. He secretly promoted the cult, especially between Bogati and Sarang, and told the people to regard him as 'king', pay him 'taxes', and send him women and gifts of pigs. Despite the contraction of his influence—which, in the southern Madang Regional, was reduced to hard-core followings around Sarang and Madang, in the belt between Bogati and Dumpu, and around a number of villages on the Rai Coast—he was still a political force. This was demonstrated in the 1964 election by the 3,000 informal votes he received in the Madang Open.

In 1968, Yali's program was equally bizarre. He nominated with the backing of three of the thirty-two Rai Coast councillors and thirteen of the nineteen Astrolabe Bay councillors. His most vocal and able supporter was Councillor Dui of Awaraing, who became his campaign manager and shared his assumption that he would be automatically returned. Dui's motivation was twofold. First, he was convinced of Yali's special powers from the cargo deities. Second, a natural orator, he often served as official mouthpiece for Yali, who was ageing and did not always explain his points clearly. He hoped thereby to further his own ambitions as a leader.

Yali's program had two levels. In front of Europeans he said that, if elected, he would make the Administration hand over the reward promised in 1943 and explain why it imprisoned him in 1950. He would demand better payment for cash crops and have factories built so that the people could learn the truth about cargo by producing it themselves. He wanted immediate self-government: Papua could remain part of Australia if it wished, but New Guinea would elect him as its king. He would seek advice from friends in Australia, America, Russia, and China,[3] and allow European officials to remain if they co-operated. But at the end of his campaign, he modified his position: realising the electors' hostility to immediate self-government, he hinted that he would implement it only in easy stages.

There was, however, another essentially cargoist platform attributed to Yali. He rarely enunciated it in front of Europeans but often alluded to it in public. When it was discussed in his presence, he invariably acquiesced. The new doctrine arose from a curious coincidence. In 1963, apart from educating the people about the new parliament, the Administration asked them to send artefacts to the Anthropological Museum on the lower ground floor of the House of Assembly. During and after the 1964 campaign, ideas began to emerge which were a continuation of the fifth (pagan) cargo belief already described. The Administration, by buying artefacts, like the Catholic mission before the war, had stolen the local gods (the cargo deities) and hidden them in the Museum, which was a cult house.[4] Should Yali be returned to the House, he would liberate the deities, who would then send cargo to the people. After his defeat, villagers near Madang raised money with which to build him his own 'House of Assembly' and cult house so that he could do this without having to go to Port Moresby. (Even

[3] Whom he claimed, somewhat vaguely, to have met during the war.
[4] For the cult house, see Lawrence (1964/67: 15-26; 1965).

people who did not hold these beliefs assumed that the purpose of the House was immediately, in some undefined way, to give them a higher standard of living.)

Between 1964 and 1968, these ideas were elaborated and spread to adherents of the cargo movement, especially around Madang. In 1967, a delegate from Kesub, a Yali stronghold near the River Gum, told the Select Committee on Constitutional Development that the people opposed elections as a waste of time, and wanted Yali to be their king and proclaim immediate self-government. Later in 1967, a group from Kesub and other villages took $300 to the District Office, hoping to buy Yali his seat in the House and so avoid an election. Twice rebuffed, the cargoists campaigned vigorously to win votes for Yali. Only Yali should go to the House, for only he could confront the Administration and free the cargo deities. So far Europeans had cheated the people by giving previous native members, who were too young and timid to rebel, spurious book learning. The European Speaker, H. R. Niall, had kept charge of the Mace, the Tamberan, the source of superhuman power.[5] Whoever controlled it, controlled the cargo deities in the House. But Yali was unafraid and old in European guile. He had *paua*—power from the local gods[6]—and would give the people *lo*,[7] a new way of life, including the European wealth they wanted. In the past, he could not use his power to the full, but this would be the culmination of his career as cargo leader. He would go to Port Moresby and do what no native Member had yet done: 'open the door' of the House of Assembly. This was the meaning of the term 'Rai Coast Open Electorate'. He would enter the House of Assembly—which either was a cult house or had a cult house (the Museum) attached—and, as Anthony Voutas would defeat H. R. Niall (the incumbent Speaker) in the Morobe Regional Electorate, Yali would occupy the Speaker's Chair, take possession of the Mace, be proclaimed king, and announce self-government. He would then die a second death and, as a superspirit, find the cargo secret in a special room. He would then free the deities, so that they could give the people wealth, and take the Mace

---

[5] In the southern Madang District, the Pidgin word *tamberan* means a spirit of the dead, and *haus tamberan* a cult house. By derivation, Tamberan in a general sense means anything that controls the cult house and the spirit-beings associated with it. In this instance, it was the Mace.

[6] As was claimed also at Sio in 1964 (Harding 1965: 205). For the genesis of the belief, see Lawrence (1964/67: 206).

[7] The Pidgin word *lo* is elusive and has obviously changed its meaning in the last decade. At the present time, it appears to mean 'the full way of life, including cargo'. Lawrence (1967: 274n.1) unjustifiably discounts this interpretation by Hughes and van der Veur (Bettison *et al* 1965: 403). Even so, the word probably derives from the English word 'law' rather than an indigenous word, as they suggest.

back to Madang and the Rai Coast as a perpetual guarantee of the millennium.

Iaga Bakuk, 36, married with six children, was born in Erima, although his father was an immigrant Sepik labourer. He was cook-boy for Yali from 1945-9 and visited Madang in 1950, when Yali was on trial. In 1951, he joined the Pacific Islands Regiment, retiring as a Warrant Officer, Second Class, in 1966. In the army, he learnt to read and write Pidgin, and a little English. He had forgotten much of the Erima language, and professed neither paganism nor Christianity. After two visits to Australia, where he saw Europeans working in various factories and on a farm, he became an adamant opponent of the cargo movement. He left the army partly to help his village attain a European way of life. He opened a trade store, bought a boat, planted coconuts, and grazed ten cows. A similar motive prompted him to nominate. He had visited the first House of Assembly while in the army. He told electors that there was no cargo inside it, and clearly described its role as a place for debate between natives and Europeans, who could then advise the Administration. He explained the meaning of the Mace as a symbol of authority *(dispela sitik emi bos)* (literally, 'this stick is boss').[8] He advocated economic co-operation with white men. He was almost entirely rejected by the people of his locality, who openly supported Yali. They disbelieved his anti-cargoist propaganda, sneering at him as 'the P.I.R. man' *(man bilong P.I.R.)*, 'white man's puppet' *(man bilong wetman)*, and simply 'bighead' *(bighet)*. Also, his father's immigrant status could always be held against him.

The campaign

The emergence of the Madang District as a discrete political region in 1968 was nowhere more apparent than in the system of alliances whereby each Regional candidate teamed with candidates in some of the Open electorates (see table 6). Team-mates were expected to provide each other with material assistance and speak for each other at meetings. One team (Team 2) was recruited technically on the basis of party (A.P.P.) allegiance. But, generally speaking, all alliances were personal associations between individuals who felt they had common political views and aspirations. No team anticipated serving any interest wider than that of the District, but all claimed that, if returned to the House, they would act as pressure groups, speaking with one voice to make sure that the District's needs were really heard.

---

[8] Although we have no evidence, it is possible that Iaga's statement suggested to Yali that the Mace was the *Tamberan*, the source of European superhuman power. Yali habitually draws from a common pool of ideas.

No team had effective liaison with politicians in other Districts, although, as will be seen, McKinnon made gestures of support for a Morobe Regional and a Kabwum Open candidate.

Both European and indigenous candidates were important in the alliances. The Europeans, with greater understanding of Western political procedure, took the initiative in organising them, and probably were responsible for the outward cast of some major policy statements and the printing of leaflets. They also provided transport (aircraft, cars, and launches). Indigenous candidates contributed many basic facts and ideas from which policies were forged. Above all, they sometimes helped their European associates to meet at least a few of the indigenous voters in a more relaxed manner than might otherwise have been possible. By the same token, they treated the alliances in a typically Melanesian fashion, fraternising with members of other teams and thereby puzzling the Europeans, who (except for Middleton, possibly because of his close ties with the people from childhood) thought in terms of exclusive groups—miniature parties on the Australian model.

The campaign in the southern Madang Regional was conducted with generally good manners as long as no controversial issue was introduced. Few of the candidates visited more than a fraction of the voters outside their own localities or the main centres, largely because of the difficulty of travelling through rugged country during the rainy

TABLE 6—CAMPAIGN TEAMS: MADANG REGIONAL AND OPEN ELECTORATES

Electorate	Team 1	Team 2	Team 3
Madang Regional	Garrett	Jephcott (A.P.P.)	Whitaker
Bogia Open	Saretofa	Bareng	——
Middle Ramu Open	Walai	McKinnon	——
Mabuso Open	Angmai	Saramuri (A.P.P.)	Bato
Sumkar Open	Middleton	——	Wadau (Kaki)
Rai Coast Open	Poe	——	Yali

season. Usually a Regional candidate—with his team-mate in the relevant Open electorate and any others who were at hand—travelled by car, aircraft, or boat to the bigger villages, sub-stations, mission centres, and councils, synchronising where possible with local gatherings such as council meetings. By covering most important places in this way, they hoped to reach influential people who would relay the talk to their own villages. Jephcott, however, visited only two or three coastal places and concentrated, despite his injury, on a campaign on foot down the lower Ramu Valley. Whitaker sent a house servant and his campaign manager inland to Konogur.

In the Open electorates, indigenous candidates generally walked around their own areas, especially where they had personal contacts. Angmai, Bato, and Yali were active also around Madang, and travelled more widely than their rivals. Kaki and Wadau barely campaigned in their home areas: Kaki visited Karkar twice; and Wadau addressed Sumkar labourers at Goroka and went to Karkar, where he called at several villages but spoke little. Middleton campaigned extensively on Karkar, and made short forays to mainland bush villages and sent out assistants from Karkar Council with tape-recorded messages. Four candidates relied on council support: Middleton was endorsed by Karkar Council; John Poe was strongly supported by most Rai Coast councillors; Yali was supported by over half the Astrolabe Bay councillors; and Kaki felt assured of the backing of Sumgilbar Council.

Apart from their individual policy proposals, most candidates followed a uniform pattern in their speeches. They gave electoral information: names and boundaries of electorates; the difference between Regional and Open electorates; names of candidates; and voting procedures. They generally included a long section on economic development. Those who opposed parties and self-government openly said so. Except for Yali until the end of his campaign, those who had other views prudently avoided these subjects, knowing the voters' fears. Most candidates stressed that they would tour their electorates more regularly than their predecessors, whom the people rarely saw and therefore distrusted. There were differences in personal style. Garrett spoke forcefully. Jephcott's frank personality easily won him friends. Whitaker spoke idiomatic Pidgin with considerable charm. Angmai and Poe were the most effective indigenous orators. All candidates (except, apparently, Togop and Iaga) had their own election leaflets and photographs, but only Whitaker used his leaflets to set out his policy. Team-mates issued joint photographs. Garrett and Jephcott posted large voting signs on trees, houses, and trucks. Garrett used a polaroid camera to give children instant snapshots at meetings, and he and Whitaker gave out T-shirts with their propaganda printed on them. Also Garrett, Whitaker, and Angmai gave out key-rings or badges inscribed with their slogans.

To this extent, by European standards, most candidates behaved with moderation. The sophisticated Madang view was that a man, having paid his $50 deposit, should be given a fair hearing and not be attacked either behind his back or to his face in public. People should listen to all candidates and then make up their minds. Whitaker, Jephcott, the Sumkar candidates, Saramuri, Bato, and Togop held to this principle, which led, especially in Sumkar, to the fraternisation between the teams mentioned. Kaki, while still technically allied to Whitaker (see p. 187), said openly that he would be happy to see Middleton (his own and Whitaker's opponent) win and helped him with transport on the mainland. Middleton publicly praised Kaki, and provided both him and Wadau with his own transport both to and on Karkar. Wadau spoke fairly about Middleton and Kaki in Goroka. Bato, although his long-standing political rival, nearly always spoke well of 'my friend Angmai'.

This comparative restraint, however, was possible only when candidates campaigned as individuals. It was shattered when they became involved in the main political issue on the mainland (although not on Karkar, which was barely affected): the struggle between the cargo movement and Western modernisation, which was made bitter by vituperation and even intimidation. From the very beginning, this issue caused widespread attention: there can have been few people in the southern Madang Regional who were unaware of it or did not feel that they had to make up their minds about it. It was the major topic of conversation among both indigenes and Europeans. Yet, before polling day, it was impossible for us as observers to assess the potential voting strength of the two sides. As will be seen, the cargoists under Yali's leadership made a great show of strength, holding the biggest meetings of the whole campaign, especially in coastal Mabuso and the western Rai Coast. As their opponents never assembled in comparable numbers, it seemed to us at the outset that the cargoists might represent the majority. This proved wrong. Without the voting figures as a guide, we did not realise the extent to which Yali's influence had waned: that (as already mentioned) he could claim hard core followings only around Sarang and Madang, between Bogati and Dumpu, and around a number of Rai Coast villages. At first, we observed his and his supporters' activities only near Madang and Bogati. Hence, like other Europeans, we were duly impressed. But when some of us began to work away from Madang and Bogati (especially along the north coast road and near Saidor), we began to realise that the cargoists had far less support in outlying areas than they boasted and we had supposed. In the event, the cargoists were clearly defeated at the polls. This does not diminish their importance. They emerged as a phenomenon to which we are daily growing accustomed in Western society: a minority sufficiently large and vociferous to make their presence felt. Throughout the whole campaign, it was they who called the tune.

The struggle between the cargo movement and Western modernisation developed around the teams of Garrett and Whitaker. Thus it is important to note how they were formed. By early September 1967, both Garrett and Whitaker had let it be known that they would stand and had decided to seek running-mates in the Open electorates. Garrett had already met the Ambenob councillors, won President Liwa's backing, and approached Angmai, whom he recognised as a dynamic younger politician. With his considerable skill in organisation, he soon added Middleton in Sumkar, Walai in the Middle Ramu, Robin Saretofa in Bogia, and John Poe in the Rai Coast. In Mabuso, Whitaker had teamed with Bato, whom he rightly regarded as a politician of experience and skill, having proved himself on Ambenob Council and in the 1964 election, and who lived near himself at Panim. But, in the other electorates, he was at a loss to find running-mates with modern skills. In Sumkar, he claimed an alliance with Kaki, but it was uncertain from the start and, in the Rai Coast Open, Poe had rejected his approaches in November 1967, when he addressed the council at Saidor. In the Rai Coast Open, he was left with the alternatives of Iaga Bakuk, little known and less supported, and Yali, a controversial figure to say the least. On 5 January 1968, after some apparent hesitation, he chose Yali, who, with Dui, was visiting Madang to campaign among Rai Coast labourers there, and around Bogati and Dumpu in his own electorate. He hoped to win the support of the cargoists, whose strength he over-estimated, even more than other Europeans, as two-thirds of the Rai Coast Open and a third of Mabuso voters. He believed that he would be able to restrain Yali from cargoist excesses in the House.

The alliance was irresponsible. It embarrassed Whitaker's other running-mates, Kaki and Bato, who were men of considerable achievement, as it coupled their names with cargoism. They ceased to support him, Kaki making a deliberate gesture of rejection and Bato making his position clear by his behaviour on the council. This is best described by tracing events in the Madang-Bogati area between 9 and 18 January.

On the morning of 9 January, Yali visited Matokar and brought Wadau into Whitaker's team. Kaki is said to have withdrawn in anger and torn down the joint photographs Whitaker had displayed. On the evening of the same day, Whitaker held a public meeting at the Native Club in Madang, at which he announced his alliance with Yali. About 1000 people, mainly Yali supporters, attended.

Dui spoke first but did no more than to tell the hundred Rai Coast people present to vote for Yali in the Rai Coast Open and Whitaker in the Madang Regional. Yali then gave a long and irrelevant speech about his wartime experiences and inner knowledge of European secrets. He was followed by Bato, who was the most important speaker.

Bato believed that the issue at stake was not mere adulation of a cargo leader but the outcome of the election in Mabuso Open. With courage and impartiality in the face of an unsympathetic audience, he expounded the implications of Yali's visit and Whitaker's decision: the stimulus to what became known as the 'Yali vote' outside the Rai Coast Open Electorate. If Yali's supporters around Madang now acted as they did in 1964, when some 3000 of them voted invalidly for him, they would seriously falsify the results of the poll because their potential votes would be lost to the legitimate candidates—including himself, who might well have been defeated by Suguman in 1964 for that very reason. Hence he told the audience that they must vote properly: Rai Coast electors for Yali, Poe, or Iaga; and Mabuso electors for their duly nominated candidates. If Mabuso people voted for Yali, their ballot papers would be useless and must be burnt. He then discussed his own policy, and praised Whitaker for his friendliness, ability to mix with indigenes, and understanding of their worries. Whitaker then spoke briefly about his own policy and threw the meeting open for discussion.

Bato's anxiety about the Yali vote seemed fully justified. Six of the nine speakers from the floor—all registered Mabuso voters—firmly announced that they did not acknowledge any separation between Madang and the Rai Coast, which were 'one place'. Yali was as much a Madang as a Rai Coast man, and they would vote only for him. Whitaker and Dui tried to explain that this was impossible in view of the electoral boundaries, but the speakers were intransigent.

If any doubts about the audience's mood remained, they were dispelled at a second meeting of cargoists held that night at Kesub, where Yali was staying in a new house built specially for his visit. Several Europeans were present. It now became clear that Yali's true platform was the new cargo belief already described. The atmosphere was one of intense expectation. Yali was the first to speak. He told the people to vote for Whitaker and Bato, even though Bato was a mere boy who had no 'power' *(paua)* and had not been to the war, whereas he himself was a spirit of the dead. But the Administration and not he had drawn the electoral boundaries, which they must therefore accept.

There was more discussion. Again the audience expressed contempt for the electoral boundaries and determination to vote for Yali. Although Europeans were present, speakers began to allude to cargo and the current belief about the House of Assembly. They reminded Yali that they had willingly paid his 'taxes', and given him pigs and food. Now he had to repay them by sending the reward for which they had waited so long. They would vote for him, in spite of the electoral boundaries, so that he could not claim that they had deserted him and he would have to fulfil his obligations. Dui replied to all these comments in a highly allusive speech. The people must be patient. Only Yali could 'open the door' of the House and establish self-government. On the Rai Coast, it was being asked: 'What is this *Tamberan* (Mace) and what else is there in the House of Assembly?' They were going to try Yali. If he failed, they would discard him. Yali then asked the people if they wanted self-government in 1968. Their approval was unanimous.

The two meetings encouraged rather than killed the 'Yali vote' in Mabuso. A letter was sent to Usino urging the council to support Yali as their only candidate. On 10 January, Yali and Dui travelled to Bom, a coastal village near Bogati. The large audience applauded Yali's promise of early self-government, an end to periodic elections, and the installation of himself as King of New Guinea. Once again, Dui's speech had an obvious cargo message. He stated that Europeans were not rich through business *('wetman ino kamap long biladi bisnis')*. By producing copra, people would get a little money. The real secret was 'power', which the missions had stolen from them but Yali had retained. Yali would 'open the door' of the House of Assembly, take possession of the *Tamberan,* and reveal the truth. At the close of the meeting, as people shook hands with Yali, they contributed $100 in 'taxes'.

From Bom, Yali and Dui went to Dumpu, and then back to Madang. On the night of 18 January, at least 1000 people (many of them cargoists) attended a second gathering at Kesub in Yali's honour. About $300 were raised in 'taxes'. It was now assumed that most people around Madang would 'vote Yali'. Even Dui, flushed with Yali's apparent popularity, admitted that he no longer urged Mabuso people to vote for Bato. He argued that one of the green leaflets told the people to vote for the person of their choice. Yali was their choice. During the evening, Yali was presented with a gift of food and reminded again of the return he was expected to make. The ceremony closed with an old man, Lemab of Silibob, crying out: 'Yali and Whitaker, there is no place for you here now. Tomorrow you must go and open this House of Assembly. You two must dismantle this cult house *(haus tamberan)* of the white men. You two must bring it back to Madang'.

There were immediate administrative and political repercussions to these events. The District Office now treated the 'Yali vote' in Mabuso as a problem demanding special electoral techniques. At a briefing session in the first week of February, the Regional Returning Officer instructed his staff that persons, other than electors in the Rai Coast

Open, wishing to 'vote Yali' should be told twice that it was useless. If they still insisted, the officer should simply write Yali's name on the ballot paper and let it go at that.

Politically, the campaign became more ruthless. Around Madang, the issue now was 'vote Madang' versus 'vote Yali'. The former was to vote for Garrett, and Angmai or Bato indifferently, and the latter for Yali, Whitaker, and the cargo movement. The anti-cargoist Ambenob and Rai Coast councillors, and Garrett, Angmai, and Poe were determined to defeat Yali. President Liwa of Ambenob warned that Mabuso votes cast for Yali would be burnt. He did not openly support either Angmai or Bato but appealed explicitly for coastal solidarity against the inlanders. The 'Yali vote' could help only the bush candidates (Saramuri and Togop), who did not understand coastal problems. On 9 January, the council's Executive Committee, including Bato (although he intended to go to the meeting at the Native Club the same evening), unanimously recommended council support for only Garrett in the Regional and the return of gifts (T-shirts and badges) sent by Whitaker for distribution. Although on 10 January the full meeting of the council rejected the motion, Whitaker's gifts were in fact returned. Bato refused to change his original vote. Incensed by the threat to his electoral hopes and the disparagement of his 'youth' at Kesub, he publicly disassociated himself from Yali even at the cost of his alliance with Whitaker. From now on, he seemed virtually certain to withdraw from the campaign.

There were other moves to counter the 'Yali vote'. Liwa and a Lutheran schoolteacher addressed two meetings after church. The Rai Coast Council sent a representative to support Ambenob Council's stand. Garrett, Angmai, and Poe consistently attacked Yali and Whitaker at Madang and on the Rai Coast: Yali was the bane of the District, the spurious 'king' who had cheated the people for twenty-three years, who had never fulfilled his promises but took their money in 'taxes'. Yali and his lackey Whitaker wanted to ruin the country with immediate self-government. Whitaker's mixing with indigenous people at the hotel was mere ingratiation, and his business achievement slight in comparison with Garrett's. Even Jephcott was attacked after his successful campaign on Karkar. Garrett, afraid that he might lose votes and improve Whitaker's position, revisited the island and with the support of a local European planter, belittled Jephcott as a mere 'cattleman' who could do the people no good. As a result, several Karkar councillors, who had been impressed by Jephcott, now changed their allegiance and campaigned for Garrett in the more inaccessible mountain villages.

Whitaker's and Yali's counter-attack was ineffective. Whitaker several times accused Garrett obliquely of trying to rob villagers of their land through his proposals for 50-acre allotments. Some Madang, Sarang, and Rai Coast people asserted that Yali was being maligned: it was he, after all, who had brought development to the District after 1945, forcing the Administration to introduce co-operatives, councils, and schools.[9] The most positive reaction came from Dui. He told Rai Coast people slow to attend his meetings that the officer in charge at Saidor had sent him to order them to vote for Yali, who, when elected, would imprison Poe's supporters in Australia, confiscating their land and coconut groves as his own property. European houses would miraculously replace the bush huts of Yali's loyal supporters. If Galek people voted for Poe, they must return to Yali the pigs, food, and valuables he had laid out for them at a feast. When the River Mot burst its banks and devastated a wide stretch of land, Dui claimed that Yali had caused this with his 'power' from the gods, to punish those villages affected for voting for Poe.

The situation was complicated when the police charged Whitaker with misappropriating Administration property while Governor of Bion Corrective Institution. Apparently the investigation began long before he announced his electoral intentions. Although the case came before the court only after the election, during the campaign the police brought him in to headquarters for questioning and conducted an inquiry among people living along the road where he had his store. Indigenous policemen appear to have leaked the information about the charges around Madang. We assess the influence of this incident, and of the personal recrimination between cargoist and anti-cargoist candidates, on voting later. Broadly speaking, although it caused Whitaker anxiety and embarrassment, it did not seriously affect the election in the southern Madang Regional. By polling day, news of it had spread through the region between Madang and Sarang, but not to Bogati, Saidor, or the Bagasin Area. As far as could be ascertained, his political opponents did not refer to it in public.

The voting pattern

The results of the polls in the Madang Regional and its five Open electorates are set out in table 10 on p. 216. They can be analysed from two broad points of view: the candidates' own forecasts of their chances in comparison with actual returns; and the politics of voting.

[9] This was a common, erroneous belief associated with Yali's Rai Coast Rehabilitation Scheme, especially his appointment of village 'boss boys' in 1947, who were mistakenly assumed to be the first 'councillors' (Lawrence 1964/67: 141-65).

Most candidates in the four electorates studied were prepared to estimate the voting pattern, although they stressed the guesswork involved because of their lack of contact with electors. In the Madang Regional, Garrett (the winner) expected about 26,000 votes, with a minimum of 21,000 and a possible maximum of 30,000. With a final total (on the second count) of 23,426, this was a fairly realistic assessment, despite some errors about particular areas, which tended to cancel each other out. He forecast his easy win in the Sumkar section of the Regional but overstressed his predominance in Bogia, where he defeated Whitaker by only 3682 to 3190. He underestimated his chances against Jephcott in the Middle Ramu (2368 to 5404) but won outright in Mabuso, where he had expected to carry only Bundi. In the Rai Coast section, which he considered unpredictable, his successes closely corresponded with those of his ally John Poe, except in the upper Ramu, where Jephcott beat him, and around Bogati, where he did better than Poe. Jephcott's hopes were naturally low after his accident but he rightly expected success in the Ramu Valley, where he clearly took the Middle Ramu Open section, and those sections of Mabuso and the Rai Coast (Dumpu and Naha-Rawo) where he was known. Although only third in Mabuso, Bogia, and the Rai Coast, he polled better than he predicted. He ran Garrett second in Sumkar.

Whitaker was the least realistic about his chances. He overestimated the total vote (of which he expected 29,000 each for Garrett and himself, and 6500 for Jephcott) by nearly 20,000 and his own share of it by about 19,000. Although correct in assuming that he would win the pro-Yali vote, he did not realise that it had been reduced to limited groups of vocal devotees and, as has been mentioned, wrongly computed it at two-thirds of the Rai Coast Open and one-third of Mabuso. In the result, Whitaker did not win in any Open section. Although close to it in Bogia, he lost by some 2000 votes in both Mabuso and the Rai Coast, where he had placed his greatest hopes. In Mabuso, he carried the Hansemann Mountains, the upper Gogol, the Jobto-Barum area across the Gogol, and the Kesowai-Usino stretch of the Ramu—all (save a few villages such as Usino) known cargoist areas. In the Rai Coast Open area, his results tended to duplicate Yali's, being most favourable between Bogati and Dumpu, and in those parts of the Saidor area where Yali still had followers.

In Mabuso, Angmai Bilas, the winner, shrewdly appraised his prospects. He narrowly defeated Bato in their natal area between Madang and the Gogol, where he guessed they would share the votes equally. He carried Bundi as he expected, because he had addressed the council and Bato had not, and because of the appeal of his Catholicism in an area greatly influenced by the Catholic mission, which also shared his progressive ideas. He did not hope to do well in the Ramu and Bagasin areas against local candidates, Saramuri and Togop, but possibly was shaken by Saramuri's heavy vote, which defeated Bato and enabled him to survive until the third count. Saramuri, too, may have been surprised: he had no idea of the electorate beyond the Ramu and could not estimate his chances beforehand. Bato shared Angmai's expectations of dividing the Madang-Gogol votes equally, and hoped for second preferences around Usino, where he had addressed the council. As well as running Angmai close in the Madang-Gogol area, he won handsomely in the Hansemann Mountains, but lost badly in the Bagasin Area, Ramu Valley and, as he expected, at Bundi, which he had not visited. We did not learn Togop's hopes. Most of his 605 votes came from his natal Bagasin Area, but even there Saramuri beat him.

In Sumkar, Middleton won decisively, especially on Karkar, as he expected. He also carried the mainland easily, although voting was comparatively low. This dashed Kaki's early hopes for a mainland victory, for he did not get the support he anticipated from Sumgilbar Council and beat Middleton only narrowly even in his home locality. Wadau had no clear picture of the election, his electorate, or modern politics, and came a bad last even in his own locality, where he picked up most of his votes.

In the Rai Coast Open, Poe could forecast his victory with greater precision than any other candidate in all four electorates, thanks to his continual liaison with the Rai Coast and Astrolabe Bay councillors who supported him. As he predicted, he carried most of the mountains on both sides of the Nankina, lost in the Bogati-Dumpu-Kesowai area (possibly a little more heavily than he anticipated), and shared the coastal votes with Yali. He gained slightly more than his estimate of half the votes in Yali's own Nankina-Mot locality. Yali, for his part, had little more appreciation of his electorate's boundaries and population than Wadau or Saramuri. Although certain that he would win, he could not specify the areas he expected to carry save the coast, especially Astrolabe Bay. His bland assumption of victory showed that he did not appreciate how much his following had shrunk. Iaga was barely known to the electorate and took most of his few votes in his own locality.

In interpreting the voting, we examine three issues: the low percentage of the population that voted; informal voting; and the reasons for people voting as they did. It is as hard for us as observers to explain these problems as it was for the candidates to forecast their chances at the polls, for we could contact the mass of the electors no better than they.

A notable feature of the election in the Madang Regional, as in the Territory as a whole, was the low voter turn-out compared with 1964. Even in 1964, the average Madang District vote, 66 per cent of those enrolled, was lower than the Territory average of 72 per cent. In 1968, the turn-out was: 58 per cent in the Regional; 57 per cent in Bogia Open; 51 per cent in the Middle Ramu Open; 60 per cent in the Mabuso Open; 64 per cent in Sumkar Open; and 56 per cent in the Rai Coast Open.[10] The 1968 average for the Madang Open electorates was 58 per cent.

The drop was probably due to a number of factors. In the first place, there was a loss of votes through rejection of ballots of absentee electors, whose names and villages could not be traced in the Master Roll. Of 1957 absentee ballots in the Madang Regional, 45 per cent were invalidated in this way. In the second place, in limited areas of Mabuso and Sumkar, some people kept away from the polls out of loyalty to Yali. They realised that it was useless to vote for him but they did not want to vote for anyone else. This most likely was true of a number of Gal-Utu villages in Mabuso, which had always opposed the Administration and councils. But it did not apply in the Rai Coast Open, where it was legitimate to vote for Yali and where cargo cult provided an incentive to vote, either to get him in or keep him out.

In the third place, throughout the whole southern Madang Regional, a number of people did not vote because of apathy and poor communications. Some had lost interest in the electoral process, which previously they had associated with cargoism or general material expectations. After 1964, there were no widespread, startling results. Only a few groups got any of the tangible benefits expected from the House of Assembly or even saw their representatives. Apathy was not counter-balanced by official effort during 1967-8. Administration officers were not sent to instruct the people in voting. Neither the councillors nor the perfunctory distribution of leaflets served as an efficient medium of political education. Radio broadcasts reached only a limited audience, especially away from the coast where there were few receivers. As noted, candidates personally contacted only a fraction of the electors, as was particularly clear in the Bagasin-Gogol area, where two groups of villages did not record a single vote, and in the Rai Coast Open, where remote mountain populations possibly never

[10] This figure for the Rai Coast Open Electorate corrects that of 35 per cent originally given in Bryant (C.E.O. 1968: 44), which Wolfers (1968d: 24) also quotes. Wolfers's suggestion that the low vote in the Rai Coast Open was due to the cultists' distrust of the House of Assembly is not justified. See our comments in the following paragraph. It should be noted that where other figures given by Bryant (C.E.O. 1968) disagree with those given here, the latter should be accepted as correct.

even heard about the election. In addition, in the Rai Coast Open, some groups which knew about the election must have found it physically difficult to cast their votes. Polling booths were set up mainly along the coast and in only eight inland villages. As a result, many people, especially in the heavily populated central montane region, were not visited and would have had to travel considerable distances along tracks which were hazardous, if not impassable, during the wet season. Under these circumstances, it is perhaps remarkable that even 56 per cent of the Rai Coast Open electors went to the polls. Problems of terrain and travel were less acute in Mabuso and Sumkar, which were far better served in this respect.

There were two kinds of informal votes: those invalid for technical reasons, the percentages of which are set out in table 7 and the 'Yali vote' in Mabuso. In the first category, some cases were due to officials who either omitted to initial the papers or neglected some other technical detail. More commonly, however, literate electors did not inscribe their papers correctly, putting ticks, noughts, crosses, or numbers without sequence, or writing the preferred name in the voting

TABLE 7—INFORMAL VOTING IN MADANG ELECTORATES

Electorate	Open %	Regional %	Amount higher in Regional	Remarks
Bogia	1·32	4·0	Three times	
Middle Ramu	0·17	4·05	24 times	
Mabuso	(1·7)*	3·3	Twice	'Yali vote' (11·3%) deducted
Sumkar	4·0	13·0	Three times	
Rai Coast	0·9	2·6	Three times	

* Estimated by deduction of known 'Yali vote'.

squares. On the whole, such informal voting was positively correlated with the degree of literacy in the electorate, with the ascending order of: Middle Ramu, Rai Coast, Bogia, Mabuso, and Sumkar. Many who thought themselves educated were too proud to use the whisper vote and then invalidated their papers.[11] This may explain also voting in the

[11] As noted on p. 170, Karkar had the highest rate of literacy in the Madang Regional. An additional factor on Karkar was the difference in approach of two poll clerks. One of them courteously made himself available to those who, even if literate, wanted to use the 'whisper vote', so that they could do so without embarrassment. The other left it to the voters to ask for his services, which, if literate, some people were ashamed to do.

Regional, except in the Middle Ramu section, not covered in this study, where abnormally high informal voting may have had some other cause.[12]

The 'Yali vote' in Mabuso amounted to about 1100 or 11 per cent of the total. It did precisely what Bato feared, depriving him of votes actually intended for the Whitaker-Yali alliance of which he was, at least technically, a member. Thus, around Mawan, where Whitaker beat Garrett in the Regional by 231 to 65, Bato received only 19 votes to Angmai's 62, although there were 318 invalid 'Yali votes', of which he might have expected a large share. The same happened at Jobto-Barum, where Whitaker defeated Garrett by 252 to 141 but Bato got only one more vote than Angmai (122 to 121). Here again there were 149 'Yali votes'. But the 'Yali vote' actually cast was smaller than many people expected and, even had it all gone to Bato, he probably would not have beaten Angmai, who reaped the large Bundi vote.[13] Even so, it might have helped him or Saramuri push Angmai harder. It had one other important by-product. Some Yali supporters in Mabuso later accused electoral officials of fraud. In some cases, the poll clerks taking the whisper votes either did not receive or ignored the Returning Officer's instructions to oblige the intransigent by writing Yali's name on the ballot. Cargoists concluded they were being cheated. (Some indigenous poll clerks interviewed after the election admitted failing to take the prescribed action because the votes would be informal in any case.) Other Yali supporters charged that, when officers did write in Yali's name, they did so at the edge of the papers (where there was most room): the officers were obviously marking the papers for burning, as both Bato and Liwa foretold would happen. The clerks should have drawn in another voting square and written Yali's name beside it together with those of the other candidates.

We examine now the ballots actually cast. On the whole, the pattern of voting reflected, and thus vindicated, the alliances between Regional and Open candidates. There was fairly equal polling, for example, for Garrett and Angmai, and Whitaker and Bato, around Madang; for Garrett and Poe, and Whitaker and Yali, on the Rai Coast

[12] This may have been the result of McKinnon's vigorous campaign in the Middle Ramu Open, where he was well known. Apart from Jephcott, who carried the area, no Regional candidate paid it the same attention.

[13] In fact, the number of people in the general Madang area who voted for Yali in 1968 had probably not dropped appreciably from the 1964 figure of 3000. Over 700 of his supporters in Sumkar transferred their votes to Wadau and, as can be seen by comparing maps 6, 7 and 8, all the villages between the Kabenau and Naru Rivers were transferred in 1968 from the old (1964) Madang Open to the new Rai Coast Open. These villages would have provided at least 1000 votes, which would have been cast for Yali on both occasions, invalidly in 1964 but validly in 1968.

seaboard; and for Jephcott and Saramuri in the Ramu Valley. Shrewd candidates, like Garrett and Angmai, did not compete with others on their home grounds—as with Jephcott and Saramuri in the Ramu—but concentrated on places like Bundi which, fielding no candidate of their own, were ready to be wooed by the most skilful. We have mentioned some exceptions to alliance voting, due to the Mabuso 'Yali vote'. A few others resulted from local factors. In Mabuso Open, in the Garia-Girawa area and along the Ramu south of Usino, Saramuri and Togop beat Angmai and Bato, in that order, although the Regional voting for the first area was for Garrett, Jephcott, and Whitaker, and, in the second, for Whitaker, Jephcott, and Garrett. This was probably due to the strength of Saramuri and Togop as local candidates, and of Yali's support of Whitaker in Dumpu.

We considered several possible voting determinants: the Administration; the Christian missions; the planters; the Madang Workers' Association and the attitudes of 'foreign' workers in Madang; local government councils; the traditional socio-cultural system; regionalism and personality; the recriminations between cargoist and anti-cargoist candidates, and the charge against Whitaker; land loss; and the ubiquitous demand for material progress coupled with the need to choose between its two rival expressions, Western modernisation and the cargo movement. Of these, the most important was the last.

As noted, the Officer in Charge, Usino Station, advised Togop against nominating because he might split the Ramu-Bagasin vote. Several officers worked hard to get 'foreign' urban workers from outside the District to enrol in Madang. Otherwise, especially with respect to voting, the Administration and also the Christian missions kept neutral. They did not influence even the Europeans, of whom 563 enrolled and 291 (51 per cent) voted, or Chinese, of whom 49 enrolled and 24 (49 per cent) voted. Planters as a whole had no organised position: some opposed, while others supported, Whitaker and Yali; and some, north of Madang, helped people with political and electoral education. As noted, one planter on Karkar supported Garrett against Jephcott. The Madang Workers' Association did nothing, and the 'foreign' workers were of no importance. Despite the Administration's encouragement to them to identify with their place of work, where many of them had lived for a long time, of the 1503 enrolled in the Madang Regional and Mabuso Open, only 162 actually voted. The local government councils, although introduced institutions, were closer to the people and more deeply involved in the election. But, as hinted, their role was sometimes equivocal: councillors had to carry out the Administration's political education and electoral education schemes, for which they were ill equipped, yet were asked or even volunteered to support particular candidates and urge fellow villagers to vote for them, as many Rai Coast councillors did for Poe. Sometimes councillors merely echoed existing opinion, giving the lead that people expected, like traditional 'big men'. Sometimes their advice was ignored. Sometimes individual councillors gave conflicting advice. In some Madang and Rai Coast villages, people criticised their councillors for endorsing candidates without consulting them. Garia informants said that councillors promised to tell them for whom to vote but either forgot or sent unintelligible messages.

The traditional socio-cultural system was of little consequence. Cognatic associations, patriclans, and political groups, except probably at Bundi, were too small to exert sectional pressure in the modern national electorates. The two large Karkar language groups expressed no rivalry but united behind Middleton and Garrett. Even the cleavage between bush and coast was used only as a rallying cry around Madang to counteract the 'Yali vote'. Interpersonal relationships outside the linguistic group were more important. As he did in 1948-50 (Lawrence 1964/67: 208), Yali manipulated distant groups through his wives—three from the Rai Coast and one from Matokar, Rebecca, true sister of Wadau, the Sumkar candidate. The trade network had comparable influence. It had always given the Bogati-Dumpu people a sense of solidarity, which they carried over into the election. Staunch cargoists, they represented Yali's largest bloc vote. When Mabuso speakers asserted that Madang and Rai Coast were 'one place', they were referring not only to the cargoist link but more especially to old trade ties. Many Garia probably voted for Garrett in the belief that he would build them a road along their traditional trade route, the Naru Valley. When, after the election, he suggested another, economically preferable route, some felt they had been betrayed: their forbears had not used it and, despite its advantages, they could not do so. Some of Yali's trade friends reluctantly voted for Poe because they opposed the cargo movement. Others, equally hostile to the movement, voted for Yali out of fear of his taunts whenever they had to go through his village to the coast.

Regionalism and personality affected all candidates' results. All did well in their home or adopted areas. Some also established associations with other localities (even overcoming the coast-inland cleavage), as did Angmai with Bundi, and Bato with Amele-Dalam through his land demarcation work. Middleton and Jephcott won votes wherever they campaigned on foot. Among the 'outsiders' to the local village scene, Whitaker exploited his affability, idiomatic Pidgin, and ability to identify with the Melanesian outlook; Garrett his obvious European competence and special knowledge of road-surveying; and Poe his command of English and Police Motu as well as Pidgin, as signs of his ability to master the complexities of modern government and as compensation for Papuan 'foreignness', which was held against him only around Bogati and by those who disapproved of cargoism but wanted an excuse to vote for Yali because of trade ties.

It is hard to evaluate the importance of the hostility between cargoist and anti-cargoist candidates, and of the charge against Whitaker. The general turbulence of the campaign affected different people in different ways. Those who adhered to either side and had been abused or intimidated by the other, welcomed the counter-attacks of their own champions and did not resent them as infringements of Melanesian political good manners. This probably did not influence their votes, which were already determined by the stand they had taken. Those who were not involved in this way made no open protest but clearly found the atmosphere of mutual recrimination distasteful. It is impossible to say how far this caused them to cast their votes for one set of candidates or the other. The police charge lost Whitaker probably at most 2000 votes, but certainly not the election, in the southern Madang Regional. As noted, by polling day, people knew nothing about it outside the relatively small Madang-Sarang region.

The two most important voting determinants were economic: alienated land; and the demand for development together with the two rival approaches to it. Land loss was a serious issue around Madang, where a large area had been resumed for the site of the town, and along the north coast road, where, as stated, European planters and the Catholic mission had extensive holdings. Some people in this region supported Yali to some extent because they believed that he would rectify their injustices over land and, possibly, prevent Garrett, with his scheme for 50-acre blocks, which they did not understand, from taking what land remained to them.

More prominent, however, was the issue that has dominated politics in the southern Madang Regional ever since European contact began in 1871: the search for European wealth. As far as we could judge, virtually everyone who intended to vote looked on material development as of paramount concern. But, on the eve of the election, the main question was: which of the two competing platforms would they support? Of the potential electors, who were in the majority, those prepared to trust the candidates who had European skills and promised economic progress along Western lines, or those who believed that by sending Yali to the House of Assembly they would achieve the instant millennium for which they had waited so long? Had the election been held in 1948, the cargoists would have swept the polls. In 1968, they were convincingly defeated. The results indicate that Yali's active following in the southern Madang Regional has contracted to the few hard-core groups previously summarised: a few pockets behind Rai Coast beach villages, including about half of the people of his own Nankina-Mot locality; the coastal and mountain region between Bogati-Bongu and Dumpu-Kesowai; the Astrolabe Bay littoral; the Hansemann Mountains; the central Gal-Utu area; and a few villages along the Gogol, in the Bagasin Area, and between Madang and Sarang.

Much research must be done before we can properly explain the cargo movement's loss of popularity during the last two decades.[14] Here we can give only tentative answers. Initially, it seems clear that the cargoists were not defeated primarily by the arguments and oratory of Garrett's team. Garrett, Angmai, and Poe, although they spoke out forcefully, did little more than reinforce views that many of the people themselves had already formed. The Karkars had long been anti-Yali because he opposed the missions, and their own cargo cults had no influence on the election, but many other previously loyal groups between Saidor and Madang had rejected him as a failure and were ready to try a new road to wealth. Many were afraid of his advocacy of immediate self-government, and some of his insatiable demands for women, which might tempt him to tear down all sex restrictions. Their attitude was helped by the awakening of new political consciousness among their leaders, the councillors, to some extent by the spread of education, and almost certainly, in a few places mentioned below, by real gains in economic development. Some councillors were renegade Yali 'boss boys', originally attracted to him by a desire for power and responsibility, which they could satisfy now in a more real way by participating in local government. Comparatively young men, they soon realised their own superiority over the ageing and illiterate Yali, whose incompetence as Council President and Conference Chairman was notorious, and were anxious to break free.[15] Education and better job opportunities, although not as effective as might be supposed, have probably helped emancipate some younger people by demonstrating the falsity of cargoism and offering a viable alternative. They reinforced the process of natural erosion: some older cargoists who died after 1950 were not replaced from the succeeding generations.

Yet the most powerful factor seems to have been economic development made possible by roads and airfields. The north coast road has brought the people cash crops and their own trucks, and has reduced the number of active Yali supporters. The Madang-Gogol motor road has reclaimed several villages. Although Yaliism is still a force in the

[14] As, for example, the studies carried out by Miss R. M. McSwain on Karkar, Miss Louise Hogg at Kauris, and Mr P. McLaren at Bongu.
[15] This does not, of course, explain the attitudes of the Astrolabe Bay councillors who supported Yali.

south-eastern Ramu Valley around Dumpu and Kesowai, it is disappearing to the north-west towards Usino, where there are the new airstrip, council, and Patrol Post. Finally, Yali's Nankina-Mot people, of whom over half supported Poe and Garrett, have shown signs of rejecting his leadership since 1958 (Lawrence 1964/67: 268). They made it clear that they were ready to try coffee production as a substitute for cargo cult provided that they were helped to build roads to transport their crops (Lawrence 1967: 274-5).

To conclude this section, we can make two general observations. First, the success of Garrett's team was not a victory of conservatism over revolutionary forces but the reverse. Whereas the cargoists and their associates would conserve traditional society, at most fostering development only at the village level and continuing to hold out false hopes for the millennium, Garrett, Middleton, Angmai, and Poe represent comparative dynamism and change, promoting highways, farming, and industry.

Second, the cargo movement has been defeated at the polls but, as with any messianic cult, we should not underestimate its powers of recuperation. Perhaps in a new form it could still prove a serious political force by regaining a greater measure of popular support. Several comments are in order. Although many have rejected Yali as a cargo leader, there is evidence that they still accept cargo cult as intellectually satisfying. They have not discarded its assumptions. They could easily revert to it, should the program of radical development for which they voted fail, and should another suitable leader arise. The Nankina-Mot coffee growers made this clear in their request for a motor road. Moreover, although the actual 'Yali vote' was smaller than many people anticipated, the potential is still large. If Yali's 3189 votes in the Rai Coast Open and 1100 informal Mabuso votes are added to the 714 won by Wadau, his protégé, in Sumkar, the total between Sarang and Saidor is 5003. This is a considerable figure, if the low voter turn-out is taken into consideration, and could have been augmented by those Mabuso and Sumkar groups which did not 'vote Yali' merely because they realised it would be invalid and thus useless. It could provide the foundation of a widespread revival of cargo cults. The cargo movement has always managed to incorporate within its intellectual or explanatory system virtually all the religious, political, and administrative institutions imported from the West. It has done this again with the latest, most important institution, the House of Assembly, by offering its devotees a plausible program in the field of modern national politics.

KABWUM AND MOROBE

As only one fieldworker was available, it was impossible to cover the campaigns in the Morobe Regional and Kabwum Open Electorates in the same detail as in the southern Madang Regional. We concentrate on Kabwum Open and that part of Morobe Regional within its borders (see map 6).

The Kabwum Open Electorate was formed by combining the eastern half of the first Rai Coast Open with a small part of the old Finschhafen Open (cf. maps 6 and 7). Although the 1967 redistribution produced a greater number of smaller electorates, Kabwum, with nearly 50,000 people and 26,000 electors, remained nearer the 1964 standard. It was the most heavily populated Open electorate in the Morobe Regional.

The area has the rugged terrain described at the beginning of the chapter. The mountain-dwellers are divided into seven major linguistic groups (Dedua, Kalasa, Komba, Selepet, Timbe, Uruwa, and Yupna) ranging from under 2000 to over 11,000 speakers. The coastal sector, containing about twelve beach and sub-coastal communities, represents less than 15 per cent of the electorate's population. In February 1968, there were nineteen adult expatriates in Kabwum: twelve Lutheran mission personnel; four Administration officers; two education officers; and one businessman.

Apart from Kabwum Station, there were administrative posts at Kalalo and Sialum. Ulap and Kalasa mission stations were linked by motor road to coastal anchorages. Another motor road ran along the electorate's east coast. Kabwum, Wasu, and Indagen had airstrips. Three others were planned or under construction. Wasu, formerly a Patrol Post, had developed into a small port town, with its own anchorage, church, mission rest house, trade stores, bulk supply stores, sawmill, Medical Aid Post, houses for indigenous residents, a new wharf (completed in July 1968), and an aircraft hangar planned by a private company. Inland coffee farmers depended on small ships calling at Wasu and many wage labourers leaving the area embarked there. In 1967, a local government council was proclaimed to incorporate 30,000 people in the central part of the electorate (Sio, Komba, Selepet, and Timbe). It will probably be extended to include the Uruwa and Yupna.

There were substantial variations in socio-economic development. At one extreme were the sophisticated Sio coastal villages. At the opposite extreme were the backward Uruwa and Yupna, patrolled only four times before 1942. Sios left home as wage labourers before 1900, and in 1968 many held semi-professional and skilled jobs. Far fewer Uruwa and Yupna emigrated, most as unskilled labourers and servants. We have only crude estimates of cash income, but Sio's per capita average was probably ten to twenty times greater than that of the Uruwa and Yupna. Most Sios were literate in Pidgin and many younger Sios knew English. According to a recent census, 52 of 1481 Uruwa and Yupna were literate in Pidgin, but none knew any English.

These contrasts implied comparable differences in political participation. In 1964, two of nine candidates in the Rai Coast Open were from Sio. Most Uruwa and Yupna had not heard of the candidates (of whom only one visited a small part of their area), and only 51 per cent voted. Yet, until January 1968, no Sios seemed aware of the new Regional electorates. Few Sios regularly listened to radio news and, despite general literacy, fewer still read a newspaper. Important news sources were visitors and letters from the towns, and second-hand reports from better informed native schoolteachers. Items of greatest interest were absent relatives' activities and local shipping. Local government and District Administration activities were of tertiary significance, just as radios and printed matter, such as the news in the Pidgin *New Guinea Lutheran,* were tertiary sources.

As noted, most Kabwum people were mountain-dwellers, outnumbering the scattered coastal inhabitants by about eight to one. This highlighted the local importance of a social attitude described in the Background section: the cleavage between bushmen and beachmen, generalised and in some ways enhanced by modern developments, and in many contexts now apparently unbridgeable. In Kabwum, this posed an obvious political problem: the mountain zone's overwhelming electoral power. A coastal candidate could hope for only a limited following among mountain people, while mountain candidates had negligible appeal on the coast. Furthermore, the coast-inland antagonism overshadowed both intra-coastal and intra-montane divisions. In the context of election politics, 'beach' and 'bush' were more important categories than ethnic groups such as 'Timbe' or 'Komba'. (As self-conscious entities, these ethnic units were modern creations, administrative census divisions.)

Beachmen and bushmen were not mutually suspicious primarily because of ethnocentric prejudice. They viewed linguistic and cultural differences as naturally complementary. Animosity had other sources, traditional and modern. Until early post-European times, coastal and mountain people often were at war. As mentioned earlier, coastal people feared inland sorcery. In modern times, cash cropping, in some areas, brought beachmen and bushmen into conflict over land, especially in formerly unclaimed or unused coastal areas. The Administration's recent program of land demarcation might ultimately resolve such disputes, but even the initiation of the program before the election put a further strain on coast-inland relations. Nevertheless, antagonism was never monolithic but apt to be most acute where social interaction and trade ties, favoured by geographical propinquity, were most intense, as between Sios and Komba in the Puleng Valley. Before contact, distant bush people in the high mountain valleys and plateaux never had direct ties with the coast. Such ties were established with pacification but, with rapid development of coffee plantations in the highland area after 1960, distant bushmen and beachmen once more drew apart.

Coastal people were painfully aware that, unless they could overcome the problem of population imbalance, they would play a minor role in both national elections and local government. Advent Tarosi, the Sio candidate, proposed a new Open electorate to consist of the littoral between Finschhafen and Biliā (near Madang), and include Long and Tolokiwa Islands, and the Siassis. This area, he said, held 'all our trade partners. People here knew my father; they know me. None of these people', he added jokingly, 'would use sorcery against me'.

The candidates and their campaigns

Six candidates nominated for the Kabwum Open, including an expatriate Education Officer, John Crowhurst. Two candidates, Stoi Umut (from the eastern Timbe and Komba area) and Advent Tarosi (a Sio), stood in the 1964 Rai Coast Open, polling first and second respectively. All were young—in their thirties or early forties—and quite well educated. Fransing Ansuang (a Komba), President of Kabwum Local Government Council, and the sitting Member Stoi Umut, went to local mission schools. Rauke Gam (a Komba) was a storekeeper, who had attended Heldsbach Teachers' College and taken a commercial course in Lae. Buaki Singery (a Komba) had been an Administration clerk, had completed Standard VI, and had briefly attended the Papuan Medical College. Tarosi completed Standard VIII at school in Malaguna, Rabaul, before the Pacific War, at the end of which he took a teachers' refresher course at Sogeri High School. Crowhurst attended university briefly before training as a teacher in the 'E' Course at Rabaul. Only Fransing and Stoi spoke no English. Buaki spoke Komba, Selepet, Timbe, Kalasa, Sio, English, Pidgin, Police Motu, and the two local church languages, Yabim and Kâte. Only one candidate belonged to a political party; Stoi had joined Pangu. As in the southern Madang Regional, parties were not popular.

Except for Crowhurst, brought up an Anglican but calling himself an agnostic, all candidates were Lutherans. Fransing was active in church affairs all his adult life but Rauke, store manager at Ulap Mission Station, was the 'official' mission candidate. Buaki and Tarosi were nominal church members. Privately, Tarosi deeply resented the extent of mission influence in the area and, in particular, the church's inordinate claims on villagers' time and financial resources. Publicly, however, he emphasised the value of the Christian social ethic and urged co-operation with the church. By contrast, Crowhurst was widely reputed to be anti-mission. In his campaign speeches, he did not criticise the church but apparently did so in response to questions and during informal discussions. Copies of a letter denouncing Crowhurst as a 'Catholic man', and urging voters to support Tarosi and Rauke, in that order, circulated widely in the Kalasa and Dedua areas. The letter was issued by the 'headmen of Kalasa' and bore the stamp of the Kalasa Circuit of the Evangelical Lutheran Church of New Guinea. At Sio, where Crowhurst taught for five years and was respected, people were concerned at his anti-mission stance, mainly because they knew it would harm his chances.

From a geographic and ethnic standpoint, the recruitment of the candidates was peculiar. All five indigenous candidates came from the central part of the electorate: one (Tarosi) from the coast and the other four from villages at the headwaters of the Kwama River. Five major linguistic groups (Dedua, Kalasa, Uruwa, Yupna, and Selepet) fielded no candidates. Until November 1967, Tarosi had assumed that only he and Stoi would stand in Kabwum Open. Having already managed to discourage three other potential candidates, he was dismayed and angry when he learnt that Crowhurst and the three Komba men had entered the lists.

Although January and February, the height of the wet season, are the most difficult and dangerous months for travel in Kabwum, several candidates campaigned vigorously on foot throughout the electorate. Crowhurst and Buaki visited all its major sections, while Voutas, the successful Regional candidate, walked through the populous core area (Komba, Selepet, and Timbe) and called in on some of the eastern communities. Tarosi did not wage an extensive mountain campaign for several reasons; physical incapacity; his dislike of leaving his family for a long period; the expense of travel; and commitments to projects already undertaken. What was more important, perhaps, he relied heavily on his informal canvassing during the inter-election years, and support from H. R. Niall, Loto Lisa (a Sio kinsman who stood in 1964), and the Lutheran mission. Moreover, he judged that energetic campaigning would produce only marginal returns. This reflects mainly his assessment of the continuing strength of traditional sentiment as opposed to candidates' statements on issues in determining voters' decisions. His campaign was a token effort, involving a few desultory trips along the coast, a brief visit on foot to Kabwum, and talks with Sios in Lae. Rauke and Fransing scarcely moved out of their home areas. Their campaigns consisted of little more than social visits to people who already knew them. Both emphasised their intention to work for a system of roads that would help the transport of coffee from the mountains to the coast. Stoi Umut did not campaign at all. He nominated from Rabaul and remained in New Britain for most of the pre-election period. Many electors apparently dismissed him: one commented that there were only five candidates, as Stoi did not count.

Stoi's popularity was at a low ebb. His poor performance as an M.H.A. is a matter of public record, but the basis of his constituents' criticism should be made clear. He won the 1964 election by capitalising on the people's cargoist expectations (Harding 1965). Their disappointment with him was due to their failure to realise these hopes. We elaborate this later on. Most frequently people complained that Stoi never came to talk to them after his election. This reflects the apparently common conception of the M.H.A.'s role: that of intermediary between the Administration in Port Moresby and the local people. But electors who were 'given talk' by Stoi during his occasional patrols were even less pleased by his swaggering conduct. He was often faulted for drunkenness. Those who had not seen him drunk had heard about his many parties, which were alcoholic orgies. Several times electors described him as a 'child of the Patrol Officers', because in his early career they had promoted him (Harding 1965). Such statements implied condemnation of the Administration: if the people's representative had failed, the Administration must share the blame, for a succession of Patrol Officers had turned a blind eye to Stoi's cargoist activities.

H. R. Niall and Anthony (Pidgin, Toni) Voutas, the two candidates in the Morobe Regional Electorate, had several points in common: both had been in the Administration, Niall recently as Morobe District Commissioner, while Voutas was a Patrol Officer; and both had been active in the first House of Assembly, Niall as Speaker. They were opposed on the role of political parties and self-government: Voutas was a foundation member of Pangu and Niall a staunch independent. These issues were less important to indigenous electors than to the numerically insignificant expatriates. Indigenous electors respected them as former Administration officers and as Europeans: after Stoi's poor showing, they doubted whether any of their own people was fit to serve in the House. But what they saw as crucial was the difference in age and outlook between the two men: Niall was 63 and Voutas 25.

Moreover, since the election, Voutas (Ward 1970: 494ff.) has described how he succeeded in creating the almost unique image of an Australian willing to immerse himself in village life—living with the villagers, eating local food, working in the gardens—and, as the sitting Member for Kaindi Open (which overlapped the new Morobe Regional), maintaining continuous communication with constituents through a network of *komitis*—a man in every village wearing his 'Toni' badge (badges being a respected mark of expatriate authority), relaying his messages to the people and reporting on their wants and 'worries'. His campaigning was also unique for a European: in Morobe, though it was impossible to establish a *komiti* man everywhere, he sent Toni badges throughout the electorate, visited on foot (as noted) every village he could reach in the available time, and dispatched a campaign team to cover other areas. He also sent circulars to all villagers at regular intervals, with two messages: 'This is Toni', and 'Toni is Pangu'. His own speeches stressed that he was a member of a team which would work together in the House, and that to vote for a team was to have a greater voice in government.

Apart from the notion that parties, and Pangu in particular, would make the House of Assembly more effective, Voutas raised two other important issues: self-government as a transitional stage to full independence; and economic development. But only the last—economic development—struck a responsive chord. This was something the indigenes could understand. By contrast, most respondents disliked the idea of immediate self-government and were confused, even irritated, by discussion of parties. Yet most people did not associate either self-government or parties with Voutas. This largely nullified Niall's tactic of striking at his rival by criticising self-government, Pangu, and parties generally, as he did in his published leaflets: 'It is no good voting for a Pangu man. I think they intend to ruin the Territory'. In other words, while many may have *agreed with* Niall, they were *attracted to* Voutas. For example, a literate and comparatively well informed Sio informant, outspokenly hostile to self-government, said he liked Voutas because he was young and opposed Niall because he had too much of the 'old way of thinking'. Voutas, however, had one cause for embarrassment in Kabwum: Stoi's membership of Pangu. On party grounds, he should have supported Stoi, but in fact he did not do so and, so little did the party issue mean to them, the electors did not associate the two men.

Niall's Kabwum campaign consisted of brief visits to places accessible by air, but he was the only Morobe candidate to suggest anything like the alliances described for the southern Madang Regional. He sought co-operation with at least two Open candidates, Tarosi and Crowhurst, proposing mutual support on much the same terms to both. Tarosi received also the unsolicited help of McKinnon (the founder of the A.P.P. and candidate in the Middle Ramu Open). McKinnon sent a Sio employee to campaign for Tarosi, and apparently spoke personally for Tarosi and Niall in Madang, where many Kabwum people were living.

Issues and the voting pattern

As in the southern Madang Regional, the electors' dominant interest was economic development. This set the tone of most village discussions of the roles of the House of Assembly, the local government council, co-operatives, Administration agencies, incumbent and prospective members, and even the election process itself. It subsumed, and even tended to distort, issues of a non-economic order, such as the question of self-government. Subsistence farmers, wage workers and entrepreneurs, the educated and illiterate, cargoists and Christians—all agreed on the significance of the question: 'How are we to progress?' Indeed, interest in and knowledge of the House of Assembly did not seem to extend beyond its potential contribution to the material advancement of community and region, which, in the people's view, was or should be the chief business of local and national government.

At times, of course, some—even many—Kabwum people, realising the magnitude of the task, have despaired of ever achieving the economic level of Europeans. Others, more reflective, have tried to reduce the problem to intelligible dimensions. Informants at Sio, the most sophisticated community in the electorate, pinpointed the main elements necessary for developing the area: people, natural resources and money, and knowledge and technical assistance.

Their first anxiety was for greater population, to achieve which some advocated the reintroduction of polygyny, and one prominent elder even the compulsory impregnation of all unmarried women. Yet they opposed the idea of foreign immigration and especially European or Asian acquisition of land. Second, they recognised the importance of basic resources—what they could plant and find in the ground—and capital as ingredients of development. Certainly, pooled cash savings and earnings among kin or village groups have been significant in financing local projects. But here people had in mind large-scale monetary capital from outside sources.

It was the third need that the people saw as greatest: knowledge and technical assistance. They wanted people trained in English and modern skills, and people from advanced countries to teach them. They compared themselves with the Papuans, who were ahead of them because of a longer tradition of Western education and a better knowledge of English.

The people criticised both the local government council and the Open candidates for the House of Assembly on this third score. Of the council, they complained that it did no more than provide minimal services and routine administration: village affairs such as bride price and pay for pigs, chickens, and betel-nut. They wanted discussions about the kinds of projects they should start and the kinds of people they should invite from other countries to help them. They saw the same deficiency in the Kabwum candidates: no local candidate, including Crowhurst, offered any detailed or comprehensive development program, although they all promised to work for much needed local schools and roads. To this Voutas, who regarded the densely populated mountain province of Kabwum as critical in his bid for the Morobe Regional seat, presented a marked contrast. He stressed the Pangu policy that New Guinea itself must develop manufacturing and processing industries. The country spent a great deal in buying tinned meat and fish, rice, sugar, tea, and coffee from foreign businesses. Pangu would work to establish these businesses in the Territory. Nothing could appeal more strongly to the people's aspirations.

Voutas's campaign brought the crucial issue of economic development into focus, but much village discussion of the conditions and means of material progress was vague. Moreover, discussion was often tinged with cargoism. Indeed, the extent to which Stoi's overwhelming victory in 1964 was due to his reputation as a cargo leader and to which the electors expected him to engineer instant large-scale development is clear from the complete collapse of his popularity. Before polling day, people in the central part of the electorate castigated him abnormally frankly and harshly as a liar, thief, drunkard, do-nothing, and even 'child of Satan'. In late 1967, Stoi's trade store empire—built largely from funds collected from constituents—was in ruins. He was in debt to both European companies and natives.

Yet malfeasance, fraud, and drunkenness were not, in most electors' eyes, Stoi's most grievous sins. They had given him thousands of dollars as 'taxes' or 'gifts of respect' in return for his authorisation to perform money-generating cargo ritual, bogus investment shares, and good luck charms. The people would have forgiven his misappropriation of these substantial sums if he had fulfilled some of his promises, but, as they charged him in Pidgin, *'emi no opim lo long mipela'*: 'he did not reveal to us the procedures by which we could achieve wealth'.[16] Clearly, Stoi's failure as an elected representative consisted largely of his failure as a cargo leader. One Timbe elder grumbled to an officer conducting a political education patrol in 1967 that his people did not want a new election: they could not afford to pay for another 'member man' like Stoi.

We now analyse the voting, first and in greater detail, in Kabwum Open and, second and more cursorily, in Morobe Regional. In Kabwum, on the first count, Rauke Gam, the winner, led his nearest opponent, Buaki Singery, by nearly 500 votes. Fransing Ansuang trailed the

[16] See note 7. The concept of *lo* seems to be a constant for the whole Karkar-Finschhafen coast.

TABLE 8—DISTRIBUTION OF FIRST PREFERENCE VOTES BY AREA, KABWUM OPEN ELECTORATE

(a) *Central (Core) Region*

	Montane		Coastal		Total	
	No.	%	No.	%	No.	%
Rauke Gam	1371	20·8	3	0·4	1374	18·6
Buaki Singery	1487	22·6	1	0·1	1488	20·2
Advent Tarosi	367	5·6	757	96·1	1124	15·2
John Crowhurst	812	12·3	7	0·9	819	11·1
Stoi Umut	1060	16·1	20	2·5	1080	14·6
Fransing Ansuang	1496	22·7	—	—	1496	20·3
Totals	6593	100·1	788	100·0	7381	100·0

(b) *Peripheral Region*

	Eastern		Western		Total	
	No.	%	No.	%	No.	%
Rauke Gam	627	22·5	412	45·6	1039	27·1
Buaki Singery	537	19·2	20	2·2	557	15·1
Advent Tarosi	483	17·3	85	9·4	568	15·4
John Crowhurst	610	21·9	349	38·6	959	25·9
Stoi Umut	518	18·6	37	4·1	555	15·0
Fransing Ansuang	16	0·1	1	0·1	17	0·5
Totals	2791	99·6	904	99·0	3695	99·0

field, 1,000 votes behind the leader. Three candidates—Crowhurst, Tarosi, and Stoi—were neck and neck with about 1,700 votes apiece. Rauke was not declared elected until the fifth count.

Voter turn-out was low, only about 46 per cent of those registered going to the polls. As was to be expected, interest ran high among the Sio and Komba, who between them fielded four candidates and of whom, excluding absentees, about 54 per cent voted. By contrast, only 40 per cent of the neighbouring Selepet and a third of the Timbe cast ballots. The people had gained too little tangible benefit from the first House with Stoi (an eastern Timbe) to be more enthusiastic. Yet, surprisingly, Stoi did better than electors' statements before polling day suggested. His loss of popularity is shown dramatically by his holding the loyalty of only some 1100 people in the montane area that netted him over 7500 first preferences in 1964. Interestingly, he won over 500 votes in precisely those parts of the Timbe region in which he had previously collected large sums for bogus investment shares.[17]

The geographical distribution of first preferences is shown in table 8. For this purpose, the electorate has been divided into central (or core) and peripheral regions. The core, subdivided into montane and coastal sectors, consists of the central census divisions (Komba, Selepet, Timbe, and Sio) making up the Kabwum Local Government Council area, to which all candidates belonged. The periphery comprises the backward Uruwa and Yupna, to the west, and the Dedua, Kalasa, and Sialum, to the east.

As can be seen in table 8, Rauke slightly trailed his two fellow Komba candidates, Fransing and Buaki, in the central (core) region. Thus he achieved his margin of victory in the peripheral region, where he outpolled the others. He was able to draw votes in all major sectors of the electorate probably because of support from the Lutheran mission, particularly its indigenous personnel. His status as 'mission candidate' placed at his disposal the only organisation which both spread through the entire electorate and operated effectively, however informally, at the grass-roots level.

In the core region, where all candidates were previously known to electors, first preferences were evenly divided. In the periphery, where only Crowhurst and Buaki campaigned, the distribution was less even. Fransing, a homebody, was simply unknown in the periphery, whereas the remaining indigenous candidates had at least some contacts there before the campaign. Crowhurst's strong showing in the periphery was certainly the result of campaigning in about half the villages. Tarosi, the only coastal candidate, received overwhelming support on the coast. Had the Lutheran mission given him more than qualified encouragement, he might have carried other areas and so won the election. As expected, the four inland candidates received only scattered votes in the coastal sector.

The degree of the candidates' reliance on localised support may be expressed in terms of their percentages of first preferences in their home areas. (This is set out in table 9.) By 'home area', we mean the linguistic group containing the candidate's natal village. As Buaki, Fransing, and Rauke were all Komba, their home areas coincided. As Stoi came from eastern Timbe and Komba, his home area over-

[17] This statement is based on financial records supplied by an expatriate informant.

lapped theirs to a considerable extent. But in the case of Buaki and Rauke, we must add 'area of residence' to home area. Both men had lived outside their natal areas on stations where they occupied key roles. Buaki had served as an Administration clerk at Kabwum and he won four-fifths of the Selepet first preferences around the station. Rauke had managed the trade store at Ulap Mission, and he got two-thirds of Selepet first preferences in its vicinity.

TABLE 9—DEGREE OF LOCAL SUPPORT, KABWUM

Percentage of candidates' first preferences received in home areas and areas of residence, Kabwum

Candidate	Percentage
Buaki Singery	69·6
Fransing Ansuang	66·4
Stoi Umut	52·9
Rauke Gam	32·5
Advent Tarosi	30·2
John Crowhurst	4·5

Of the indigenous candidates, Tarosi's support was least localised. Even so, he polled 100 per cent of the vote in Sio, his natal community. Moreover, if the Puleng Valley Komba, who live immediately inland from the Sios and compose many of their trade friends, are included in Tarosi's home area, his index of local support rises from 30 per cent to 46 per cent. Although he lived for over six years at Kalalo and Sio, and was headmaster of the Sio primary school for five years, Crowhurst received only 82 votes at Kalalo and none at Sio. Finally, because of ethnic affiliation, kinship, or trade ties, all five indigenous candidates had a major stake in the Komba area Fransing, who campaigned least outside his home area, scored most heavily here, getting over a third of the Komba vote.

In the Morobe Regional, Voutas defeated Niall, outpolling him by over two to one. He scored heavily in all areas where he campaigned. Niall received a third of his votes in Tarosi's stronghold, the coast and Puleng Valley. Voutas's youthful vigour and, especially, emphasis on economic development won him overwhelming support in the area that had experienced the most rapid commercial growth in recent years. Around Kabwum, the economic as well as the administrative centre of the Open electorate, he won 1167 votes against Niall's 27. Yet Niall outpolled him by 942 to 113 at Sio and around Ulap Mission. The people of these areas realised the economic potential of cash crops and wage labour in earlier years, but thereafter settled down to an equilibrium from which they were loath to be disturbed.

What was the significance of the election in Kabwum? In contrast to 1964, when Stoi Umut's victory seemed assured at the close of nominations, few informed observers were willing to hazard a firm prediction before the 1968 poll. In the electors' view, most of the candidates were men of proven competence, who had served in responsible positions: two had been teachers, one a storeman, another an Administration clerk, and another President of the local government council. Stoi Umut had been M.H.A. and apparently his old charisma had not completely evaporated. Even those who criticised him nevertheless averred that he was a good businessman. Buaki, who had been disgraced by dismissal from the Administration and imprisonment, was characterised by a few as a 'trouble man', but even the critics did not take this too seriously. Crowhurst did not try to emphasise his superior qualifications but rather adopted the modest and restrained approach that characterised his indigenous rivals.

The effect of individual campaigns is difficult to assess. Crowhurst was probably most successful in vote-getting, but the overall results seem to confirm Tarosi's judgment that, in areas where a candidate was already known by name and reputation, campaigning would be of limited usefulness. His own case bore witness to this: the whole Sio population, as noted, supported him, although his canvassing was desultory. Yet despite anticipations to the contrary, this was the only bloc vote. Even the populous Timbe divided their loyalties between four candidates.

Material development was the crucial issue. All the Open candidates stressed the importance of meeting the electorate's educational and economic needs. But it was Voutas who capitalised on the desire for development by presenting what appeared to be novel and imaginative proposals. He made a deep impression because he had no rival. As in the southern Madang Regional, indigenous electors saw cargoism and secular economic development as alternative approaches. Whether cargoist attitudes were actively expressed or subordinated to discussion in secular Western terms depended largely on the candidates. In 1964, Stoi Umut's campaign and election evoked considerable cargoist expectations, whereas, in 1968, candidates and electors discussed development mainly in pragmatic terms, because Stoi was absent in New Britain.

Thus cargoism was less important in 1968 than in 1964, not because it was on the wane but because no candidate sought to mobilise cargoist support as Stoi had done in the first election. Moreover, Stoi's failure may have convinced many voters of the futility of relying on local, especially indigenous, representatives to achieve material progress. This, as suggested, helps to explain voter apathy. One man remarked: 'Before we had an election and we got nothing. Now we are voting again. If nothing happens this time, we won't have any more elections'.

CONCLUSIONS

We now examine briefly our initial statement that the chief interest of the election between Karkar and Finschhafen centred on the influence of the revision of electoral boundaries in 1967 on the development of a hitherto consistent political tradition. This tradition grew from the common values and beliefs of the indigenous socio-cultural and trade systems in response to uniform experiences under colonial rule, found its expression in cargoism, and culminated in the 1964 campaign for the House of Assembly.

In 1968, the persistence of this common tradition in both the southern Madang Regional and Kabwum was obvious in the pre-eminence of economic development as the election issue and in certain attitudes deriving from indigenous socio-cultural systems. In both areas, the people opposed political parties, which they saw as divisive, the antithesis of their own consensual ethic, and further alienation of land, which they regarded as an inviolable concomitant of living. In both areas, regional ties and the rivalry between coast and inland were voting determinants, although they appear to have been more pronounced in Kabwum than in the southern Madang Regional.

Beyond this point, however, there were three marked differences between the campaigns in the two areas: in the alignments of candidates; in the method of campaigning; and, above all, in the interpretation of the crucial issue of development. In Morobe and Kabwum, ties between the Regional and Open candidates were far more rudimentary than the formal alliances in the southern Madang Regional and its Open electorates. Niall proposed mutual support to both Crowhurst and Tarosi, but Voutas ignored his Pangu tie with Stoi Umut. Otherwise, there were the tenuous links between Niall, Tarosi, and McKinnon (who was not standing in any Morobe electorate). Again, in the southern Madang Regional, relatively little campaigning was done on foot, except by the indigenous candidates in their own immediate localities, and Middleton and Jephcott in mainland Sumkar and the lower Ramu Valley respectively. In the main, European members of the alliances provided mechanised transport both for themselves and their indigenous running-mates. As a result, they were restricted to the motor roads and airfields, and thus had only limited contact with voters. In Kabwum, in the absence of elaborate alliances, candidates tended to operate as individuals and therefore relied far less on mechanised transport. Crowhurst, Buaki, and Voutas campaigned extensively on foot and, although their movements were comparatively laborious and slow, were far more intimately known to the people. They penetrated the villages and met the electors on their own ground.

The most significant difference occurred in the interpretation of economic development. In the past, between Karkar and Finschhafen, there had developed a cargoist tradition sufficiently uniform for Yali and Stoi Umut, who campaigned between Madang and Sio in 1964, to be given a fairly stereotyped response. Both candidates were regarded as exponents of a viable program of economic progress.

In 1968, however, although the people's desire for economic progress remained unchanged, their conceived means of achieving it were superficially more varied. As seen, there were two main interpretations of the problem, which the people regarded as alternative approaches: cargo cult and Western modernisation. In the southern Madang Regional, the *leit-motif* of the campaign was the rivalry between the two ideologies, whereas in Kabwum the candidates stressed only Western modernisation. This represented a change of circumstances rather than of popular outlook. It was made possible largely because of electoral redistribution. There was no cargoist candidate to campaign in Kabwum and exploit the people's continuing belief. Stoi was discredited and absent in New Britain for most of the period. What was perhaps more important in view of the recent elaboration of cargo doctrine found in the southern Madang Regional, Yali had no occasion to visit Kabwum as his ties with the area had never been binding and few, if any, of his supporters were living there. Thus he left Kabwum to the orthodox politicians, and directed his campaign towards the Madang area, with which he had very close links: he was an affine of the Matokars; the Madangs, who had originated the cargo movement, were largely responsible for his becoming its leader; and many Rai Coast people were working in Madang town or on nearby plantations. Yet there is no reason to suppose that this will be always the pattern. New redistributions will promote new variations. For instance, the campaign would have developed very differently if Tarosi's suggestion for a littoral electorate (which Yali's followers around Madang would have strongly supported) had been adopted.[18] Orthodox politicians probably would still have won the poll, but the manifest cargo vote might have been proportionately larger, with cargoism recognised as a proportionately more powerful force.

[18] This would not have been feasible: a littoral electorate of this kind would have meant the creation of inland mountain electorates, which would have had no social, political, or economic rationale.

TABLE 10—THE ELECTION RESULTS ON THE NORTH-EAST COAST

Madang Regional	1st count	2nd and final count
J. J. Garret	22,120	23,426
Bruce Jephcott	12,298	14,688
E. J. Whitaker	10,376	Excl.
Informal	2703	—
Exhausted	—	6680

Bogia Open	1st count	2nd count	3rd count	4th count	5th and final count
J. Meangarum	2765	2841	2999	3456	3943
R. Saretofa	2311	2346	2483	2886	3102
L. Mondolau	2118	2132	2167	2269	Excl.
J. Sakiap	1176	1221	1306	Excl.	—
J. Bareng	490	505	Excl.	—	—
F. Nabura	228	Excl.	—	—	—
Informal	122	—	—	—	—
Exhausted	—	43	133	477	2043

Middle Ramu	1st and final count
J. McKinnon	6271
Walai Toba	1790
Taptap	579

Mabuso Open	1st count	2nd count	3rd and final count
Saramuri Sinamaiba	2367	2828	2947
Togop Siburia	605	Excl.	—
Angmai Bilas	3642	3721	4050
Bato Bultin	1977	2010	Excl.
Informal	1282	—	—
Exhausted	—	32	1594

Sumkar Open	1st and final count
Kaki Angi	1538
John (Jon) Middleton	7410
Wadau Marun	714
Informal	402

TABLE 10—continued

Rai Coast Open	1st and final count
Yali Singina	3189
Iaga Bakuk	140
John Poe	5409
Informal	79

Kabwum Open	1st count	2nd count	3rd count	4th count	5th and final count
Rauke Gam	2558	2708	2796	3369	3980
Stoi Umut	1820	1914	1991	Excl.	—
Fransing Ansuang	1549	Excl.	—	—	—
John Crowhurst	1834	1930	2144	2418	Excl.
Buaki Singery	2073	2139	2255	2503	2958
Advent Tarosi	1860	1886	Excl.	—	—
Informal	306	—	—	—	—
Exhausted	—	1117	2508	3404	4756

FREE ELECTIONS IN A GUIDED DEMOCRACY

H. K. and Peta Colebatch, Marie Reay, and A. J. Strathern

WESTERN HIGHLANDS was the most populous Regional electorate with 162,810 voters enrolled. It comprised nine Open electorates ranging in voting potential from 11,100 (Jimi) to 23,936 (Hagen). Jimi reached into Chimbu, and Kandep-Tambul into the Southern Highlands, but the Regional electorate coincided closely with the Western Highlands District (map 9). Our areas of intensive study (Wahgi and Mul-Dei), together with Hagen, produced most of the coffee that, despite economic diversification over the previous decade, dominated the commercial activities of local people. Expatriate electors, about 500 in all, were concentrated here and economic transformation had been faster than in the harsher altitudes further west and the rugged, roadless Jimi. This chapter emphasises the Regional election because it is the only election here in which any political opposition emerged and because of its relevance to the absence of political issues in the Open elections.

Segmented, named groups with strongly agnatic traditions but

All team members were in the field from mid-January to the end of polling. Both Reay and Strathern had been there during 1967 but no team member was present while nominations were open. With much exchange of ideas and information, H. K. Colebatch concentrated on Kaibelt Diria M.H.A.'s campaign in Wahgi Open, Peta Colebatch on the Regional candidates and their campaign, Reay on the 'non-campaign' of the Minj candidates for Wahgi Open, and Strathern on Mul-Dei with emphasis on Dei. Several anthropologists who had worked in the region but were not directly studying the election helped us in various ways. W. L. Rowe co-operated in recording voting patterns for Hagen and arranging for the transport of used ballot papers to Canberra for analysis. D. P. Sinha and Marilyn Strathern provided particular items of information and discussed with team members matters pertaining to politics and elections. Ted Westermann kindly supplied observations on the election in Wapenamanda. We acknowledge with thanks the assistance of Claire Hocking in the compilation and calculation of voting figures. Various residents of the region helped us both directly and by giving us privileged access to information and facilities. We ourselves, however, are solely responsible for the interpretation of the data presented in this chapter.

varying in composition and size provided the arena for local politics all over the region. Tribes and/or phratries, often several thousand strong, ranged from highly unified groups that warred before contact to sets of separate patriclans loosely linked by sharing a name and a tradition. Pacification had frozen some unusually large tribes in a position of dominance with smaller groups attached, and these retained a high degree of external political unity. Such tribes, however, tended to have a proliferation of leaders. Former enemies had had to co-operate over the previous decade in local government planning and public works. Some 'native' councils were already operating by 1964 and ten larger councils had been established by 1968. The new developments extended the old inter-group rivalries to opposed new groupings of unprecedented span. Disputes in a public bar or on a plantation sorted men by council area, Sub-District, District, or even broader region (Highlands versus Sepik or Papua), for disagreement divided the universe of principals and bystanders into solidary units. Western Highlands M.H.A.s identified themselves with Papua and New Guinea (*wantaim* [together with] Australia) in differences with the United Nations or Indonesia. A road death in 1967 became a question of redress between Mul and Dei council areas, and by 1969 a land dispute had set Dei and Hagen councils against each other. Candidates in 1968 estimated their chances and pursued their campaigns in terms of the segmentation of their electorates, basing this variously on geographical, administrative, and council areas, tribes, language areas, and mission affiliations. Competition between council areas had already played a part in the 1964 election for Minj Open (Strathern 1964; Reay 1965). This time it dominated both candidates' ideas of support and constituents' ideas of representation in the new electorates of Mul-Dei (where the Dei council area had been part of Minj Open) and Wahgi (the rump Minj Open).

'Big men' of the region used segmentary opposition to climb to prominence on the suppression of rivals, the advantages of being a near agnatic kinsman of a former leader being traditionally greater in the east. They were polygynists, orators, financiers, entrepreneurs, adjudicators, and planners. Successful councillors had used 'big man' skills in council elections, making constituents disassociate their previous record from the obligation to vote for them and, recently, suppressing intended counter-nominations to get elected unopposed. The uneasy ambiguity of representing government to the people and the people to higher authority paralleled the traditional leader's dual task of steering and deferring to public opinion (Reay 1959b: 129-30). 'Big men' seeking office within the council, however, had to curb qualities that attracted the support of fellow councillors to win that of the influential

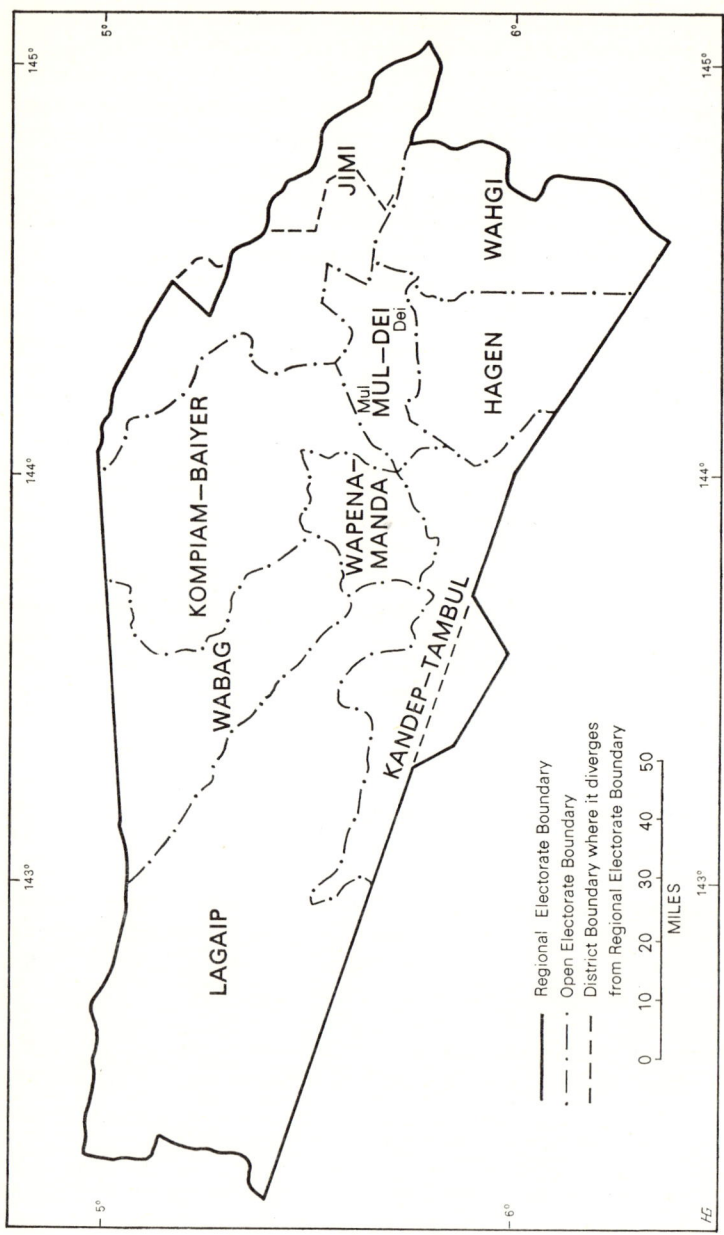

9 Western Highlands Electorates

administrative adviser. Disputes over women, pigs, and (in the west) land preoccupied officially unrecognised councillors' courts where litigants sought economic and political gain. The absence of formal rules brought those with a reputation for fair court hearing (usually former *luluai*s [government-appointed headmen] and interpreters) power and popularity of a kind that surprised expatriates. Ten former Administration interpreters and five former *luluai*s contested Open seats in the region. Where offences were involved, councillors' courts had no power to mete out penalties but had to refer cases to the *kiap* (administrative officer) for a time-consuming fresh hearing. Councillors had to lead their people sometimes in unpopular tasks and envied the *kiaps*' authority to jail or fine persons for disobedience. Further, the Administration had promised that councils could make rules that would have the force of law, but these had to be approved and gazetted first and the delay was seemingly never-ending. By 1968 the councils had no power to impose penalties to be attached to rules on bride wealth, baby clinics, or roadwork. Local authority was an issue of grave concern but people did not connect it with the election, seeing it rather as being internal to the affairs of the council.

House of Assembly and council politics, however, were only separated conceptually in two Open electorates. In Kompiam-Baiyer, Traimya Kambipi romped home on a rational campaign conducted by deputies (in his absence at the Christian Leaders Training College) and based on his special qualifications, which contrasted with the 'big man' skills of council politicians. In Wabag, Tei Abal had cultivated the idea of councillors and M.H.A.s having complementary, not competing, roles at least equal to each other in status and importance. Elsewhere, elections for council president were, in the words of the Regional Returning Officer, 'a kind of pre-selection for candidature in the House of Assembly elections', executive office in the council marking career hurdles on the way to the plum post available to ambitious local men. Six council presidents and vice-presidents stood for Open seats, and all the Wahgi Open candidates had had presidential experience.

THE PRE-ELECTION SCENE

The role of members

The Administration had a clear interest in seeing that some of the indigenous members of the first House (an élite group well tutored in the ways of government) achieved re-election. 'What we are here for', Tei Abal told the House on its last day, 'is to learn. The government is here to teach us'. The gradualist, conservative cast of these members reflected their realisation that their District was more backward and more populous than most: therefore *'Westan Hailan'*, Kaibelt Diria declared, *'em i as bilong Papua-Niugini'* (*as* meaning 'foundation'). This view seemed to get official support from Tom Ellis, the only District Commissioner to be appointed an Official Member of the House of Assembly. His appointment in 1966 looked like a step to check a potentially rebellious House by mustering a group of members who could be counted on to support the Administration in a crisis. Under his supervision the Western and Southern Highlanders tended to vote with the Administration more consistently than any other group. They considered themselves to be 'Tom Ellis's men' and conferred with the D.C. before each sitting of the House. Kaibelt Diria described the procedure thus (in Pidgin):

> I know what people are saying, and if it is a big problem they are talking about I can bring it to the attention of the government. I ask the D.C., or talk to the A.D.C. first and then ask the D.C.; and if the D.C. tells me to take it to Port Moresby, well I take it to Port Moresby. And if the answer is yes, I can come back and tell all the people about it, and the people see this going on and so when the election comes they vote only for me.

When one member described Ellis as 'God *bilong mipela*', the others understood him to refer to a proven omnipotence in bringing economic development to the District. Benefits visible in the Highlands Highway, the Hagen Show, massive overseas investment, and a little money in everyone's hands were directly associated with the laconic District Commissioner who could settle a man's fate with a growl or a shrug and could stand up in church and tell the congregation 'God *i makim mi Nambawan bilong yupela*' ('God has placed me in authority over you'. Cf. Romans 13:1, revised standard version).

Preparations for the 1968 election began in 1966 with the indigenous M.H.A.s' review of their chances of being re-elected. Ellis had made it plain that in return for their support of the official line of development they could expect the Administration to help them learn the skills they needed and bring benefits to their electorates. Now, with their term half over, some who had been counting on Administration support in 1968 learned that this help must cease when nominations came in and the Administration had to fulfil its electoral duty to give all candidates an equal chance. Hitherto they had seen themselves as apprentice politicians rather than as parliamentarians elected to govern the country: government and Administration were identical, though as representatives of their electorates they were free to vote against the official members on matters not affecting general policy. They now sorted themselves into career politicians who had to secure re-election by any means available and drop-outs who were due to be replaced by more effective members.

The only certain way of ensuring success, they decided, was to make sure no one nominated against them. They could overcome constituent dissatisfaction by touring their electorates and seeing that benefits they had brought were widely known. They could try to allay the political ambition of known rivals. The local *kiap*s could effectively further these aims, but if they opposed a particular member's return, as Leme Yangalyo (Wapenamanda) alleged in his own case, they could at least ensure that others nominated against him. The M.H.A.s, with Tei Abal as informal leader, also discussed how to win against other candidates, pooling ideas gleaned from their *kiap*s, any other expatriate supporters they had, and fellow members. Hoping to enhance their credibility in their electorates, they invited one another to visit and speak on their behalf; but these visits made no impact.

Members explaining to councils their progress in getting things for their electorates introduced the idea that, although the government was good and wise in matters affecting the country as a whole, they themselves were competing with one another and also had to 'fight' the powers in Moresby to get any special consideration for their own areas. This new notion took such firm root that a common view of the member's role, explicitly promulgated in election speeches in Mul-Dei though rarely formulated as a coherent theory of political representation in Wahgi, was:

> The House of Assembly is a strong place of bricks and cement, filled with strong *mastas* [white bosses] who have bald heads, ties, and glasses. No playboy must go there, but only a strong, brave man without shame, like a pickaxe or a crowbar, who can break into it and bring back *bisnis* [opportunity for profitable enterprise] for us. He must say to the white man's government there, 'You, Government, must give much money to my area. I have many people and we have not enough money. And you must give us plenty of bulldozers to relieve my people of hard work and injury on the roads and allow them to work at this *bisnis* instead.'

This formulation draws upon concepts shared by people in several parts of the Western Highlands: permanent buildings as an index of stable prosperity; the relevance of personal appearance and apparel to political behaviour; release from the forced labour of roadwork for progress and wellbeing; and, above all, the importance of *bisnis*.

'*Bisnis*' stands for any profit-making enterprise—cash-cropping, commercial activity, investment, or, collectively, economic development—any means by which a person, group, or population can make money by independent effort, without being beholden to a boss. The task of the M.H.A. was to get 'the white man's government' to introduce new *bisnis* opportunities and remove impediments from those already existing.

Candidates needed experience of working for or with Europeans to be eligible for this task. The prosperity of European planters and businessmen had been presented as the model for the economic aims of every person and the wages offered for coffee picking (recommended, for example by the Mul Council Survey, as a major source of increased income) seemed paltry to people who were themselves growing coffee. Europeans had stimulated consumer demands and there was discontent with wages, the low prices paid for coffee and tea, and the high charges for repairing motor vehicles. The M.H.A. should be a forceful negotiator.

Contradictory images of the ideal member held in Dei and Wahgi in 1964 were now reversed. Key men in Dei had seen him as a super-councillor with some of the power of the *kiap*, acting as boss of the councillors to forward road-building, sawmills, and coffee-growing, but by 1968 Dei candidates were declaring that they would be the people's 'servants' as all the candidates for Minj Open had assured voters whoever they elected in 1964 would be. Wahgi people were disillusioned with the earlier propaganda that the M.H.A. would be '*boi bilong ol*' (servant of the people); candidates and constituents assumed that the Administration shared some of its power with him. Kaibelt Diria was to campaign on his achievements; Tumun Dubura hoped to bring to the south the advantages the north had enjoyed through having a northern member; Mugap Baugum promised to bring bulldozers and iron bridges to the coffee roads and access roads as well as highways. Mugap, challenged on his ability to get this done, said he would tell the *kiap*s that it was necessary, for they had to heed what the M.H.A. said.

Political parties

From the days of the Legislative Council to April 1967 there had been expatriate attempts, all abortive, to form a Highlands Party. In June 1967, however, Tom Ellis called a meeting in Mt Hagen of the M.H.A.s and the council presidents and vice-presidents, with Keith Levy as chairman, to discuss the nature and functions of political parties. The council men reported to a second meeting that they and their constituents were not yet ready for political parties. Seven of the nine candidates in our two adjoining Open electorates associated parties with self-government and/or independence, and wariness about self-government led people to reject the notion of parties without debate. All who had attended the briefing sessions in Mt Hagen had heard of Pangu and knew that there were at least two parties, one formed in Port Moresby and one in Wewak. Prominent council men who had not previously heard of political parties gained the impression that they were all subversive and Pangu particularly so. This may have been an inference from statements indigenous M.H.A.s were making that the region did not need political parties yet because 'we Western Highlanders' were 'the government party'. Kaibelt Diria, who attacked Oala Oala-Rarua in the House immediately after the first meeting of the United New Guinea National Party in 1965 and made three more attacks on parties in 1967, saw them as part of a threatened new political order in which his present position of power and prestige would be devalued in favour of new forms of authority and in which Highlanders generally would be at a disadvantage.

The indigenous candidates for the Regional (excepting Phillip Matuakan, who had been to school in Australia) had learned about political parties through newspapers, radio, and conversation. All saw them as groups of people with similar ideas. They were cautious in discussing them and their opinions tended to be unfavourable, at least for now, though two had friends or relatives in Pangu Pati and one of these had friends also in the United Christian Party. All were aware of expatriates' repeatedly voiced suspicion of Pangu.

The only favourable reactions to parties, however, that fieldworkers observed among indigenous people in the region also concerned Pangu. Several high school pupils home on leave spoke of the party with enthusiasm as a means of launching themselves on lucrative and exciting political careers. Otherwise only some educated Papuans stationed in the region were heard giving even qualified support to any party, and that invariably Pangu.

James T. Ovia, a carpenter from Yule Island, who had lived in Wahgi for several years and wanted to stand for the Open there, described himself as 'the father of Pangu' and said the founders of the party had derived the name from a letter he had written to the Australian Broadcasting Commission. He was the only person known to have sported a party badge and he removed it during the nomination period on the advice of the A.D.C. who was Returning Officer.

Electoral change

Ian Downs, the Highlands Special Member, was a Goroka planter prominent in the Highland Farmers' and Settlers' Association, a former D.C. for the Eastern Highlands, and an active member of the old Legislative Council. No candidate from the Western Highlands had stood against him in 1964. Long before his term was over, however, the interests of the Eastern and Western Highlands had diverged sharply. Further, benefits that came to Goroka (Eastern Highlands District) in the way of education and health services, improved roads, and more permanent buildings were easy to associate with having an able M.H.A. ostensibly representing the Highlands as a whole but 'really' looking after his own part of the electorate.

In 1964 voters in Hagen and Minj had confused giving first and second preferences with electing both an expatriate and a local candidate for the Open electorate, interpreting warnings that only one man could win as information that the man who came second would work with the member as teacher-adviser (if white) or pupil-observer (if black). Minj chose Kaibelt Diria as its pupil-member and Hagen chose Keith Levy as its teacher-member. The splitting of the massive Highlands Special into four Regional electorates corresponding closely with the administrative Districts was still being foreshadowed when Levy, as the only expatriate M.H.A. from the District, began to act as if he were Special Member for the Western Highlands, using his particular skills and position as a European to guide the Open members from his region. Downs took a leading part in debate and, as an elected Member, frequently opposed the official nominees, but Levy preferred to work behind the scenes and encouraged the indigenous M.H.A.s to support the Administration in their speeches. These 'pupil-members' saw him as being finally answerable, like themselves, to the D.C.

By 1968 council elections had taught voters that only one man would win the Open election and that one other man (in Hagen, Mul-Dei, and Wahgi, specifically a white man until Iambakey Okuk began campaigning) would be elected for the District. Both Wahgi and Dei councils had, in addition to the ordinary 'local' wards, special 'regional' wards in which, by informal agreement, only expatriates competed in the first elections. The plummeting failure of the multi-racial experiment in Wahgi and the lukewarm acceptance of it in Dei, coinciding with recent waves of anti-European sentiment (mild compared with other parts of the Territory, but novel here) led expatriate candidates to confine themselves to competition for the Regional, leaving the Open electorates free for ambitious local men.

Only one European (Roland Freund, agricultural officer for the

Lutheran mission in Wapenamanda) and one part-European (John Leahy, a planter in Mt Hagen) stood for Open seats. Both were sons of pioneers and both spoke vernacular languages. Freund polled better than any of Leme Yangalyo's indigenous opponents, but Leahy had no chance in Hagen, where electors plainly wanted one of the men already prominent in their affairs. Leaders in Hagen and Mul complained that Levy had not helped them as he had led them to expect. Rumours were rife that he got elected by plying voters with liquor and making false promises or by electoral officials directing voters, altering ballots, and manipulating results. He was an obvious target for dissatisfaction with the Special Member, with expatriates generally, and with his own record as Open Member, and he was reluctant to stand for the Regional, though expatriate friends (including Ellis) urged him to do so. Tas Hammersley, who had resigned his post as District Education Officer to be a private farmer, nominated in his stead. Levy changed his mind, however, and Hammersley withdrew— too late to recall electoral agents who continued to urge electors in remote areas, well after polling began, to vote for a non-candidate.

Four of the eight Regional candidates were Europeans. Between them they had a wealth of experience in most of the District's formal organisations. Keith Levy had withdrawn from these on being elected, but had served on the House of Assembly Works Committee. John Colman, a 1964 opponent, had been chairman of the Town Advisory Council, and John Watts president of the Chamber of Commerce. Nol (that is, Noel) Rutledge, the only Regional candidate with experience in local government, had been southern vice-president of Wahgi Council. To qualify educationally, Highlander candidates were necessarily young and relatively inexperienced: they were aged 23 to 30, whereas the Europeans were 37 to 47. Phillip Matuakan belonged to the Wabag-Lagaip Development Committee; otherwise the indigenous candidates had affiliations only with sporting and religious groups.

The European candidates were planters and businessmen; the indigenous candidates included one mechanic (Iambakey Okuk), a junior business executive with the Lutheran Waso marketing organisation (Phillip Matuakan), a teacher at a Lutheran school (Nita Wapurao), and a lecturer at a Catholic teachers' college (Philip Wamell). The Europeans, seeking election to secure their investments and continued presence in the Territory, proposed to retain their present means of livelihood if elected. All the indigenous candidates, however, saw the job of M.H.A. as a superior alternative career. None was entirely satisfied with his present work. All expected a seat in parliament to bring added status and prevent them from being left behind by an emerging generation equipped with more and better education.

Both sets of candidates expected to help uneducated Open members to translate bills and interpret procedures, but they differed in their views of the electorate. The indigenous candidates saw it as an expanded Open electorate, and indeed three had considered standing for an Open. They thought the Regional and Open members would be wanting the same things and working for them in much the same way. They saw no reason why Europeans should get votes, even in their home areas; Iambakey alone was aware of uneducated Highlanders' dependence upon Europeans and their susceptibility to European propaganda, and he was the only indigenous candidate who had pondered the implications of the size of the electorate. The European candidates, by contrast, saw the Regional electorate as a contracted Special electorate geared to the unity of the District: the Regional Member, a European, would co-ordinate or 'steer' the indigenous Open Members to this end. They did not see the indigenous candidates as serious competitors: *kiap*s quoted indigenous M.H.A.s as saying that a European should represent the District, and Hagen councillors affirmed on 14 February that they wanted a European member for the Regional and a native member for the Open.

No Regional candidate was well known throughout the electorate. Colman had stores at Baiyer River, Mt Hagen, Laiagam, and Wabag and had operated earlier at Kandep, Kompiam, and Minj but the other candidates thought the votes he obtained through these links would be negligible. Levy, having already acted as if he represented the District, could claim credit for benefits that had come to the Western Highlands as a whole but indigenous electors confused him with the Special Member other candidates were criticising. Watts was unknown outside Mt Hagen and Rutledge known only in Wahgi. All the indigenous candidates had school friends, people they had trained with, and more recent contacts scattered through the District but these were not usually influential persons. In Mt Hagen, where Wamell had lived for two or three years, he was unknown outside the Catholic educational institutions. Matuakan's father-in-law, Poio Iuri M.H.A., was prominent in Lagaip. Iambakey Okuk was the son of a Chimbu policeman who had lived at Nondugl in Wahgi for several years and he had been with his parents earlier in Kudjip (Wahgi), Mt Hagen, Dei, and Tambul. He had been working as the only indigenous mechanic in Wabag. Voters in the east would be sympathetic towards 'Corporal Okuk's son', and indigenous operators of motor vehicles in the west knew 'the mechanic' well. Further, as a prominent footballer he was well known to all Soccer Associations in the District.

For campaign purposes the candidates saw the Regional electorate as a combination of the nine electorates and considered their chances in each. Alternatively, it comprised three main language groups, each coinciding with a broad cultural uniformity. Matuakan reasoned that since over half the population of the Western Highlands was Enga-speaking the election could be won in the populous western part of the electorate, and he alone did not try to cover as much territory as possible. The European candidates, and also Iambakey, acknowledged in a different way the importance of the western area. Believing that the influence of Tei Abal, already re-elected unopposed for Wabag Open, spread throughout the Enga-speaking world, they assumed that a Regional candidate who had Tei's support could win. Iambakey embarrassed Tei by making it known that the M.H.A. had asked him to stand and alleging publicly that Tei supported him. Conversely, however, the M.H.A.s knew that asking an influential person to stand for the Regional would secure his support for themselves.

Issues and attitudes affecting the Regional election, and by implication the Open elections also, centred upon the charismatic District Commissioner. Tom Ellis was appointed Director of District Administration before dissatisfaction with his régime on the part of some expatriates crystallised into any organised opposition. Wahgi men had criticised Ellis for favouritism towards Kaibelt but trusted his judgment on policy matters. Some expatriate businessmen in and about Mt Hagen, however, had many complaints. People within the District referred to him as 'God' and critics thought him domineering and opinionated—more concerned with increasing his power than with promoting the economy. He was mean, they said, with road maintenance funds for their areas in spite of a verbal concern with the total region. They alleged that he used hard-sell tactics instead of the reasoned economic arguments necessary to convince investors. They suspected him of using his administrative power to help some enterprises in which they alleged he had a private financial interest. (This allegation was untrue.) They read sinister overtones in his determination to direct policy and change in the District after his departure. They thought his political and electoral education program was slanted to ensure the election of his supporters.

These expatriate businessmen had been active in the formal organisations of the area and also constituted an informal 'study group' along lines suggested by a visiting officer of the Australian Country Party, and now they decided to develop a political arm to ensure the stability of their investments. They persuaded John Watts to stand for the Regional. They suspected that the Administration was rigging the election in favour of Levy and they collected sworn affidavits to produce in the Court of Disputed Returns if he won. They alleged pressure on electoral staff to influence assisted voting and threats of economic reprisals against Watts supporters. They referred to the D.C. by his surname, seeming to reduce him to human proportions in order to do battle with him, and thought Ellis would stop at nothing to get Levy re-elected. (They acknowledged later that this assumption was incorrect.) In this climate a planter who had talked with the Regional Returning Officer brought the news into Wahgi that Levy was now standing, and a rider that 'so of course' Noel Rutledge would not stand made it impossible for Rutledge to withdraw, though he might otherwise have done so in favour of Watts.

THE REGIONAL CAMPAIGN

The campaign already set in motion by Tas Hammersley before he withdrew was unique in using a grass-roots approach. He had prepared his truck as a campaign vehicle he could sleep in while spending a few nights with different groups; he had walked from Kompiam to Baiyer and was prepared to walk further through the electorate. He sent out about thirty-six schoolboys bearing his photograph and instructions on what to tell people they met. These youthful agents came from places as far apart as Jimi, Laiagam, Porgera, and Tambul in all parts of the electorate and would be operating in their home areas.

Other candidates adopted a less imaginative approach. European Open candidates in 1964 had used council meetings as a means of contacting electors and this time both European candidates and administrative officials assumed that the council would be the chief instrument for getting local people to know the candidates and for the latter to communicate any platforms they held. All four used the Australian method of campaigning by making speeches and justifying their policies. At council meetings each gave an address in Pidgin telling something of himself and what he proposed to do if elected, then this talk was translated into the vernacular by an official interpreter or a prominent councillor. They received courteous speeches-in-reply that thanked them for their trouble and attributed the outcome of the election to *samting bilong resis* (a matter of [who won] the competition for votes). They assumed that the councillors would decide for whom their people would vote as a bloc. The context of the formal meeting, however, ruled out the response in expressions of support or dissent that is so much a part of candidates' meetings in Australia. The indigenous candidates, who faced the same problem of how to contact a massive number of people and woo their votes, also addressed council meetings but did not see these as a very effective means of communication; the major part of their campaigning was carried out informally and away from the public eye.

All the candidates excepting Philip Wamell and Nita Wapurao had posters printed bearing their photographs and instructions to vote first preference for them; those of Rutledge carried also a promise to work hard for the electorate. Iambakey Okuk drove from east to west of the electorate distributing his posters personally as well as handing out some at council meetings. Keith Levy, Philip Wamell, and John Watts sent out letters requesting support. In June 1967 Wamell sent out roneoed letters to all Catholic mission teachers and friends everywhere reminding them of a promise he had secured from them the previous year, when he had told them of his intention to stand for election, to spread his name and get in touch with the people for him. Levy wrote to every local government councillor in the District, all missionaries and business people, all Health Department, Police Department, and Department of District Administration staff, and the Open candidates. John Watts sent letters to teachers of Primary 'T' and mission schools,[1] council presidents, heads of mission congregations, planters, the Banz Farmers' and Settlers' Association, and the Wabag-Lagaip Development Committee. The most specific letters, those of John Watts, stressed three things: 'the maintenance of law, order, and industrial peace'; 'security and opportunity for development for all'; and 'intelligent and freely offered co-operation with the native peoples and the Administration in acceptable policies'.

The indigenous candidates did not have the money to spend lavishly on posters, pamphlets, and campaign workers. They did not have their own vehicles, though Iambakey managed to obtain the use of a pickup for the campaign period and Philip Wamell's subclan allowed him some use of a group vehicle. They had to rely on informal ties with kin and friends. They wrote personal letters to people they knew in all parts of the electorate. All hoped to capture the absentee vote in Port Moresby. Nita Wapurao had gone there in October 1967 and told people he was intending to stand. Iambakey claimed to have about twenty medical students campaigning there for him, and both Matuakan and Wamell wrote to people they knew there. Lacking the European candidates' ability to pay electoral agents to 'speak out' for them, they depended upon relatives or friends to do so after a church service or a council ward meeting or at one of the town markets. The impact of such speaking out varied, of course, with the standing

[1] 'T' schools (with Territory curriculum) are the government primary schools for indigenous pupils, as distinct from 'A' schools (with Australian curriculum) which expatriate children attend (usually in company with a few highly selected mixed-race and/or indigenous pupils).

of the speaker in the group he was addressing; but also a voluntary supporter, no matter how vocal, could change his mind later on exposure to other candidates.

There was no marked difference between the platforms the European candidates communicated to electors. All were concerned with economic development of the type Tom Ellis had already promoted and although Levy and Watts differed radically in the methods they judged to be appropriate for promoting it this difference was not apparent to uneducated people. Candidates' speeches at council meetings were similar in format and contained little that was distinctively memorable when given one after another, and reports of these by councillors to their constituents were garbled and confused. Distinguishing gimmicks proved to be more successful in identifying candidates than individual variations in the ideas they expressed. Rutledge, for example, stressed the setting up of a District-wide committee to help and advise the elected members and secure 'one voice' for the Western Highlands. Watts had also introduced this idea (which invited interpretation as a more 'democratic' attempt than Tom Ellis's to establish a Western Highlands voting bloc and as a proposal to reduce the power of the District Commissioner) but gave up mentioning it when it seemed to lack popular appeal. Watts reiterated his main theme that money is the basis of government and *bisnis* the source of money, but he also made a point of driving his distinctive new blue fastback sedan wherever he could to distinguish him from other European candidates.

Whereas the indigenous candidates relied upon their own personalities and policies to gain as many votes as possible from people who knew them, the European candidates relied at first upon the persuasive powers of the councillors they addressed at meetings. The Europeans sent out car-teams to spread their names and campaign materials and vied with one another to get the help of influential indigenous supporters. Watts scored a victory in Wahgi when he arrived in company with a Hagen leader well known to prominent Wahgi councillors, and another when voters recognised the voice of their favourite radio-announcer from Radio Mount Hagen issuing from his tape recorder. Tape recorders, fitted with tapes in Enga, Melpa, and Wahgi (the three main languages of the region), as well as in Pidgin, were an effective means of getting this candidate known: the car-teams delighted in playing them and audiences gathered quickly to hear recordings of their own language in which the simple and memorable name 'Jon Wos' recurred as a frequent refrain. Another successful device was the distribution of how-to-vote cards coloured blue, as the electoral education campaign had informed voters the Regional ballot papers would be: in one part of the electorate people hoarded these cards and tried to use them as ballot papers.

The control European candidates could exercise over indigenous campaigning on their behalf was limited. A candidate telling people through an influential interpreter, for example, to vote first preference for him alone had no means of knowing whether the interpreter slipped in a caution that they had to make up their own minds. The vernacular tapes used by Watts's car-teams included material he himself would presumably not have permitted in an English or Pidgin version: in Wahgi his reference to the Highlands Special Member looking after his own part of the electorate to the detriment of the Western Highlands came over unmistakably as an allegation that he was filling his pockets with ill-gotten money; cautiously worded offers to work for the electorate invited construction as guarantees of particular material and other benefits—money, good roads, cars that would differ from those presently available in not requiring expensive repairs, along with big schools, big hospitals, more agricultural extension officers, regular consultation with ordinary constituents as well as with council, and true partnership between the races. A stress on money and increasing *bisnis* opportunity seemed to imply that he would raise the price of coffee and bring other good things besides. Candidates' car-teams added extra elaborations of their own, often deliberately improving upon what they had been briefed to say in order to help the white man who had made their touring possible. They got to widely dispersed courting ceremonies and other sing-sings and made some new friendships and exchange partnerships on their own account.

Being locally known actively damaged Rutledge's chances once the indigenous car-teams sent out by the other candidates entered his home area. Confident of local support, he failed to secure his home area by scotching rumours that he epitomised all the faults of expatriate councillors. He kept up with the other candidates, so far as finance allowed, in attempts to cover the electorate that were costing them all much more than they had anticipated. It was soon apparent that the seemingly inexhaustible funds John Watts was able to muster strengthened his chances of getting votes everywhere. The European candidates timed their personal tours of the electorate to take in council meetings, and one A.D.C. signalled the Returning Officer that the council was meeting on a certain date to ensure that all Regional candidates could attend. As the campaign progressed, however, they still went to council meetings but, according to Watts, this was to avoid having a mark put against them rather than to gain more votes as they had hoped earlier. The candidates were now concentrating on going to meetings arranged by local people in different areas and on getting local people to campaign on their behalf. The European candidates had got around to using the indigenous candidates' original tactics—reliance on friends and informal contacts in each area.

Philip Wamell was concerned about the number of children in the District who were not attending school and expressed his desire to get more schools established. Phillip Matuakan stressed the need for further unity and development before independence. Iambakey Okuk, in taking this point further and making it one which the others could not ignore, was the only indigenous candidate to turn the common expectation that a European would be elected into political capital. At council meetings he said that coastal people such as Oala Oala-Rarua were wanting early independence but the Western Highlands did not want it yet. The United Nations would wish to hear the people's views on this. If Europeans with successful businesses and cars alleged that the people did not want independence they would not be believed as the United Nations would think the Europeans only wanted to stay in the Territory to make more profits. The people should elect one of the natives as their representative because only a native would be believed.

This approach forced replies from the European candidates and also made the question whether to elect an indigenous or expatriate candidate a basic issue. It did not, however, serve Iambakey's own purpose. Many expatriate electors, including some officials, associated his advocacy of 'black' representation with an anti-European, anti-Administration stance and, despite his insistence that having a native as spokesman would increase the credibility of the belief he shared with them that the Western Highlands people did not want independence yet, the impression spread among expatriates that he was in favour of self-government and secretly associated with Pangu Pati. At the January meeting of Wapenamanda Council the D.O. questioned Iambakey on his links with the party and on his future intentions; he answered strongly that he was a Western Highlands man and thought the same way as the people of the District did, but the questioning could have implied to councillors that their D.O. had doubts about the candidate and this could easily have put doubts in their minds too. Iambakey's message that it would be an advantage to have a native member did little to convince people that he himself was a suitable man for the job but it helps to account for the extent of support the indigenous candidates received in their home areas. Opinion leaders in Wahgi who had been assuming that an expatriate would win the Regional, and had hitherto dismissed the Minj man, Konumbuga Philip Wamell, as a *manki* (a mere lad) of no importance reacted to Iambakey's campaigning by deciding to support Wamell.

Iambakey's campaigning affected both the course of the election and the political climate of the period. Anonymous urban vandals began to scrawl 'RACIST' across photographs of European candidates pinned outside chambers in Mt Hagen and 'PANGU' (just as deadly a smear word here) across that of Iambakey. Police Special Branch officers were obtrusively touring the electorate with ears cocked for the expression of 'anti-Administration' sentiments (one even alleging that anthropologists could be expected to 'stir up racial strife' because their work required them to 'mix with natives'). Expatriate supporters of Levy deplored the administrative chaos that would result if 'that mechanic from Wabag' should win, and European bookmakers were now rating Iambakey's chances as high as those of the least likely European (Rutledge). The concern of Watts's committee with changing the style of government in the region gave way to a more conservative stress on the aims they and the Ellis administration shared in policies of economic development.

John Watts and Keith Levy used one unusually sophisticated means of viewing the electorate, drawing up projected voting figures for each of the areas. Watts's supporters did this early in order to assess the desirability of exchanging preferences; Levy conducted his analysis near the close of polling simply to assess his likelihood of success. Both analyses showed that the candidate concerned could win. The accuracy of both projections depended not only on the calculation of the candidate's own support but also on a proper assessment of support for each of the other candidates. Watts's group divided the electorate into three (Hagen, Wabag, and Wahgi) and worked through the hypothetical results, keeping a careful record of the anticipated elimination of each candidate in terms of the numbers of votes exhausted at each count and the allocation of second preferences from the votes he could get in each area. They decided that it would be worth while for their candidate to exchange preferences with Rutledge in Wahgi but not elsewhere. They therefore printed two different sets of 'how-to-vote' cards, one with 'JON WOS (1), Nol Rutledge (2)' for distribution in Wahgi and the other with simply 'JON WOS (1)'. When it became clear early in polling that Rutledge was not pulling the votes they had assumed he would get in his home area they hurriedly stopped associating their candidate with him. Levy's analysis set out, by Open electorate, the maximum number of votes he could possibly get against the numbers the other candidates might attract. He arrived at a rough estimate of the number of votes available by taking eligible voters to be half the total population and assuming a turn-out of 75 per cent. In some areas, such as Kandep-Tambul and Kompiam-Baiyer, he had very little information to guide him and divided up the votes as best he could;

in the former, for example, he divided the votes equally between himself, Watts, and Colman.

There is little evidence of the Christian missions giving positive support to particular candidates. The Holy Trinity College (Mt Hagen) had roneoed Philip Wamell's letters but the priests both there and at Fatima College (Banz) were ignorant of his whereabouts and activities in January 1968, which would seem unlikely if they were sponsoring him as a candidate. Nita Wapurao, the Lutheran mission schoolteacher, said that the mission at Yaramanda was not in favour of his candidature. The Wabag Lutheran newsletter of 10 January 1968, however, carried advice in Pidgin to 'Choose men who are members of Wabag Lutheran Church', indicating which Open candidates for Lagaip and Wapenamanda were Lutherans. It listed only two Regional (*Hailan Spesal*) candidates: it mentioned Phillip Matuakan but not his connection with Waso and drew attention to Iambakey Okuk's association with the Lutheran Elcong. The omission of Nita Wapurao's name seems to confirm the candidate's own account. More generally, missionaries emphasised particular qualities they thought appropriate in an M.H.A., advising converts to pray for a good man to win or for guidance in voting in a way that would make this possible. Missionaries who used their influence in this way allowed converts to decide for themselves to exclude Open candidates repugnant to particular missions.

Candidates canvassed missions along with other groups, but only Levy made a point of visiting prominent missionaries of different denominations in the various centres hoping to benefit from any information they gave people about the election. No Regional candidate relied upon sponsorship and open support from any of the missions, but some of the candidates did expect those with clear mission affiliation (Lutheran or Catholic) to get support from people of the same religion, particularly in their home area. The indigenous candidates relied upon the missions as focal points where people gathered and took the opportunity to address them after church services. Similarly, however, Philip Wamell attended meetings convened by the Administration for electoral education, stepping forward after the officer's talk to deliver a policy speech. (Some other candidates did this also, but more rarely.) Thus the indigenous candidates showed willingness to address assemblies of people brought together for some other purpose. Both Iambakey and Wamell addressed crowds at the town markets but did not convene meetings of their own. The arrival of the European candidates' car-teams seems to have usually stirred at least a rustle of interest; but those of John Watts could draw a crowd by playing the speeches taped in the vernacular.

THE OPEN CAMPAIGN IN WAHGI AND MUL-DEI

Wahgi: the sitting Member

Kaibelt Diria had resigned the presidency of the northern 'native' council to stand for the House of Assembly in 1964.[2] An ardent advocate of the amalgamated multi-racial council proposed late that year, he was northern vice-president from 1965 then became president in October 1967, this time retaining the office throughout the election. His role was essentially that of an indigenous equivalent to the *kiap* adviser, initiating and guiding discussion within formal meetings on the basis of knowledge he shared with officials. Uniquely experienced and skilful at dealing with Europeans, he expected the Wahgi people to appreciate the advantage this gave him over others in getting things done for the electorate. He listened sympathetically to the ideas and complaints of expatriates and took official guidance on which of these to take to Port Moresby. He modelled his coffee *bisnis* on an expatriate plantation, with himself as boss rather than leader among equals. Local councillors resented the difference between his stipend and theirs when they saw his *bisnis* benefiting. By 1966 he was ready to buy a motor vehicle and his *kiap* supporters persuaded him to get a *bisnis kar* (commercial motor vehicle) for transporting passengers and goods instead of the private sedan he desired: this would make him known all over the electorate and earn the extra money he would need for his 1968 campaign. He had 'KAIBELT DIRIA M.H.A.' painted in large red letters across the front of his truck.

Twice Kaibelt used his position as M.H.A. to influence officials who appeared to be condoning expatriate privilege, but he did not refer to these events when campaigning on his effectiveness as member. In 1965 he secured a ban on the conscription of women for roadwork. Nopnop Tol, who had stood against him in 1964 and hoped to defeat him next time, expressed the view (which traditionalists supported) that this was an attempt to alienate women's votes over which their menfolk had rights of disposal. Kaibelt did not, however, mention in his campaign the acceptance and development of women's clubs, for which he had worked with energy and enthusiasm. He opposed trenchantly the tax rise proposed by the council adviser in 1967. Phrasing his objection

---

[2] Kaibelt told Reay in 1963 that he had worked as an Administration interpreter, but he was never formally employed as such and evidently he was referring to having assumed the task of interpreting for *kiap*s (as any council president has to do at some time or other) on occasions that were then important to him. He had first impressed expatriates with his organisational skills and readiness to learn when employed as foreman in the Malaria Control Unit and on a plantation. (Cf. Reay 1965: 155-9)

in terms of the desirability of gradual development ('slowly, slowly, we are still infants'), he nevertheless insisted that taxes should not be raised before 1968 [sic] and councillors and ward committeemen told constituents that Kaibelt was blocking a tax rise in order to win votes at the next election.

Kaibelt knew that his strongest opponents were far less acceptable than he to his *kiap* advisers and was reasonably hopeful that official support would help to keep him in power. The A.D.C. stressed to him that he himself had to campaign actively to win the election of 1968 and by late 1966 had discussed with him a plan to ensure success.

Kaibelt's plan was to exploit the now traditional opposition between north and south, the former 'native' council areas. He would nominate early then appeal to his known rivals in the north to stand down in his favour rather than splitting the northern vote and allowing a southerner to be elected. In the south he recognised Tumun Dubura as his most serious rival but he was counting on the nomination of other southerners splitting the southern vote.

Political ambitions in Wahgi

In 1966-7 nearly every man who controlled a motor vehicle saw himself as an immediate potential rival to Kaibelt or at least as building up his *bisnis* before entering Territory politics. Most of the 'big councillors' on both sides of the valley had considered unseating the member. Their primary aim appears to have been to capture the pinnacle of the local prestige system simultaneously for themselves, their particular clans or tribes, and their parts of the council area. Despite the inclusion of the East Kambia, the Open electorate was essentially equated with the council area and the office of M.H.A. was seen as the highest of the positions of mingled prestige and power available to prominent men in local government. Councillors discussed among themselves the most equitable distribution of the higher positions (M.H.A. and council president) between north and south and of the lesser positions on either side ('regional' vice-president and 'regional' member) between the many men available to fill them. Principles of fairness faltered on their private ambitions to obtain (for themselves, their own groups, and their own areas) a unique convergence of as many positions as possible. Nearly all the southerners wished to obtain for the south the advantages they thought the north had enjoyed through having its own M.H.A., and men in all four corners of the valley wanted to secure representation for what they thought were neglected parts of the council area. All saw Kaibelt as the official nominee (excepting Mugap Baugum, who thought he himself was favoured) and some contrasted Administration sponsorship with their own position as popular leaders.

Several saw themselves as more deserving of the prestige and perquisites of office than Kaibelt because of criticisms their supporters had made of him. Some expected the M.H.A.'s stipend to enable them to employ managers for their *bisnis* activities while they took the unparalleled opportunities the job afforded for travel. Few saw the work of the M.H.A. as being exacting: indeed, one who tested his chance for the House of Assembly by standing for a 'regional' seat in the council election of October 1967 shrugged off his defeat by saying that visiting polling centres had at least made him better known, so he could expect more votes next time, and in any case $50 deposit was a small price to pay for the chance to win an assured income with nothing to do for it but talk and travel. After the council election fifteen men who had played some part in local politics were still intending to challenge the M.H.A. Nine were roughly contemporary with him, ranging in age from just over 40 to about 55. Twelve were present or past councillors. Of nine currently in the council, eight had served continuously from the inception of 'native' councils. Eight, including two now out of the council, had been 'big councillors'. Three had been presidents, and both the current vice-presidents wanted to stand. Two ward committee men hoped mistakenly that their councillors, not themselves potential candidates, would support them.

Seven of the older men and half of those still in their thirties were polygynists. All were coffee farmers and nearly all had had motor vehicles. Six ran trade stores and four of the younger men kept a few head of cattle. Four older men had been in paid employment at some time or other. Ten of the fifteen were southerners, at least seven of whom hoped to bring to the south the advantages they thought the north had enjoyed through having a local M.H.A. All the northerners and two southerners came from places where constituents felt they had benefited little from local government because of a centralist bias in favour of Minj in the south and the Banz-Kerowil area in the north. They believed that Kaibelt, coming from Talu in Banz-Kerowil, promoted his own area to the neglect of theirs, and they trusted that having a local M.H.A. would give them a powerful voice in the council.

Nopnop Tol (aged about 50) had stood in 1964 (Reay 1964:248-50; 1965:162-4) and intended all along to challenge Kaibelt again. He was still influential in his own Konumbuga tribe and in relations with immigrant settlers. Nop was a genuine, though unlettered, intellectual who brooded upon the future and articulated popularly acceptable prophecies from widespread but fragmented hopes. He maintained a more varied base for his ideas (and, by implication, for potential support) than any other intending candidate through paying attention to pronouncements of traditionalists and ideas discussed by educated youths. He had been president of Minj 'native' council since its inception but had not served on the amalgamated Wahgi Council. When his plan to re-enter council politics in 1967 misfired his supporters ceased to regard him as a credible candidate for the House of Assembly.

Bag Kum (aged about 45), another former 'big councillor' from Konumbuga tribe, managed to get back on the council at this time. He hoped that as M.H.A. he could secure official approval for a coffee factory he wanted to establish in competition with expatriate enterprise. He led a group his father had formed of men incorporated, like himself, from other clans. With land demarcation committees advising groups to resume land held by non-agnates, Bag and Amban (a younger non-agnate who was an innovator in *bisnis* and had ten wives) were under pressure to review and declare their group identification before contesting the election.

Half the southerners opposing Kaibelt had their home base in a single tribe. Realistically the M.H.A. saw Tumun Dubura, currently the most eminent Konumbuga councillor, as his only serious rival in the south. Tumun, a former Administration interpreter and later *luluai*, had been vice-president of the 'native' council and refrained from nominating in 1964 on official advice that he would split the Konumbuga vote. Tumun had been the first president of Wahgi Council but by mid-1966 had clashed with the council adviser, who considered him 'not a fit person to hold office'. Officials thought a council president should be above reproach and an exemplar to his people in every way, but constituents dismissed the lapses they knew about as the actions of a 'real man', the way they themselves might act if placed in a position of power. Missionaries saw the influence of a heavy drinker like Tumun as necessarily evil and many expatriates thought him a trouble-maker when he primed individuals to insist upon just rewards for work. Lacking formal education, he had a wide reputation for fairness in informal court hearing and early in his presidency he was selected for training as an Assistant Magistrate (*'olasem* [just like a] Judge'). Threatened with dismissal from the presidency, he agreed to resign only after obtaining an oral assurance, which was not honoured, that this training would not be denied him.

Tumun's official downfall made him no less prominent and effective in the council, but it affected other councillors' anticipations of the 1968 election. As a reminder that the Administration imposed an arbitrary ceiling on the power permitted to local leaders, it gave them confidence that official sponsorship of Kaibelt would end before it could block his replacement as M.H.A. They thought, however, that the *kiaps* were persecuting Tumun, the obvious man to replace him, in order to ensure that he himself did not win. They now weighed the chance of getting official support for their own candidature. Tumun, however, took official disapproval as a challenge to demonstrate that he did not need sponsorship by *kiaps* to win elections. He planned to gain the South Wall 'regional' seat in the council and get back the presidency before crowning his ambition by becoming M.H.A. He won the 'regional' seat easily. The presence of an intimidating array of senior Administration officials, and a clear indication from the A.D.C. that he wanted Kaibelt for president, made him signal to the other councillors a last minute decision not to contest that office and he accepted the southern vice-presidency.

Mugap Baugum was well aware that he had succeeded Tumun as president in November 1966 through the influence of a former council adviser rather than by popular choice. He construed this as the Administration's intention to groom him to replace Kaibelt as M.H.A. and took to touring the valley in council transport with the object of getting widely known as the *kiaps*' choice before standing for election. Educated to Standard III at a Lutheran bush school and now leader of the mission congregation, he coerced the men of his council ward (including traditionalists and Christian converts of all denominations) into doing 'council work' (the supply and haulage of materials for his new church, 'voluntary' roadwork, and attendance at unusually frequent ward meetings) under threat of being jailed for defaulting. Mugap achieved re-election to the council but was not subsequently re-nominated for president. He assumed, however, that the council adviser (who became Assistant Returning Officer) was a powerful ally who would ensure that he won the House of Assembly election.

Ambitions to unseat Kaibelt had been burgeoning also in the north. Here the M.H.A. had already persuaded likely contenders in the Banz-Kerowil area that he alone would be able to defeat candidates from other parts of the electorate. Ngunts Gigma, a Catholic councillor who saw himself as a better Christian and a better traditionalist, had also persuaded local rivals to stand down and seemed certain to draw a bloc vote at the foot of the mountains north of Banz. Talu Bor and Kambia Mogul, leaders of different groups in the north-eastern Nondugl area, appeared to be joint heirs to the vote that had saved Paulus Waine's deposit in 1964 (Reay 1965:161-2, 178). Paulus himself contemplated standing again when an official asked him whether he intended to do so, but no one took him seriously. The two current leaders had strikingly different political styles. Talu, a former *tultul* in his forties, was imposing in stature and had made his name by sporting a dramatic innovatory arrangement of traditional decorations at his group's pig festival. His emphasis on plumes (particularly those of the Princess Stephanie bird of paradise, *kai mek*) as political symbols helped councillors to whip up constituent solidarity in ridding the council of expatriate members in 1967. His flair for personal influence found more congenial expression in the absence of officials than in formal meetings and in 1967 he was elected northern vice-president after posing a serious informal threat to Kaibelt's bid for the presidency. Kambia, though only 35 and with a little schooling behind him, seemed to constituents to be developing into a real leader of men. His *bisnis* activities included substantial trucking interests as well as a tradestore and a tea block. In 1967 he won the North Wall 'regional' seat in the council, which Kaibelt did not risk contesting, from the sitting expatriate. He was building a European-style house and preparing to entertain expatriate guests at the opening as Kaibelt had done in 1964 (Reay 1965:179).

Alone among the Member's northern rivals, Mek Gorop of Kimil in the west was assured of a large enough undivided local vote to threaten his success in a narrowed field. An ex-*tultul* with a tradestore and the first *bisnis kar* in his home area, he had recently applied for eighty acres to extend and diversify primary production. As the acknowledged *bisnis* leader in the area adjoining Dei, he found that all the people here (including a group which had threatened to secede from Wahgi Council if it could not have its own councillor) were glad to support him against a Banz-Kerowil M.H.A. they rarely saw.

Kaibelt Diria nominated one and a half minutes after the opening, Tumun Dubura nominated on 16 December, and Mugap Baugum did the same six days later. In the south the A.D.C. called the known intending candidates and 'all the councillors' into his office and according to several who were present, spoke to them as follows:

> If a large number of candidates stood many would lose their deposits. Election for the House of Assembly was a serious matter, not to be approached in a spirit of gambling, and $50 was a substantial sum to risk at a time when coffee prices were low. Kaibelt was the only northern candidate and if they insisted upon opposing him they should agree among themselves to present only one or two candidates from the south; otherwise many deposits would be lost, the work of the electoral officials would be made harder, and the election would be spoilt.

The southerners gathered nearby and reached rapid consensus to present a single candidate who, with the southern vote assured, could expect to defeat Kaibelt because of the numerical superiority of the south over the north. Tumun was the obvious choice. He was currently the most eminent of all southern leaders and, since he had stood down in 1964 for his tribesman, Nop, he should have his chance of securing representation for the south. Mugap alone insisted that he had a right to stand for election himself. One of Tumun's tribesmen threatened reprisals if he nominated. Mugap suffered repeated humiliations in the public bar of the hotel, bashings on his way home at night, and various insults from open taunting to stony refusals to acknowledge his presence. He thought he had powerful allies in the council adviser (the Assistant Returning Officer) and all the Protestant missionaries, mistaking courtesy and sympathy for support, but eventually he tried to withdraw his nomination. He knew the closing date by rote but did not realise that this date had passed when he went to see the Returning Officer three days too late.

Men who were at the meeting that chose a southern candidate said that the A.D.C. had already held a pre-selection meeting for Kaibelt in the north. According to a northern account, he summoned 'all the people' from Nondugl to halfway to Kimil to attend. He announced that ten men from the south and four, besides Kaibelt, from the north wanted to contest the Open seat. He asked those present whom they wanted to elect and they all said Kaibelt, to which he replied that that was good because Kaibelt had been a good member and he himself liked him too. Kaibelt himself discussed with most of his northern rivals the fact that he had already nominated and the possibility of a southern man winning if they stood against him.

The Open campaign in Wahgi

A wet spell just before polling was marked by mass movements of Wahgi people in a 'mud-slinging' which both echoed Kaibelt's campaign and presaged the result of the Open so closely that it appeared to have been planned with his re-election in mind. Wahgi traditional custom permits the expression of conflict in ritual games staged between different groups and categories of people (Reay 1959a). The 1968 game ranged (non-traditionally) whole communities against each other and took from some of the old games the practice of using lumps of mud as missiles. Towards the end of January Kaibelt's Tsengelap tribe became involved in a snowballing enlargement of the traditional mud-game. Claiming an unacknowledged victory over fringe groups of Nondugl people, they proceeded to 'fight' with mud the various groups along the North Wall, eventually scoring a clear win against the people of the Kimil area in the west. With the north symbolically secured for their candidate, some Tsengelap and others they had incorporated by 'conquest' straggled untidily along the road to Kudjip in the south, so plastered with mud from previous battles that they looked like traditional mourners. They defeated the Kudjip people before more northerners crossed the Wahgi near Minj, to be rebuffed by Tumun's tribesmen. The Konumbuga then set out to conquer all the other southern groups in

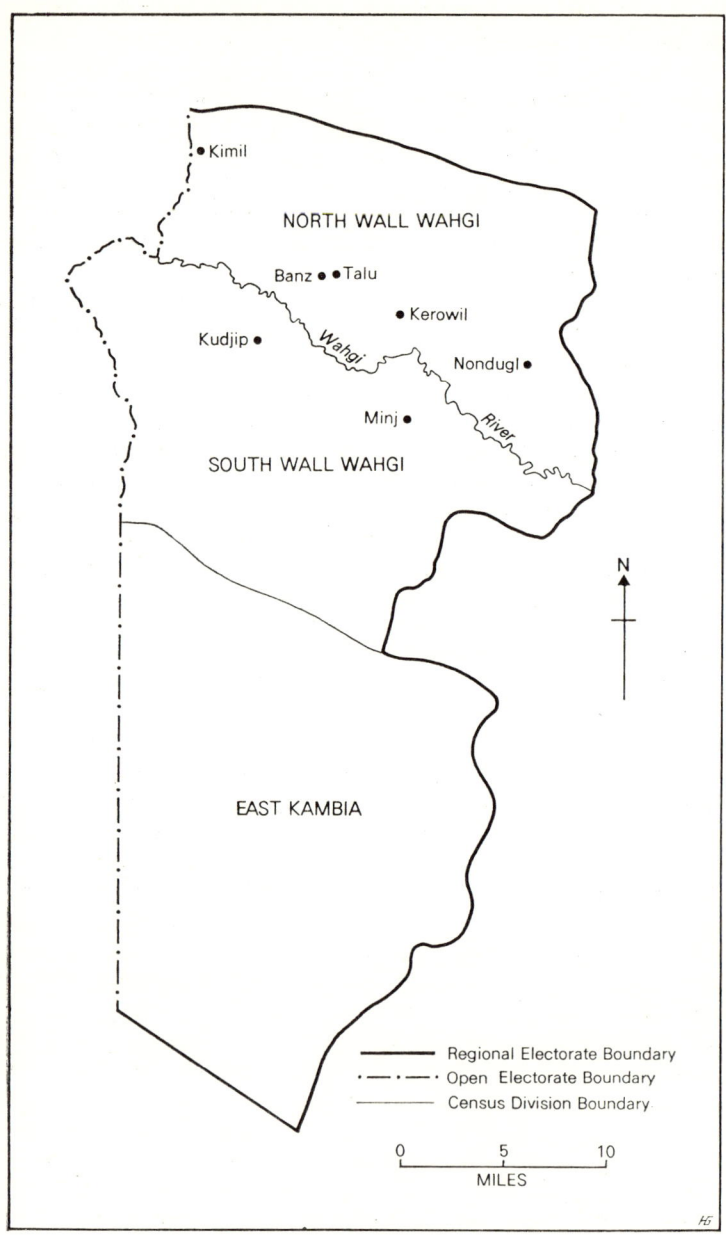

10 Wahgi Open Electorate

both directions before tackling the north. Their path was blocked, however, when a man was injured in a westerly fray and stones wrapped in mud smashed the windscreen of a *bisnis kar* in the east. Missionaries had the game stopped when the muddy armies reached the mission strongholds east and west of Minj. Whether by accident or Machiavellian design, Tumun's battalions had no chance to engage the renegade southerners of Kudjip who had been snowballed into an 'alliance' with the north.

Kaibelt Diria was the only Wahgi candidate to mount a campaign. For practical purposes he divided the electorate into three areas, each requiring a different strategy. On the North Wall, his home ground, he could make certain he won the overwhelming majority of votes once he had secured his position as the only northern candidate. He saw the South Wall east of Minj as Tumun's home ground (the third candidate being no threat to either him or his southern rival) and took every opportunity to visit this area informally when the weather allowed but did not engage in formal campaigning there. He saw the South Wall west of Minj as a no-man's-land in which hard campaigning could attract a significant number of votes away from the councillors' earlier token endorsement of Tumun.

Kaibelt held a series of mass meetings along the North Wall. At those observed, about half a dozen local figures (not necessarily councillors or ward committee men) addressed a crowd at their usual assembly place. They dwelt on Kaibelt's work in promoting development of roads, bridges, and schools and, in particular, the building of the Highlands Highway which, being largely maintained by the Public Works Department, had eased the pressure of roadwork on villagers. A vote was taken and Kaibelt was endorsed by a show of hands. He himself then made a mild-mannered speech stating that he was well-liked, that development was proceeding but much more was needed to make the area strong, and that with schooling, hard work, and the help of a beneficent Administration all would be well in the end. These meetings seemed ritualistic, as if all present accepted Kaibelt's qualifications and regarded the meeting as having been called only for form's sake.

Kaibelt also held meetings on the South Wall west of Minj. He appears to have put his case more forcefully here. He claimed credit for major public works, particularly roadwork (the new south road to Mt Hagen, then nearly completed) and the steel bridges already linking Kudjip with Banz and about to be installed along the south road. He promised to see that the council tax was not raised while coffee prices were low. He was able to tell people truthfully that he himself had blocked the last tax rise, that the council had only been able to pass it while he was absent in Port Moresby, and that both Tumun and Mugap had supported it. A man who kept taxes down and persuaded the government to build steel bridges might be powerful enough to get the price of coffee raised, and rumours spread from Kudjip in the west of the South Wall that Kaibelt had promised to do this if elected. The steel bridge linking Kudjip with the northern township of Banz made the southerners of the west less dependent than they had been on Minj, that part of the south which they saw as having benefited most from the development and activities of the council. Kaibelt exploited their dissatisfactions with the council by associating drawbacks with having Minj men in positions of power. He reminded the women that he had released them from conscription for roadwork.

It is possible to relate Kaibelt's electoral success to this extra benefit he offered women voters. In fact he polled enough votes at other southern centres to pick up the few hundred he needed to win an absolute majority, given his hold on the north. Kaibelt aimed to win the election in Kudjip, however, and it seems that he did so. The westerly Kudjip-Aviamp area was the only place in the south where he polled a majority and the only place in the south where he campaigned as intensively as he did in the north. The men here would not have voted for him on the issue of women's roadwork; indeed many might have voted against him if this had been the only issue, but the importance of taxes and steel bridges must have made it irrelevant to their choice. The slump in coffee provided an important incentive for Kaibelt to activate there but he could not have done this if he had not convinced them on other grounds of his power to do things for them, and although the law concerning women's roadwork had been unpopular with the men it demonstrated to them that he did indeed have this power. In Wahgi as a whole the turn-out for men was 18 per cent higher than that for the women, but Kudjip was an exception: here the turn-out for women was 6 per cent higher than that for the men and more than half the votes there were cast by women, though men outnumbered women on the electoral roll. This does not, of course, demonstrate that Kaibelt won the election on the women's vote. But the implication is inescapable that his appeal to the women was successful, that there was indeed a bloc 'women's vote' for him as he had hoped, and that women were beginning to realise that they could influence events on something of an equal footing with men—to gain, in Dahl's terms, a sense of political efficacy (1963:61).

Kaibelt did not make Tumun's mistake of assuming that the endorsement of his candidature by other leaders in his half of the electorate was final; he campaigned even more assiduously throughout his home area than outside it. All three candidates knew that boundary revisions had reversed the 1964 numerical superiority of the north over the south and Tumun took this to mean that it was the turn of the south to be represented. Kaibelt construed the proportion of electors in the two regions as a necessity to capture as many votes as possible that could otherwise be expected to go to his southern opponent. His campaign meeting at Kudjip ended successfully, as those he had held in the north had done, with a demonstration of mass support by a show of hands.

The Member had been hoping to hold similar meetings all along the South Wall, but his reception as he moved eastward was more mixed and prim assurances that people would be voting as they themselves decided took the place of the usual demonstrations of support. The last group he addressed west of Minj was one belonging to Tumun's own Kuma phratry. A crowd of about 150 assembled, some to hear about the election and some to observe or participate in an informal court investigating an accusation of witchcraft. When Kaibelt paused in his speech several men commented that polling day was the time to talk about voting and now they wanted to resume the witchcraft inquiry. He did not carry out his intention to visit the Minj River division of Konumbuga then proceed eastward from Minj holding campaign meetings. Tumun himself, however, had reiterated what he knew of Kaibelt's talk to electors at Kudjip in order to dismiss it as a pack of lies and thereby inadvertently spread it in places where the Member himself found it prudent not to campaign personally.

Kaibelt was acutely aware that his vehicle must be roadworthy to enable him to carry out his campaign as planned. His largest single expenditure for campaigning was on a set of new tyres and, proceeding single-mindedly towards re-election, he was a constant visitor to the council garage for regular servicing and correction of minor flaws. He was the only candidate who had a serviceable vehicle for the electoral period. His use of it as a tool for winning the election contrasts strikingly with the record of the two southern candidates.

Tumun had usually had a controlling interest in at least one *bisnis kar*, which he operated more widely than most, but when nominations closed he had disposed of his latest vehicle. In November 1967 the *kiap*-controlled council garage had suddenly stopped extending credit and in mid-January its yard was full of indigenous-owned vehicles awaiting expensive repairs. Among these were several Tumun could otherwise have commandeered when lacking his own transport. He explained to a fieldworker that he had no time to travel around the electorate even if he had needed to do so, because he was working full time at Minj. He expected to be visiting all the polling centres with the electoral teams. Stranded without a regular means of getting to polling centres, he obtained some rides with Regional candidates and some in the few local *bisnis kars* still operating. Just after he had arranged with the owners of one such truck to carry him regularly to polling centres they had to tell him that the *kiap*s had unexpectedly commissioned it to provide extra transport for the electoral team and had forbidden them to carry any of the candidates. The five-ton truck Mugap had arranged for his adopted clansmen to buy arrived just as the election started and he pressed it into service to transport him to polling places. Unwieldy and heavy on fuel for a campaign vehicle, it broke down after a few days and henceforward Mugap relied upon getting lifts to the centres with Regional candidates' car-teams. He struck up a personal friendship with members of John Watts's car-team and walked hand-in-hand with these men about the various polling places, smilingly oblivious to the opportunities this gave him to contact electors.

Tumun had been working full time with a police sergeant on preliminary hearings of disputes between local people, helping him to decide whether to refer these to the *kiap* or the police officer. He was expecting payment, which he alleged had been delayed in Port Moresby. Asked whether he knew that paid government employment was incompatible with candidature, he said he would ask the Returning Officer who (as A.D.C.) had employed him. He continued his court work to just before polling but would not say whether he had ever received the payment he had been expecting for it. He gave 'election talks' to the people involved in the disputes, but did not try to canvass votes: he simply gave them information about the election. The A.D.C. contracted with Tumun for the Konumbuga to work on the airstrip for the two weeks before the election and the candidate convened a meeting of his tribesmen to address them on this work and the coming election. He told them when polling was to begin, in what order the teams would visit the various groups in the electorate, where they themselves had to go to lodge their votes, and what candidates were standing for the two electorates. He listed the four European and then the four indigenous candidates for the Regional and said of the Open candidates that they were three good men whom all his listeners knew: 'my brother-in-law, Kaibelt on the other side [of the Wahgi]; myself; and Councillor Mugap of the Ngeniga'. People had to think about the candidates and vote for the one they liked. Whoever was going to win was a matter of how people voted. He spoke at greater length about the work the Konumbuga were to do, detailing the payment they would receive and how the work would be allocated among the various groups. He interpreted Pidgin speeches into the vernacular for Regional candidates visiting Minj but did not overtly canvass votes. The nearest Tumun went to delivering a campaign speech was a personal explanation to Regional candidate John Watts halfway through the election:

> This is the way it is [he said in Pidgin]. I have spread John Watts's talk and I have spread my own talk for Nol [Rutledge] and I have listened to talks on behalf of John Colman and Keith Levy, and a certain indigenous man Iambakey, Philip Wamell, this whole group [of candidates], I have listened to the talk of all and delivered it. As for myself, I can travel from the Chimbu boundary to Hagen, to the Tuman River and the Kimil River and the Ga River, and it is not as if I would be travelling there for the first time. Everyone knows that I began as a government interpreter at Minj in the early days and all the people know me. I left interpreting and became *luluai* and everyone knew. When the council began in 1961 I was still in office. 1963, 64, 65, 66, 67 have passed and now we are beginning 1968 and I am still in the council. That is the way it is and it would not be good for me to travel around giving [campaign] speeches and my talk not go strongly in the House of Assembly, and it would not be good for all the villagers to abuse me. That is the way I am thinking and I have merely become a candidate. Everyone can vote for me or not. It is a matter of the way people vote, and we shall see later.

The council adviser told Mugap in November that if all the Lutherans voted for him he would have a good chance of winning, and Mugap took this to mean that he was assured of the Lutheran vote and could not lose. He got odd lifts in January to visit Lutheran pastors and northern councillors so that he could tell them that he was standing, leaving messages for those who were absent when he called. He visited the headquarters of the Swiss Evangelical Brotherhood and came away with the rosy expectation that the missionaries would see that all their converts voted for him. An official advised him that a visit to Port Moresby would be worthwhile because of the potential absentee vote. He told several Wahgi men there that they must return home immediately in order to vote for the candidate they wanted; 'three good men'—Kaibelt, Tumun, and himself—were standing. Several men had already left their jobs in Lae to come home and vote for Tumun. Mugap met during his journey a former M.H.A., a Lutheran councillor like himself, who encouraged him in his candidature and criticised Kaibelt trenchantly as being unpopular with the other members, lazy, fond of beer, and a passive tool of the *kiap*s.

Mugap was alarmed to hear on his return that his entire council ward had decided to vote: 1. Kaibelt, 2. Tumun, 3. Mugap, in precise order as on the ballot papers, and that he himself had been generally agreed to be a drunken fool. At this time, two weeks before polling, people were tired of interrupting their usual activities to traipse dutifully to the assembly place and hear a few more details about the arrangements. They had had their fill of elections anyway. No candidate could do more than any other if elected.

The Swiss Evangelical Brotherhood was pursuing a temperance campaign in the vicinity of Minj which Tumun construed as a more subtle method than that the mission had used in 1964 to make sure that Kaibelt defeated the Konumbuga candidate. He admitted freely to his own robust thirst (though he prided himself on drinking only when he was not working and on being a sober and courteous driver) and knew that Kaibelt drank moderately. The A.D.C. had warned Tumun and Nop in 1967 that if they were convicted once more for any offence defined by excessive drinking they would be charged with habitual drunkenness, convicted on their existing records, and disqualified from standing for both the 'regional' ward in the council and membership in the House of Assembly.[3] All the Konumbuga leaders had a reputation for 'strength', both physical and political, which included an ability to drink other men insensible. Mugap had been a teetotaller before becoming council president. Thereafter, as a frequent visitor to the public bar, he became an easy prey to challengers among the 'strong' drinkers who resented his replacing Tumun as president (and, later, his refusal to put personal ambition aside as they themselves had done in the pursuit of a common goal) and liked to humiliate him in public. To Kaibelt and Tumun, his susceptibility was a demonstration of inadequacy. Mugap saw his own weakness as the ordinary condition of mankind and rationalised his continued visits to the bar as courageous confrontations with the forces of evil. Kaibelt visited the public bar several times when the temperance campaign was at its height, to meet the Regional candidate Rutledge and share a drink with Minj men he might have a chance of influencing. Apparently he did not realise that these visits confirmed many Minj people's impression that he drank to excess when away from his electorate. All the candidates drank, so all were equally unsuitable for election; for many Minj voters this reduced the Open election to a ritual gesture of signifying support for the group the candidate represented.

Mugap called a ward meeting a week before polling to spread

---

[3] This threat of disqualification for *candidature* contrasts strikingly with disqualification for *membership* in British colonial practice: a winning candidate for the Legislative Council in Fiji in 1963 repeated his electoral success in a by-election held because he was found to be ineligible to occupy the seat (Meller and Anthony 1968: 48, 58).

more information about the election. He described the visit of Regional candidates to the council meeting and what he had heard of Kaibelt's campaigning at Kudjip, not openly criticising the M.H.A. but saying that he and Tumun, as Minj River men, were agreed. One man stated:

> It does not matter whom we vote for. All three of you are mindless drunks. Whoever wins will eat a lot and drink himself to sleep in Port Moresby and only wake up to listen to what the *kiap* wants him to say in the House of Assembly.

Patrols before the 1964 election had warned people against being misled by candidates' persuasive manner and hollow promises. Advice to vote for someone they knew to be a good man rather than an upstart *man bilong gris* (plausible talker) persuaded the Minj people that campaigning was improper and officially frowned upon. Tumun went to Kudjip to learn at first hand whether what he had heard of Kaibelt's talk was accurate, but he called no meetings of his own and made no public speeches, there or elsewhere, to counter his rival's arguments. The Minj people thought Kaibelt was scoring unfairly over the southern candidates by reawakening the tax issue: it was wrong for one candidate to malign the others and *gris* (persuade) people to swing their allegiance from their own man, for the point of the election was to find out whom the majority wanted as their representative.[4] The pejorative *gris* was the only term used for 'electioneering' or 'campaign speech'. The southern candidates construed advice to 'give talks about the election' as instructions to impart electoral information, not permission to canvass. Tumun told a fieldworker that he proposed to report to the A.D.C. what Kaibelt had said at Kudjip and ask whether the northerner should be disqualified. He himself was careful not to criticise the others in public, not to make promises, and not to *gris* electors either by soliciting votes directly anywhere or by trying to alienate votes committed to other candidates. Whilst Kaibelt and Mugap mingled with voters in the vicinity of the booth, Tumun kept well away from the prohibited area in case officials assumed that he was surreptitiously canvassing and found an excuse to disqualify him.

Tumun judged that a leader who was well known had no need to explain himself to voters. Both he and Mugap knew that appearing at polling centres as a visual reminder that he was standing had helped him to sweep the poll in his 'regional' ward for the council and they

---

[4] Cf. Weber's statement: 'It is very common for the will of a minority to attain a formal majority and for the majority to submit. In this case majority rule is an illusion' (1947: 120); see Reay, Beyond Democracy: avoiding the gamble of the ballot box. *J. of Administration Overseas* (in press).

both thought it important to be present at as much of the polling as possible. They knew also that 'buying votes' was prohibited. Kaibelt was careful not to bribe voters outright but he was prepared to spend as much money as might be needed on an energetic campaign and the election cost him $800 (11·67 votes per dollar). Mugap spent about $200 (3·3 votes per dollar), mostly on his trip to Port Moresby, but this included little of his own money: the Lutherans and the Ngeni-Muruka were to elect him and he saw it as their responsibility to meet his costs. Tumun saw no reason why the electorate's exercise of its choice should cost him anything and his expenses came to $19 (83 votes per dollar).

The voting in Wahgi Open relates the quasi-traditional 'mud-slinging' directly to the campaign. The Nondugl people did not acknowledge the victory the Tsengelap claimed over them in the mud-game; so Kambia and Talu refused to instruct their constituents to vote only for Kaibelt but told them to vote for Kaibelt or Tumun as they liked and Tumun received more votes there than elsewhere in the north. The Tsengelap victory in the Kimil area was complete; so also was Mek's guarantee of support for Kaibelt, who received 98·3 per cent of the votes there, a greater proportion than he obtained anywhere outside his own council ward. The Tsengelap mud-slingers and their enforced allies besieged Kudjip with the same success as Kaibelt's campaign speeches had had there but they did not carry their triumph eastward. The infiltration of Tsengelap and allies directly across the Wahgi River near Minj was easily rebuffed by the Konumbuga, over 96 per cent of whom voted for Tumun; the southern favourite's tribesmen picked up the Ngeni-Muruka on their way east, scarcely pausing to 'fight' with Mugap's adopted clansmen at all—but no one excepting the Assistant Returning Officer, one missionary, and Mugap himself had really taken the latter's candidature seriously; and the Konumbuga's victories were halted in places where Tumun's majorities were lowered by a significant vote for Kaibelt. (See table 11.)

The Open campaign in Mul-Dei

The combination of Mul and Dei council areas in a single Open electorate reflects the intention of the Administration, expressed as early as 1964, to amalgamate the two councils. Dei councillors had opposed this, fearing a Mul take-over. In April 1967 the *kiap* who was to be Returning Officer related this issue directly to the election by telling the councillors that they and their eventual M.H.A. would decide. Mul and Dei had been associated with the first House of Assembly through members from Hagen and Wahgi respectively. This time the member would come from either the council area itself or the other area paired with it in the Administration's planning and in the re-arrangement of Open electorates. This pairing, which implied the possibility of competition between representatives of Mul and Dei (as distinct from a competition between individual candidates coming indiscriminately from all over a unitary electorate) constituted the major political cleavage throughout the period affecting the election.

TABLE 11—LOCATION OF CANDIDATES' MAJORITIES, WAHGI OPEN, expressed as percentages of total valid vote

Kaibelt Diria		
Own council ward (Talu)	100	minus 1 vote
Kimil (area of Mek Gorop)	98.3	
Other northern groups without Nondugl	96.6	
Nondugl (area of Kambia Mogul and Talu Bor)	74.0	(Tumun 27.4)
Southern groups west of Kudjip (intensive campaigning)	64.7	(Tumun 35)
Kudjip (intensive campaigning; criticism of Tumun and Mugap)	87.2	(Tumun 11.3)
Tumun Dubura		
East Kambia (only candidate who had ever visited)	97.5	
Own Konumbuga tribe	96.2	
Vicinity of Minj (minus Konumbuga and Ngeni-Muruka)	77.8	(Kaibelt 12.6)
East part of South Wall (Tsigmil to Kugmarl)	75.1	(Kaibelt 20.3)
Mugap Baugum		
Ngeni-Muruka (own adopted clan)	87.2	(Tumun 11.9)

The Dei president, Peruwa Kuri, alleged that Mul Council had deceived his own over an aid-post the two bodies had jointly established in Mul territory. In August he pronounced that the councils should remain separated for two years to allow for the completion of projects already begun. One of these was the construction of a permanent council house, for which councillors were not envisaging an alternative use, in Dei. President Peruwa, who had held office continuously since 1966, saw himself as being uniquely qualified for the job of member. His selection for an Australian political education tour in the year preceding the election was seen as preparation for this new role.

Early in October a Mul driver who had accidentally hit a deaf man in Dei was attacked there by the clansmen of the victim and some others and died from head injuries. By the next day Dei was in crisis. Rumours alleged that Dei men had already been killed in revenge. The driver's kinsmen were declared to have placed his body on a high trestle (to mark not only their grief but also their intention to avenge his death) and to be making emotional speeches in Mul. The Dei council adviser forbade vehicle operators to leave their area. Labourers working at Banz came home. A week after the driver's death the councillors met and agreed that Dei council must raise money and the killer's clan provide pigs and pearlshells for a death compensation. If this were not done, they felt, 'the election would be ruined'. The compensation was promptly gathered and paid over, but the Dei councillors were not satisfied that the men of Mul would forgo direct retaliation. They wanted a Dei man to win the election, but candidates were afraid to canvass individually in Mul. President Peruwa, just back from Australia, knew that he himself was an obvious target and would not even accompany the formal campaign into Mul when the candidates toured the electorate collectively. He did not share the doubts of the councillor from his pair-clan that he might have difficulty in serving as M.H.A. and council president, doing two jobs at once. He was confident of official support, and the only expatriate still a council member in 1968 was a scrutineer for him. Councillors were now privately hoping that the councils would not join, despite their public protestations to the contrary. By mid-January doubts expressed earlier about Peruwa being over-bearing and arrogant were suppressed as men of Dei realised the need for unity if they were to defeat the popular Mul candidate, Mek Nugintz. Peruwa's visit to Australia had led to his opposing vigorously the idea of early self-government, and this too made him an eminently suitable successor to Kaibelt Diria as his councillors' voice in the House of Assembly. They credited Kaibelt with having stopped roadwork for women, secured iron bridges, and ended card-playing (which used to take up much time and money), but now they wanted more positive improvements in *bisnis*, which should come before any talk of self-government.

Only six candidates nominated, although eight others had been likely contenders in mid-1967. Four who had withdrawn (three in Dei and one in Mul) said they had not wanted to spoil the election by having too many candidates and splitting a council or a tribal vote. Those who nominated included four from Dei (Peruwa, Warike, El, and Pim) and two (Mek and Pung) from Mul. Two erstwhile contenders from Dei made it clear that they had stood down for Peruwa who, feeling he was officially favoured to win, nominated early. So also, however, did Mek of Mul, who did not seem to be or to feel so favoured. Table 12 sets out information about the candidates.

The two council presidents, Peruwa and Pung, tended to think they had a better right to stand and a better chance of winning because of their close association with the council adviser. Unlike Peruwa, however, President Pung of Mul had only held office since January 1968 and rumours had it that the *kiap* had changed the votes in the presidential election to ensure his success. Mek declared to a fieldworker that he himself was the people's unofficial choice, that Pung's candidature following on his own was unwelcome to electors, and that his rival would poll only a few hundred votes. Mul Council as a whole seems to have informally endorsed both the new president and his rival. The election looked like being a contest between these three men —two of them council presidents and the other, though lacking official position in the administrative hierarchy, well experienced in using governmental authority as overseer of roadworks. They had other things in common with one another *vis-à-vis* the other candidates (see table 12). They were all of much more forceful demeanour than the rest. Mek was the son of a 'big man' and well on the way to being one himself, and both Pung and Peruwa were already powerful figures in the traditional exchange system. The importance of local government in the election in Mul-Dei has already been stressed. If this had been the only significant factor, Pung might have had a better chance of winning. Given Mek's personal abilities, however, his standing outside the council system could be turned to advantage. Since he had not been involved in the competition for the council presidency, he was not hampered by the resentment engendered within the most numerous Mul tribe by Pung's defeat of their own man. In any case, considering the hardening hostilities between the two council areas and the multiplicity of candidates from Dei, one or other of the Mul candidates seemed best placed to win. Peruwa knew that the candidature of three other Dei men, each with his own local area of support, would hamper him in his contest with Pung and Mek but he felt he was destined to win.

All candidates stood for good coffee prices, iron bridges and bulldozers, schools, hospitals, and *bisnis*. The question was who was most likely to obtain these things. Candidates saw councillors and their clans, rather than the larger units, as the decision-makers and hoped that a few clans in various areas would vote for them even if the others favoured a local candidate. The civility of councillors and the ambiguity of the promise 'We shall vote for you' encouraged this hope, though at least one candidate, Warike in Dei, realised that a favourable response from councillors might simply indicate politeness and that in any case they could not guarantee votes. In 1964 the areas that were later declared 'regional' wards for Dei council had already shown some grouping of tribes in response to the two candidates who went there, the

TABLE 12—MUL-DEI OPEN CANDIDATES

Name	Age (approx.)	Occupational experience	Political experience	*Bisnis* experience	Other data
Peruwa	30	Various jobs with Europeans in early youth; farmer	Vice-president Dei Council 1963-6, president 1966-	Coffee, store, formerly vehicles	Young 'big man', polygynist; new house, smart clothes
Warike	40	Interpreter during war; plantation foreman; now council interpreter	Council employee	Coffee	Educ. Standard I; two wives
El	30	Lutheran mission teacher (Pidgin)	Nil	Coffee	Educ. Standard IV; attends Lutheran District Conferences as representative
Pim	30	Businessman, craftsman	Nil	Entrepreneur, formerly had Admin. contract for supplying traditional artefacts	Widely travelled in District
Pung	40	Formerly interpreter, medical orderly, plantation foreman; farmer	President Mul Council 1968-	Coffee	'Big man', polygynist
Mek	30	Roadwork overseer with P.W.D.	Nil	Coffee, store, *bisnis kar*	Young 'big man', polygynist; ran away early from S.D.A. school; neat clothes; vehicle actually serviceable and used for campaign

Mala tribes supporting Ian Parsons and the Tiki groups, other than those at Tiki itself, Kaibelt Diria. These two wards coincided closely with the local areas of influence associated with the two principal Dei candidates, that of Peruwa the council president including Tiki and that of Warike the council interpreter including Mala. The third ward, Gumants, contained the much smaller home bases of the weaker Dei candidates, El and Pim. Each candidate respected the territories of the others and was polite to them there.

Local areas of influence corresponded closely to the tribal affiliations of candidates and to traditional inter-group alliances (see Strathern 1970:139-41). Warike's tribe and its subsidiaries dominate Mala; while that of Peruwa, with over 2500 persons (Tipuka tribe) carries most weight in Tiki. His alliance is opposed to an even more powerful chain of three tribes (5500 people). The common link in this chain of alliance is Kombukla tribe, and from this group came El. On this basis El stood to gain most votes. However, he seemed unlikely to do so. He had lived for many years away from his own people, among Peruwa's Tipuka, where he was completely overshadowed by the more forceful and experienced council president. In addition he could lose some votes in his own area to Pim, the fourth Dei candidate, whose home is close to Kombukla territory.

The two Mul candidates were close patrilateral relatives, so neither could count on an undivided vote even from his own clan. Their shared home base was extensible, however, to the entire council area and even beyond it. One clan in Dei was an emigrant segment of their tribe that had moved away perhaps twenty years ago when the candidates' clansmen had killed one of its men. Despite the circumstances of the migration, the Mul candidates could hope to pick up some votes in the opposed council area. Mek campaigned successfully in the area of Pim, the weakest candidate, but the campaign focused surprisingly little on the part of Dei bordering with Mul. Pim did not get the votes he expected in the Mul area and the other Dei candidates, more realistically, were not expecting any. Warike listed twenty-seven Dei councillors who would support him. He received group votes from those in his own 'regional' ward and from three he listed in the Jimi, but was overoptimistic in listing ten councillors in Gumants and six in Tiki.

Both the Mul candidates listed nineteen councillors in their area who would support them; Pung (the council president) listed seven and Mek (the ultimate winner) nine in Dei also. The names of six in Mul and one in Dei occurred in both lists. It was reasonable for them to lay equal claim to and in the event share the votes in their own council area, where the voting for them was close, but their estimates for Dei were heavily optimistic. A common idea was that a candidate would win if he obtained first preferences in his own council area and second preferences in the other. Mek's supporters hoped for this, and the men Peruwa sent into Mul must have had this in mind when they stressed that he was just like Mek in appearance and ways; one of them returned with a new wife obtained through Mek's good graces. Mek's success came, however, from most of Pung's second preferences staying within the council area.

The candidates began by moving about the electorate to assess their chances of support. The Mul men had already done some solid auspice-taking and patrolled on foot and by vehicle in their council area. Pung had patrolled with the *kiap*. Mek now travelled through Mul and along the Highlands Highway by car and walked unobtrusively through a part of Dei. Peruwa had told everyone in Dei about his Australian visit and there seemed little point in making a second patrol. El said he had patrolled through many parts of Dei. Candidates' platforms and their criticisms of one another were already well known.

The candidates then used the Dei council truck to make a joint whistle-stop tour through the main census points of Mul and Dei. At each point they and various councillors and supporters would leap off, round up an audience, deliver a few speeches, and move on. The accompanying supporters included both old, respected men and Pidgin speakers. Mek was a regular member of the entourage but drove his own vehicle over to Dei and back. Pung joined in occasionally and in Dei, where he had a reputation for courting activities, he unbent and entertained his audience. Pim and El rarely had a chance to say anything in Mul, for Mek or Warike had always said it all first and then it was time to go. Peruwa went everywhere with the joint campaign in Dei but, though he sent two councillors to represent him, did not go to Mul— ostensibly because of illness but really, according to Warike, through fear of poison in revenge for the Mul driver's death. Perhaps also he found joint campaigning undignified and wished to disassociate himself from the general run of candidates, for both he and Pung kept themselves rather aloof in the first part of the campaign; early in February he found a private vehicle and sought votes in Mul with a speech that emphasised his visit to Canberra, his knowledge of where money was manufactured, his presidency, and his boosting of taxation revenue in Dei.

Peruwa announced premonitions of success by referring to dreams and other signs. Dreaming that he caught a Raggiana Bird of Paradise in his hand symbolised success in the election, and it had a Princess Stephanie plume beneath it, meaning that Mek (named after that Bird of Paradise) would come second. As he voted on the first day he heard a *kot* bird cry, and mysteriously this made him vote for Keith Levy instead of John Watts as he said he had intended. He recounted this as an omen of Levy's success, though he continued to support Watts and give honourable mention to Iambakey. Informants suggested that all this was 'hidden talk' which really conveyed that the *kiap* had told him both he and Levy would win. This discreet propagation of omens was plainly meant to influence voting.

The candidates were polite to one another in public but their agents spread derogatory and sometimes salacious accounts of the characters and records of their rivals. Peruwa's agents suggested Iambakey for the Regional, though he had been publicly supporting the European candidates. Those he sent into the Jimi, where Warike and El had gone earlier, obtained assurances that the people there would vote for him. In fact, however, those nearest to his own tribe supported him or El and those nearest to Mala ward Warike.

The campaign changed its character with the onset of polling. Candidates began to make sharper speeches in border areas where they were hoping for votes, and to co-operate more with the Regional candidates. Peruwa and the ward committee man he had sent into the Jimi accompanied the election patrol. He addressed voters at Kotna just before they filed into the booth:

> One man shoots birds in the bush, another misses. Some of us are strong, but others just copy us. They would go to the House of Assembly and return to tell us lies. The *kiap* knows who is good and who isn't. At the fourth election only the councillors will decide whom to send. The Mul men are different from us, a little like the Hagen men. There are four of us from Dei itself, but forget about Pim, let him lose. If he went he'd forget to attend the meetings and sell axes instead. [Pim had recently been selling axes from the Jimi to tourists.] On the other side of the Kwiya river they're electing Warike; here you must elect me.

John Watts arrived with a bundle of pamphlets for Peruwa to distribute in his area but Peruwa had already left for Mul with Keith Levy so El took the pamphlets on his behalf. Open candidates, only one of whom (Mek, the ultimate winner) had a serviceable vehicle, were now anxious for lifts to see how the voting was going, and Regional candidates could provide these. The Regional candidates, for their part, hoped for last minute consolidation of local areas through *rapprochement* with Open candidates and councillors. Councillors co-operated willingly so long as vehicles or grants for subsistence were available, and rumours of money gifts from Europeans to Open candidates multiplied. The Open candidates were careful, however, not to make support of any Regional candidate a specific part of their platforms since, in Dei at least, no Regional candidate was overwhelmingly popular. Colman campaigned successfully in Warike's area despite the latter's approval of Levy; but Peruwa's support of Watts, Pung's of Colman, and Mek's initial approval of Levy may have helped the candidates.

Pung and Peruwa seem to have been effectively hindered by their awareness of their position as council presidents and their conviction that they were officially favoured. They saw themselves as government officers and for some time were inclined, like Tumun in Wahgi, to wait for destiny to take its course. Mek, experienced in command but outside the official hierarchy, was not inhibited in this way and was free to take advantage of kinship and any other connections that might help him. His maternal kinsmen were tribesmen of the driver who had been attacked in Dei, and this link with the cleavage between the two councils could draw votes away from Pung in Mul. The election of Mek Nugintz, however, was not mechanically determined by kinship and tribal affiliations and inter-council opposition. Like Kaibelt Diria in Wahgi, he was the only candidate who made sure that he had a roadworthy campaign vehicle and he was prepared to use a strong voice and the money he needed (here over $200, yielding about twenty-five votes per dollar) to build up a team of supporters and present himself convincingly to electors.

VOTING BEHAVIOUR

Early in the polling, officials became concerned at the prevalence of null and single preference Regional votes, especially in areas where voters should have had ample prior experience of council elections. Had something gone wrong with the elaborate and detailed program of electoral education so that voters had failed to grasp the importance of preferences and the distinction between Open and Regional? Tally clerks reported that voters were indeed confusing the two electorates: they were uttering a single sequence of names drawn from both sets of candidates as if arranging them in a single set of preferences. They had done this in 1964 (Reay 1965:174-5); had they learned so little from the experience of the intervening years and from the recent deliberate efforts of the Administration that their earlier misunderstandings remained?

In Wahgi, however, and possibly elsewhere, this behaviour was coming about through confusion of a different kind. Voters were well aware that they were to elect two members—one for 'the District' and another for 'the place' (council area or Sub-District)—and they knew which candidates were standing for each electorate. Electoral education talks and subsequent electoral information patrols had repetitively emphasised these facts. One item, however, had been neglected. Care was taken to impress upon voters the necessity for calling the name of the Open candidate they wanted before voting for the Regional and this instruction, designed to make doubly sure that the two electorates were conceptually separated, misfired. Many offered their first choices for the two electorates before uttering a second preference of any kind, not realising that tally clerks concentrating on recording a completed Open vote might hear the first name chosen from the Regional candidates as a second preference after the first Open candidate named. In trying to ensure that the Open vote was completed first, some over-assiduous clerks drifted into requiring a full set of preferences for all Open candidates before asking the voter about the Regional electorate. Interpreters, by now under grave suspicion of having misled people both during electoral education and in the booth, had less opportunity than they had had in council elections to make certain on their own initiative that voters construed questions correctly.

The hazards of assisted voting make it impossible to reach many firm conclusions about voting behaviour. This section uses some of the results of an examination of the ballot papers to analyse the structure of candidates' support. Also, we relate some aspects of the patterning of preferences on the ballot paper to electoral education, the campaign, and the politics of the area. The ballot papers examined were those used in all nine Open elections and in the Western Highlands Regional. Of the 114,647 Regional papers, 93,619 were examined, those that were unavailable including mainly 9000-odd from Lagaip, 8000-odd from Kompiam-Baiyer, and 3000-odd from Hagen (see table 13).

Official results show that 3·2 per cent of the Regional votes and 0·45 per cent of the Open votes were invalid ('informal'). The higher proportion of these in the Regional has a simple explanation. Everywhere voters were issued with two ballot papers, one for each electorate, when their names were ticked off the roll. No provision was made for persons who wished to vote for one electorate and not the other. All but 29 of 1224 informal Regional ballots examined showed no preferences and were unmarked apart from bearing the initials of a presiding officer; and comments from electoral staff confirm that our sample of about one third is representative of the total in being overwhelmingly composed of 'no preference' votes. Informal voting in the Open, however, was predominantly a reflection of incompetence on the part of a minute proportion of voters who were unassisted and of carelessness on the part of an occasional fatigued tally clerk. The 29 informal

TABLE 13—PERCENTAGES OF SINGLE PREFERENCES IN EACH CANDIDATE'S VOTE WESTERN HIGHLANDS REGIONAL

	Hagen	Jimi	Kandep-Tambul	Kompiam-Baiyer	Lagaip	Mul-Dei	Wabag	Wahgi	Wapena-manda	Western Highlands
Nol Rutledge	28·21	5·57	82·50	n.a.	49·20	3·70	2·29	55·81	6·67	31·03
John Watts	29·87	12·06	99·03	n.a.	87·88	61·39	9·80	67·10	21·50	61·72
Phillip Matuakan	21·43	5·56	91·74	n.a.	77·49 incomplete	—	14·54	50·00	31·53	46·69
Keith Levy	19·82	4·26	99·07	n.a.	n.a.	51·74	4·48	60·45	8·26	44·73
Iambakey Okuk (Meknik)	20·69	1·45	92·08	n.a.	44·31	77·83	10·27	72·57	7·50	30·55
Nita Wapurao	—	2·20	97·77	n.a.	49·35	—	16·88	56·44	20·70	25·08
Philip Wamell	17·09	2·58	70·00	n.a.	41·56	12·50	8·11	75·83	7·05	70·41
John Colman	18·63	1·42	83·05	91·97	84·58	26·90	8·67	67·65	20·95	37·48
Mean single preferences in total valid vote	25·58	3·68	98·36	90·29 incomplete	77·34 incomplete	47·10	8·57	71·78	22·63	48·49

n.a. = not available (see p. 261).

Regional ballots of this kind included 24 showing multiple (two or three) first preferences, three marked with a cross instead of a numeral, and two showing no first preferences but a single preference marked '2'. Occasionally, both in the Regional and also in Opens with a large number of candidates, a later preference was duplicated, invalidating subsequent preferences, and on one ballot only alternate preferences were marked.

Nearly half those who voted cast a single preference (table 13). Electoral education talks had instructed voters to think about the men who were standing for election and vote for the one they liked. Whether particular candidates elaborated this kind of instruction or not, some voters of every degree of sophistication decided not to allocate preferences. Peruwa in Mul-Dei had been counting on getting second preferences from Warike, which would have helped him considerably, but the other candidate's tribesmen decided that if their own man did not win they would certainly not help another to do so and 77 per cent of the votes they cast showed single preferences. The official leaflets, and also the radio talks based on these, encouraged voters to fill in all their preferences; the only explanation for this advice, however, was that it was 'for the good of the country', an opinion that would have suited Peruwa but which Warike's tribesmen would presumably have contrasted with their own good if any of them heard it. Kaibelt in Wahgi instructed some groups to vote for him alone, but he had no real need to do so when his own hard campaigning and the timidity of his only serious rival ensured him a majority of primary votes. Half of his supporters cast single preferences as against Tumun's 43 per cent and Mugap's 15 per cent. Voting behaviour in council elections had already suggested that the winning candidate in Wahgi would get the most single preference votes. Regional voting there showed an identical trend: Wamell, with 59 per cent of the total Wahgi vote, polled more single preferences there than any other candidate (table 13). This trend can also be discerned in the region as a whole if we consider only the leading three candidates (Watts, Levy, and Colman), but winning candidates in the other Opens did not get the most single preferences. The attitude of Warike's tribesmen in Mul-Dei suggests that tribalism is the key determinant of single-preference voting and that Kaibelt received most single preferences in Wahgi because he extended his 'tribal' unit to embrace the northern 'native' council area. Tumun's expectation that southern voters would give preferences to both the southern candidates was not realised in his own tribe. He gave them no instructions on how to use their votes apart from repeating the electoral education talk that they should vote for the man they liked, and 75 per cent of his own tribal vote was by single preference. Mugap's reference to himself and Tumun as 'Minj River men' in addressing the council ward that included the clan that voted for him appealed to a more narrowly based loyalty than he needed but explicitly suggested voting for them both. Also, although he saw the imparting of information about the election as the duty of a candidate, he had no occasion to repeat the electoral education talk to people elsewhere as Tumun did.

A first preference can be interpreted in two ways: it may be a judgment of first in a numerical sequence, the assumption of the Australian 'alternative vote' system; or it may be a choice between one candidate and the rest of the field. Some of Tumun's supporters reasoned that since only one man could win he would be either a northerner or a southerner and they wanted a southerner so this ruled out the possibility of voting any kind of preference for the northern candidate; further, Tumun was the southerner they wanted so this ruled out giving any kind of preference for Mugap. The electoral information patrol had grouped the Regional candidates as four white men and four black men, and Wahgi people considered whether it would be preferable to have an expatriate or indigenous member, the choice they had already exercised in the 1964 Open. Seventy-four per cent decided in favour of an indigenous man for the Regional, 80 per cent of these voting for Wamell and 19 per cent for Iambakey. The latter received few of their second preferences. After plumping for Wamell the second choice was not an alternative to him as a candidate but an alternative to having an indigenous member: 93 per cent of Wamell's second preferences in Wahgi went to expatriates (mostly to Colman and Watts rather than to the local planter Rutledge).

Two electorates, Jimi and Kandep-Tambul, contrasted strikingly in the extent to which voters used their preferences. In Jimi 75·64 per cent of voters allocated all eight preferences available for the Regional and only 3·68 gave single preference votes, whereas 98·36 per cent of Kandep-Tambul voters plumped for a single candidate and only 0·19 per cent gave eight preferences. (Indeed, only 0·2 per cent gave six or more). Similarly, single preferences for Open candidates in Kandep-Tambul ranged from 66 to 96 per cent of their total vote, whereas no candidates for Jimi Open received more than 3 per cent single preferences and none received less than 90 per cent showing all seven preferences. Comparing Jimi with Wahgi (where voters voiced a mean of 1·37 preferences) could have suggested a correlation between single preference voting and relative sophistication in voting procedures, but the allocation of preferences in Kandep-Tambul on the one hand and Hagen on the other does not support this. The most likely explanation for the contrast between Jimi and Kandep-Tambul lies in the

TABLE 14—LOCALISATION OF CANDIDATES' SUPPORT, WESTERN HIGHLANDS REGIONAL

	Hagen	Jimi	Kandep-Tambul	Kompiam-Baiyer	Lagaip	Mul-Dei	Wabag	Wahgi	Wapena-manda	Western Highlands
Noel Rutledge	40	1672	123	77	340	32	218	1625	98	4225
John Watts	9708	859	8809	4055	3053	3536	1835	1302	414	33,571
Phillip Matuakan	13	37	121	11	1835	1	337	10	2864	5229
Keith Levy	4180	1843	4461	876	8263	3372	2170	175	219	25,559
Iambakey Okuk (Meknik)	556	1037	241	917	303	217	3072	2172	1648	10,163
Nita Wapurao	5	184	221	964	92	6	75	160	4053	5760
Philip Wamell	130	426	10	11	88	10	37	9322	153	10,187
John Colman	1858	3671	287	3328	786	3506	1347	722	789	16,294
Informal	214	257	377	1211	741	303	37	399	120	3659
Total	16,704	9986	14,650	11,450	15,501	10,983	9128	15,887	10,358	114,647

differing interpretations Administration personnel could and did place upon their authority to instruct people how to use their vote. Various officials in the region showed on the one hand an easy tolerance of people giving as many preferences as they wished, often combined with a concept of administration that favoured the least possible burden for those who had to count the votes, and, on the other, an eager concern that an underdeveloped area like the Western Highlands should display a degree of understanding of the electoral process that would fully justify the time, trouble, and money spent on political and electoral education.

Only 27·3 per cent of persons casting valid votes in the Western Highlands preferred indigenous candidates to Europeans. The Europeans received their heaviest support in areas that did not have indigenous candidates (table 14). All the indigenous candidates polled poorly in Hagen, the home base of the three strongest Europeans, and in adjoining Mul-Dei and Baiyer. Komp, a prominent councillor standing for Hagen Open, urged electors to choose 'one man only' to beat the large 'Wabag' (that is, Enga) vote. They could take this advice literally or understand it to mean that the choice lay between one of the Europeans from their own area and the indigenous candidates from other places.

Regional candidates had no unique local base, simply areas of relative strength. (Even Iambakey, the only candidate settled in Wabag, was Chimbu by descent, had his father in Wahgi, and was introduced by Peruwa in Dei as a 'sister's son' of Hagen.) For the Open candidates the task was to ensure a large number of first and second preferences in their home base and to expand the base as far as possible. In assessing the extent to which candidates relied upon and gained local support, we have to follow Western Highlanders' own construction of events and view the election as a segmentary situation. The 'home area' of each candidate was capable of much extension. The most meaningful unit for comparing the extent of local support for the three candidates in Wahgi Open was different in each case—a council ward, a tribe (developed here from a grossly expanded clan), and a clan. The places of these units in the overall segmentation of the electorate are clearer when we view them as segments also of the council ward system. Talu was a single-member ward with Kaibelt as its representative; Minj-Kamang ward had three councillors, all Konumbuga, including Tumun; Ngeni-Muruka clan had sturdily supported Mugap in two council elections for Pugamil (a single-member ward) against a candidate from a minority clan. Kaibelt's council ward, Tumun's tribe, and Mugap's adopted clan were the local units they could rely upon for some measure of especial solidarity and the units their ward committee men rustled out in strength to the poll. The more inclusive former 'native' council areas were also 'home areas' to all three.

The northerners who voted for their own Open candidate were prepared, as Wahgi people, to support a southerner, Wamell, in the Regional. Similarly the Mul-Dei Open 'home vote' was, in different contexts, the vote of a candidate's clan, clan-pair, tribe, 'regional' council ward, or total council area. With more candidates actively campaigning than in Wahgi, but all more tentative than Kaibelt in their attempts to break down known segmentary opposition, the most effective local loyalties were to the council areas, with Mul candidates picking up a few cross-votes from near the border. With the accent on these larger unities, Dei tribes without candidates turned out in greater strength than those of the candidates themselves and within the tribes of the two main candidates from Dei other clans turned out in greater strength than that of the candidate. East Kambia voters (Wahgi 'southerners' located outside the South Wall itself) supported Tumun even more strongly than his own tribesmen did, and Kaibelt's strongest support outside his own council area came from a distant part of the north (table 11). One group there that had periodically threatened to secede from Wahgi council and seek incorporation in Dei asserted its identity as a northern group rather than voting for a southern candidate.

The Hagen vote (16,704) was large enough to be split three ways and still allow all three Hagen candidates for the Regional to poll well there. Clearly, however, they would need to attract strong support elsewhere to have a chance of winning. Expatriates living outside Mt Hagen township were part of the European community served by and identified with it: thus Keith Levy, though resident in Mul-Dei, appeared to voters everywhere to be one of three candidates from Hagen and all three had approximately equal access to votes both there and in adjoining electorates. John Watts obtained 58 per cent of the Hagen vote, but this was only 28·92 per cent of his own total vote. His support from the two relatively small adjoining electorates (4055 votes from Kompiam-Baiyer and 3536 from Mul-Dei) contributed less to his success than that from Kandep-Tambul alone (8809 votes). His lowest poll was 414 in Wapenamanda, where the two local candidates captured the bulk of the votes (67 per cent between them). Levy's 8263 votes from Lagaip, where he stayed for two weeks just before the poll, constituted 32·33 per cent of his total vote and included only 195 less than those he polled in Hagen and the adjoining electorates. He polled well in Mul-Dei with 3372 votes, but Watts and Colman both did better there with over 3500 each. He himself attracted 818 more in Hagen than in his 'home' electorate. He obtained useful support in Kandep-Tambul (4461) and Wabag (2170) and, like Watts, received some votes everywhere, his lowest poll (175) being in Wahgi. In two parts of the electorate where he had a slight edge over Watts another candidate polled better, Colman beating him easily in Jimi and Iambakey doing much better in Wabag. Colman drew 53·34 per cent of his total vote from Hagen and adjoining electorates; indeed he polled better in Mul-Dei (3506) and Kompiam-Baiyer (3328) than in Hagen itself (1858). He obtained 22·53 per cent of his total vote (comprising 165 more votes than in Mul-Dei) in Jimi, but found little support elsewhere. Rutledge also was rather better supported in Jimi than in his home electorate.

Iambakey Okuk ('Meknik' on the ballot papers) obtained 21·51 per cent of his vote in Wahgi on the score of local loyalties due to his father rather than himself. His votes there came largely from people around Nondugl, where his father was stationed and also where disaffection with the M.H.A. enabled them to support a different Regional candidate from the one Kaibelt's following chose. (In giving a measure of support to Tumun in conjunction with Iambakey, they reversed the pattern in other northern groups of voting for a northerner in the Open and a southerner in the Regional.) Iambakey led all candidates in his home electorate, which contributed 30·63 per cent of his total vote.

With Iambakey and the two Wapenamanda candidates, the 'home area' could also be considered to be the populous Enga-speaking area that included (as well as Wabag and Wapenamanda) most of Kompiam-Baiyer, all of Lagaip, and parts of Kandep-Tambul. This was certainly Phillip Matuakan's view. He himself obtained 54·77 per cent of his vote from his own electorate, where he was competing with another local candidate, and 35·09 per cent from Lagaip, where his father-in-law was helping him; he did not poll well, however, among Enga elsewhere. Nita Wapurao gained 70·36 per cent of his total vote from his home electorate, leading Matuakan there by 1,189 votes, and won nearly 1,000 votes in Kompiam. Iambakey's support was more widely based than that of the other indigenous candidates, though not strong enough anywhere but in his home electorate to make him a serious competitor with the top three Europeans. Of all the candidates who polled best in different areas, Iambakey in Wabag was the only one to attract a clear majority (57·75 per cent) of second preferences from the supporters of the other candidates. The other three indigenous candidates polled an aggregate of under 5 per cent of the Wabag vote, but he himself collected 16 per cent of Wapenamanda and nearly 14 per cent of Wahgi (table 14). Wamell did not poll well outside his home electorate.

The explanation offered earlier for Iambakey's failure to reap a substantial proportion of second preferences in his father's (in traditional terms, his own) adopted electorate did not apply in Wapenamanda, where both the local candidates commanded nearly 50 per cent (in each case the greatest proportion) of each other's second preferences. This appearance of an 'exchange' needs to be related to their being obvious rivals. At no time did they solicit each other's preferences; they were commonly thought to be fielded by rival Lutheran organisations; and whereas Matuakan stood for the conservative interests of an established businessman, Nita was a radical intellectual. Supporters of Levy in Wapenamanda favoured Matuakan with 43 per cent of their second preferences, nearly twice the proportion of Watts supporters who did so. If Levy can be said to represent the *status quo ante* and Watts a 'new look' in the administration of economic development, Colman could be said to stand for continuity and stability leavened, perhaps, by more direct and less formal relations between expatriates and local people. Matuakan drew a majority (52·21 per cent) of Colman's preferences in Lagaip, where his influential father-in-law could well have associated the two. Nita, by contrast, tended to get the most second preferences from indigenous candidates. In addition to his support from Matuakan voters in his home electorate, he gained the greatest proportion of Iambakey's preferences in Jimi (66·5 per cent), Wapenamanda (44·32 per cent), Mul-Dei (35·55 per cent), and Lagaip (35·2 per cent) and most of Wamell's second preferences in electorates with Enga speakers. These patterns of voting suggest that a decision to vote for solely indigenous candidates (a choice exercised by only 16·34 per cent of voters) may express a less conservative viewpoint than that of most Western Highlanders at the time of the election.

CONCLUSION

Constituent views of the candidates, the latters' expectations of support and the patterns of voting were continuous with traditional politics in being based on the segmentary opposition of groups of varying span. Bloc voting based on consensus was also continuous with traditional methods of making decisions. Traditional custom impinged on the election in the use of dreams and omens in Mul-Dei and the quasi-traditional 'mud-slinging' before polling in Wahgi. Throughout the period embracing the election, pigs were moving in steady procession between Dei and Wabag, first in one direction and then in the other as the *tei* and *moka* ritual exchange cycles proceeded. While polling was in progress Leme Yangal-yo, M.H.A. for Wapenamanda, a prominent figure in *tei* exchanges, threatened to call in all his debts if he did not win the election. In so doing, he threatened the very basis of Enga life. If he had carried out his threat the *tei* would have collapsed and the still valid traditional basis of Enga life would have crumbled.

The Open election in Wahgi was for power in the local government council as much as for representation in the House of Assembly, though people there valued the right to have representation in the seat of government. In Mul-Dei it was essentially a competition between two council areas resulting, as Dei had feared, in a Mul take-over. Experience of councils had taught people to value representation (Reay 1970) but what concerned them was the representation of populations and communities, not of points of view. The chronic issues in local politics (bride price; the time spent on informal courts; and, in many areas, insoluble land problems exacerbated by continuing boundary demarcation) were not felt to be the concern of the House of Assembly and did not form the basis of electioneering. These issues did not concern the Regional candidates. Open candidates, if pressed, might have had to express conflicting views on them and controversial issues were implicitly taboo. No candidate was willing to alienate the vote of those who saw issues differently, even to secure the support of like-minded people. In the realm of *bisnis,* where there was general agreement that the member should press for higher coffee prices and lower costs for the purchase and repair of motor vehicles, voters tended to interpret promises to do so as claims to superior ability, not firmer intention, to fix prices. Some voters said that they would wait and see who won and then tell the member firmly that this was what people wanted from him, though it seemed unlikely that they would trouble to do this after the election was over. Voters did not see the election of a member as something they themselves could control. For one thing, they believed some candidates to be officially favoured. Clans and sometimes council wards held meetings to decide whom they would vote for, but in Wahgi the stress on the secrecy of the ballot prevented them from making their collective decisions known beyond the boundaries of their own groups, so their estimates of candidates' chances were uninformed. Consensus worked with less certainty, too, in a paper poll than by a show of hands (a procedure formerly followed in council elections in Dei and Wahgi and seriously suggested by many Wahgi groups as an alternative to the present system). Each person was still free to vote differently by individual choice and, when a group had decided upon one or two candidates, give variant later preferences.

The 1968 general election was an unusual event for those who conducted it. Council elections from 1964 onward had called for similar procedures and had to be reported to the Electoral Office as well as to local government authorities, but this time a U.N. Visiting

Mission was proposing to observe the election at first hand and the outspoken comments of the Liberian delegate in the last mission were still the subject of uneasy joking among officials and their expatriate acquaintances. Some officials with experience of conducting council elections had developed a sophisticated expertise. (For example, they were able to correct the Deputy Chief Electoral Officer's version of how to count preferences when he visited Mt Hagen to brief them on their duties.) Many officials wanted certain candidates to win; indeed, considering the assistance already received in promoting the Administration's policies, it would have been remarkable if they had been able to view all candidates impartially. But impartiality was only legally required from the Issue of the Writ to the Declaration of the Poll, the period of the actual election as defined by the Act. The Ellis administration knew very well that much could be done to determine the course and outcome of the election before it began. To some extent it was possible for *kiaps* who knew that they were going to be electoral officials to bring about the kind of election they wanted.

There was no legal barrier to the Administration gearing its program of political education to its official policies of economic development and the advancement of particular politicians who could be relied upon to champion these in parliament. The Administration's concern with 'political education' during the year preceding the election mixed teaching the alphabet of politics with persuading local men to support the official ideology of economic development before self-government. The use of the local government council and the sitting member (where he had shown himself to be pro-Administration) as instruments of political education increased the significance of the council for the election and entrenched the sitting member's identification with the powerful Administration.

Briefing on the nature and functions of political parties had consolidated the carefully encouraged popular view of self-government and/or independence as undesirable for the region. This could not become an electoral issue when no one was willing to oppose it publicly.

It was not hard, however, to discredit an educated indigenous candidate by putting him under suspicion of being privately opposed to it. Despite Iambakey's protestations that he was a good Western Highlander, did not want political independence for the Territory, and belonged to no political party, his name became inextricably associated with that of Pangu. Pangu itself was unequivocally identified in the region as being 'anti-Administration'. The Police Special Branch asked a European Regional candidate whether Iambakey had said anything against the Administration and also hoped that the study team would inform them of 'anti-Administration talk'.

No expatriate actually expected Iambakey to win. (Some even went so far as to say that the Administration would not let that happen.) But the agitation over what might occur if he should do so was an admission of this possibility. So far as expatriates in the Western Highlands were concerned, the elections for Moresby Open and East and West New Britain Regional were satisfactorily decided when only 'good white men' nominated; and the contest for Morobe Regional interested many of them more vitally than that between Levy and Watts, for the possibility of Voutas winning for Pangu against Niall for the Administration appeared to threaten the entire colonial order and their own livelihoods. A win for Iambakey would demonstrate that a massive native population preferred a fellow native to one of themselves—not simply to squabble with other indigenous representatives about the proper distribution of roads and bridges, but also to bring the dreaded future closer.

Iambakey had talked of representation at the U.N. and of overseas trade. An indigenous man who concerned himself with other than strictly parochial matters without cutting himself off from the uneducated populace was dangerous because he betrayed a sophistication that put him outside expatriate control. There was no 'Yessir' in Iambakey's political vocabulary: he was prepared to argue with the European candidates and stand up to cross-examination. He was a reminder that the control that did exist—witnessed by the confidence with which the Administration could rely upon any Western Highlands M.H.A. or council office-bearer to voice the official line on independence, and the agreement of Hagen Council that it was 'no good' to have an indigenous member for the Regional in addition to one for the Open—was really quite tenuous.

In Hagen Open a traditional leader of some local eminence died. The Administration did not insist, as might have been expected, that the lengthy mourning ceremonies customary in the area should be curtailed to fit in with the important work of a national election. Instead, it went out of its way to offer every facility for all groups even slightly affected to express their grief in traditional fashion. This meant that Regional candidates trying to secure support were rudely rebuffed. The Hagen people were inaccessible to the campaigns of the main European and indigenous candidates, and thus the compliance of their leaders with the idea of electing a European was effectively frozen.

Iambakey's arguments invited rebuttal and discrediting because expatriates who knew the region expected them to stir up trouble. This could not happen, of course, if Western Highlanders were as deeply and unanimously committed to the official line as the public statements of their spokesmen had continually asserted. The voting in Wabag and

Wahgi suggests that Tei Abal and Kaibelt Diria, Tom Ellis's own star pupils, lent more support than anyone expected to Iambakey's plea to 'vote black' for the Regional. Even the threat that the Europeans would be leaving the Territory on the attainment of independence would lose its coercive force if people reached the conclusion that they could do things well enough themselves, as Iambakey seemed to be saying. The 'Yessir' compliance with privately galling political domination by expatriates could be nearing its end.

Few indigenous electors discerned political dissent in the competition Watts offered the 'official' candidate, Levy; some expatriates, too, failed to recognise that the Watts position entailed power shifts in the administrative structure. It was left to Iambakey to introduce genuine political opposition as an issue on which to vote. The opposition was to the advisability of having a European representing the District, but the expatriates who panicked at the implications of Iambakey's campaign were quick to brand him as a secret supporter of Pangu, the party that had opposed the Administration explicitly on the question of self-government. The question itself could not become an issue: it was permissible for a candidate (Matuakan) to use the official advocacy of economic development before political independence as an electoral platform, but not for a would-be M.H.A. (Ovia) to wear a Pangu badge. It is hard to see how any other issues could have emerged when political opposition was equated with subversion.

What did the bogey of 'self-government' really mean? Neither expatriates nor local people construed it as the gradual indigenisation of the Public Service and the increasing assumption of responsibility by indigenous national leaders. Many expatriates conjured visions of violence and chaos, spontaneous local attempts at expropriation, and mob rule with the removal of control. Local people liked the prospect of self-government but were appalled at the many skills they still lacked to undertake it: hence their continued reliance upon Europeans and their often reiterated statements that it was 'something for my grandsons, not myself'. If it came too soon, before the people of the region were ready, outsiders from more developed parts of the Territory would take the place of Europeans and they would resist this strongly. If the Europeans wanted to stay after independence they could do so on the local people's terms. Local government councillors would be *kiaps*. According to one of our Open candidates, the M.H.A. would take the chair and office of the D.C. in Mt Hagen and the flag would fly in a village with his house at its head; both Europeans and local people would live in the village. This image identified elected representation with the indigenisation of power and incorporated in the projected residential arrangements the idea that whites and natives should work together.

TABLE 15—THE ELECTION RESULTS IN THE WESTERN HIGHLANDS

Regional	1st count	2nd count	3rd count	4th count	5th count	6th count	7th and final count
Noel Rutledge	4225	Excl.	—	—	—	—	—
John Watts	33,571	34,740	35,232	35,436	36,167	38,595	43,613
Phillip Matuakan	5229	5284	Excl.	—	—	—	—
Keith Levy	25,459	25,992	26,237	26,462	26,634	27,702	33,236
Iambakey Okuk	10,163	10,522	11,151	12,125	12,905	Excl.	—
Nita Wapurao	5760	5806	6836	Excl.	—	—	—
Philip Wamell	10,187	10,571	10,685	11,178	Excl.	—	—
John Colman	16,294	16,683	17,013	17,383	18,248	20,996	Excl.
Informal	3659	—	—	—	—	—	—
Exhausted	—	1290	3734	8304	16,934	23,595	34,039

Mul-Dei Open	1st count	2nd count	3rd count	4th count	5th and final count
Peruwa Kuri	2315	2374	2456	2909	3108
Wareke Wema	1172	1191	Excl.	—	—
Mek Nugintz	3029	3223	3249	3338	5675
Pung Nimp	2567	2633	2640	2707	Excl.
El Rop	1401	1499	1665	Excl.	—
Pim Koropie	456	Excl.	—	—	—
Informal	47	—	—	—	—
Exhausted	—	20	930	1986	2157

Wahgi Open	1st and final count
Kaibelt Diria	9440
Tumun Dubura	5811
Mugap Baugum	601
Informal	35

A TOWN AND ITS HINTERLAND

Murray Groves,
R. M. S. Hamilton and Margaret McArthur

PORT MORESBY, the present capital of Papua and New Guinea, was first established as an administrative centre more than eighty years ago. Until World War II, it was a small, sleepy colonial town inhabited by a few hundred expatriate Europeans, mainly Australians, and some immigrant Papuan workers employed mostly under indenture. It was a white man's town, functioning as headquarters of the Administration and as a transhipment and service centre for the rubber and copra plantations of the hinterland. Several nearby villages of the Motu and Koita peoples, the indigenous owners and occupiers of the land around Port Moresby, began to supply the town with urban workers increasingly in the 1930s but still maintained economies based primarily on gardening, fishing, hunting, and trade in pottery. Before the war all other Motu and Koita villages depended entirely upon their traditional economic institutions for subsistence. Europeans owned and managed copra plantations along the Papuan coast both east and west of Port Moresby and rubber plantations on the Sogeri plateau inland from the town and on mountain foothills at the head of Galley Reach some thirty miles away. Labourers on these plantations came under indenture from remoter areas.

Since World War II, as headquarters of the Administration for the entire Territory of Papua and New Guinea and its major financial

Margaret McArthur supplied most of the data in this chapter on the Goilala Open Electorate and on the campaign of Andy Anderson for Central Regional. R. M. S. Hamilton supplied data on the campaigns of Chatterton and McCarthy for Moresby Open. Acknowledgments are also due to George Obara of the University of Papua and New Guinea and Andrew Taylor of the Australian National University for notes that they supplied on the election campaigns at the Roro village of Tsiria and the Motu village of Tubusereia respectively. For all other data in this chapter, for the overall analysis of the data and the main argument developed in the chapter, and for the final text, Murray Groves is alone responsible.

and commercial centre, where a high proportion of the Territory's enormously enlarged revenue is spent on wages, buildings, and services, the town of Port Moresby has expanded as rapidly as the Territory's annual revenues have increased—from $4,965,358 in 1946-7 (Territories *P.A.R.* 1946-7: 24) to $135,891,701 in 1967-8 (Territories, *P.A.R.* 1967-8: 104; *N.G.A.R.* 1967-8: 298). Over this period population growth in Port Moresby has been rapid and continuous as the growing town has engulfed the nearby villages of the Motu and Koita people and attracted immigrants in steadily increasing numbers from other parts of the Territory. At the 1966 Census there were 41,848 persons within what was then defined for census purposes as the Port Moresby urban area (Census 1966: Table 23). The town's physical expansion has also been spectacular: the built-up areas have spread out around the harbour, along the coast, and inland to new suburbs some miles from the sea, eating up the traditional hunting and gardening lands of the Motu and Koita people, which they have sold to supplement inadequate urban wages.

Port Moresby is a centre of rapid social change. With quantitative changes such as population increase and territorial expansion there occurred also, at some point within the last decade or so, a profound qualitative change. Local villagers who had abandoned their subsistence economies and immigrants from other areas who had severed their most intimate links with their home villages began increasingly to identify with the town and to embrace whole-heartedly an essentially urban way of life. The town acquired a new function: no longer merely an Australian colonial outpost, it became an integral part of Papuan and New Guinean society, inhabited predominantly by indigenous workers who now supply not only essential manpower for the urban economy but also essential goods, services, money, and ideas to kinsmen and fellow tribesmen in the hinterland. A vital, exciting, distinctively urban sub-culture and new, complex, rewarding social networks have developed among Papuans and New Guineans in Port Moresby, which is now, for them, their own town rather than a white man's town, though the white men themselves have been slow to notice this change.

By almost every relevant measure of modernisation, the indigenous people of Port Moresby and its immediate hinterland are the most advanced in Papua and New Guinea. Though data are not available at present to substantiate all of the following statements, it seems nevertheless safe to say that this population has higher levels of educational attainment, a stronger commitment to urban life, a more complex differentiation of status and role, including greater occupational specialisation, a more extreme dependence on wage

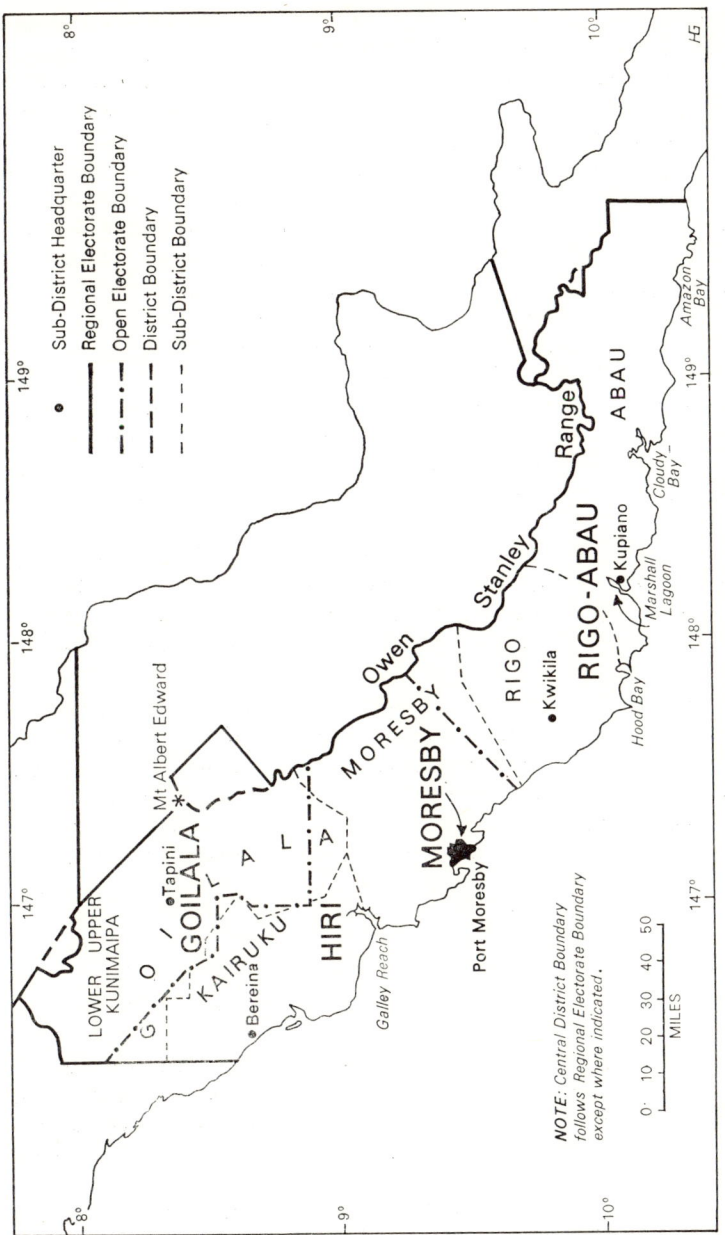

11 Central District Electorates

labour at the expense of traditional means of subsistence, a larger number and greater variety of voluntary associations, more frequent and more intensive exposure to mass communication media, and a greater diversity of new institutions, ideas, and opportunities, than any other indigenous population in the Territory.

Furthermore, at Port Moresby and on plantations in the town's immediate hinterland there is the largest concentration of expatriate European immigrants in the Territory. They have brought with them to Port Moresby skills, norms, experiences, and values, including those of a specifically political kind, acquired in the communities from which they have come—mainly Australian cities.

From considerations such as these, it is plausible to expect that the people of Port Moresby, more advanced in so many other respects, might also prove more advanced in their use of the parliamentary political system in which they now participate, and that electoral politics in the Port Moresby area at the time of a national election might in many ways prove more sophisticated than elsewhere in the Territory.

In the first place, it seems not unreasonable to expect, from both candidates and voters, more sophisticated ideologies than those of the parish-pump kind to which backwoods rural politicians in Papua and New Guinea have usually appealed. In Port Moresby there are many expatriates with university degrees or other professional training, and also an indigenous intelligentsia comprising for the most part students at the University and the Administrative College, schoolteachers, and other professional or semi-professional civil servants. Newspapers, magazines, and radio continually introduce the alien ideological concerns of the world outside, and Port Moresby is also the Territory's major market-place for the exchange and distribution of local ideologies.

Secondly, surrounded by the largest, most complex, and most diverse formal organisations in the Territory, including all the headquarters departments of the Territory Administration, some agencies of the Commonwealth Government, the Territory head offices of many commercial firms, and the offices of diverse local, national, and international voluntary associations, candidates in the Port Moresby area, many of whom have themselves worked in these bureaucracies, might be expected to develop campaign organisations somewhat more sophisticated than those of the candidates in other electorates.

Thirdly, since national political decisions crucially determine many vital aspects of the lives of urban workers, including the nature and adequacy of their livelihood and the shape and utility of their physical habitat, whereas most rural villagers look to the national government merely to provide a cash icing for the cake of their subsistence economies or in other ways marginally to improve the quality of a life that they could sustain well enough without any intervention from the national government, it might be expected both that interest in a national election would be keener in Port Moresby than elsewhere and that major campaign issues would be more numerous.

Fourthly, as a corollary of the first three points, political parties might be expected to succeed sooner in Port Moresby, since ideology, formal organisation, political commitment, and campaign issues are the essential ingredients of successful party politics.

Fifthly, the basic rural status differences of age, sex, kinship, locality, religious affiliation, and ethnic or linguistic group are supplemented in Port Moresby by other extremely important differences of income, occupation, educational attainment, membership of voluntary associations, Territory of origin (Papua or New Guinea), and caste (European, mixed-race, Chinese, indigenous). Since differences such as these have often been found to influence political behaviour in other countries, we might reasonably hope to identify for the Port Moresby area some correlations between such things as income levels, occupational categories, voluntary association memberships, and caste affiliations on the one hand, and support for particular candidates on the other hand, whereas a search for such correlations would seem futile in most rural areas.

In an attempt to test these expectations, this chapter concentrates on the three electorates that in 1968 included all, or some parts, of the Port Moresby urban area and its immediate hinterland: Moresby Open; Hiri Open; and Central Regional.

THE ELECTORATES

The Moresby Open Electorate consisted essentially of the town of Port Moresby—minus a number of residential communities within the town boundary inhabited mainly by Motu and Koita people, the traditional owners of the land on which Port Moresby now stands, who were excluded from this electorate and included for electoral purposes with rural Motu and Koita villagers in the Hiri Open Electorate, presumably on the ground that they had more interests in common with their fellow tribesmen than with their fellow townsmen (see p. 41).

Of the 41,848 persons enumerated at the 1966 Census in the Port Moresby urban area, 31,983 were classified as 'indigenous' (Census 1966: Table 23). The 'non-indigenous' population included 9080 expatriate Australians and other Europeans, 452 mixed-race, and 247 Chinese (Census 1966: Table 30). 'Indigenous' people enumerated at the Census included both Motu and Koita inhabitants of those villages excluded from the Moresby Open electorate and placed in the Hiri Open electorate at the 1968 election, and also immigrant workers, their wives, and their children, who have migrated to Port Moresby from every administrative District in the Territory and now greatly outnumber Motu and Koita in the town.

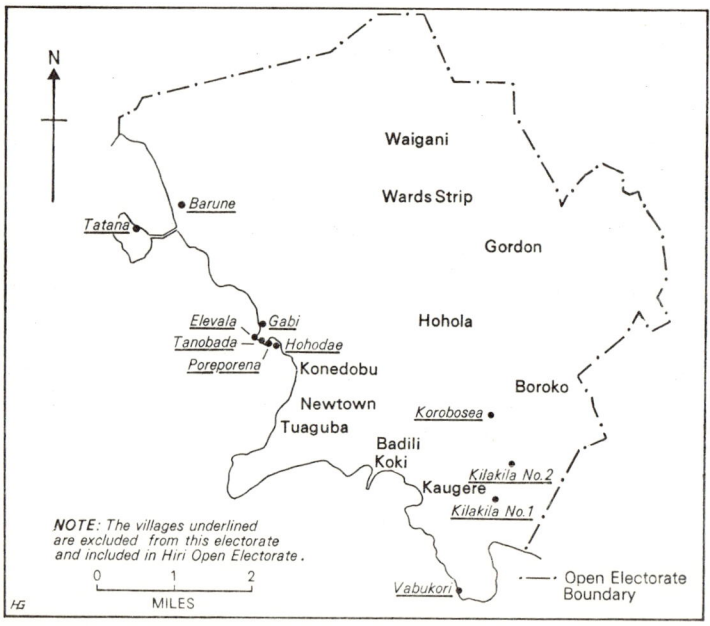

12   Moresby Open Electorate

The European population live in expensive residential areas high upon all the hills immediately overlooking the harbour and the sea, in a fashionable housing settlement for senior Administration officers a mile or more around the harbour from the old commercial centre of the town, and in several new suburbs, predominantly housing lesser grades of expatriate public servants, which sprawl out across the plains beyond the coastal hills, three, four, five, and six miles inland from the centre of town.

Some of the indigenous immigrants included in the electorate live in rows of two-roomed or three-roomed concrete boxes at Hohola, another inland suburb, and others live in somewhat worse conditions at Kaugere and Sabama, government sponsored working-class suburbs closer to the sea several miles east of the town. In addition, scattered throughout the urban area there are 'squatter' shanty settlements built of old timber and corrugated iron from post-war scrap-heaps on land to which the residents have no title—often just out of sight and hence, to most Europeans, also out of mind. A list of these shanty settlements compiled by the Sub-District Office in about 1964 identified twenty-two of them, inhabited by a total of 6346 people.[1] Other immigrants live on houseboats at Koke waterfront, or in domestic servants' quarters scattered throughout the European residential areas. Unmarried male immigrants also live in labour compounds situated in various parts of the town.

Deducting from the total 1966 Census figures the populations of the Motu and Koita villages excluded from the electorate, and allowing for population growth since 1966, we may estimate that the population within the Moresby Open Electorate at the time of the election comprised over 10,000 non-indigenous people and over 26,000 indigenous people. Altogether 13,422 electors were finally enrolled in this electorate.[2]

Many indigenous immigrants living in town enrolled in their home electorates rather than the Moresby Open Electorate, but a significant number preferred to vote in Moresby Open (Obara 1968) and their problems received considerable attention during the campaign.

The Hiri Open Electorate basically comprised all of the Port Moresby and Kairuku Sub-Districts minus the Port Moresby urban area, which was cut out to form the Moresby Open Electorate. As noted earlier, however, certain Motu and Koita village communities located within the boundaries of the Moresby Open Electorate were treated for electoral purposes as part of the Hiri Open Electorate. The inhabitants of these urban villages share the same way of life and have many of the same problems as other urban workers in Port Moresby, but still have bonds of kinship, custom, and sentiment

[1] The list was kindly made available by the staff of the Sub-District office, to whom thanks are due.
[2] Before the election, electoral staff in Port Moresby contacted 10,251 immigrant adults to enrol them, giving them a choice of enrolling in Moresby Open or in their home electorate. Of these 10,251 electors, 5838 chose to enrol in their home electorates and 4413 enrolled for Moresby Open. (These figures were kindly supplied by the Returning Officer for Moresby Open.)

linking them to their fellow tribesmen in rural villages. As things worked out, they probably preferred to vote in the Hiri Open Electorate, where they crucially affected the result in a very close contest.

Outside the town of Port Moresby, the Port Moresby Sub-District comprises five Census Divisions: East Coast, which incorporates all predominantly Motu and Koita villages east of Port Moresby as far as Gaire; West Coast, which incorporates all Motu and Koita villages west of Port Moresby; Vanapa River and Mountain Koiari, containing small settlements of Doura, Koiari, and Mountain Koiari people; and Sogeri Valley, in which there are a number of rubber estates owned and managed by expatriates employing indigenous labourers from other parts of the Territory under contract.

The Kairuku Sub-District comprises seven Census Divisions each populated by the people after whom it is named. They are Kabadi, Nara, Roro, and Waima-Kivori, which extend westwards in that order along the coast from Galley Reach past Yule Island to Cape Possession, and three inland Divisions, Bush Mekeo, Mekeo, and Kuni. In addition to indigenous villagers who maintained their traditional subsistence economies with cash supplements earned mainly by marketing rural produce in town, there are some large expatriate rubber estates at the head of Galley Reach in the Kabadi Census Division and expatriate copra plantations strung out along the beach in the Kabadi and Nara Census Divisions.

Ultimately 20,423 electors, 11,256 male and 9167 female, enrolled in the Hiri Open Electorate. Since most plantation labourers enrolled in their home electorates, these electors were for the most part the traditional inhabitants of the area, divided politically between those administered from Port Moresby and those administered from Bereina, divided ethnically into nine or ten main groups, and divided also between Catholic adherents of the Sacred Heart Mission at Yule Island, most strongly represented among the Mekeo, Bush Mekeo, Kuni, Doura, and Roro, and Protestant adherents of the Papua Ekalesia, formerly the London Missionary Society, most strongly represented among the Motu, Koita, and Gabadi (Kabadi).

The Hiri Open Electorate at the 1968 election comprised a large part of Port Moresby's immediate rural hinterland, closely linked to the town. Though Port Moresby's expansion since the war has been financed by Administration expenditure rather than the productive capacity of its hinterland, the expatriate rubber and copra plantations of the Port Moresby and Kairuku Sub-Districts have used the town as an entrepôt and have thus made some contribution to its economy. Also, indigenous villagers throughout the two Sub-Districts have

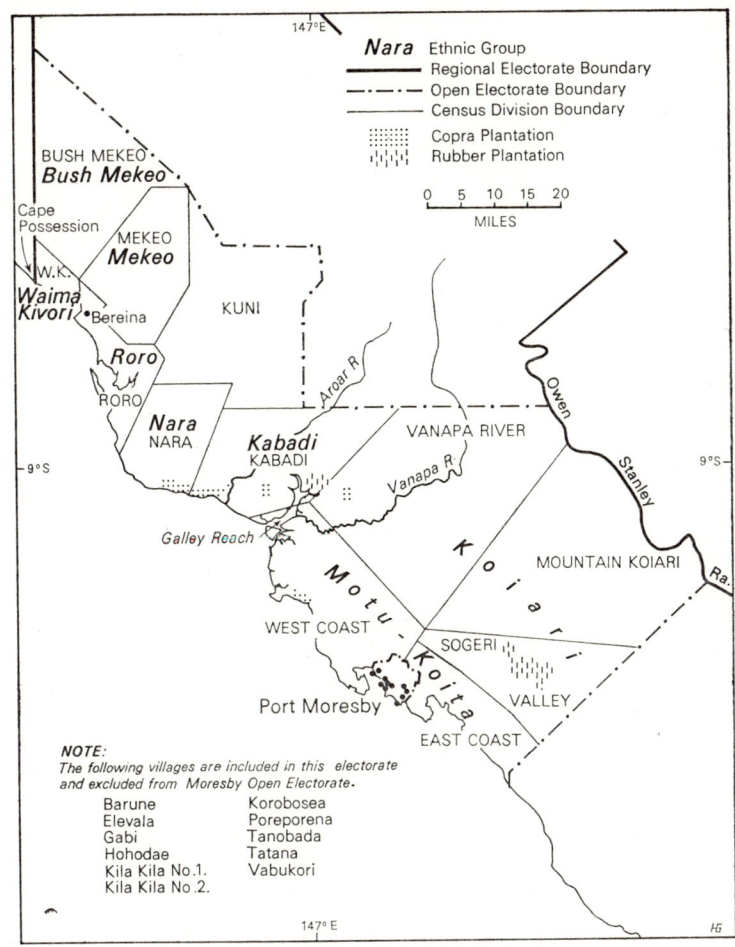

13 Hiri Open Electorate

supplied increasing quantities of fruit, vegetables, fish, and betel-nut to Port Moresby consumers as the town has expanded. There are workers from most rural villages in the two Sub-Districts working in town, and their rural kin frequently pay visits to them by canoe, motor vessel, or truck.

The boundaries of the Central Regional Electorate at the 1968 election coincided with those of the Central District, one of the

Territory's eighteen major administrative Districts. This Regional electorate comprised four Open electorates: Moresby Open and Hiri Open, already described, and Goilala Open and Rigo-Abau Open, each of which must now be described very briefly to make the campaign for the Central Regional Electorate fully comprehensible.

The Goilala Open Electorate coincided with the Goilala Sub-District, an inland mountainous region north-west of Port Moresby rising from several thousand to 12,000 feet above sea level, administered by an Assistant District Commissioner at Tapini, 3250 feet up, where during the wet season from November to April the airstrip is usually closed by cloud except for a few hours a day. The Sub-District's other airstrip at Woitape, further east at about 6000 feet, is also often closed by rain and cloud. There are 35 miles of jeep road from Tapini, frequently blocked by landslides during the wet. The main valleys are traversed by graded tracks which link most villages, and they too suffer from slides and washaways during the rainy season, though at other times many of them are good enough to carry motor cycles. In this terrain campaigning was difficult, and bad weather over the voting period kept people at any distance from polling stations away from the poll.

There are three main linguistic groups among the Goilala: the Fuyughe, Tau'ade, and Kunimaipa. All depend on subsistence agriculture with sweet potato as their staple. There has been virtually no economic development in the area except for the sale of vegetable produce flown in small quantities to Port Moresby and the introduction of cattle on a small scale. French priests and nuns of the Sacred Heart Mission have worked extensively throughout the area and most of the inhabitants are Catholics, though the London Missionary Society also has a station among the Kunimaipa, staffed by Papuans.

The Goilala Open Electorate was a backwoods electorate linked to Port Moresby by an air service and an administrative chain of command, but remote from the town in every other way.

The Rigo-Abau Open Electorate in 1968 extended from Gabagaba, the furthest Motu village east of Port Moresby, just on the Rigo side of the boundary between the Rigo and Port Moresby Sub-Districts, eastwards along the coast for more than 150 miles, past Hood Point and Marshall Lagoon and Mailu, to the boundary between the Central and Milne Bay Districts at Orangerie Bay. The inland boundary of this long, narrow, predominantly coastal electorate followed the peaks of the Owen Stanley Range at distances varying between about twenty and fifty miles from the sea. Various places within the western half of the electorate, including the Rigo Sub-District headquarters at Kwikila, are linked to Port Moresby by road.

Primary produce, rural sightseers, and immigrant labourers pour into Port Moresby along this road. There is also considerable canoe traffic between Port Moresby and the coastal communities in this electorate, and copra scows make regular runs from town to plantations along the beach in several parts of the electorate. Like the Hiri Open Electorate, Rigo-Abau Open can be viewed as an integral part of Port Moresby's immediate hinterland, supplying the town with labour, local produce, and export crops by road and sea.

THE CANDIDATES

Two Europeans, J. K. (Keith) McCarthy and Percy Chatterton, were the only candidates for the Moresby Open Electorate. This seemed perfectly proper to most of the European electors, one of whom said in an interview, 'after all, this is a European town', sublimely unaware that in fact Papuans and New Guineans outnumber Europeans in the town three to one. Nor was it a cause of any widespread complaint among indigenous electors. Many Papuans knew and trusted one of the candidates, Chatterton, as well as they would have known and trusted any of the likely Papuan candidates, which perhaps explains why several Papuan politicians who might otherwise have stood in this electorate chose to stand elsewhere. McCarthy, who had spent most of his career in the former Territory of New Guinea, had similar repute among some of the New Guinean immigrants to the town, though its extent in his case is difficult to estimate.

The two candidates for Moresby Open were both experienced, able, and widely-known. Both had become legendary figures in Papua and New Guinea, Chatterton as a teacher, missionary, translator of the New Testament, and urban welfare worker, McCarthy as a pre-war Patrol Officer, wartime hero, and post-war Director of Native Affairs. Both had served in the last House of Assembly, Chatterton as elected member for the Central Special Electorate and McCarthy as a nominated official member. Retired from their professional posts, both had elected to live in Port Moresby, Chatterton in a very small weatherboard bungalow near an indigenous housing estate at Kaugere and McCarthy rather more elegantly in a high-covenant housing area. Chatterton admitted that as a retired missionary he stood to gain more than others financially from his member's salary, but the obvious dedication that he showed in serving the Port Moresby community and the sense of achievement and purpose that he found in politics were unquestionably major motives in his decision to stand. McCarthy's career had also shown considerable dedication to the welfare of the Territory and its people, and at times he too seemed a man with a mission, really eager to contribute his knowledge, experience, and vision to the development of the Territory, but it was widely thought that the desire to occupy some official niche in Port Moresby society after his retirement was also a motive for his candidature. For whatever reasons, it was quite clear that both men badly wanted to win—but neither felt sure that he would.

Chatterton took up duty as a mission teacher at Port Moresby in 1924. By 1968 he had spent forty-four years in the Port Moresby and Kairuku Sub-Districts, where he was widely known and respected by local Papuans. In the first House of Assembly he built up a formidable reputation as a champion of his constituents' rights and interests, particularly those of Port Moresby's indigenous population, and as a vigilant critic of the Administration. His door was always open to constituents and many with grievances found him a ready ally.

McCarthy came to the Territory as a Patrol Officer in 1927. His rise through the ranks was steady: Assistant District Officer in 1935, District Officer in 1947, District Commissioner at Rabaul in 1949, and in 1960 Director of the Department of Native Affairs (later to be called the Department of District Administration). His war record was equally distinguished, and earned him the M.B.E. His personal qualities and experience were unquestioned but unlike Chatterton, who could show that he had criticised the Administration with useful results, McCarthy found great difficulty in projecting anything except an establishment image.

In the Hiri Open Electorate, there were six candidates: three from the Mekeo area in the Kairuku Sub-District and three from Motu villages near Port Moresby.

Toua Kapena, a Motu leader from Hanuabada, combined long experience in the white man's world with high prestige among his own people. During the 1930s he worked for the Administration as a medical orderly. After the war he joined the headquarters staff of the Education Department in Port Moresby as a clerk, and remained the senior Papuan clerk in the Department until 1964 when, somewhat disillusioned with wages and working conditions in the Public Service, he resigned to become bar manager of the Kone Tavern, where Papuan public servants at Konedobu and the men of the Hanuabada village cluster do much of their drinking. When he made this move he was already thinking of standing for the House of Assembly in 1968 and felt that his position at the Tavern, where he came into contact with large numbers of indigenous workers, would enhance his electoral prospects. Since the war he has been continually prominent in the affairs of his own community, as a Director and at one time Chairman of the Poreporena and Hohodae Co-operative Society, a member of the Port Moresby Town Advisory Council, chairman or other executive member of numerous sporting and social clubs, and President of his local government council for many years—first when it was limited only to the Hanuabada village cluster, later when it took in other nearby Motu and Koita villages to become the Fairfax Local Government Council, and more recently when it expanded to include all rural Motu and Koita villages from Manumanu in the west to Gaire in the east, under the misleading name of the Port Moresby Local Government Council.

Another Motu candidate, Allen Rabura of Vabukori Village, stood as the endorsed candidate of the Napro (National Progress) Party. Aged 30, he had been working as a clerk in a large commercial firm ever since he left school at Standard VI, the senior standard in Territory primary schools. He also owned and operated two trucks which gave him additional income. He had not held any public office and had no prior political experience before joining the Napro Party, which he was persuaded to do by the Chairman and founder of the party, a close personal friend, some months before the election. Though pre-selected at a general meeting of party members, he had to finance his own campaign.

There was a third candidate for Hiri Open from a Motu village, Manuel Albaniel of Tatana, an elderly man who did no campaigning outside his own village and played no effective part in the election.

Two candidates from the Mekeo area in the Kairuku Sub-District were both confident that they had solid support in their home base and thought they could build on this elsewhere sufficiently to win.

Aisa Nguu of Inawaia Village, aged 42, educated to Primary Standard V at the Yule Island Catholic Mission Station, had been President of the Kairuku Local Government Council since 1962 and still held this office at the time of the election. He had also been a member of the Central District Advisory Council since 1963. In 1950, when he was working as a Field Assistant for the Agriculture Department among the Mekeo, he represented Papua and New Guinea at the South Pacific Conference in Suva, Fiji. Leaving his job with the Administration in 1953 he returned to village life and described himself in 1968 as a 'subsistence farmer', though in fact he also owned a truck and made money from a transport business. Six months before the election Aisa Nguu received a letter from the secretary of the newly formed Pangu Pati, who had been impressed with his performance at a District Advisory Council meeting, asking him to visit Port Moresby and discuss 'policies and plans for the future of the country', as he put it later in an interview. After these discussions, in which the names of other élite indigenous politicians who had already joined Pangu Pati were mentioned and the major aim of the party, to unite all the diverse indigenous groups throughout the Territory into a cohesive nation, was debated, Aisa Nguu agreed to join the party and stand for election in the Hiri Open Electorate. The party did not provide funds, nor did it offer at that stage any detailed political platform. Its appeal to Aisa Nguu lay mainly in the calibre and dedication of its leading members and the call to national unity as a necessary condition for the advancement of his people.

The other leading candidate from the Mekeo area, Charlie Maino Aukey, 44 years old, part-Mekeo and part-European, was a man of quite a different kind: an extroverted, generous, successful small businessman, trained as a mechanic in Port Moresby after an earlier unfinished period of training for the priesthood, now the proprietor of a successful trucking business at his village, Inawi, a frequent and convivial visitor to Port Moresby, known widely throughout the Kairuku and Port Moresby Sub-Districts.

There was also a third Mekeo candidate, George Mapai, a Co-operative Officer who had worked in Port Moresby but was working far away from home in the Milne Bay District at the time of the election. George Mapai did not return to the electorate at any time during the campaign, so far as we could discover, but he did arrange to have a mimeographed 'Policy and Platform' in both English and Mekeo distributed throughout his home area.

In the Central Regional Electorate there were five candidates: three Papuans, all Motu, and two Europeans.

The leading Papuan candidate, Oala Oala-Rarua, though still quite young, was a seasoned campaigner who had long prepared himself for political office. The son of a respected London Missionary Society pastor from the Motu village of Pari, and married to a woman from an influential Hanuabada family at Port Moresby, he enjoyed by birth and marriage important connections and prestige among the Motu and Koita people. A schoolteacher, he came early in his career under the influence of Kwato Mission, representatives in Papua of the Moral Rearmament movement, under whose auspices he once visited Europe. Subsequently he met and impressed the then Assistant Administrator who took him into the Public Service as a personal assistant. When he moved to Port Moresby in 1962 to take up his new post with the Assistant Administrator, he joined the Papua and New Guinea Workers' Association, became its president, and in

1965 resigned from the Administration to work full time for the Association and for a Territory-wide Federation of Workers' Associations which was proposed at that time. By 1968 this Association was defunct and Oala Oala-Rarua was working for a private business firm, but during his presidency of the Association he became widely known among urban workers in Port Moresby and received credit for the Association's achievements, such as they were, under his leadership. As a public servant and later as a trade union leader he made a number of visits to Australia and visited Europe a second time. A matriculated student of the University of Papua and New Guinea, where he has successfully taken several subjects part time, he has established friendships with a number of Australian intellectuals and professional men, with whom he is at ease. He had sought election to the national legislature twice before 1968, first in 1961 when he was narrowly defeated by a man from the Western District of Papua in an electoral college ballot for a seat on the then Legislative Council, and again in 1964 when he was defeated for a House of Assembly seat by a Goilala man.

The second Papuan candidate for the Central Regional Electorate, Gavera Rea, was born at Hanuabada, one of the Motu villages now within the Port Moresby urban area. Aged 31, married, and like Oala Oala-Rarua the son of a well-known London Missionary Society pastor, he was well connected among the Motu, but not well known among them for he had grown up away from his own village—first as a child, when his father was stationed elsewhere in Papua, and later as an adolescent at school in Australia. After school in Australia he studied for and obtained matriculation qualifications at the Administrative College in Port Moresby, but instead of accepting the place available for him at the University of Papua and New Guinea he decided on a career in business and commerce and accordingly took a post with the Papua New Guinea Corporation in Port Moresby. At the Administrative College he founded and became Vice-Chairman of the Papua and New Guinea Tertiary Students' Federation, for its time a distinctly radical and outspoken student organisation. A foundation member and one of the eight initial committee members of Pangu Pati, he ran for election in 1968 as the party's endorsed candidate in the Central Regional Electorate.

The third Papuan candidate, Sevese Morea, a radio announcer and disc jockey in his early twenties, was born at Vabukori, another Motu village within the Port Moresby urban area. He stood for the Napro Party, to which, like his fellow villager Allen Rabura, he was recruited by personal friends among the party's founders.

Frederic David Anderson, an Australian, aged 43, appeared on the ballot paper for the Central Regional Electorate as 'Andy Anderson,' the name by which he was most widely known. A former Assistant District Officer in the Goilala Sub-District, since leaving the Administration in 1957 he had acquired a hotel at Tapini and a farm in the Goilala area. He was narrowly defeated by Percy Chatterton for the Central Special seat in the House of Assembly at the 1964 election.

The other European candidate, Ron Slaughter, also in his forties, had been prominent for many years at Yule Island and among the Mekeo as a trader, shipowner, and businessman, and he had once been one of the three elected European members of the Legislative Council, which was replaced in 1964 by the House of Assembly. He had fairly recently entered into partnership with local fishermen in a crayfish enterprise, and was well liked and well respected by Papuans in the Kairuku Sub-District.

Considering the candidates for all three electorates together, we may ask in what ways they were or were not representative of their communities or of the electors whose votes they sought. The answer is that in most cases they were very exceptional men, of unusually high achieved status among their peers.

The four European candidates were all men of long experience in the Territory, each having spent all or most of his entire working life there. Each owned property in the electorate for which he stood, even if in Chatterton's case it was only a humble cottage. Each had previously participated in national politics: Chatterton, McCarthy, and Slaughter as members of former legislatures, and Anderson as a candidate for election. Each regarded the Territory as his permanent home. Each had enjoyed long and close contact with indigenous villagers at the grass-roots level: Chatterton as a missionary, Anderson and McCarthy as field officers in the Department of Native Affairs, and Slaughter as a trader and business partner. None of them had taken a university degree, though Chatterton had taken tertiary courses in teacher-training and theology, but all four were thoughtful, intelligent, articulate men of independent mind. Chatterton has translated the New Testament into Motu and has in recent years contributed a lively and searching monthly column to the *Pacific Islands Monthly*. McCarthy has published two books. In all of these respects the four candidates were exceptional among expatriate whites in the Port Moresby area, the majority of whom are more recent arrivals, own no property, certainly do not intend to stay forever, neither know nor care much about the indigenous people among whom they live, and rarely cerebrate. Of course, only exceptional white men enjoying wide repute among the indigenous electors had any chance of winning, and it would have been unrealistic for others to stand.

The Papuan candidates were almost all men with exceptional experience of the white man's world. None of them was either a hereditary leader of his lineage or a 'big man' who had achieved status at village level through gift exchanges, feasts, etc. They had all achieved their status through their success in manipulating modern institutions. Each of them had advanced through the school system to the highest level of secondary education available in his generation. Two had gained university matriculation. As a group, they were probably rather more affluent than the average Papuan in and around Port Moresby. Most of them had held posts of some responsibility in the Administration or in other influential organisations. Two of them had long been active in their local government councils, of which they were both chairmen. Two others had played some official part in trade union affairs, and yet another had organised workers informally in an industrial dispute. At least three of them had travelled abroad.

In offering themselves for election, these men seem to have acted on the assumption that the electors would wish to be represented in such a new, modern institution as the House of Assembly by men who were exceptionally well acquainted with the institutions of the modern world.

Why did the candidates decide to stand?

In a majority of cases, the principal motive was no doubt the pursuit of further status. The four European candidates were all men to whom a seat in the House would have provided an *official* status, a place in the public precedence list, so to speak, which otherwise they lacked. For the Papuan candidates who had already participated in public life—Toua Kapena, Aisa Nguu, and Oala Oala-Rarua—a seat in the House was the next step in their political careers, the next rung on the ladder of achieved status, for which they had already prepared themselves. In some cases, also, there was definitely a zeal for public service, a genuine desire to promote the welfare of others, but in this matter it is not always easy to separate reality from rationalisation. Some of the candidates with previous political experience simply enjoy politics and public life. For several, including Chatterton and Oala Oala-Rarua, it might be said that they needed the job, in the sense that their abilities and personalities could not have been so fully fulfilled in other jobs available to them.

For whatever reason, most of the candidates badly wanted to win and thought that they could. The ultimate results showed that Anderson, Chatterton, Oala Oala-Rarua, Slaughter, McCarthy, and

Charlie Maino were justified in thinking that they could win. In close contests, each of them managed to mobilise the support that he expected and each came within hailing distance of the winning post. In calculating their support, they counted on established loyalties, both ethnic and sectional. Four others—Aisa Nguu, Gavera Rea, Sevese Morea, and Allen Rabura—must have known that they lacked any natural power base, but they were all members of political parties and doubtless expected their parties to have a much more potent appeal than in fact they did. They also made the mistake of believing that hard campaigning and rational argument might count for more than established loyalties at the polling booth. Only two candidates—George Mapai and Manuel Albaniel—seem to have been inexplicably unrealistic about their chances. In the event, Manuel Albaniel was the only candidate to lose his deposit, but Allen Rabura and George Mapai had narrow escapes.

THE CAMPAIGNS

Most candidates financed their own campaigns, though Toua Kapena, Oala Oala-Rarua, and Chatterton received some assistance from well-wishers. The basic costs were for travel within the electorate and for publication of leaflets and posters. Most of the Papuan candidates reported that they spent about $300 on their campaigns. European candidates probably spent more: Chatterton and McCarthy waged an advertising war in the *South Pacific Post* which must have cost them money, and Slaughter travelled widely in his own light aircraft making leaflet drops and whistle-stop appearances.

Most candidates relied upon close relatives and friends for whatever help they needed during the campaign. Only three of them established any formal campaign organisation at all. They were Chatterton, McCarthy, and Toua Kapena.

Chatterton's campaign was managed by Leo Buckman, of the British and Foreign Bible Society, who had twice stood for pre-selection as an A.L.P. candidate for Western Australian seats before World War II, but in 1941 had resigned and severed his links with Labor. Although he had never joined any other political party he had retained his interest in politics. He had managed Chatterton's campaign in 1964 and knew him well as a missionary, as a translator, and as a man. His unshakable belief in Chatterton's victory must have been an enormous source of comfort to both Chatterton and others of his supporters, and Buckman spared no efforts to turn this belief into reality. His enthusiasm, if at times unbridled, was also infectious and he welded together a hard-working, effective group of Papuan and European supporters including several European lawyers, a lecturer's wife from the university, several prominent Administration welfare workers, a number of public servants, both European and Papuan, some members of the United Church, and some Papuans who had been associated with Chatterton at various stages of his missionary career. This campaign committee was broadly representative of the community, though it lacked any representatives from the business firms or from among the ranks of senior Administration officers, and within it Buckman instituted an efficient division of labour. Chatterton's campaign organisation was in fact more effective and sophisticated than that of any other candidate in any of the three electorates discussed in this chapter.

McCarthy's campaign manager, Craig Kirke, was a successful barrister and solicitor in Port Moresby who had himself held several public offices, first as the elected member for the Papuan Mainland Electorate in the old Legislative Council and also as an appointed member of the Port Moresby Town Advisory Council for many years. He had offered his services to McCarthy as campaign manager when McCarthy nominated, but seemed to lack the enthusiasm for the work which Buckman displayed. The other men whom McCarthy considered as members of his campaign committee or as close supporters included a number of Port Moresby businessmen, though none from the larger business firms, a senior New Guinean in the police force, a leader of Port Moresby's mixed-race people, a retired plantation owner, a Papuan medical officer, and an influential member of the Public Service Association. These men were not organised, several of them probably did not consider themselves to be members of a campaign committee in any formal sense, and it seemed evident that, unlike Chatterton, Keith McCarthy had to do most of the work himself, or with his wife, who was his most active and enthusiastic helper.

Some months before the election Toua Kapena assembled his campaign committee with representatives from all sectors of the Hanuabada village cluster, his own community, including a number of men long prominent in community politics. The major aim of these men was to ensure that the Motu and Koita people, unrepresented in the last House of Assembly because the mountain Goilala people had outnumbered them in the electorate to which on that occasion they were allocated, should this time gain representation in the House. Toua Kapena was their candidate for Hiri Open and Oala Oala-Rarua, the defeated Open electorate candidate in 1964, was this time their candidate for Central Regional. There was a tacit agreement among the leading citizens of the Hanuabada village cluster and among the members of the Port Moresby Local Government Council that, to avoid a split vote, no-one else among them should stand.

The two political parties fielding candidates provided no organisational support for these candidates within the electorates. The Napro Party designed and supplied a standard election leaflet for Allen Rabura and Sevese Morea. These leaflets displayed a calendar, rare in Papuan houses and therefore likely to be pinned on the wall, a photograph of the candidates and a few brief slogans from the party's list of objectives, such as 'Primary Industries and Production', 'Self-Help Housing Schemes', 'Stable National Government', 'Security of Investments', and 'National Development Schemes'. Pangu Pati gave its candidates no logistic support whatsoever, but by personal arrangement Gavera Rea and Aisa Nguu campaigned together throughout the Hiri Open Electorate, so that each was able to establish entrée for the other in villages where he was known. Neither party had any branches or any grass-roots membership outside the town of Port Moresby. The party candidates were perhaps misled into believing that it is the idea or image of a political party rather than its organisation that brings electoral success.

McCarthy and Chatterton in Moresby Open had no logistic problems, since the town itself constituted the entire electorate. Within this small area each campaigned intensively, seeking by one means or another to make contact with every elector. One of the features of the campaign was that there were no attempts to stage public meetings similar to those organised in Port Moresby during the 1964 election. Before the beginning of the campaign the *South Pacific Post*, Port Moresby's only newspaper, had announced that it would not report public campaign meetings as such, and this was coupled with a general feeling by all concerned that only the converted attend public meetings anyway. Canvassing played a big part in the campaigns of both candidates.

Chatterton's strongest support was thought to lie with the Papuans in Port Moresby, upon whom he concentrated enormous effort. There were two problems: first to persuade indigenous immigrants to cast their vote in the Moresby Electorate as they were entitled to do under section 130 of the Electoral Ordinance 1963-1967; and then, secondly, to persuade them to vote for Percy Chatterton rather than Keith McCarthy. In the middle-class Kaugere and Hohola residential settlements Chatterton used the standard doorknock technique with which most Australians are familiar. In the shanty settlements, however, he used a different approach: he would visit one of the elders of the community, engage him in conversation outside his hut, and continue chatting until a crowd had gathered. He would then explain that he was a candidate for the forthcoming election and that he would appreciate the people's support. More often than not it was forthcoming, sometimes in the form of a promised bloc vote. Chatterton did not confine his efforts entirely to the Papuan community, but also exhorted the New Guineans: 'Those of you who think like New Guineans, vote in your home electorates; but those of you who have lived for some time in Port Moresby and who are interested in this town, vote *here* and vote for Chatterton'.

McCarthy believed that he would attract support from a wide cross-section of the community but primarily pinned his hopes on the expatriates and the New Guineans. He canvassed accordingly. On Saturdays he could be found mingling with the crowds at Koke Market singling out Pidgin speakers, who can almost always be assumed to come from New Guinea, and engaging them in conversation. On Sundays, he and Mrs McCarthy could be found outside the Lutheran Chapel in Koke speaking to the New Guineans as they emerged from church. His approach to a section of the European community was to appear at parties given in his honour and by his supporters, or hold parties himself. This 'cocktail campaign', as it became known, no doubt had something of an impact with those who attended; but as one regular attender complained, there always seemed to be the same people at each party. McCarthy must also have felt a forlorn hope that some Papuans, especially Papuan public servants at Konedobu, might vote for him, for he was seen once drinking in the Kone Tavern, where they usually drink. The gesture misfired: several Papuans expressed resentment at what they considered a blatant election ploy from an expatriate who had never previously been sighted in any of the town's predominantly Papuan bars.

Four of the six candidates for the Hiri Open Electorate travelled widely within their electorate and visited most of the villages within it. Of them all, Toua Kapena seems to have travelled most widely. He began his campaign among the Mekeo, at the far western end of the electorate. A stranger there, he could not use the machinery of the Mekeo Local Government Council to assist him, since the President of the Council was a rival candidate, and he therefore found it difficult to gain entrée into the villages. He visited about a dozen Mekeo and Roro villages, addressed small meetings in about half of them, but received little support. He then spent a week campaigning in Motu and Koita villages near Port Moresby, where councillors of the Port Moresby Local Government Council usually arranged his entrée, and some days in the Galley Reach area west of Port Moresby, where he held a meeting in the Motu village of Manumanu, addressed a church gathering which he fortuitously found assembled at the Koita village of Gorohu, and made a one-day tour through the villages of the Gabadi people under the auspices of the Manumanu member of the Port Moresby Local Government Council, whose wife came from Gabadi. In the following weeks he continued to alternate meetings in the Motu and Koita villages near Port Moresby with quick trips inland, once to the Doura and Koiari villages across the Vanapa River, once by truck to the Sogeri plateau, and once by air to the villages of the Mountain Koiari.

Allen Rabura, Charlie Maino, and Aisa Nguu had similar itineraries. Understandably, they and Toua Kapena all concentrated more effort on their own home areas than on the areas in which they were strangers, but they did make an effort to penetrate into alien territory. Their main campaign technique was the public meeting, in which usually they presented themselves to as many villagers as they could assemble, made a short speech, and then answered questions. The precise form of these meetings was often determined by the host villagers rather than the candidates. The meetings were seldom long, and in a single day candidates often moved rapidly through several villages some distance apart. Most candidates valued these meetings for their whistle-stop function, the opportunity they gave the constituents to see and meet the candidate, rather than the opportunity they gave for the candidate to present policies and propaganda. As in the traditional politics of the peoples in this electorate, personalities were more important than issues.

Candidates for the Central Regional Electorate had little hope of campaigning intensively throughout the entire electorate.

Anderson chose to campaign intensively throughout the Goilala Sub-District only, and made no visits elsewhere. Calculating that the people of the Goilala Sub-District in which he lived outnumbered any other potential local or sectional group, and hoping that the other candidates would split the coastal vote, he decided to campaign only in his own area and thus attempt to secure overwhelming support there. For ten weeks he went around on foot accompanied by two or three local people, averaging about 25 miles per day. For most of his campaign he was also accompanied by one of the candidates for Goilala Open. To secure votes beyond his own area he sent some Goilala men to Port Moresby to campaign among their urban kin and friends, and wrote letters soliciting support from individuals whose influence he thought might be helpful.

Oala Oala-Rarua visited many villages along the coast in the Port Moresby and Kairuku Sub-Districts and a few villages in the Rigo Sub-District. He made a perfunctory attempt to campaign among the Goilala, where he addressed one village from which in fact he eventually received a few valuable second preferences, but returned to Port Moresby, discouraged by his reception, after only a day or two. To some of his supporters his campaign seemed somewhat lethargic: he counted on the fact that he was already widely known among the Motu and Koita and the urban workers of Port Moresby, rather than his personal appearances and campaign oratory, to secure votes. Sevese Morea also concentrated his campaign mainly upon those Motu and Koita villages in which he was known. He did not even manage to visit the villages in the Kairuku Sub-District which other Motu candidates visited. A university student at Yule Island wrote in his journal:

> Sevese Morea, a candidate for Central Regional, sent his pamphlets to a councillor at Tsiria for distribution among the people. Some people remarked that candidates who do not present themselves personally to the electors should not be voted for at all. Another elderly man commented that we cannot know their policies, see their physical appearance and know them as candidates, so the best thing is to number them last on the ballot paper. (Obara 1968)

Two other candidates for the Regional electorate did make some attempt to cover most of the ground. Gavera Rea held meetings throughout the Port Moresby and Kairuku Sub-Districts jointly with his fellow Pangu Pati candidate for Hiri Open, and in the Goilala Sub-District with the Pangu Pati candidate for Goilala Open. Unfortunately for him, the Pangu candidate for Goilala Open was a retiring member whose inactivity in the first House of Assembly had so angered and disappointed his electors that when the votes were counted at this election he mustered only 600 votes and came second last in a field of eight candidates. Walking from Goilala area down to the coast Gavera Rea campaigned in some Goilala villages on his own, and subsequently at the poll obtained more votes from those than from other Goilala villages, thus establishing beyond doubt that his association with his Pangu associate was more hindrance than help. He also campaigned in the Rigo-Abau Electorate. The remaining Central Regional candidate, Ron Slaughter, left his own power base among the Roro and Mekeo, whose local government councils had indicated their support for him, and flew a small aircraft widely throughout the rest of the electorate, making personal appearances and leaving leaflets in as many villages as he could reach and dropping his leaflets from the air on villages that he could not reach. He did not conduct meetings or make speeches. His sole aim was to get his leaflets, bearing his photograph, into as many hands as possible.

The major organisational problem for most Papuan candidates was that of gaining entrée to alien villages. They were of course perfectly free to walk uninvited into any village in their electorate, but even today it is not customary for Papuans to enter villages in which they have neither kin nor trade partners; they feel ill at ease in such villages, and they cannot expect either a welcome or a hearing there. Campaigning together, Gavera Rea, a Motu, and his Pangu Pati associate in the Hiri Open, Aisa Nguu, a Mekeo, doubled the number of villages to which either one could have obtained a ready entrée alone. Toua Kapena, a Western Motu, used his fellow local government council members to provide him with entrée to Eastern Motu villages. Without such contacts, candidates entering alien villages might ask a local government councillor to call a meeting on their behalf, in the belief that election campaigning is a form of government business which local government councillors are obliged to facilitate, but in fact these councillors were not under any such obligation. In other words, ethnic barriers are still sufficiently strong, even in Port Moresby's immediate hinterland, to impede electoral campaigning.

Another most notable feature of the Papuan candidates' campaigns was their reluctance to attack their opponents. Very few of their speeches ever contained any references to other candidates, and such disparaging references as did occasionally occur were always delicately and obliquely worded, as when Oala Oala-Rarua referred in his campaign leaflet to his two Papuan rivals as 'mere youths' and to his two European rivals as men who lacked 'experience in working for the needs of Papuans'. The Papuan candidates seem to have viewed the election not as a contest between candidates but rather as an act of choice by the electors: the candidates were merely volunteering their services. In this way, no-one stood to lose face in defeat.

The European candidates saw it otherwise. Anderson among the Goilala relentlessly attacked the other candidates for Central Regional as men who would promote the interests of the coastal rather than the mountain peoples. McCarthy and Chatterton fought a fierce electoral battle with few holds barred. The two men's personalities were at issue as much as their policies, and personal attacks were therefore inevitable.

The battle was fought mainly in the pages of the *South Pacific Post*. The Chatterton camp was convinced that the editorial policy of the paper was sympathetic to the McCarthy cause and pointed by way of illustration to the coverage given to McCarthy on his retirement, on his departure for leave, and on his return. A report of a visit by McCarthy to one of the worst of the shanty settlements, situated near the Administration offices at Konedobu, particularly annoyed Chatterton and Buckman. McCarthy described the housing conditions there as 'shocking', and promised, if elected, to get something done about housing in the Moresby area. As Buckman pointed out, this settlement was probably visible from the window of the Director of District Administration's office, and yet for seven years McCarthy had not spoken out on housing, which had been one of Chatterton's main concerns throughout his four years in the House of Assembly. Chatterton responded in the next issue of the *South Pacific Post* with an advertisement headed 'WHO'S INTERESTED IN HOUSING', comparing his record on this topic in the previous House of Assembly with that of his opponent. He followed this with a series of mini-ads or slogans, each with a sting in the tail. Samples included: 'WHAT ARE YOU VOTING FOR? SENSE WITH PERCY—SENTIMENT WITH MAKATI'; 'WHAT ARE YOU VOTING FOR: ACTION WITH PERCY OR INACTION WITH MAKATI?'; 'PERCY NEVER RESTS ON PAST ACHIEVEMENTS —PERCY NEVER RESTS'; 'PERCY NEVER STOPS WORKING FOR YOUR WELFARE—PERCY NEVER STOPS'. In the final week before the election a series of three advertisements were inserted entitled 'Percy Prefers Performance'. They depicted 'before and after' scenes and were meant to illustrate how Chatterton's campaign in the House for cheaper appliances, better housing, and better roads had met with success. They were probably less effective than the mini-ad, but also far less offensive. Buckman's handling of this aspect of the campaign showed his flair and sense of purpose. McCarthy handled his own press advertising and by contrast was restrained. Using variations on his picture poster he plugged his record, his integrity, and his knowledge of the Territory. It was not until the last week that he inserted two hard hitting advertisements headed 'IT'S NOT ALL TALKING' and 'TRUTH IN ADVERTISING'. It looked at last as if he was going to take off the gloves. The first was an incitement to vote for a man of action: 'When the talking stops you need a man for Moresby who will make sure the wheels start turning'. The second was an answer to Chatterton's claims about performances on housing in the House of Assembly, which were denounced as 'half-truths'.

POLICIES

Most candidates' policies had no ideological content whatsoever: no general ideas about political progress, reform, or development; no notions of social and economic justice; no commitment to basic rights and liberties; no visions of the future. Some candidates did refer to the future political independence of the Territory, but only to say that they did not want it for quite some time to come, if ever. On this particular issue Chatterton was the only candidate who made any specific proposals about independence, but that is not to say that his proposals were very radical, as the following statement from his 'Five-Point Programme' demonstrates:

> PLANNING FOR INDEPENDENCE. I believe that very few Papuans and New Guineans want to rush into independence. But nearly all of them want to feel that steady and meaningful progress is being made towards that goal. A step-by-step plan for this progress should be worked out now and explained to the people of the Territory. It will then be for them, through their elected representatives in Local Government Councils and in the House of Assembly, to make their wishes known as to the speed at which these successive steps forward should be taken.

The two Pangu Pati candidates referred to their party's desire for early 'self-government', deliberately choosing this word rather than 'independence', but they did not develop the point.

Apart from these occasional references to self-government or independence, few candidates offered any policies for the nation as a whole, and those who did often contented themselves with vague and innocuous pieties espousing such worthy causes as 'closer co-operation between all people of the Territory', 'equal opportunity for all people of the Territory', 'equal opportunity for all people to progress with the Territory', 'honest and progressive government', 'equality of opportunity for all men', and 'a dedicated and efficient public service' (McCarthy); 'support for primary industries and production', 'stable national government', and 'national development schemes' (Allen Rabura). Like the Queen's Christmas message to the Commonwealth such policies were unexceptionable but uninformative.

Chatterton's were unquestionably the most coherent and most thoughtful of any candidate's views on the nation's future. In his 'Five-Point Programme' one could detect several implicit ideological notions: the idea, for example, that a fair share of the economy should be reserved for local people, and the notion that eternal vigilance is the price of civil liberty.

While few candidates offered the voters ideological positions or national policies, all of them without exception promised parochial good works. Their overwhelming emphasis was on the local needs of their electorates and the provision of material assistance to meet these needs. The same promises recurred with monotonous regularity: more roads (Charlie Maino, Oala Oala-Rarua); public housing schemes (Allen Rabura, Toua Kapena, Oala Oala-Rarua, Sevese Morea); more government schools (Toua Kapena, Charlie Maino, Oala Oala-Rarua, Sevese Morea); better health services (Toua Kapena, Oala Oala-Rarua); encouragement and assistance for primary industries in the electorate (Toua Kapena, Gavera Rea, Aisa Nguu); better wages and working conditions (Toua Kapena, Oala Oala-Rarua, Gavera Rea); encouragement and support for co-operatives (Toua Kapena); improved market facilities (Charlie Maino, Oala Oala-Rarua, Gavera Rea, Aisa Nguu); and improved and expanded facilities for technical education (Aisa Nguu, Gavera Rea).

Two candidates, Oala Oala-Rarua and Gavera Rea, both of whom had participated in trade union activities, expounded policies for urban workers in some detail. In policy speeches within the Port Moresby urban area, Oala Oala-Rarua referred to his desire to assist his fellow urban workers to solve the welfare problems of urban wage-labourers, both individually and collectively, and recalled his leadership of the Port Moresby Workers' Association. His campaign leaflets also stressed his role as a workers' leader, referred to his achievements as President of the Workers' Association, and promised to work for increased wages, housing, leave entitlements, job security, improved training schemes, sick leave, retirement benefits, and compulsory unionism for all urban workers. Gavera Rea promised reform of the arbitration system and appointment of a workers' adviser.

BASES OF SUPPORT

Though the candidates' policies were monotonously similar, their approach to the electors and the kinds of image they tried to project varied greatly.

In Moresby Open the past career and affiliations of the candidates influenced the strategy of the campaign. Both camps were well aware of the value of parading past performance. The respective records of the two candidates were impressive and were therefore brought out of storage and polished up for the occasion. Whilst there were those who doubtless respected the image of the *kiap,* the old-style native affairs officer, the McCarthy camp probably relied too heavily on the 'old McCarthy magic', his past record as a native affairs officer with charisma, and not enough on the present man and his policy. By contrast, Chatterton's campaign manager, Buckman, well aware of the frailty of the mission image, was much more circumspect in his use of Chatterton's mission background. Chatterton ran on his record as a politician rather than his earlier record as a missionary.

In Hiri Open, most candidates relied upon the ethnic loyalties of their fellow tribesmen to give them their basic strength, but hoped to attract some additional votes outside their own ethnic groups.

Though he travelled widely throughout the electorate, Toua Kapena essentially counted on a strong bloc vote from his own Motu and Koita people to put him in. At meetings among his own people he spoke briefly and in a low key.

> I shall not waste your time with words [he would begin]. You all know me. You know my record as a leader of your Local Government Council. The work of the House of Assembly is important work, building upon but more important than the work of Local Government Councils. You need good men for such work. I offer myself, but I am not going to make promises that I cannot fulfil. The people are angry with politicians who have been elected because of promises that they have failed to honour. I don't want that kind of reputation, and therefore make no promises except to do my best for my people.

He relied upon the benefits that these villagers had already obtained from the Port Moresby Local Government Council to establish his *bona fides*. This tactic paid dividends. At Manumanu, where the council had provided an outboard motor for the villagers to run a powered canoe service to Port Moresby, one man summed up Toua Kapena's appeal in a fishing metaphor: 'We know that he will help us, for we have already shared in the catch from his net'.

At Hanuabada, his own village and the largest of all Motu villages, Toua Kapena's campaign committee organised a final rally at which all important village leaders spoke in turn before the candidate himself closed the meeting with his own short speech. It was an ethnocentric, soul-searching tribal rally of the Motu and Koita peoples; a lament and inquisition on their failure to get any of their own people into the legislature at the last two opportunities, when in each case they had split their vote; and an appeal for all Motu and Koita people, especially those of Hanuabada, to turn out and vote and thus ensure that at long last, by electing Toua Kapena, they would regain the political influence and prestige that they had enjoyed for generations but had recently lost. Every man who had figured at all prominently in Hanuabada village politics since World War II spoke at this rally, and each played variations on the same theme.

Charlie Maino hoped that his affable personality and wide network of personal contacts outside his own home area would give him enough votes for success even though it seemed likely that the Mekeo vote would be split between himself and Aisa Nguu. He campaigned in most Motu and Koita villages, visiting some of them twice. Some of his visits to villages in his own home area were merely whistle-stop appearances, as at Tsiria, on Yule Island, where a Papuan university student made the following note:

> Charles Maino, one of the candidates from the Mekeo area, came to Tsiria personally and distributed his pamphlets to the village people. The people were glad to see Maino face to face but unfortunately he did not stay long, neither did he give his campaign speech. (Obara 1968)

Nevertheless, he made himself widely known, his personality was appealing, and many people outside his own area felt well disposed towards him.

Aisa Nguu and Gavera Rea held joint meetings at which they both spoke. Their speaking style was didactic, hammering out and elaborating five or six numbered points in sequence. At Tubusereia,[3] for example, Gavera Rea introduced Aisa Nguu to the Motu villagers and outlined his career. Aisa Nguu then spoke in Police Motu, on roads, improvements to Koke market, the provision of post-primary technical education to provide careers for those who are now 'dropouts' at the end of primary school, and Administration subsidies for the work of local government councils.

In his campaign speeches, Allen Rabura referred to his Napro Party affiliation, and elaborated on the five points in the party platform. Speaking softly, sometimes inaudibly, he was usually given a polite but unresponsive hearing.

George Mapai did not visit the electorate during the election. Public opinion concerning his prospects at one village in his own Sub-District was summarised by a villager as follows:

> Another Mekeo candidate, George Mapai, sent his pamphlets and his policy platform to a councillor in the Kairuku Local Government Council for distribution among the Tsiria people ... Mr. Mapai, who works for Native Co-operative Societies, has been away from the Kairuku Sub-District for almost fifteen years and this means that he does not really know the difficulties of life faced by his home people. Moreover, he is now stationed at Samarai ... All of the

[3] Information on this meeting at Tubusereia was kindly supplied by Andrew Taylor.

above factors bar him from being elected by the Kairuku Sub-District people, especially the Mekeo and Roro people, although he has been all over the world and is an intellectual, well-educated. (Obara 1968)

The candidates for Central Regional also varied greatly in their approach to the electors.

Ron Slaughter offered no message at all. He counted on his personal repute among the Roro and Mekeo, his contacts among the Europeans of Port Moresby, and possibly some dividend from his leaflet distribution in areas where he was unknown, to secure him a majority.

Andy Anderson's message was simple, parochial, and forceful:

> There is no money for the Goilala. When I go to the House of Assembly, I'll speak out strongly ... Don't vote for men from the coast. They wouldn't look after us.

He made the point that he was not attempting to 'steal' the Papuans' own electorate, Goilala Open, urged them to elect a Papuan in that electorate, and promised that if elected he would help to teach their Papuan member about the working of the House. He also made a strong, clear and insistent appeal for them to vote only for him in Central Regional and not to allocate preferences. 'Don't give the names of any of the other candidates. They are all coastal people.' This tactic, which he chose because he felt that discussion of preferences might confuse the electors, had a decisive influence upon the final result of the poll.

As in his 1964 campaign, Oala Oala-Rarua's policy speeches among his own people were often instructional, explaining the electoral boundaries and the differences between Regional and Open electorates, identifying the candidates, discussing electoral procedures, and analysing in general terms the major welfare problems of his constituency as he saw them. He explicitly hammered out the theme that he had no specific policies to offer, but was offering rather whatever political dedication, skill, and experience the electors might consider him to have. He counted on substantial support among his own Motu and Koita people in Hiri Open, a solid vote from Papuan workers and some support from European electors in Moresby Open, and possibly some votes from Rigo-Abau Open, where he was known in some places and there were no local candidates.

One further point needs to be made about campaign styles. Though they had made numerous promises in their leaflets, most of them admittedly rather vague, two of the Motu candidates, Toua Kapena and Oala Oala-Rarua, repeatedly said in their speeches that they preferred not to make specific promises which they were not sure they could honour, and therefore proposed to make no promises at all. Their campaign speeches—particularly those of Toua Kapena —were indeed remarkably empty of any content whatsoever. They were composed in fluent, impeccable Motu, much of it impossible to translate effectively because it was intended to communicate style, personality, and cultural attainment rather than information. The medium was the message. The policy speech was a ceremonial occasion, like an old-time feast with dancing, in which these two candidates put their repute, their *personae,* what in Motu would be called their 'name', symbolically on display. What the audience saw and heard was the candidate's style and bearing, but like the produce on view at a feast, these were in each case merely the end-product of a successful career and substantial accomplishments, and it was ultimately these accomplishments that the candidate was offering to the voters.

THE POLLING

In Moresby Open Electorate the poll lasted one day only. In the other Open electorates polling was staggered and mobile teams took the polling booths to the voters. In Hiri Open, mobile patrols were out from 17 February to 15 March, when the last of them completed its work.

Though canvassing within 20 feet of a polling booth was prohibited, there was nothing to prevent the candidates from visiting villages and campaigning there at the same time as the mobile polling teams, during the month over which the polling extended, but Anderson was the only candidate who made full use of this opportunity. Most candidates in effect closed their campaigns on the first day of polling.

Voting was not compulsory. In Moresby Open, only 5036 (37 per cent) of the 13,422 persons enrolled turned out to vote. After a lively campaign, with eighteen polling booths conveniently located in all the major population centres of a small town, and on a fine day, such apathy was difficult to explain. It seems likely that a higher proportion of Europeans than Papuans failed to vote, since the overall turn-out was much better in the predominantly Papuan Central Regional Electorate. Perhaps the expatriate Europeans felt no strong involvement in Territory politics. Perhaps they felt that either candidate would do as well as the other, thus freeing them from the necessity of choice. Perhaps they were simply unwilling to take time off from their usual Saturday pursuits. We cannot really know. Among sixty-seven people enrolled in the Moresby Open Electorate whom we interviewed before the election, thirty Papuans and thirty-seven Europeans, fifty-seven said that they intended to vote. It may be significant that nine of the Europeans but only one of the Papuans intended not to vote, though the people we interviewed did not in any sense constitute a representative sample of the electorate.

In Hiri Open, 11,852 (58 per cent) of the electors voted, in Rigo-Abau Open, 11,446 (50 per cent), and in Goilala Open, 11,713 (69 per cent). The overall figure for the Central Regional Electorate was 39,358 (54 per cent).

Polling procedures were in all important respects identical throughout the Territory, and there seems little point in describing the procedures as we observed them at particular polling booths. There is, however, one observation worth noting. Outside Port Moresby, most electors used the 'whispering ballot' procedure, indicating the photograph of the candidate of their choice to a poll clerk, who marked the ballot paper accordingly. There was great variation between poll clerks, and even in the performance of the same poll clerk on different days, as to whether they sought to elicit any preferences after the first, and if so how many. Voters seldom stated a second, third or further preference unless specifically asked to do so, in which event they usually did. Since the result hinged on preferences in two of the three electorates under discussion, the whims of the poll clerks in this respect may have affected the results.

One other fact is possibly noteworthy. In Moresby Open a far higher proportion of the men on the roll voted (43·5 per cent) than of the women (28·9 per cent). In the other Open electorates and in Central Regional there was no significant difference between the proportion of male electors and the proportion of female electors who exercised their right to vote.

VOTING PATTERNS

The result in Moresby Open was a comfortable win for Chatterton (2691 votes) over McCarthy (1801 votes). There were also 544 informal votes cast. It is impossible to make more than an intelligent guess as to the sources of each candidate's support. No clear patterns emerged from our pre-election interviews. Individual tallies were obtained for each of the eighteen polling booths, and by combining some knowledge of Port Moresby's social geography with the assumption that most people voted at the booth nearest their home,

TABLE 16—INITIAL RETURNS IN MORESBY OPEN ELECTORATE BY INDIVIDUAL POLLING BOOTH

Polling booth	Chatterton	McCarthy
Guide Hall, Konedobu	242	98
Welfare Office	167	135
Sub-District, Ela Beach	318	393
Everyman's Hut, Koke	589	231
Games Office, Badili	107	90
Konebada	221	130
Taurama Hospital	99	31
Murray Barracks	22	33
Hohola	203	52
Teachers' College	34	13
Jackson's Airport	17	21
Coronation School, Boroko	65	96
Salvation Army, Boroko	231	201
Bavaroko School, Boroko	212	159
Administrative College Annexe	30	25
Gordon	30	18
Koke Primary 'T' School	13	11
Kila Kila	4	0
Total	2604	1737

it is plausible to guess—but not possible to establish—that McCarthy's support came more from Europeans than from Papuans whereas Chatterton obtained solid support from both communities. The European vote appears to have been shared by the two candidates fairly equally, with perhaps a slight advantage going to Chatterton: returns from the booths at Konedobu, the Welfare Office, and the three Boroko centres, all in predominantly European residential areas, showed both men polling well. The Papuan vote, on the other hand, seems to have favoured Chatterton, who gained his largest majorities in two predominantly indigenous residential areas (Hohola and Konebada) and in two predominantly indigenous gathering-places (Koke and Taurama Hospital), but also polled well at the Boroko booths, at two of which in fact he had majorities. The relevant figures (compiled after the first count, before the inclusion of postal and absentee votes) are shown in table 16.

Hiri Open Electorate produced a very close result. After the first count the outcome depended on preferences, and at the final

TABLE 17—HIRI OPEN ELECTORATE: FIRST PREFERENCES BY CANDIDATE AND LOCATION OF BALLOT BOXES

Location of ballot boxes	Candidates					
	Aisa Nguu	Toua Kapena	Allen Rabura	Manuel Albaniel	George Mapai	Charlie Maino
Motu-Koita Villages in Port Moresby						
Hanuabada	36	1161	14	23	14	13
Kila Kila	19	117	78	4	3	5
Vabukori	7	34	78	8	2	17
Other Motu-Koita Villages						
West Coast	92	1154	96	127	14	79
East Coast	31	711	139	19	7	8
Other Parts of Port Moresby Sub-District						
Koke Market	56	20	4	5	3	88
Brown River/Vanapa	18	57	8	5	3	28
Mountain Koiari	2	114	2	52	1	1
Sogeri Plateau	10	310	30	11	4	18
Other	19	135	18	2	4	9
1. Total Port Moresby Sub-District	290	3813	467	256	55	266
Kairuku Sub-District						
Nara and Gabadi	181	198	26	25	21	437
Kuni	7	2	4	0	64	332
Roro	61	8	6	9	40	662
Waima-Kivori	125	34	42	5	313	296
Mekeo	734	13	17	20	95	927
Bush Mekeo	10	1	1	1	12	506
Other	8	18	9	8	2	3
2. Total Kairuku Sub-District	1126	274	105	68	547	3163
3. Absentee and Postal Votes	25	61	8	5	28	55
Grand Total (1 + 2 + 3)	1441	4148	580	329	630	3484

distribution of preferences the eventual winner, Toua Kapena, watched the progress figures go up on the board with great anxiety.

The returning officer for Hiri Open recorded both the results from each ballot box separately and the place or places in which each numbered ballot box was used. It is therefore possible to draw up a reasonably precise and detailed summary of the locations from which each candidate gained his first preferences, as in table 17.

Toua Kapena obtained a landslide vote in his own community, Hanuabada, where there was a large voter turn-out; overwhelming majorities in all other Motu and Koita villages except Tatana and Vabukori, where the local candidates, Manuel Albaniel and Allen Rabura respectively, picked up votes; a very high proportion of the votes cast in the remaining inland villages and on the rubber estates in the Port Moresby Sub-District; a useful number in the villages of the Nara and Kabadi census division; a majority of the few votes cast on the rubber estates at the head of Galley Reach; but very few votes among the Roro, Waima-Kivori, Mekeo, or Bush Mekeo. He also polled poorly at Koke, where many Mekeo immigrants or transients in the town voted. Massively supported by his own ethnic group, the Motu and Koita, he also managed solid majorities in the rest of the Port Moresby Sub-District and made successful intrusions into the nearer census divisions of the Kairuku Sub-District. His support was doubtless founded essentially on ethnic and local loyalties, but his hard campaigning and his wide repute as a council leader and member of the indigenous élite enabled him to bring out the vote where the other candidates from Port Moresby, Manuel Albaniel and Allen Rabura, failed.

Aisa Nguu and Charlie Maino obtained far less support than Toua Kapena outside their own home areas, though they campaigned almost as hard as he. They put paid to each other's chances by splitting the Roro and Mekeo vote, for as shown in table 19 a significant proportion of the electors failed to indicate any preferences after their first. If Aisa Nguu had not stood, Charlie Maino probably would have won.

The Central Regional Electorate produced an even closer finish and the eventual winner had to wait even longer and with even more misgivings than Toua Kapena before he could finally savour success. A parcel of ballot papers from the Goilala Open Electorate was lost in the mail, causing the returning officer to delay the final distribution of preferences for several weeks in the hope that they might turn up. If the final result had been so close that the missing ballot papers might have altered it, a new election would have been necessary. This issue was in doubt until the very last count of preferences.

After the count of first preferences, the candidates stood as follows: Slaughter, 10,536 votes; Oala Oala-Rarua, 10,488; Andy Anderson, 10,045; Sevese Morea, 3666; Gavera Rea, 2807. There were 1816 informal votes cast.

Oala Oala-Rarua seemed assured of a substantial lead after distribution of preferences from the two other candidates from Motu villages, but throughout the count it always seemed likely that preferences from Slaughter or Anderson would ultimately put the other in. In the event, Anderson's campaign strategy decided the issue. At his meetings he had deliberately and persistently instructed the Goilala not to allocate any preferences beyond their first, fearing that the preferential system might confuse them and cause them to lodge informal votes. They obviously did as he suggested. The result was victory for Oala Oala-Rarua.

Table 18 shows the support for the Regional electorate candidates in the component Open electorates. It can be seen that Anderson drew the greater part of his support from the Goilala Open Electorate, but gained some votes in Moresby Open, possibly from European acquaintances, and a surprising number in Rigo-Abau Open, where he was totally unknown and conducted no campaign. (It has been claimed that electors inland from Rigo mistook his photograph in the polling booth for that of a local European known to them.) Oala Oala-Rarua drew his support from the Hiri Open, Moresby Open, and Rigo-Abau Open, in all three of which he polled strongly. A breakdown of votes by individual ballot boxes in Hiri Open showed that his support there came from those sections of the electorate in which Toua Kapena was also strongly supported: the Motu-Koita villages and the inland villages of the Port Moresby

TABLE 18—CENTRAL REGIONAL ELECTORATE: FIRST PREFERENCES BY CANDIDATE AND LOCATION OF BALLOT BOXES

Location of ballot boxes	Candidates				
	Ron Slaughter	Gavera Rea	Oala Oala-Rarua	Andy Anderson	Sevese Morea
Moresby Open Electorate	1841	203	1487	323	419
Hiri Open Electorate Motu-Koita Villages	149	478	2464	19	298
Hiri Open Electorate Other parts of Port Moresby Sub-District	714	224	1089	134	209
Hiri Open Electorate Kairuku Sub-District	3589	229	1017	25	393
Goilala Open Electorate	847	610	605	8702	612
Rigo-Abau Open Electorate	3396	1063	3826	842	1735
Total	10,536	2807	10,488	10,045	3666

Sub-District. In Moresby Open his work as a union leader doubtless won him the votes of Papuan workers. It is significant also in this connection that almost half of his votes from the Rigo-Abau electorate were absentee votes cast at polling booths in Moresby Open, presumably by immigrant urban workers. Slaughter gained most of his votes from the same three electorates. In each, he and Oala Oala-Rarua ran neck and neck. Slaughter's following in Moresby Open was probably more European than Papuan, and Oala Oala-Rarua's almost certainly more Papuan than European. In Hiri Open, Slaughter's support came from the people of the Kairuku Sub-District where he was well-known. From his own account of his leaflet dropping campaign in the Rigo-Abau Open, his large vote there would seem to testify to the electoral effectiveness of his photograph.

CONCLUSION

We began this chapter with a number of expectations which the data have failed to fulfil. We expected to find ideological commitments of some sophistication, but found almost none at all. We thought that urban candidates might develop complex campaign organisations, but the organisations of most candidates were quite rudimentary. We anticipated keen interest in the election and vigorous debate on a variety of campaign issues, but in the Moresby Open Electorate voter turn-out was exceedingly low, in Hiri Open and Central Regional the turn-out was lower than in many entirely rural electorates, and there were no campaign issues about which any of the candidates really disagreed. It seemed likely that political parties, especially Pangu Pati which originated in Port Moresby among the indigenous urban élite, might have some substantial success, but neither of the parties which ran candidates made much impression. In this connection it is interesting to note that the Pangu Pati, which failed here, succeeded in several rural electorates a long way from Port Moresby. Finally, we thought it likely that socio-economic differences other than those of locality and ethnic group might influence voting behaviour, but the data have forced us to conclude that when candidates whom they could identify with their own locality and/or ethnic group were available, most voters preferred such a candidate to outsiders.

Some of these conclusions, however, need qualification. Though in general our expectations were unfulfilled, by closer examination of the data it is possible to discern some early signs of a developing political sophistication which may very well mature at the next election. In other words, our mistake may have been a mistake about the *timing* rather than the *direction* of political change in the Port Moresby urban area. There were, for example, ideological issues lying just beneath the surface of political discourse, especially issues concerning race relations, political independence, indigenous socio-economic expectations, and national identity, which occasionally came to light in informal discussions among electors and were sometimes, though more rarely, hinted at in candidates' speeches. Several of the candidates, especially the two Pangu ones, held clear views on important ideological issues, but seem to have felt—rightly, it would seem—that the electorate was not yet ready for any ideological commitment. In the matter of organisation, several candidates in the course of their campaign became increasingly aware of the need for organisational solutions to the problem of entrée into alien communities at election time, and also of the need to build up support in effective grass-roots organisations, such as trade unions and local government councils, for some years before an election. Also, there were hopeful signs that Papuan electors may before long learn to consider factors other than local or ethnic loyalties when casting their votes. It is true that most of the votes for Papuan candidates outside their own local areas or ethnic groups came from places where no candidate with any local identification stood, but nevertheless in Central Regional the three Motu candidates between them obtained nearly two thousand first preference votes in both the Goilala and the Kairuku Sub-Districts. Admittedly the local candidates were in each case white men, and also there may have been a 'donkey-vote', but unquestionably *some* of these votes came from electors who were impressed with these 'foreign' candidates' campaign speeches. Further, there is clear evidence that a substantial number of Papuan workers voted for Oala Oala-Rarua because they regarded him as a workers' leader. And finally in Moresby Open, where ethnic and local loyalties were not at issue, those who voted were forced to base their choice on other criteria.

Having made these qualifications, we must still admit the possibility that our expectations were false as to the *direction* as well as the *timing* of political change. The model of the sophisticated Australian-type parliamentary system which administrators in Papua and New Guinea have implicitly chosen as their goal, and from which to some degree we derived our expectations for the 1968 election, may have been excessively idealised. If voting were not compulsory in Australia, what percentage of electors would vote? To what extent are Australian electors influenced by ideological concerns rather than appeals to their pockets? Are personalities not as important as campaign issues in Australian politics?

TABLE 19—THE ELECTION RESULTS IN CENTRAL DISTRICT

Central Regional	1st count	2nd count	3rd count	4th and final count
Ron Slaughter	10,536	10,827	11,425	12,841
Gavera Rea	2807	Excl.	—	—
Oala Oala-Rarua	10,488	11,290	12,407	13,306
Andy Anderson	10,045	10,211	10,959	Excl.
Sevese Morea	3666	3972	Excl.	—
Informal	1816	—	—	—
Exhausted	—	1242	2751	11,395

Hiri Open	1st count	2nd count	3rd count	4th count	5th and final count
Aisa Nguu	1441	1461	1500	1600	Excl.
Toua Kapena	4053	4113	4305	4339	4654
Allen Rabura	580	587	Excl.	—	—
George Mapai	630	641	667	Excl.	—
Charlie Maino Aukey	3485	3508	3568	3733	4370
Manuel Albaniel	336	Excl.	—	—	—
Informal	1327	—	—	—	—
Exhausted	—	215	485	853	1501

Moresby Open	1st and final count
Percy Chatterton	2691
J. K. McCarthy	1801
Informal	544

Even if we have not unduly idealised the electoral politics of Australian and other Western parliamentary democracies, a further crucial question arises. Why should we expect Australian political modes to prove acceptable to the peoples of Papua and New Guinea, whose traditional cultural inheritance and experience of social change have been so different from anything familiar to Australians? To meet this question intelligently, we must examine the politics in the years preceding independence of those colonial societies which seem most closely comparable to Papua and New Guinea. This is no place for an essay in the comparative politics of colonial societies, but the last years of British rule in some relevant African and Asian countries do seem to have generated, at least among indigenous urban élites, precisely the kind of politics that we looked for in Port Moresby but failed to find: fierce ideological conflict, tightly organised political parties and pressure groups, burning issues, considerable rank-and-file enthusiasm, and some shift from ethnic to other loyalties. If this impression is valid, then the most important questions about the 1968 election in Port Moresby still remain to be answered. Why were there so few ideological issues, such rudimentary campaign organisations, such a poor voter turn-out, so much of the indigenous peoples' traditional political style in the candidates' campaigns, so little conflict, so much uncritical acceptance of Australian colonial rule, and so little indignation in the face of evident and inexcusable inequalities and injustices in Port Moresby's caste-ridden colonial society? If there is merely a local time-lag in the late-colonial processes of political development, then electoral politics in Port Moresby should be very different at the next election, or the one after. Otherwise, the data in this chapter leave a great deal for sociologists concerned with late-colonial societies to explain.

FROM DEPENDENCE TO AUTONOMY?

R. S. Parker

IN drawing conclusions from the preceding field studies, we first try to characterise the Territory politics of 1968 in terms of the kinds of political resources which candidates drew upon in the election campaign. Next we look for indications of 'national politics' emerging, as the rate of political integration helps to shape (though in no simple way) the prospects of 'self-determination'. In the light of these findings we then assess the diffusion, assimilation, and legitimation of the introduced political institutions, and seek to identify the more important signs of further change.

POLITICAL RESOURCES IN 1968

Here we classify political resources and estimate the extent to which the different types operated as positive or negative supports to potential and actual candidates. We compare the evidence on three dimensions: as between the several study areas; as between Territory and Australian electoral processes in a few appropriate cases; and as between 1964 and 1968. These comparisons should provide a first measure of the rate and nature of political change and its distribution, and of the differences between New Guinean and Western perceptions of formally similar institutions.

Group relationships of candidates

The most direct resource for an election candidate is a substantial number of committed votes within the electorate, and in nearly all

---

Although the author is responsible for the final text, this chapter broadly represents the joint views of the Editors, and owes most of its leading ideas to numerous discussions with both A. L. Epstein and Marie Reay. Thanks are also due to E. P. Wolfers for many improvements to the final draft and for supplying material for the section on parties; to members of the Institute of Development Studies at the University of Sussex for criticisms of early drafts at its Staff Seminar; and to the Institute itself for the Visiting Fellowship which enabled the work to get done.

self-governing countries votes are committed in this way by adherence to a political party. In New Guinea there were no bloc party votes in 1968, but many of the indigenous candidates (who numbered sixty-six out of the eighty-nine in our research areas) nevertheless commanded a more or less automatic bloc vote. Its core was usually to be found in their own or their more notable relatives' kinship or clan groups. However, these groups were too small to have a decisive effect on the election, except where a large number of groups each put up its own candidate—there were sixteen in each of four Highland electorates—when the result could depend on the chances of preferential voting. Normally, the core groups had to bring with them, or be supplemented by, some larger following if a candidate was to achieve a majority.

Some larger blocs of committed votes came from other residents in the candidate's 'home area' where he was known from birth, and sometimes from adherents in an 'adopted area' if the candidate had lived and worked for some time away from his natal area. With few exceptions, mainly in the Milne Bay District, indigenous candidates seemed to score well in their home or adopted areas. In addition, some candidates won bloc votes from one or more of the larger 'solidarities' which had become established in the various areas at the time of the election. Some of these were linked to the past, such as the trading networks, and the 'beachmen' and 'bushmen' divisions of the north-east coast. But the more important kinds of supplementary bond figuring in the election nearly always sprang from some fact or common experience arising from European occupation: a cargo cult, localities served by a single road, sometimes religious denomination. The most prevalent and important of these larger solidarities seem to have been generated by the spread of local government councils. They provided a focus for wider group loyalty or inter-group rivalry, as reported from the Western Highlands; they helped to create—or at least to give expression to—an increasing awareness of public issues beyond the village's concerns; and they provided a medium for the transmission of political information about the election.

Naturally, two or more candidates from the same 'home area' were likely to be weakened by splitting its vote. On the other hand, shrewd candidates from other areas could pick up extra votes in places which fielded no candidate of their own. Thus Garrett and Angmai concentrated on Bundi rather than compete with others on their home grounds, and similar areas provided most of the votes for Papuan candidates in Central District electorates, outside their own local areas or ethnic groups.

Candidates' political skills and attributes

One asset mentioned in the area chapters as frequently as 'home base' and 'adopted area' is 'to be known' or 'to become known' in the electorate. A few candidates managed this, without much effort, during the campaign. Paul Lapun in South Bougainville was 'known' for his prominence as a member, and for the very mystery with which he surrounded his person. After his brief visit early in the pre-election period, he could afford to leave his image to be propagated by a few representatives and the cargoist grapevine. Matthias ToLiman in the Gazelle relied on the strategic appearances he made on ceremonial occasions while a Parliamentary Under-Secretary. Rauke Gam won in Kabwum though he scarcely moved out of his home area, because he was well known in all sections of it at the beginning, and was reputedly supported in all sectors by the indigenous members of the Lutheran mission. On the other hand, a candidate lacking such assets as these three had, who did not appear in his chosen electorate at all during the campaign—like Mapai of Hiri—could not be regarded as a serious contender.

To be known, then, the average candidate wanting to win had to campaign in person through the electorate, or find some other way of planting his identity in the electors' minds. Even in the difficult north-east coast area, where few candidates visited more than a fraction of the electors outside their home bases and the main centres, most of them walked over their own areas and at least one or two other sections.

The commonest mode of addressing electors personally was at gatherings in the villages—sometimes in the evening and sometimes after the church service—conducted with varying degrees of formality. Except in the Western Highlands, the use of 'traditional' avenues of approach, such as trying to win bloc votes or at least influence electors through clan or other community leaders, was comparatively rare and then usually ineffectual, unless the leaders concerned were associated also with non-'traditional' institutions such as local government councils. The reason is possibly that in the non-Highland areas modern channels reached larger numbers of people, and were more open to new-fangled purposes such as mobilising votes for a House of Assembly election. On the other hand, the area reports mention few attempts by candidates to plan a campaign on the basis of careful estimates of their voting strength in particular sectors of the electorate.

When they could afford it, candidates supplemented their own efforts by distributing leaflets, posters, printed shirts, and trinkets. In this some were helped by agents sent out to remoter parts, or by local government councillors—and in at least two cases candidates dropped leaflets from aircraft.

The more expensive methods were naturally confined to European candidates who, like the few others who lacked any kin-based core vote, had to rely on their identification by residence with one or more localities in the electorate, and strive the harder by other forms of campaigning. Propagating the name or face alone could be important in vote-getting, as was shown positively by the success of Slaughter's leaflet-dropping in Rigo-Abau, negatively by the fate of Francisco Kalade whose photograph was missing from the polling booths in Esa'ala, and generally by the showing of candidates who dispensed with platforms and programs and even speeches, and concentrated on impressing their identity on the memories of electors. Impressing their personality was better still, if it showed orthodox qualities such as 'moral uprightness', being 'a good Christian', hospitality and generosity. This all underlines the general conclusion that the 1968 election, like that of 1964, was fought, as chapter 3 puts it, by independent candidates on individual lines, by individual means and largely through individual contacts.

As to the impersonal attributes which helped candidates to win, and distinguished candidates and winners from those of 1964, we shall confine ourselves to a few general comments, since detailed comparisons have been published elsewhere (Wolfers 1968b: Tables I, III, IV. Cf. Bettison *et al.* 1965: 447-9, Tables 1-3). Europeans predominated as candidates and winners in the seven Regional electorates in our areas. In the fifteen Opens, five of sixty-two candidates were Europeans, two being elected.

Table 20 lists on the right the electorates covered in the present study, with the members elected in 1968. The left-hand column shows the Special electorates which included the areas studied here, with the Open electorates roughly corresponding to those on the right, and the sitting members in these areas in 1968. Members re-elected in 1968 are shown in italics in both columns.

A number of points illustrated by the table are, in fact, typical of the 1968 election as a whole. About one-sixth of the outgoing members did not seek re-election. One-half of those who did stand again were defeated. The average level of achievement and legislative experience among expatriate elected members did not rise—Stuntz, Barrett, Niall, and Downs were a weightier group in these respects than any four expatriate elected members in the second House. The level of conservatism among expatriate elected members, however, declined somewhat—in our areas the outgoing six included at least

TABLE 20—ELECTED MEMBERS IN THE STUDY AREAS, 1964 AND 1968

First House		Second House	
East Papua Special	Stuntz	Milne Bay Regional	Abel
Milne Bay	*Guise*	Alotau	*Guise*
		Esa'ala	Evennett
Esa'ala Losuia	*Watson*	Kula	*Watson*
New Guinea Islands Special	Grose*	Bougainville Regional	Lue
Bougainville	*Lapun*	South Bougainville	*Lapun*
New Britain Special	*Ashton*	East and West New Britain Regional	*Ashton*
West Gazelle Special	Barrett		
Rabaul	*ToLiman*	Gazelle	*ToLiman*
		Kokopo	Tammur
		Rabaul	Epineri
Madang-Sepik Special	Martin	Madang Regional	Garrett
		Mabuso	Angmai
		Rai Coast	Poe
Madang	Matibri*	Sumkar	Middleton
North Markham Special	Niall	Morobe Regional	Voutas†
Rai Coast	Stoi	Kabwum	Rauke
Highlands Special	Downs*	Western Highlands Regional	Watts
		Mul-Dei	Mek
Minj	*Kaibelt*	Wahgi	*Kaibelt*
Central Special	*Chatterton*	Moresby Open	*Chatterton*
Moresby Open	Rarupu	Central Regional	Oala
		Hiri	Kapena

* Outgoing members who did not stand in 1968.
† Voutas was an outgoing Member of the first House, but for an Open electorate.

three outspoken opponents of early self-government, while the incoming four included two Pangu Pati leaders. Finally, the Western-style qualifications and capacities of non-European elected members rose appreciably—compare the comments in preceding chapters on the outgoing Matibri, Stoi, and Rarupu with, say, those on the incoming Lue, Tammur, Poe, Oala, and Kapena.

What kind and direction of political evolution are indicated by the comparison of candidates' and winners' attributes at the two House of Assembly elections? Observations at the electorate level have shown that both contests attracted candidates drawn from the most prominent people, indigenous and European, in each area—prominence in fact being based on experience (backed where available by formal training and education) in expatriate-influenced aspects of social, political, or economic life. A number of the indigenous members elected on both occasions might have achieved important status in their own communities by traditional standards, and some owed their election in part to the prestige of older relatives who enjoyed such status. But among the candidates as a whole, elected or rejected, the 'big man' by earlier standards who had no European connections, skills, or occupational experience was conspicuous by his absence. Thus, as Wolfers notes for the election generally, 'the men who stood and, to an even greater extent, those who won, were men with some experience of the forces of change in Papua and New Guinea' (Wolfers 1968b: 17).

This represented an intensification of trends noted in 1964. In Milne Bay, Methodist Christian virtues were an asset to candidates in both elections but they were much less in demand than the pragmatic qualities sought in 1968. In Kokopo, Oscar Tammur realised that by traditional standards he was too young to count, but his secondary education and technical training in Australia gave him the mark of sophistication which helped to outweigh the handicap of his youth, while his leadership at Raniola presumably protected him from the stigma attached in a cargoist community to that other 'P.I.R. man', Bakuk—and Tammur was elected. In the Central District, all the Papuan candidates had achieved success in manipulating modern institutions, and certainly the elected Regional and Hiri candidates were pre-eminent in their experience of these institutions.

These facts are no doubt due in part to changes independent of the new political institutions. Traditional 'big men' had become less significant for various reasons, and there was a steady increase in the number of people coming out of Australian-sponsored schools and training institutions and into Australian-generated types of employment and enterprise. But the field studies contain a number of hints that there was also a general feeling that the elections, and the House of Assembly which gave rise to them, were essentially 'white man's business', and therefore that those who became involved in them needed some acquaintance with white men's ways and interests.

Let us now examine another kind of political resource. By noting the extent to which the candidates and their electoral behaviour were thought to conform, consciously or otherwise, with well-established values and attitudes of the bulk of electors, the field chapters help to show the nature and relative strength of such norms at the time of the election.

Values and attitudes of electors

Most chapters give examples of mutual aid among candidates in the course of campaigning. The commonest form this took was the sharing of transport and of 'platforms' at election meetings. But there were also cases of candidates financing the printing of leaflets for others, or introducing a fellow candidate to villages where he was not known. Such aid was unremarkable as between candidates in different electorates, especially if they were co-operating in a political party or other alliance. In so far as candidates extended some of these courtesies to rivals in the same electorate, the field teams noted it as an example of a peculiar mildness—compared to the practice in industrial countries—that seemed to characterise electoral competition in New Guinea.

Another point, cited in the majority of the studies as evidence of such mildness, was the relative lack of public recrimination among rival indigenous candidates, compared with the direct denigration by European candidates of one another, and sometimes of indigenous candidates even in other electorates. It appeared that the indigenous style was much preferred by most electors. In Kula, Patterson was criticised for his personal mud-slinging contest against Watson. In the Gazelle candidates generally avoided confrontation with their opponents. In the Madang area, political groups, associations, and relationships were said to emphasise consensus of interest and outlook, and discourage controversy. In Kabwum, Crowhurst adopted the 'modest and restrained approach that characterised his indigenous rivals'. According to chapter 7 the same phenomenon was a notable feature of the Papuan candidates' campaigns. There an interpretation similar to that in other chapters is given, but going one step further:

The Papuan candidates seem to have viewed the election not as a contest between candidates but rather as an act of choice by the electors: the candidates were merely volunteering their services. In this way, no-one stood to lose face in defeat (p. 298).

Some of these extracts hint at a traditional origin for the observed behaviour, and indeed its occurrence in the more traditionally influenced elections of the Western Highlands would seem to support such an interpretation. But the same chapters show elsewhere that it is part of a more complex pattern. For one thing, as suggested in chapter 2, the avoidance of open confrontation may be due as much to a sense of vulnerability on the unfamiliar ground of contemporary issues and legislative policy, as to the observance of customary conventions. For another thing, the convention may lie not so much in a taboo on conflict itself as in the regulation of its method—perhaps in memory of how easily conflict passed over into violence in former times. Kaibelt Diria's criticism of the other Wahgi candidates may have seemed improper to men of Minj but it contributed to his win, and the Mul-Dei candidates could afford to be polite to one another when they left the task of casting direct aspersions to their agents. At least two chapters acknowledge that disparagement by insinuation was practised with skill and apparent impunity.

But some accounts do report overt conflict which was not disapproved. Elliott Elijah's direct criticisms of 'three white men' brought favourable responses. In the Madang conflict over 'cash crops or cargo', adherents of either party 'did not resent the counter-attacks of their champions as infringements of Melanesian good manners'. Perhaps there is a clue to the paradox where chapter 5, describing the Bundi groups, refers to the strong rivalry between patriclans and major political groups which is a constant feature of their political life. At the 1968 stage in political evolution, the election candidates represented no substantial political parties or other organised groups in direct confrontation. It may be that unless an issue like the cargo controversy in Madang-Rai Coast is joined, they do not feel themselves to be members of rival collectivities. Candidates in the Western Highlands had much more in common with one another, as potential negotiators with the government on behalf of an entire electorate, than with their own supporters *vis-à-vis* other candidates and theirs; and in many other areas the candidates appeared to maintain the conventions appropriate to 'in-group' behaviour, with the distant government—and sometimes expatriates in general—as the corresponding out-group.

Cargo beliefs of constantly varying incidence and content are endemic in many parts of New Guinea. The assertion of the Chief Electoral Officer that they played a smaller part in the 1968 election than in 1964, finds some support in that cargoism figured explicitly in only two areas studied and in one of these the 'cargo candidates' met decisive defeat. Cargoism is not, however, on the wane, even here; rather it is a continuing response to the common experience of colonial rule. Its smaller role in the 1968 election does not, then, express reconciliation with this experience but merely an unwillingness of candidates to exploit it—partly, perhaps, from signs of electors' disillusionment with the results, or lack of results, of trusting cargoist candidates in 1964. On the other hand, support for the overwhelmingly victorious candidate in South Bougainville was very strong in the most cargoist, anti-European segments of the electorate. In New Britain Koriam Urekit, re-elected with an overwhelming majority, has insisted that he is no cargo cultist, but anthropologists who have worked among the people he has led are unanimous in identifying his influence with such a cult. This suggests that the official discrediting of cargo cults may have persuaded indigenous politicians to denounce 'cultist' activities and 'cargo' thinking overtly, while tacitly recognising cargoist expectations in their own electorates.

Underlying both cargoism, and the obsession with Western artefacts and knowledge that triggers it off, are the pervasive norms of the indigenous culture, outlined in chapter 5 but common to all the areas of our study:

> Social values are materialistic and egalitarian. Economic considerations dominate political life ... possessions are a prerequisite of social relationships ... Religion, too, stresses materialism ... To ensure economic success, man must harness the power of gods and spirits by means of ritual (p. 168).

Herein may lie the key to the ambivalence which emerges from the various field accounts of indigenous electors' attitudes to expatriates, and expatriate ways and skills, in the context of the election. This is not a simple question.

First there is the matter of local attitudes towards expatriate people as inhabitants of the Territory—whether European or Asian, private businessmen or Administration staff, planters or missionaries. These vary with locality. In South Bougainville and on the Gazelle, expatriates in any of these guises are increasingly seen as expropriators of land, business rivals, and unpredictable wielders of arbitrary power. Wherever population growth and economic development exacerbate land shortage and employment problems under the colonial régime, increasing tension is likely.

Thus in Bougainville the activities of C.R.A., and the seeming inability of the Administration to prevent or curtail them, had only confirmed past dissatisfaction with Europeans and their behaviour towards villagers, shown by the refusal of many Nasioi and others to vote for any European in 1964. During the 1967-8 election campaign, even the more sophisticated and less cargo-ridden Buin people, not directly affected by C.R.A., pointed out that Europeans had no roots in the island and, in a crisis, might again return to Australia; and they drew the contrast between European campaign promises and past performance. The European candidates themselves attested the prevalence of these sentiments in South Bougainville, and voting patterns in the 1968 election for Bougainville Regional confirmed it.

Where some of this tension had taken cargoist forms, the feeling was stronger and was expressed more overtly in electoral behaviour. In a cargoist area on the Rai Coast, Iaga Bakuk's own neighbours sneered at him as 'the P.I.R. man' and 'white man's puppet', while Yali's oratory called forth from a follower the cry: 'You ... must dismantle this cult house of the white men'—referring to the House of Assembly. But even in the Western Highlands, indigenous hostility to the multi-racial councils was linked to a novel wave of anti-European sentiment and led expatriate candidates to withdraw to competition for the Regional.

Attitudes to the Administration varied with the length and nature of contact, but generally seemed more equivocal than those towards Europeans as such. In an area of relatively recent contact like the Western Highlands, people saw its officers as maintaining physical security, imposing exotic laws and customs, and pointing the way to new forms of desirable wealth. In an area like the Gazelle this image had long since given way to a mixture of expectations of further aid and education, disappointment and frustration over current shortfalls in performance, and disillusion over the hard bargains, especially over land, driven by the Administration in the past. Hence it told against a candidate like ToBaining to appear as an Establishment figure who sided with the Europeans against his own people and depended on the Administration for patronage. Similarly Epineri argued—apparently to good effect—that candidates like ToBunbun and ToPatiliu, who were employees of the Administration, could never be good representatives while he himself, an independent contractor by occupation, and regarded as a consistent spokesman for the Tolai, voicing local dissatisfaction with the slow rate of development and change, was elected with a handsome majority over these two candidates.

Attitudes to individual expatriates as candidates for the House involve other issues again. In several areas in this second House of Assembly election, reaction against the sitting Member (which we will discuss further in other contexts) took the form of favouring candidates of another race. But this worked both ways. In Esa'ala, dissatisfaction with Lepani Watson as M.H.A. created a climate of opinion which favoured a European candidate, successfully exploited by Evennett. Similarly, in Kabwum, indigenous electors respected Niall and Voutas (the Morobe Regional candidates) as former Administration officers and as Europeans: after Stoi's poor showing, they doubted whether any of their own people was fit to serve in the House.

But in Milne Bay Regional, Elliott Elijah won some favour by arguing that Stuntz's apparent indifference proved that Europeans were not concerned to represent local interests, and that Watson could hardly be blamed for inefficiency under such poor tutelage. Similar reactions produced more dramatic results in some other parts of the Territory—notably in the East Sepik Regional, where alleged neglect by the sitting Special Member, Frank Martin, accounted in part for a tide of anti-European feeling which swept in a supposed 'outsider', Michael Somare, youthful leader of Pangu.

The interesting point about this two-way phenomenon is the apparent tendency to see the problem of unsatisfactory representation in racial terms.

Where the situation was not unduly complicated by factors such as these, the dominant consideration was the possession of relevant experience and skills—and this meant, of course, some familiarity with European ways in government, as practised by the Australian Administration. Other things being equal, this would give a clear advantage to an expatriate candidate, especially in areas where indigenous opportunities to acquire these attributes had been limited by remoteness or the recency of contact. But it was the attributes in themselves that people sought, not representation or governance by the European as such. Thus in the Madang Regional and Rai Coast Open respectively, Garrett, the Australian, was able to exploit his obvious European competence and special knowledge of road-surveying, and Poe, the Papuan, his command of English and Police Motu as well as Pidgin, as signs of his ability to master the complexities of modern government. 'Race' did not matter so long as the 'know-how' was there; but if a Papuan or New Guinean had it, so much the better, for he might be a more reliable spokesman for the bulk of his constituents.

However, if sophistication of this kind was a necessary condition of success for indigenous candidates, it was not a sufficient one, as shown by the ignominious fate of Kalade, who had all the relevant qualifications. The fact was appreciated by his successful opponent Evennett, who said that the *desiderata* for an elected member were: 'education, knowledge of political processes in the capital and the electorate, ability to understand and talk to Europeans (the "real governors") and a permanent home in the electorate with a knowledge of local people and their needs'.

Organisations and associations

Another kind of resource for election campaigning anywhere is the potential support of organisations with a popular base, whether governmental agencies or private associations. Such organisations played a part in the two House of Assembly elections, and probably a greater part in the second. But by 1968 there had been comparatively little development of any vigorous associational life, political or otherwise, even in areas of longest contact and greatest development.

This was particularly true of organisations specialised for electoral activity, such as political parties or candidates' campaign committees. Outside a handful of towns, there was little sign of the 'political parties' so hastily inaugurated during 1967. Parties figure in the area chapters mainly as objects of uncertainty or hostility. Hopes that the abortive Agriculture Reform Party might do a service by pre-selecting candidates were disappointed. The other parties did little more than find some candidates willing to stand. At best they provided their candidates with some leaflets and a few talking points. At worst, especially in Pangu's case, it was an electoral liability for a candidate to be publicly associated with them, and candidates—almost to a man in the New Guinea Territory—avoided or even denied such association. Candidates 'sponsored' or 'endorsed' by parties (and few could say what these terms meant) had in all cases to finance their own campaigns like anyone else. (The few figures we have for this—apart from the deposit of $50—range from $19 to $800 for indigenous candidates, and up to $4500 for one expatriate campaign.)

As for candidates' own 'campaign committees'—as distinct from the 'agents' and 'campaign managers' described earlier—very few are mentioned in the team reports. In the Western Highlands Regional, the backing of John Watts, the winner, by a group of prosperous businessmen was thought to have helped him get votes everywhere while other Regional candidates' campaigns had to be curtailed when funds ran short. The only other such organisations in our areas, those of Chatterton, McCarthy, and Toua Kapena in Moresby and Hiri, provided one example at least of campaigning in the Central District being more formalised than in the rest of the Territory.

Other organisations were much more important as resources in the 1968 election. They are summed up in the claim of John Guise that he enjoyed widespread support—from local government councillors, women's clubs, co-operative societies and churches, some members of Kwato mission, and Anglican and Catholic churchgoers. The area studies in general present evidence almost exclusively on local government councils and religious groups, and even on these the evidence is not always clear as to what constitutes 'support'.

For example, it almost invariably indicates that the managements of 'missions', as such, were careful to dissociate themselves from any overt part in the election by way of supporting or opposing particular candidates. An unknown number of individual missionaries advised their flocks about the merits of the respective candidates. We do not know what proportion of this advice was unsolicited; we do know that some was not on denominational lines. In this context it is difficult at first sight to interpret the statement that Rauke was the 'official' mission candidate in Kabwum, or that 'opposition to a candidate by organisations such as churches and councils meant defeat' (p. 129). It is easier to follow Komoro's assertion that in 1964 'some missionaries' told their parishioners not to vote for him, and the conjecture that a letter from the Methodist mission head suggesting prayer for guidance about voting could have had an important bearing on Watson's success in Kula, since neither of his rivals was a churchgoer.

The usual meaning of references to 'mission opposition' or 'support' is probably best conveyed by the reminder in chapter 4 that individual priests (and the same may be said of indigenous lay preachers and catechists) enjoy considerable independence on their own stations and can make their attitudes known in a number of subtle ways. A common religious bond can attract a voter's allegiance to one of a field of otherwise unknown candidates, and 'the communication network provided by mission stations and schools looms large ... where other channels are so inadequate'. Such networks of indigenous mission people helped to organise Methodist support for Watson in Kula, Catholic support for Lue in Bougainville, and Lutheran support for Rauke in Kabwum. In some places, with or without organised support, there were blocs of denominational votes, just as there were blocs of clan votes and locality votes. It was on this assumption that the Catholic sector of the Kiriwina population was said to be strongly behind Patterson, while people at Sio thought Crowhurst's anti-mission stance would harm his chances. In all this there was no appreciable change from 1964, except possibly an increased tendency in certain areas for denominational differences to be subordinated to secular ends.

Caution is also needed when interpreting references to local government councils as a political resource. The field reports contain a number of statements in the form: 'Middleton was endorsed by Karkar Council'; 'Roro and Mekeo ... local government councils had indicated their support for [Slaughter]'; and 'Patterson was persuaded by the Louisiade Local Government Council into nominating for the Kula Open'. But the accounts also make it clear that bloc votes did not necessarily follow in such cases. Patterson received only a small proportion of the votes in Misima; Kaki did not get the support he anticipated from Sumgilbar Council; and so on. There is no evidence to suggest that 'councils' went back on their collective word. This raises the question whether they really made a corporate decision in these instances, and the field reports nowhere say so explicitly.

An incident very early in the run-up to the election well illustrates the divergence that can arise between official constitutional conceptions and the pressures of politics in New Guinea. During March 1967, impressed by the need for more concerted opposition to the Administration in the House of Assembly, James Meangarum, M.H.A. for Ramu Open, spoke publicly and later wrote to local government councillors in his area urging them, with others, to form a political party. Later in the year Tony Voutas, M.H.A. for Kaindi, took up the idea of a party based on local government councils, and in a circular letter to all councillors in the Territory apparently said he had been officially told there was no objection to their voting funds for the purpose. It appears from chapter 2 that the notion aroused some interest on the Gazelle, at least. Naturally (from the government's point of view) the Director of District Administration had to point out, by circular and a statement in the House, that a council as such could not legally devote funds to a political party (*South Pacific Post*, 4 September 1967).

We do not know at what point the 'support' of a 'council as such' for a national election candidate would become *ultra vires*. But whether or not councillors or their advisers took note of the legal niceties, it seems likely that the forms of council participation in the 1967-8 election campaign would rarely, if ever, be definable in legal terms. The actual pattern varied everywhere as described for the north-east coast. Councillors actively canvassed for particular candidates; or merely echoed prevailing opinions; or gave confused or conflicting advice to voters, who sometimes ignored it and sometimes criticised councillors for endorsing candidates without consulting them.

The complex nature of councils as political resources is analysed clearly at the end of chapter 3. 'A wiser course was to treat these bodies as collections of individual voters'. At the least, council meetings, like church services and the gatherings of other public bodies such as co-operative societies, provided a handy forum for presenting the candidate's person, and his message if any, to the maximum number of people with the minimum of travel and speechmaking. In addition, councillors and church workers—especially the former—are the main channels of information between the 'politically insulated' villagers who make up a majority of the voters, and the outside world. By virtue of their accepted role as messengers between 'the government' and the people, councillors in particular could be expected to pass on some account of the candidate, even if it was neutral or inaccurate. If they did no more than this, councillors were probably helping the candidate. If they actively recommended or opposed him, their opinion could be decisive. But, as the division within Astrolabe Bay and Rai Coast councils over Poe and Yali exemplifies, in general 'councillors acted as individuals in favourable positions of influence, and not as members of corporate bodies' (p. 129).

Candidates varied greatly in their use of such influential connections. What is clear is that the local government council and the mission community were easily the most significant—in many areas the only significant—groups available for this purpose. It is conjectured in chapter 7 that Oala's work as a union leader won him the votes of Papuan workers. If so, this owed nothing to organised activity by the Port Moresby Workers' Association, which, as indicated in that chapter, was moribund. The only other reference to any such body is the terse remark in chapter 5 that the Madang Workers' Association did nothing. Associational life in this as in other spheres was, indeed, underdeveloped in Papua and New Guinea in 1968.

Issues and interests

It is characteristic of politics in Australia for the contestants to use policy issues and conflicts of interest as resources in their campaigning. As noted in chapter 7, even in the Territory's capital the 1968 election was almost as devoid of such issues and conflicts as that of 1964.

Only a minority of the candidates disputed with each other over questions of policy. If they raised them at all, it was usually to say that if elected they would advocate schemes for the development of their own electorate and District, and about these there was rarely room for serious differences of opinion. Hence disputes over policies scarcely offered rewarding means of support for one candidate as against another.

The number of candidates who raised issues broader than the material needs of their own locality was smaller still—and included a disproportionate number of the unsuccessful. In Esa'ala, Kalade, more than any other candidate, concerned himself with country-wide issues —and he came a bad last. In Kula, Watson alone discussed the public service, the Five-Year Development Plan, or the political future of the Territory. In Bougainville, the two candidates—Lee and Komoro—who offered specific programs were defeated; the two victors did not, for all practical purposes, campaign at all. The burning issues to a Western observer—European utilisation of mining and timber resources—only affected the election as two of many examples of perceived European 'oppression'. In New Britain, there appeared to be little to choose between either the Regional or Open candidates in terms of ideological orientation. The question of the Territory's political development was raised—by the voters as well as by the candidates—but Epineri alone was credited with advocating early independence, and it seemed that he won in spite of this. On the north-east coast there was much talk of various measures to promote economic prosperity in the region, the only specific dispute being about the proper route for a road to the Highlands. The great 'issue' was over 'cash crops or cargo', and it was the handful of members of the cargoist alliance alone who talked of localising the public service, immediate self-government, and early independence—and went down to defeat. In the Western Highlands, all expatriate Regional candidates stressed the same platform: the kind of economic development that District Commissioner Ellis had promoted. No-one disputed this, and no other issues were raised. And in the shadow of Port Moresby itself: 'Most candidates' policies had no ideological content whatsoever: no general ideas about political progress, reform or development; no notions of social and economic justice; no commitment to basic rights and liberties; no visions of the future'. Pangu candidates conscientiously mentioned self-government—and were rejected.

In so far as it did receive some discussion in most areas— especially by disapproving European candidates—the question of self-government was, perhaps, a widespread 'issue'. But it was one on which opinion seemed overwhelmingly on one side. The success of Abel and Voutas, despite being as Pangu men openly on the 'wrong' side in this issue, seemed to be—like Epineri's—only an example of the voters' addiction to other criteria than platforms in choosing their representatives. Other overt issues of wider importance were cargoism in Madang District, and the European record in Bougainville and the Gazelle. But at this point the discussion moves from issues to interests.

The peculiar relation of interests to the 1968 election may be developed from a section of chapter 2 which begins:

> Quite early on in the campaign an educated Tolai had remarked to one of the research team that we should not expect issues to play a central role in the election, which would quickly resolve itself into a simple clash of personalities. Nonetheless, questions put to the candidates at village meetings suggested that there were a number of matters which were the subject of deep concern throughout the community (p. 75).

These matters included wages of mission teachers; relationships between Papua and New Guinea, especially 'spreading around the wealth of the Tolai'; the duties of the member to his constituents; the increase in the council tax; and the land problems of the Gazelle.

Such sophisticated questions were rarely raised in other areas. Real group interests are at stake here, except in the matter of member-constituent relations—and even that reflects concern about proper representation of the electorate's interests at the seat of government. But this brings out a crucial point. The questions actually raised were not about clashes of interest among groups of local people within any one electorate or District. They involved the interests of the people of one region versus those of others, or the interests of indigenous people generally versus expatriate interests. Raising teachers' wages, for example, calls for higher Administration subsidies, not re-distribution within the District. The only case of a candidate playing off group interests within an electorate against each other was Anderson's warning to the Goilala against the 'coastal candidates'. In general, then, interest-questions could hardly function as differential supports for rival candidates in the election—since in the absence of parties rivalry was only at the electorate level. Only the Administration, or concerted political pressure upon the Administration at the centre, could resolve the conflicts of interest uppermost in people's minds.

Hence, while the election brought such interest-conflicts out into the open, it was not apparent that the outcome of the election could do anything to settle them. It was perhaps because they were thus made aware of the problems, but still felt ignorant and impotent about the means of resolving them, that many Tolai approached the election in a state of uncertainty, anxiety, and confusion.

Not unnaturally, most candidates shared with the electors this sense of impotence. Taurega was early advised by his European confidant to make no promises. 'No promises', said Oala; 'no promises', said Kapena—'the people are angry with politicians who have been elected because of promises that they have failed to honour'. For the majority of the villagers, when a Tolai candidate dutifully recited the headings of his platform, the effect was frequently soporific. What is the point of having a platform when the aspiring candidate has no party, and so can make no convincing promise of legislative performance?

'NATIONAL POLITICS'?

According to its editors, the main work published on the 1964 House of Assembly election was planned in the belief that national politics would not emerge in time for the elections, and there would be 'fifty-four separate and distinct electoral skirmishes rather than a territorial battle'. At the end, they concluded that this assumption was the correct one (Bettison *et al.* 1965: 388). In a sense, of course, this situation would accord with the legal theory of Australian elections. That still assumes that each electorate comprises undifferentiated voters who choose a person to 'represent' them according to his individual lights, in what is literally called merely a legislative assembly or a house of representatives. But the conception does not accord with the political facts of the case. General elections are contests between nation-wide (or State-wide) political organisations— the main parties—for the right to control a national (or State) government. The 'legitimacy' of such a system implies widespread awareness and acceptance of some kind of interdependence transcending all electorate boundaries.

Plans for constitutional development in Papua and New Guinea have assumed that the House of Assembly would become the focus of a similar awareness and acceptance. At the general election of 1964 there were few signs that this hope would be realised. In this section we scan the field chapters for any further signs that may have appeared by 1968, under what seem the most likely headings: co-operation between candidates across electoral boundaries; the role of expatriates in the political process; the role of organised associations —especially political parties; the political horizons of the electors; and the expectations of candidates and electors from the 'national' institutions of elections and House of Assembly.

Co-operation between candidates

'Alliances' for mutual support between two or more candidates in different electorates usually involved a Regional candidate's name being linked with that of one or more candidates for Open electorates within the same District. The most notable case was in the Madang Regional Electorate, where all three candidates had their allies in several of the Opens, issuing joint handbills and posters and speaking for one another in the campaign. The Lue-Lapun association in Bougainville was less formal but apparently effective in generating support for the younger man. Niall's link with Tarosi in Morobe and Kabwum, Anderson's and Rea's in Central with Open candidates in Goilala and Hiri, and Abel's with Patterson in Milne Bay and Kula, were more tenuous, and the latter's results were probably negative. The nearest approach to such arrangements in the Western Highlands was Rutledge's abortive—indeed backfiring—scheme to take indigenous candidates around the Regional area in return for local introductions.

The usual pattern was for the Regional candidate to initiate these 'alliances' as, even where he was not an expatriate, he stood to gain more (and in most cases did so) from the Open candidates' intimate associations with places away from his 'home area', than they did from his name, his sharing of transport or his financing of posters—if he had these to offer. The cases of Patterson, Kaki, Bato, and Kaibelt, indeed, show that some associations could be regarded as a liability for the Open candidates concerned.

The Western Highlands offered an interesting variant of the alliance theme, in the agreement by sitting member candidates to support each other in their respective electorates. In general, the 'alliances' contained the promise of widening political horizons only where they appeared under political party auspices, as with the Jephcott-A.P.P. group in Madang, and Gavera Rea and his Pangu allies in Central. But the 'parties' were so unorganised and so unpopular that in practice all alliances, including common party membership, fitted pretty well the description given for those of Madang, as being essentially personal associations between individuals who felt they had common political views and aspirations. We are not far from the 1964 situation when our chapter 3 concludes that in Milne Bay the three Open electorates could have been many hundreds of miles apart for all the interaction and mutual influence there were between them. On the other hand, the same chapter shows how Elijah's later campaign tactics led electors to see the contest as one between two firm Regional-Open coalitions — which did represent movement beyond 1964.

Expatriates in 1968 politics

Another variant of the inter-electorate alliance introduces a different facet of Territory politics. There are hints in the field reports of occasional co-operative action beyond even Regional electorate boundaries. The loan of an aircraft enabled Stuntz to cover more ground than his rivals. McKinnon, the successful candidate for Ramu Open within Madang Regional, sent a Sio employee to campaign for Tarosi in Kabwum (within Morobe), and some Sepik workers into Morobe to help Niall, and spoke himself for Tarosi and Niall (Morobe Regional) to the immigrant Kabwum workers in Madang. Earlier on, an aircraft had been lent from the Eastern Highlands to help in the formation of the All People's Party.

The common feature of this inter-Regional activity is apparent: it was sponsored by European well-wishers of European candidates or their allies, and associated with sustained public attacks on Pangu Pati and the 'radical' ideas attributed to it. It can be inferred—indeed they often said so—that the Europeans concerned, usually well-known planters or businessmen, felt that, whoever was raising issues like early home rule and self-government, these might become widespread or even 'national' issues. Hence it was thought worth while to help like-minded election candidates, even in distant parts of the Territory, to combat such ideas and defeat candidates who held them.

It might be thought that European private economic interests thus formed a potential Territory-wide political force, facing the uncertainties of pending political change. Many Europeans were uneasy about ToLiman and Tammur because they expressed indigenous concern over the land problem. As seen in chapter 1, the Highland planters, through their publications and spokesmen, European and indigenous, had consistently opposed all talk of further constitutional change, and attacked political parties in general because in a sense they were all harbingers of change even if not, like Pangu, espousing it. The candidacy of Watts in the Western Highlands Regional was sponsored by Mt Hagen businessmen who were concerned about the stability of their investments. Merely by being an indigene standing for a Regional electorate in the Highlands, Iambakey aroused alarm there. A similar alarm apparently lay behind the electorally risky theme pursued by Stuntz in Milne Bay: 'Self-government would lead to independence and the latter reduce Australian influence in the Territory to negligible dimensions. Did village people think that they could run their own country?' (p. 123).

Nevertheless, Europeans in general evidently did not see the 1968 election as an arena for united political action. The nearest approach to a conservative European party was the All People's Party which sponsored about fifteen candidates altogether and got two elected, compared to Pangu's twelve. In the areas covered by this book, expatriate voters showed little interest in the election. In Moresby Open, containing the biggest concentration of expatriate residents in the Territory, it was estimated that fewer than 37 per cent of enrolled Europeans took the trouble to vote. Though it does not apply to Moresby, a plausible reason for other areas is suggested in chapter 2: expatriates saw that their numbers were too small to affect the outcome. A further factor is that a high proportion of the expatriates are Australian public servants, most of whom have no long-term stake or interest in the Territory. So the 'business and settler' expatriates form a very small minority—and the elections are based on a non-discriminatory common roll.

If the expatriates are to have any lasting influence on the political future of Papua and New Guinea, it can only be by winning the electoral support of indigenous voters, or through channels outside the electoral process altogether. At the height of the campaign in 1967, their current position appeared to Ian Downs, the most prominent European elected M.H.A. but not himself a candidate in 1968, as follows:

> Other countries have clearly shown that expatriates and small minority groups cannot expect to maintain political control and influence indefinitely without creating resentment ... It has always seemed to me to be a reasonable proposition that the expatriate minority should relinquish political ambition for high office in order to secure a climate of tolerance and acceptance for economic security ... From this, there emerges the picture of an expatriate politician of restrained ambition who has the role of representing private enterprise (rather than a particular race of people) with an advisory capacity in the House rather than a need to lead the opposition. (*South Pacific Post*, 18 December 1967)

Thus on the evidence available at the time of the 1968 election, the 'expatriate interest' did not seem likely to provide a strong integrating factor in New Guinea politics.

Organised associations: political parties and missions

After three years of a partly elected Legislative Council with a non-official majority, and four years of the House of Assembly, and with a growing number of younger people conscious of social and political tensions in the air, one might have expected political parties to be developing as an important integrating force. Economic groupings might be too fragmented and associational life still too feeble to support interest-based parties. But there might have been a demand for parties to mobilise opposition to unpopular aspects of the colonial administration, or even to create and express 'national' aspirations for self-government; and these might have appealed to adherents scattered through the Territory, if not at first numerous.

In fact, the varied groupings calling themselves political parties during the 1968 election had been formed only during the preceding year, in direct preparation for that event, and scarcely looking beyond it as yet. Three of the five that figured in the election claimed the adherence of some sitting members of the old House. The fifteen members of Pangu's 'parliamentary wing' met openly to discuss policy, though their tendency to vote in the House against the government was only about as consistent as it had been before the party was established. Most other members were chary of formal identification with any party in advance of the election. The few who associated themselves with parties, overtly or otherwise, did so with mixed motives: in the hope that a cautious mention of the fact might attract certain types of voters, or out of curiosity about parties in general. As indicated in chapter 1, the formal constitutions and platforms of the parties (where they existed) bore little relation to what their leaders did or how they made decisions. Similarly, association with a particular party was not necessarily consistent with a man's political convictions or aims. 'Membership' itself was a tenuous relationship, and party sponsorship of election candidates was even more so. Leaders of the same party did not always agree on which candidates were 'with us', and some prominent candidates were claimed by several parties.

Yet two of the parties seemed for a time, at least to their promoters, to hold some promise of becoming 'national' organisations, and all at first gave rise to interested speculation. Both Pangu and the United Democratic Party sent emissaries to centres in distant parts of the Territory, and were soon announcing the formation of 'branches' with large numbers of 'members'. The appearance of the parties provoked discussion among the more sophisticated politicians, in areas of local rivalry or latent unrest, and among younger people with formal education. On the Gazelle, the Agriculture Reform Party was seen as a possible means of controlling nominations: pre-selection could avoid vote-splitting among the Tolai (which might let in a Chinese or a half-caste); it was also thought it could forestall other, Papuan, parties getting a foothold in the area. The party was used by some politicians as an excuse to fend off overtures from party recruiters from outside the Gazelle. On the other hand, this was one of the places where in the early stages some potential election candidates became associated with several parties simultaneously, as a kind of political insurance. Here also there were people who, in private conversation, showed a keen interest in the larger possibilities of political parties. Even in the Western Highlands a few schoolchildren and some educated Papuans were found who gave at least qualified approval to one party—and that Pangu.

As time went on, however, formidable obstacles to the growth and acceptance of political parties became apparent. On the Gazelle, parties initiated elsewhere came to be seen by some as a device whereby people on the mainland might come to dominate New Britain. One Rabaul candidate, aware at first hand of the consensual basis of 'big man' leadership, criticised parties as enabling an individual without strong popular support to gain political power which should only come direct from the electors. Such suspicions shaded over into enmity with the comment, explicitly recorded in Milne Bay, New Britain, Madang, and the Highlands, that parties would be a source of division between different parts of the country, whereas progress lay in all sections working in co-operation with each other and the Administration. Suspicion and hostility gained strength from the derogatory statements of the Minister, some Administration officers, planters and businessmen, and the more conservative politicians, both expatriate and indigenous—which so skilfully juxtaposed parties, Pangu, self-government and independence, and Australian abandonment of the Territory. Several field chapters report in almost the same words that by voting time many electors disliked political parties in general, and were downright fearful of Pangu Pati in particular.

Candidates who had been associated with parties soon realised how unpopular they were; most of them ceased to publicise their affiliation, if not actually disclaiming it, and tried to avoid the subject as a whole. A case in point was that of ToBaining and ToBunbun who, after being publicly announced as members of Pangu's executive, avoided any overt reference to the matter throughout the campaign. Others, whose affiliation was never in doubt, such as John Guise (Pangu, Alotau Open), or Jephcott (A.P.P., Madang Regional), did not campaign as party men at any stage. Finally, there were those who like Bato Bultin (Mabuso Open) had restrained an inclination to join Pangu because of the increasingly adverse attitudes to parties.

At first sight the intensity of these attitudes seems inconsistent with other reported aspects of the election. For example, while the greatest anxiety was focused on the radicalism of Pangu, yet in the Territory as a whole more Pangu candidates were elected than for all the more conservative parties together, and in our research areas Pangu men won four of the eight seats they contested. A glance at the narrative suggests that in the electorates concerned the notion of

Pangu as a vague, abstract political menace was less vivid to voters than the individual personalities of the candidates. The Pangu winners were exceptionally able and congenial politicians, all of whom except Voutas avoided obtruding their Pangu allegiance but could well afford not to deny it. The case of Voutas is more striking since he expressly avowed his Pangu affiliation in an area which disliked self-government, was 'irritated' by parties and rejected at least one Pangu candidate in an Open electorate — the discredited Stoi — and yet soundly defeated Niall who harped on the orthodox anti-Pangu theme.

Thus even when they avowed a party connection, candidates could escape its stigma by campaigning as independents. In general they had to do this because the parties were electorally and organisationally ineffectual—another feature hard to reconcile with the antipathy they evoked. As instruments for engaging even the attention, much less the support, of rank-and-file voters they had little chance against the persistent dominance of primordial ties and local loyalties, and the need for candidates to appeal primarily to them. Indeed, most of 'their' candidates offered the parties far more in terms of popular support than any of the parties offered them. A candidate's party affiliation was almost everywhere of less account than his other political resources—as orator, 'big man', *wantok,* putative supporter of the *kiap,* and so on. The parties, as organisations, had but a slight impact on the election by way of mobilising votes for particular candidates. The campaign help given to Voutas and Somare by educated, indigenous Pangu Pati members at weekends or on leave from Port Moresby, Lae and Wewak, was quite exceptional. Even where fellow-members of a party stood together in an Open and the corresponding Regional electorate, the notion of a party ticket was unknown. Such groups performed little better, and often far worse, as teams, than did the 'alliances' we have noted which were not called parties.

Furthermore the parties, as organisations, failed to become widely established among the village communities—or indeed anywhere outside their headquarters centres. Their leaders seemed either to attach little importance to mobilising the ordinary voters as party adherents, or to have only vague ideas on how to go about it. Interviews with some of the party leaders suggested that the considerable sums collected in the first enthusiastic flush of enrolments had been largely dissipated in air fares and postage, expended in the initial efforts to establish branches and maintain contact with them. Napro printed handbills for some of its candidates. By the time the campaign was in full swing, our field teams could find no trace of the branches supposed to have been set up in various centres. The report on

Napro and Pangu in Central District is typical. Their candidates financed their own campaigns. The parties provided no organisational support for these candidates within the electorates. Neither party had any branches or any grass-roots membership outside Port Moresby. As candidates generally preferred not to be identified with their parties, it is not surprising if most voters were aware of the latter only by hearsay.

Indeed, the field chapters record general ignorance and confusion about the subject, and confirm that parties played little direct part in the campaign. In Milne Bay, political parties were universally misunderstood. In Bougainville, few candidates mentioned parties in their talks, or claimed to have seen any signs of party activity; villagers rarely knew much about political parties; there was no indication that parties would be a factor in voting; Pangu had become topical by being inextricably confused with cargoism, opposition to C.R.A., and the charismatic *persona* of Lapun. In Kabwum, most respondents were confused, even irritated, by discussion of parties—and did not associate them with Voutas. In Madang, parties played no part in the campaign, even though two parties were supposed to be sponsoring candidates. In the Western Highlands, after the briefing session organised by the District Commissioner in Mt Hagen, prominent councillors gained the impression that all parties were subversive and Pangu particularly so.

Thus, although a number of 'radical' party candidates were elected; although the parties were organisationally weak and not directly 'visible' at the grass-roots; although the electors had little precise knowledge about them—yet 'political parties' were the subject of widespread debate and considerable apprehension. Repeated denunciation by the 'anti-party party' had given the term, if not its meaning, general currency, and associated it with quicker constitutional change, opposition to government policy, and disruption. 'Parties' had acquired a real, if intangible, presence in the election. This presence had been strengthened by the efforts of candidates (more than of party organisations) to induce electors to think of themselves, or of other candidates, as members or non-members of a 'party'. Both party candidates and their opponents had stimulated many voters to think more seriously about party politics than they might otherwise have done—indeed, to think beyond the man, and his 'primordial attachments' in an area, to what he stood for. The nature of the process is illustrated by the stereotype created by the opposition to Pangu, which capitalised on widespread fears: of urban—especially Papuan—leadership; of an educated town élite; of radical constitutional change; and of anti-government agitation. It was, among other things, because they could see few local signs of their existence that many prominent Papuans and New Guineans believed the parties, especially Pangu, to be well organised in other parts of the Territory, notably in Papua. In places like South Bougainville the vagueness of Pangu's local organisation, the confusion of traditional ties, cargoism and orthodox policies through which its supporters were mobilised, and the rumours circulated by friends and enemies alike, gave the party a disturbing, uncertain image that may have been different only in degree from the dim way in which parties in general were perceived in other remote areas.

It would seem that the debate over parties, and the parties' own activities, had made most Papuans and New Guineans at least distantly aware of the existence of party politics, while confirming a general mistrust of party aims and activities. While the fate of the parties as organisations held little early promise for them as integrators of Territory politics, their very existence, and the wide diffusion of the anti-party syndrome (as of the anti-self-government and dependency syndromes), represented significant changes from the politics of 1964. The significance of the latter change lay in the speed with which an integration of political ideas, if not of organisation, could be generated throughout the Territory, given the appropriate type of appeal and a voice of sufficient authority. It was a crucial fact of Papua and New Guinea politics to 1968 that except over very restricted areas no political voice had yet been heard which could rival that of the Administration.

As already suggested, the only other associations conceivably capable in 1968 of contributing to political action at a level above the individual electorate or District were the Christian denominations —once the Administration's clarification of the law had ruled out the possibility of a 'local government party'. Earlier in this chapter we have summarised the field evidence on the subtle and varied nature of mission involvement in the political process. This does not support any simple notion of a mission interest acting in a co-ordinated way on anything like a Territory-wide basis, denominationally or inter-denominationally. Of course, those in charge of individual missions have long been involved in local politics—as when agitating for royalties for the Nasioi in the C.R.A. dispute, and pressing for higher Administration subsidies for mission schools and teachers. These activities would put the missions in the category of separate, sometimes rival, 'pressure groups', in various parts of the Territory. It was too early to say whether mission organisations or denominational groups would ever become political movements with a potentiality for contributing to the integration of politics in the Territory as a whole.

The range of political horizons

So far we have been dealing with various forms of political organisation as possible indicators of political integration. We now examine the range of political information at the disposal of candidates and electors generally, and the extent of their political horizons.

Attention has already been drawn to the wide spectrum of economic development, literacy levels, and political awareness to be found in each of our areas of study. As pointed out in chapter 3, there is not only a gradation from the educated workers in the townships and government stations to the non-literate subsistence gardeners in the hinterland, but also the usual tendency, not without its exceptions in the Territory, for younger people generally to be more receptive to change and older people on the whole to be more tradition-bound. Even among the election candidates there were wide variations in intellectual horizons although as a whole their acquaintance with the world beyond the village was well above the Territory average.

Nevertheless, the general picture presented by the foregoing chapters is of a vast majority—of both electors and candidates—whose horizons did not yet extend beyond their own local government council area, or electorate, or at most the District. The people were often unfamiliar with the working of the governmental system outside these limits. Among the 'alliances' in the Madang District, no team anticipated serving any interest wider than that of the District, each promising that, if returned to the House, it would voice the District's needs as a united pressure group. In the Central District, candidates without exception promised nothing but 'parochial good works'. The exception that proved the rule was in the Western Highlands, where Iambakey made what was, for an indigenous candidate, unprecedented play with the United Nations and overseas markets, to argue the need for an indigenous rather than an expatriate voice in international councils.

Furthermore, as in the first reactions to political parties, there was more suspicion of other parts of the Territory, than belief in sharing a common destiny. For Milne Bay electors, the idea of independence was associated with fears of an Armageddon between Papuans and New Guineans. Paul Lapun's unusually well-informed agent in Kieta, 'Matthew', saw Pangu's 'unity' plans as welding together the islands and mainland parts of the New Guinea Territory, separately from Papua; while many of his fellow islanders thought Bougainville's future lay with the British Solomons and not with the 'Australian' territories at all. The Tolai were worried about being mulcted to subsidise development in Papua. Yali was acclaimed when he said that if he were elected Papua could remain with Australia, but he would see to it that New Guinea got immediate self-government with himself as king. In the Central District, almost the only policies offered by candidates for the nation as a whole were 'vague and innocuous pieties, . . . unexceptionable but uninformative'. The exceptions were topics like self-government, or the need to give Papuans and New Guineans a greater say in decisions affecting them, or the obligation to reserve for them a fair share of the developing economy: such themes created unease rather than enthusiasm.

Consistent with these restricted horizons is the ignorance of the voters about the functions of the House of Assembly and the potential political purposes of the election. The government, the House of Assembly, and the upshot of the election, seemed remote from the practical concerns of the bulk of ordinary people. This is something different in quality from the now well-known inability of many electors in industrialised countries to score highly on questionnaires about the identity of their member, the political party programs, the procedures of the legislature, or the contents of the constitution. Most of them have a shrewd idea that elections are contests for governmental power, and that the resulting legislative majority makes a predictable difference to some of the things which will be done with that power. Thanks to the press and broadcasting they also have some picture of the relations—and differences—between the ordinary elected representative and the members of the government. The situation in many parts of New Guinea may be visualised from the description in chapter 3, of how isolated villagers allowed their councillors to do their election thinking for them because their acknowledged task was to mediate between the people and all aspects of the world outside—particularly anything to do with the government.

This would seem to be primarily the result of the underdeveloped state of communications of all kinds throughout the Territory, combined with the low levels of education and literacy that limited the impact of what communications there were. There were no regular channels for disseminating accurate reports of House activity to villagers. In any case, as indicated in several chapters, printed media were scarce and few people over 25 could have taken advantage of them.

During the four years since the first House of Assembly election, neither the members nor the Administration had succeeded in raising appreciably the level of electors' understanding of the new political institutions. All the area reports mention the general failure of sitting Members to visit the whole of their electorates, and the ineffectiveness of the Administration's attempts at mass political education. If electors were better informed on the mechanics of voting ('electoral education'), this was probably because the efforts of the Administration could here be relevantly supplemented by practice in local government council elections and by the help of councillors and candidates themselves, such as it was.

The intentions of the political and electoral education programs as planned at Port Moresby are outlined in chapter 1, but not even the intentions were manifest to some of our research workers in the field. To the Bougainville team, political education in south Bougainville never consisted of more than local government council activity on the one hand, and the crash course immediately preceding the *1964* election on the other, and there appeared to be no consistent follow-up effort to expand villagers' extremely limited understanding of the House. To the New Britain team, it seemed that the Administration had largely confined its political education programs to the mechanics of voting. To some other teams, it appeared that political education was a task of distributing leaflets, entrusted to local government councils but often stopping short at that point.

Where attempts at political education were more visible, they seemed to assume that candidates and councillors would bear much of the burden. In Esa'ala, the pre-electoral patrols by Administration officers had little impact, owing to other duties and staff shortages, and they were unable to reach a majority of the villagers. Government pamphlets assumed a higher level of political comprehension than was general in the D'Entrecasteaux, but had not reached the villages. The candidates were the most important source of political education; and local government councillors were the main channels for diffusing this information to the many unable to hear the candidates for themselves. On the north-east coast, Administration officers were not sent to instruct the people in voting. Neither the councillors nor the perfunctory distribution of leaflets served as an efficient medium of political education. Radio broadcasts reached only a limited audience. Political education was sometimes confused with other issues. In the Western Highlands, the Administration mingled the alphabet of politics with the official ideology of economic development before self-government. The use of the local government council and the sitting member as instruments of political education increased the significance of the council and entrenched the sitting member's identification with the Administration. Talks about the House of Assembly during council elections confused the two in some electors' minds.

Some aspects of 'electoral education' also seemed to be delegated to candidates and councillors. In south Bougainville, the efforts of Administration patrols were unsuccessful among Nasioi. The Administration apparently expected Buin speakers to learn through local government councillors; officers made no special patrols. Generally, the candidates seem to have provided the most effective electoral education. On the north-east coast, most candidates usually began their campaign speeches with electoral information. In the Central Regional, Oala's policy speeches among his own people were often devoted to explaining the electoral boundaries and the differences between Regional and Open electorates, identifying the candidates and discussing electoral procedures. These were the items generally figuring in candidates' efforts at electoral education, and the Milne Bay, Bougainville, New Britain, and north-east coast chapters all specifically report that very few of the electors interviewed retained much reliable information on the first three items. However, in complying with the formal procedures for casting their ballots, the voters of Papua and New Guinea performed efficiently on the whole.

Expectations: from the M.H.A., the House, and the election

To the articulate indigenous voters in the Territory the failure, as political educators, of the elected members of the first House was more serious than that of the Administration's programs. Many of them were hardly aware of the latter's existence, whereas they believed that one of the member's primary functions should be, as with the councillor at the local level, not only to convey their wants and 'worries' to the government, but to bring them information about the government's decisions and doings at the centre, and about their own activities there as members. In all areas the complaint was heard that since 1964 most elected members had not only failed to keep their constituents informed, but had not even been seen by the majority of them. This disappointment was expressed about many members who were popular enough to be given a second chance in 1968, such as Lepani Watson, Paul Lapun, ToLiman, and Kaibelt, as well as about those rejected, such as Stuntz, Stoi, and Levy.

In addition to failing to keep them informed, many members of the first House had failed to live up to two other expectations of the people about the behaviour of a model representative.

One of these was that the M.H.A.'s prime role should be to further the interests of his electorate, and to this end should be that of intermediary between the Administration in Port Moresby and the local people. During the 1967-8 campaign this view was strikingly illustrated by a common reaction to the experience of being represented by men like Lepani Watson and Matthias ToLiman, who had been singled out by the Administration to be Parliamentary Under-Secretaries in the first House. The former constituents of such men repeatedly asked candidates to promise that if elected in 1968 they would not become whatever was to be the equivalent of an Under-Secretary in the new House. Constituents did not see it as either an honour or an advantage for their member to be diverted from his proper function as messenger between themselves and Port Moresby, to be drawn into the inscrutable activities of the Administration and perhaps become merely a government puppet. It meant nothing to them that he might thus occupy one of the few positions in the central government that could afford an indigenous representative the opportunity of some little participation in real political power. Perhaps they had not yet envisaged the possibility of indigenes sharing in such power. Perhaps they had some inkling of how little power, for their purposes, these positions really carried.

An example of the other expectation was the image projected by Epineri Titimur, of the ordinary villager who knew the difficulties and worries that confronted people in their daily lives—one who talked out about the problems facing the community as a whole, and not simply his own. This was the kind of member that many voters felt they had all too rarely secured in 1964. As a typical Tolai voter said:

> See, at the last election the candidates said all sorts of fine things, made all sorts of promises, but they forgot all about them when they got to the House. They were concerned only with their own salaries, and the style of life this made possible, and they ceased to think about the people who sent them there (p. 73).

Rarupu's inactivity in the first House of Assembly had so disappointed his electors that he mustered only 600 votes in 1968. The reaction reported from the Western Highlands (though one not confined to that region) took a more cynical form: 'Hearsay about the Members' performance in Port Moresby was consistently damaging to their reputations but confirmed the impression constituents had from their sudden accession to affluence that the job was an enviable one.'

A corollary of disappointment with the members was disillusionment about the House of Assembly itself, and several chapters testify to the mixture of ignorance, misconception, and hope deferred which was frequently expressed in this way. There was the Timbe elder who grumbled to the field officer on a political education patrol in 1967 that his people did not want a new election: they could not afford to pay for another 'member man' like Stoi. There was the other Kabwum man who remarked: 'Before we had an election and we got nothing. Now we are voting again. If nothing happens this time, we won't have any more elections.' There were the groups in Madang (and elsewhere) who did not vote because of apathy and poor communications:

> Some had lost interest in the electoral process, which previously they had associated with cargoism or general material expectations. After 1964, there were no widespread, startling results. Only a few groups got any of the tangible benefits expected from the House of Assembly or even saw their representatives (p. 194).

And there were the many people in West New Britain who, if they knew they had a member, felt that he had done nothing for them and held few expectations of gaining anything by voting again (p. 50).

From this picture of disappointed expectations about the House of Assembly and its members we may begin to reconstruct, with the help of further observations in 1968, some conception of what candidates and electors may still have been expecting from the second election.

As to the candidates, it seems that goals ranging beyond personal ambition or beyond furthering the interests of particular electorates or Districts were rarely specific, though many candidates expressed some general emotional concern for the future of the Territory as a whole. There is no way of saying precisely how many were 'party' candidates, but in the whole Territory the number of those who most clearly acknowledged membership and were claimed by the parties was about sixty, half of these being Pangu members. It is equally difficult to say what proportion of these candidates nurtured as serious (i.e. conceivably attainable) aims the policies of 'national' import listed in the respective party platforms or in their own handbills (often copied from the party documents without the party name). It is even harder to guess at the relative strength in these cases of the candidates' public and private goals—'to separate reality from rationalisation' (p. 291). There are similar uncertainties about those non-party candidates—mostly Europeans like the 'progressive' Chatterton or the 'conservative' Stuntz—whose motives did seem to include sincere concern, favourable or otherwise, about self-government, or about the relations between the two territories, or the status of the races. But it does look as though such issues were genuine and meaningful to only a small proportion of the 484 candidates in the 1968 election as a whole. Otherwise, when impersonal motives were attributed to candidates at all in the field chapters, they took such forms as 'finding an acceptable channel to express the needs of his people' (p. 108) and 'serving the Port Moresby community' (p. 285).

Personal motives are mentioned much more frequently in these chapters than impersonal ones. They range from Taurega's impulsive pique at Watson's insinuations, to the pursuit of further status (p. 291). Elliott Elijah's reason for standing appears to combine a question of principle (free expression) with concern for an occupational interest group (the public service); if this deduction is correct, the case is unique among our field studies. The Western Highlands opinion again sounds a severely practical note, characterising membership of the House simply as 'the plum post available to ambitious local men'. This must indeed be a very important consideration in most areas, since membership of the second House carried, along with its unrivalled status, a salary of at least $3000 *plus* electorate and travel allowances, and the probability of trips at government expense to Australia and perhaps abroad.

What evidence we have about the candidates, therefore, suggests that very few saw the 1968 election as a possible opportunity for the pursuit of objectives with other than local or personal significance.

What expectations led the electors themselves—or over 60 per cent of those enrolled—to take part in the electoral process? There appeared to be a spectrum of relevant motives. Many people in remoter areas still thought it a matter of group prestige, if not an order of the Administration, to appear in strength for the ritual of balloting. At the other extreme were groups like those in east New Britain who feared to vote lest it somehow make them more vulnerable to incorporation in a local government council.

However, the commonest interpretation of voter attitudes in the field studies refers to their concern with economic development as a highly desired goal, but one only to be pursued effectively with the material aid and under the continued tutelage of the Australian Administration. The strength of this concern may be measured by the apparent anxiety of most electors everywhere to postpone all talk of self-government and independence, because of their association with the end of Australian administration and the departure of Europeans from the Territory. For many the prospect was frightening. Even Yali modified his program of early emancipation for New Guinea, realising the electors' hostility to immediate self-government. More timid spirits had long since prudently avoided these subjects, knowing the voters' fears.

In the context of such a widespread syndrome of dependency on the Administration, it is possible to picture a majority of the electors still vaguely associating the House of Assembly, and therefore participation in the election, with the enhancement of the Administration's development effort in the District concerned. Here is a typical statement:

> Economic development ... set the tone of most village discussions of the roles of the House of Assembly, the local government council, co-operatives, Administration agencies, incumbent and prospective members, and even the election process itself ... Interest in and knowledge of the House of Assembly did not seem to extend beyond its potential contribution to the material advancement of community and region, which, in the people's view, was or should be the chief business of local and national government (p. 208).

A view which would presumably be shared by most Australian voters.

DIFFUSION, ASSIMILATION, AND CHANGE

We should now be in a position to draw some general conclusions from the preceding analysis. Under the heading of 'diffusion', we turn to the apparent aims of the Australian government in establishing the House of Assembly and conducting the elections of 1964 and 1968, and the problems of implementing them in the circumstances of New Guinea. Under 'assimilation', we examine the ways in which these Australian procedures seem to have been modified by local factors; how far they were used to serve local, as distinct from Australian, purposes; and the extent to which they had been 'legitimised' among Papuans and New Guineans. We conclude by asking what indications of political change emerged from the study.

Diffusion

Although it is not possible to examine the motivations behind Australian policy, four overt aims can be identified from numerous official statements: transplanting the Westminster system; maintaining a role of neutrality in internal New Guinea politics; administering the election process efficiently and impartially; and demonstrating to the outside world its strenuous efforts to advance the Territory politically, in this case by eliciting popular interest and participation in the general elections.

It may be noted in passing that some of these aims were not entirely consistent with each other. For example, it is difficult to reconcile 'neutrality' with the imposition of one particular form of government, while the Australian canons of electoral rectitude did not always conduce to indigenous identification with or enjoyment of the process. Administrative action, also, was not always consistent with the individual aims. Most exponents of the Westminster system on its native ground would regard strong and stable political parties as an essential ingredient. An attempt to establish that system might therefore call for encouragement, rather than official disparagement of political parties, of which examples have been given in previous chapters.

Considering the fate, however, of attempts to leave behind some version of the Westminster principles in other former British colonies, there would seem to be more fundamental difficulties. A historical approach to these might be fruitful. The process whereby the present parliamentary system evolved in Britain and Australia has been reversed in terminal colonial situations like that of New Guinea. In Britain the process of 'nation-building' and the winning of political power from the monarch by Ministers in Parliament preceded the grant of popular suffrage. The Australian colonies obtained self-government before manhood suffrage was established. In both cases, therefore, popular elections immediately involved the ordinary voter in a contest between candidates for real political power. This was a tangible incentive for parties to be formed to organise the vote, and for citizens to take part in elections: these could change the government, which in turn could not ignore majority opinion in the legislature.

In New Guinea in 1968, popular elections on a universal franchise had been established, but those elected could not change the government and few believed they could even influence the Australian Administration against the latter's will. This was partly inherent in the colonial situation. It was partly due to the gap in communications between electors in the village and government in Port Moresby, and to the social and economic distance between the New Guinea villager and, say, the Australian elector. On the evidence of the present study, neither the colonial framework nor the width of these gaps had changed sufficiently since 1964 to lower appreciably the sense of dependence of most elected members. Our predecessors concluded about those of 1964: 'The representative goes to Port Moresby to get wealth, not to be the instrument or maker of national policy' (Bettison et al. 1965: 514). In 1968 it still seemed that up to this time 'they had seen themselves as apprentice politicians rather than as parliamentarians elected to govern the country: government and Administration were identical' (pp. 222-3).

This is not a criticism of the establishment of an elected House of Assembly, but a reminder that elections were taking place in New Guinea under conditions fundamentally different from those in which the Westminster system works in Britain or Australia. It is this unavoidable fact which threw doubt upon any assumption that the Westminster system was being planted in Papua and New Guinea.

Indications of the goal of 'neutrality' included official exhortations to those conducting the political and electoral education programs as well as the election itself, and intermittent drives to forestall any tendencies to 'political involvement' on the part of government employees. This reflected a belief that colonial administration can be politically neutral because it is government by public servants.

The very fact that the Administration was the government compromised its political neutrality in the legislature and the country, though not necessarily its technical neutrality in the conduct of the elections. As Cecil Abel, the Member elected in 1968 for Milne Bay Regional, said a year later:

> We have had a political party in the House of Assembly for five years. It has leadership, a clear cut policy, is highly organized and is disciplined, all the hallmarks of a party. That's the Administration party. It's a fact of life. (*South Pacific Post,* 31 March 1969)

It was a paradox of the colonial structure that this government 'party's' performance and plans were not put at stake in the general election. It was dominant but electorally immune. However, it was obliged to play a committed political role precisely because of its 'clear cut policy', which was included in many a Ministerial statement over a decade or more:

> Before self-government can be effective in a country as primitive socially and as undeveloped economically as Papua and New Guinea is at present, considerable social changes and economic progress will be required. These changes can only be brought about by major efforts by the Australian Government. (Hasluck 1960)

That policy, consistently followed, led the Administration to attempt to retain control of the House of Assembly and of political activity in the Territory at large, lest any local initiative to substitute other priorities should hinder the 'major efforts of the Australian government' to promote social and economic development in its own way. Chapter 1 describes how the government had retained its veto power over the House of Assembly, and omitted the four most important portfolios when first creating Ministerial Memberships. Chapter 6 describes how the Administration worked to maintain a politically loyal bloc of Highland members in the first House.

What is questioned here, again, is not the government's view of its responsibilities, but the fiction that any final governmental responsibility can be compatible with political neutrality.

Neither candidates nor electors were under any illusions about this in 1968. Kabwum electors described Stoi as a 'child of the Patrol Officers', and such statements implied condemnation of the Administration. Minj electors alleged that their M.H.A., Kaibelt, was merely a *boi bilong Tom Ellis,* though this implied no criticism: the District Commissioner and his officers were 'real men' who could be expected to manipulate any fools who proved useful to them. Expatriate electors took it for granted that the same District Commissioner would 'stop at nothing' to get Keith Levy re-elected.

The area chapters contain a number of examples of Administration officers being directly involved in the politics of the election itself—sometimes involuntarily. These include influencing some individuals to become candidates, and dissuading others; advising some candidates on their campaign, and allegedly influencing electors for or against others. On the whole, the motives were assumed by informants to be well-meaning: encouraging some 'backward' group to participate, discouraging another from splitting its vote. Occasionally the interventions were seen as moves in a power game. Even the well-meant enlistment of a diffident new candidate might threaten the chances of an established politician, as ToLiman's might have been threatened by a switch of Bainings votes to Mualat. In addition, there were the attempts of field officers in several of our electorates to persuade migrant workers in the towns to enrol in their current place of residence, rather than in their 'home areas', even though that right had been deliberately retained in the Ordinance on the recommendation of the Select Committee. Most of these acts were contrary to headquarters policy; that they were often the work of more conscientious officers is a measure of the unreality of a search for neutrality.

Considering the circumstances, the conduct of the 1968 election, like that in 1964, was successful and on the whole efficient. The circumstances, however, necessarily made the operation less precise than in Australia, although the system is based on Australian models. As in some African and Asian countries, it is impossible to compile a reasonably accurate and up-to-date electoral roll. The people's habit of changing their names means that many cannot be found on the roll at election time. This problem is multiplied by allowing people living away from their original homes to enrol in their former home area; large proportions of migrant workers in the towns availed themselves of the privilege, but after long absence, many had no notion of the distant candidates 'at home', and thousands were disfranchised by the impossibility of reconciling the names under which they voted with those inscribed on the roll at the time of registration.

Voting was not compulsory, and turn-out in many areas fell below the 1964 level, partly, it seemed, because more people were aware of this, and partly from a general decline of interest. Reaching a polling place in the hinterland could often be difficult both for the mobile polling patrols and for voters, owing to the terrain and to holding the election at an unsuitable time of year. Non-voting and informal voting were sometimes deliberate—for example in non-council areas from fear that voting might somehow subject the people to an unwanted council, or in other areas to avoid voting for a European. Some may still have been due to misconceptions about, or even a refusal to recognise, the distinction between Open and Regional electorates. Paradoxically, informal voting tended to be higher in more literate areas, through more people thinking (mistakenly) that they could dispense with the 'whispering ballot'.

Some observers have criticised the whisper ballot as open to manipulation (e.g. Bettison et al. 1965: 235, 405-6, 507; van der Veur 1966: 61-2). The field chapters indicate that chicanery was rare, as in 1964, but the use of optional preferences varied widely in different places, partly because polling officers followed no standard practice in reminding voters of this option or in giving them opportunity to record additional preferences. Indeed, but for the preferential system it would be possible to replace the whisper ballot by some less chancy method for the non-literate majority to record their votes. Photographs could be significant—but sometimes misleading—in identifying candidates; and the lack of a candidate's photograph at the polling booth might handicap him severely. Ignorance of the mechanics of the preferential system was probably not much greater than in Australia—but there the deficiency is supplied by political party 'how-to-vote' cards. The system has been defended for New Guinea as against 'first-past-the-post', which offers no means of offsetting the advantage of a candidate supported by the largest descent group in his electorate, however small his proportion of the total vote. If the preferential system were retained for this or other reasons, most of the vagaries of the whisper ballot would have to be endured until increasing literacy removed the need for it.

Despite these problems, Papuans and New Guineans on the whole have readily acquired the techniques for going through the formal act of registering a valid vote—or have shown that they can acquire them with the help of appropriate drill or training. But as this in itself is a purely mechanical process which can also involve arduous journeys, more electors may lose interest in it unless it offers more tangible results than in the past.

If the Administration wished to elicit popular interest and participation, its perfunctory approach to political education between 1964 and 1968 is hard to explain. Don Barrett, the unsuccessful candidate for East and West New Britain Regional, who had been chairman of the Public Accounts Committee in the first House, pointed out at the end of the election that in the budget year 1966-7 the Department of District Administration had not fully spent its modest allocation of funds for political education. This does not mean that there are, in fact, obvious techniques for political enlightenment which only require more money and manpower for their success.

Be that as it may, instead of 'interest' and 'participation' the words most frequently characterising voter reaction as a whole in the area reports are 'concern', 'bewilderment', and 'disillusionment'. We have mentioned the vague hopes that the election might in some indirect way lead to further or faster economic development. But there was a conspicuous lack of hard debate about any specific aspect or policy of development beyond individual electorates. For example, we have no record of either the economic or the political implications of C.R.A. ever being mentioned outside Bougainville.

It can be noted that the shortfall from this aim of the Administration, even as compared with 1964, gives cause for concern in the Chief Electoral Officer's Report on the 1968 election. He concludes: 'If steps are not taken to alleviate the present situation I have no hesitation in prognosticating a further drop in voting percentages in 1972' (*Report* 1968: 31).

Assimilation

The functions of the elected member, hence the criteria for choosing him, and hence the function of the election, are not seen in the same ways in the Territory as in Australia. Entering into these different perceptions are some 'traditional' elements, and many others which reflect the contact and colonial situation.

Upon the functions of the M.H.A. there appeared in 1968 to be a range of views. Only a small minority saw the position as a vantage point from which to criticise and exert organised pressure upon the Administration to change its policies. Fewer still then saw the House of Assembly as a conceivable matrix for a future independent government. A number of candidates valued membership for its material advantages—as stepping stone or climax to a *bisnis* career. But the member did not seem to be regarded as a new kind of political leader in the local community. He had not replaced—perhaps not even rivalled—the *kiap,* the councillor, the pastor, or the 'big man', as the case might be. His role was most often viewed as complementary to that of the local government councillor, as an intermediary between the community and the Administration. The councillor of course has other functions as well—and perhaps a few members had acquired some of these, such as holding informal 'courts' at the local level. In the election, it was the effective delegate and *rapporteur* who was valued, not the power-seeker.

Correspondingly, the criteria and methods that prevailed in the election contest were different from those in an industrialised country under the Westminster system, but there were indications of change. Personality, moral virtues, proved readiness to 'speak for the people', were more important than policy or program, clashes of interest, or competition between organised groups such as parties. Support was drawn both from customary and from newer kinds of political resource, with signs of the balance shifting in favour of the latter. Not many candidates in our research areas seemed able to exploit a personal position in some traditional institution, as Yangalyo used his in respect of the *tei* ritual. Nor do we have many instances of support being mobilised through practices like the mud-slinging contest in Wahgi. Many groups of Highland men assumed that their womenfolk would vote as instructed. A few older men compared Lapun to a traditional 'chief' who ought to be re-elected for life. Cargoist supporters of Lapun and Yali tried to influence voters by invoking arcane, superhuman forces and sometimes making fictitious threats in the name of the Administration; we do not have similar reports from other areas. Pre-selection by group consensus, and the treatment of polling as a ritual appropriate to dealings with the government, were probably quite widespread in areas of more recent contact and in less accessible areas generally. Educated young aspirants in the Western Highlands Regional were at first discounted as *mankis* by local 'big men', who nevertheless later supported them as the only available indigenous candidates from their areas. A number of youthful candidates were elected in the Gazelle and elsewhere. Tammur was apparently typical in presenting himself, not as an iconoclastic 'new man', but as a broker between the generations.

Group support mingled kinship and locality ties with the larger solidarities evolving from expanding communications, mission loyalties, and local government councils. The difference from Australia here was that these were demographic or geographically bounded groups, not stratified groups based on class, occupation, or status, spreading over the whole country, and represented by country-wide political parties. This, and the fact that the New Guinea support groups were rarely even electorate-wide, caused campaigning methods to be based on the individual personality—getting one's identity known through the village meeting, or its European version the McCarthy 'cocktail circuit', or merely by scattering one's name and photograph over the landscape.

Thus there were many attempts to adapt familiar social structures and practices, as well as new or evolving institutions, to the formal operation of the electoral system introduced from Australia. But it seemed in 1968 that that system had not been generally accepted as an instrument for furthering the purposes of the local societies. Some groups by their actions seemed to be deliberately rejecting the election. Usually these were dissident minorities, like Yali's audience at Bom who applauded his proposal for an end to periodic elections and the installation of himself as King of New Guinea. Similar groups refused to vote, or asserted their intention to vote informally, like the cargoists in south Bougainville who were told by their leader to vote for Lapun in both the Open and Regional, or those who insisted on voting for Yali, the Rai Coast candidate, in Mabuso. In the non-council or anti-council villages on the Gazelle, the people saw no useful connection between participation in House of Assembly or council elections and their own problems as they diagnosed them. However, in that same 'advanced' Gazelle region, at least around Rabaul, there were few indications that the election had generated a great deal of enthusiasm among the Tolai. The public mood remained elusive, but suggested at times 'a somewhat tired scepticism'.

It seemed that to the voters at large the election would not make any foreseeable difference to the welfare of any major group. On the other hand, it did not appear to compete or conflict directly with any existing institution. It was additional, extraneous, and in some areas time-consuming. The Administration's 'model' of the electoral and legislative processes differed from what can reasonably be called a typical indigenous model of political life. The former postulated a superordinate central authority, linking the small traditional political communities into a power system exceeding their previous conceptions. It cast the elected member in a specialised role for a specified time, whereas traditional leadership was more generalised and its tenure depended more on intrinsic performance. The differentiation of the elective process (for appointing legislators) from other modes of recruitment (of the church, the judiciary, or the police) contrasted with the integrated criteria and methods for filling indigenous positions of responsibility. The secret ballot was strikingly different from traditional modes of collective decision-making, where the individual's influence was overt, and varied with his personal and ritual status. All this made the Administration's model more unreal and less interesting to indigenous electors. But we have no evidence that differences between the models prevented indigenous politics and general elections from operating side by side.

Summarising to this point, it appears that neither the legislative, representative, nor electoral aspects of the Westminster system had been substantially diffused or assimilated among Papuans and New Guineans between 1964 and 1968. They were simply accepted as part of the pattern of dependence on Australian power and expertise. On the other hand, the electoral process both revealed and helped to generate impulses toward political change not necessarily connected with the Westminster system at all. Such as they were, they pointed away from dependence and toward autonomy.

Change

The main study of the first House of Assembly election ended with the sentence: 'Papua-New Guinea is still in that stage of colonial history in which a junior partnership is not only accepted but actively sought, and the 1964 elections are likely to remain unusual in many respects' (Bettison *et al.* 1965: 517). Yet on comparing the Conclusions of that book with the foregoing pages, one sees more similarities than differences. The concepts of the role and desirable qualities of the M.H.A.; the limitations of most electors' political horizons, knowledge of, and interest in the election; the undeveloped condition of 'national' politics—all these and many other elements show very little movement from 1964 to 1968. The 1964 election may have been unusual, but it was not to remain unique.

A variety of factors was still inhibiting political evolution in 1968. We have noted the powerful influence of the Administration; the 'dependency syndrome'; the 'anti-party syndrome'; the low levels of literacy, education, and economic development despite improvements from even lower levels; the almost complete dearth of a self-conscious political élite; and the lack of a 'vigorous associational life'.

On the other hand, there was no evidence of any purposeful attempts by Papuans and New Guineans, except in some forms of cargo cult, to resist social or political change as such. While some candidates urged the preservation of long-established institutions alongside the new, none proposed to reject any development towards an industrial society, provided there was prospect of an indigenous stake in it. Where an apparent political conservatism fended off talk of self-government and independence, this was based not on a desire to protect any traditional *status quo* but on the fear of inhibiting economic change. In fact, if signs of political evolution in 1968 were few, they were not negligible, and they seemed to signal the emergence of new relationships with the colonial power, diverging from the main patterns prevailing since European contact began.

Of these, the pattern associated with initial contact and 'pacification'—but often continuing to overlap or interweave with subtler relations developed later—was one of dominance and submission. Where European religious values, economic interests, or administrative arrangements were incompatible with local custom, the power of the colonial rulers necessarily prevailed. Indigenous leaders had not the resources to compete with it and, realistically, did not usually try to organise any direct political confrontation. People welcomed the protection it enforced from physical attack by their enemies while resenting the loss of autonomy it entailed. The dilemmas of this relationship help to account for the present-day ambivalence towards Europeans noted so widely in the area chapters. In addition, by establishing unified control of areas many times greater than the largest of the indigenous political units, the first colonial administrations created (as it were in a political vacuum), and immediately occupied, a new arena from which autonomous local political leadership was automatically excluded. The Australian government, as heir to this power, imposed its own forms of political leadership and proceeded to make all crucial decisions for the Papuan and New Guinean societies it ruled, including decisions to introduce new political structures.

But almost from the beginning, the activities of European missions, planters, and administrators were interacting in a more complex and less one-sided way with the local culture. Indigenous values were modified, on the ethical side; on the material side, their emphasis on economic wellbeing widened to embrace European goods and services, which fostered an ardent pursuit of the practical means of obtaining them. For the sake of these new interests most people were able to suppress the animosities and political resentments associated with colour. On the whole they accepted Australian tutelage, partly in the hope of tangible benefits and partly because they had no alternative. After 1950, this acceptance was strengthened by the more positive developmental activities of Australian governments, themselves under pressure from external forces of change.

In this way politics for Papuans and New Guineans became a matter of accommodation, mediation, and administration. As Australian influence spread or intensified, people wished to understand what improvement of their condition it promised; they needed intermediaries to make the government's demands and their own mutually intelligible; and they were induced to take part in the application of its policies, if only by way of helping to build roads or playing the modest roles of *luluai*s, constables, and councillors. Where new public functions required governmental structures, the Australian Administration had the initiative in designing them, if only because (as shown in chapter 1) indigenous political structures and the earlier indirect forms of 'native administration' were equally unable to cope with these functions, or to provide a stock on which appropriate structures could be grafted. Paternalistic colonial politics and development administration called for larger units and novel techniques. So there appeared in turn the central bureaucracy, the local government council, the new Legislative Council, the House of Assembly, and the Parliamentary Under-Secretary. But since these structures were serving functions mostly different from those of indigenous political, social, and economic institutions, many of the latter could continue side by side with the new ones and, as we have also seen, could be drawn upon as resources in helping to work the new mechanisms. These were the basic patterns which still prevailed at the time of the 1968 election.

At the same time, however, there were unintended consequences of culture contact, colonial rule and development programs which gave rise to social stresses—normally the activators of political change. The election narratives show how and where some of those stresses were brought to the surface during the campaign: in Bougainville the resentments over C.R.A. and apparent neglect of indigenous development; on the Gazelle Peninsula the effects of population explosion, shortage of land and urban employment, and disappointment with the Administration's record; along the Madang coast, the anxieties reflected in cargoism and the concern over the Highland Highway's check to trade; in several places an emerging sense of competition with expatriates for economic resources, markets, and jobs. By 1968, formal schooling had begun to produce a generation which could articulate some of these discontents and perhaps cradle a political élite able and willing to make new uses of the structures introduced by the Australians. Indeed, the elections themselves had fostered some political changes, for example, by inducing people to act in larger groupings, by calling political parties into being, and by stimulating thought about the country's future and its relations with Australia. The changing social and economic climate had begun to lift some of the inhibitions on the tension inseparable from any situation of colour-dominance. (It is a common paradox that race consciousness blossoms precisely as discriminations are being recognised and removed.) In addition, many people seemed to have decided that in their current form, the introduced political structures —in particular the House of Assembly—were not fulfilling their expected roles, and this disillusion itself became part of the pattern of latent stresses behind the observed indicators of change. We conclude with a tentative list of these indicators.

First, the ubiquity of the anti-party and anti-self-government syndromes, at least among the better-informed minority, indicated a significant speed-up in the communication of political ideas. Helped by an increasing mobility of people within the country, and the emergence of a university student population, this acceleration in the circulation of ideas, though acting predominantly in a conservative direction in 1968, pointed to an unprecedented rate of political development if the content of the ideas should alter.

Second, what could transform their content was the increase in Western-style experience among indigenous politicians—which showed some growth in the tiny nucleus of a new kind of political leadership, drawing on a wider and more effective range of political resources than the exploitation of 'big man' skills and connections alone.

Third, the election marked a further stage in the evolution of new political groupings. Besides the larger solidarities based on local government units and denominational loyalties, already active in the 1964 election, there were more systematic inter-electorate alliances among candidates, and the rudiments of a number of political parties. True, the parties did not capture the support of ordinary voters, and it remained to be seen how long those which survived the election could last, under universal suffrage, without a popular following or the backing of 'party-generating associations' outside the legislature (cf. Hodgkin 1961: 47, cited in Bettison *et al.* 1965: 508).

Fourth, a more urgent question about the pattern of voter loyalties was raised by their 'limited horizons' and the lack of 'national' identity. The 1968 political parties, other than Pangu, could not transcend their District or region of origin, in terms of organisation or support. True, it was no part of their purpose to foster inter-regional suspicion or hostility. But their mere appearance on the scene (and Pangu was not exempt from this) helped to evoke reactions of that kind which must have been already latent. In chapter 1 we have noted how the scope and focus of people's loyalties shifted back and forth, but rarely embraced the Territory as a whole. In other chapters we have seen evidence of regional chauvinism in Bougainville, among the Tolai, and on the Rai Coast. These solidarities do not necessarily coincide with the 'primordial ties' of which Geertz warned in this connection (Geertz 1963: 105-57), but they are none the less significant for that: the divisive forces that have rent new states elsewhere have rarely worked along purely 'traditional' fault lines. If it was doubtful in 1968 whether New Guinea politics were evolving toward the Westminster system of responsible government, it was even more uncertain whether they were in transition towards one polity or many.

Finally—and especially in areas like Bougainville, the Gazelle Peninsula and the Madang coast where the tensions were stronger—people were being impelled to loosen at least the psychological bonds of dependence. Some groups deliberately rejected the election ritual —by abstention or informal voting. On the Gazelle, the sources of tension were openly discussed by voters and some candidates, even though it was not generally thought that the election itself could do anything to relieve them. In Milne Bay, Bougainville, and Morobe there was overt talk and some voting against Europeans as such, or their protégés, or the Administration and 'the old way of thinking'. In Milne Bay and on the Gazelle, some of the most 'radical' candidates who stood were elected. A latent scepticism about the blessings of 'Westminster'—whether in its colonial or post-colonial form—was becoming articulate. From Iambakey in the Western Highlands to Tammur in east New Britain, the spokesmen of change were feeling their way toward the politics of autonomy.

APPENDIX I

RESEARCH TEAMS AND PLANNING COMMITTEE

Milne Bay District
    Mr W. E. Tomasetti (Team leader) — Staff member, University of Papua and New Guinea
    Dr Olga Gostin — Research Assistant, Department of Anthropology and Sociology, Research School of Pacific Studies, A.N.U.
    Mr Michael Young — Postgraduate student, Department of Anthropology and Sociology, Research School of Pacific Studies, A.N.U.
    Mr Benjamin Toyola (Student observer) — Undergraduate student, University of Papua and New Guinea
    Mr John Noel (Student observer) — Undergraduate student, University of Papua and New Guinea

Bougainville District
    Dr Eugene Ogan (Team leader) — Associate Professor of Anthropology, University of Minnesota, Minneapolis, U.S.A.
    Mr Leo Laita (Student observer) — Undergraduate student, University of Papua and New Guinea
    Mr James Rutana (Student observer) — Undergraduate student, University of Papua and New Guinea

East and West New Britain District
    Dr A. L. Epstein (Team leader) — Professorial Fellow, Department of Anthropology and Sociology, Research School of Pacific Studies, A.N.U.
    Dr Ann Chowning — Senior Research Fellow, Department of Anthropology and Sociology, Research School of Pacific Studies, A.N.U.
    Dr T. S. Epstein — Visiting Fellow, Department of Economics, Research School of Pacific Studies, A.N.U.
    Dr Jane Goodale — Associate Professor of Anthropology, Bryn Mawr College, Massachusetts, U.S.A.

Mr Ian Grosart — Senior Lecturer, Department of Government, University of Sydney
Miss Susan Klein (Research Assistant) — Tutor and Postgraduate student, Department of Government, University of Sydney
Miss Judith Mahony (Research Assistant) — Postgraduate student, Department of Government, University of Sydney
Mrs S. Mueller (Research Assistant) — Postgraduate student, Department of Government, University of Sydney
Mr Ansgau Palauva (Student observer) — Undergraduate student, University of Papua and New Guinea

Madang District

Professor P. Lawrence (Team leader) — Professor of Anthropology and Sociology, University of Queensland
Dr Thomas Harding — Associate Professor of Anthropology, University of California, Santa Barbara, California, U.S.A.
Mr A. Jarman — Senior Lecturer in Political Science, Department of Government, University of Queensland
Miss Romola McSwain — Senior Demonstrator, Department of Anthropology and Sociology, University of Queensland
Mrs F. Lawrence (Research Assistant)
Mr P. McLaren (Research Assistant) — Postgraduate student, University of Sydney
Mr John C. Taylor (Research Assistant) — Postgraduate student, University of Queensland
Mr and Mrs H. Holzknecht (Research Assistants) — Undergraduate students, University of Queensland
Mr Kambau Namaleu (Student observer) — Undergraduate student, University of Papua and New Guinea

Western Highlands District

Dr Marie Reay (Team leader) — Senior Fellow, Department of Anthropology and Sociology, Research School of Pacific Studies, A.N.U.
Mr H. K. Colebatch — Tutor in Politics, School of Social Sciences, La Trobe University
Dr Andrew Strathern — Fellow of Trinity College, Cambridge
Mrs Peta Colebatch (Research Assistant) — Postgraduate student, Department of Politics, La Trobe University

Central District
> Professor M. C. Groves (Team leader) — Professor of Sociology, University of Singapore
> Mr R. M. S. Hamilton — Lecturer in Political Science, Department of Government, University of Queensland
> Dr Margaret McArthur — Lecturer in Social Anthropology, University of Sydney
> Mr Terry Griffiths — Postgraduate student, Department of Sociology, University of New South Wales
> Mr George Obara (Student observer) — Undergraduate student, University of Papua and New Guinea

Unattached Team (Parties, Associations and Interest Groups)
> Mr Edward P. Wolfers (Team leader) — Postgraduate student, University of Sydney P.N.G. Correspondent, Institute of Current World Affairs, New York, U.S.A.
> Mr Allan Healy — Lecturer in History, Wollongong University College, N.S.W.

Members of Steering Committee (not included in field teams)
> Dr R. G. Crocombe — Executive Officer, Australian National University New Guinea Research Unit
> Professor C. A. Hughes — Professor of Political Science, Department of Government, University of Queensland
> Professor K. S. Inglis — Professor of History, University of Papua and New Guinea
> Associate Professor Henry Mayer — Associate Professor of Political Theory, Department of Government, University of Sydney
> Professor R. S. Parker — Professor of Political Science, Research School of Social Sciences, A.N.U.

APPENDIX II

BRIEFING DOCUMENT FOR RESEARCH WORKERS

1. *Characteristics of the electorate*

    (a) Geographical: physical characteristics, particularly those relevant to communication and economic development;

    (b) Social: the number and distribution of the people; their ethnic and cultural diversity, and the broad characteristics of their traditional systems;

    (c) Communications: the physical basis of the communications system in topography and made means (e.g. roads, airstrips); personal communication through traditional contacts (e.g. trade routes or fighting relationships, or new patterns of physical movement through the electorate and its immediate area); the linguistic complexity of the electorate, including the use of any *lingua franca;* extent of mass media use (e.g., one radio per village, mission news sheet in Pidgin).

    (d) Historical: economic innovations in the area since contact (e.g. Australian monetary system; cash cropping; market for labour) and degree of local involvement; innovations in government (native authorities, councils) and degree of local involvement; any discernible phases in the history of race relations and relations with neighbouring and separated peoples; missions and local response; occurrence of cargo cults and similar movements; prior elections held in the area. (For elections held earlier than 1964, note method of voting.)

2. *The pre-election scene*

    (1) Familiarity with the political system and its operation at the local and territorial level, and understanding of the purposes of the election. These may be clarified by asking questions of the following sort:

    (a) If you want to get something important done for your village/this area, whom do you ask to help? If a purely local figure (e.g. councillor, *luluai* or 'big man', or Patrol Officer), is named, then ask whether he would have to seek help from someone, and try to follow the chain until the respondent cannot answer or has reached the Commonwealth Treasury. Ask what goes on in Port Moresby—and try to establish whether there is any familiarity with government above the patrol post or District level. If there has been some development in the area of inquiry, medical aid post, new jeep, ask who was responsible for it coming. How familiar are electors with the major public works (e.g. roads), not immediately visible to them?

(b) What does the House of Assembly do? Has it been a good thing for people around here? Has it made any difference? Will it make life better for your children? Who are the people who belong to it? Try to get some idea of the balance of numbers between indigenes and expatriates who are members. Has anyone heard of the Under-Secretaries or the Administrator's Council?

(c) Who is the local Member? What is known about him? Has he been in this area, and how often? Do electors go to him with problems or for any other reason? Has he set up any sort of grass-roots organisation for maintaining contact? Are electors familiar with his pay and what do they think about the amount? Do they think it an important job? More important than local councillor? Has the local man done a good job?

(d) What is the structure of local government in the electorate and how long have the councils existed? Is there any tendency to merge; why or why not? How has multi-racial local government gone? Why have some areas not yet received local government? What is the record of achievement or failure of local councils? Much of a turnover of councillors where there have been two or more elections? Have the councils produced any men with reputations wider than their own areas?

(e) Do the people know that indigenous Patrol Officers and public servants exist? What do they think of the idea?

(f) How far is there awareness of a New Guinea national identity, national symbols like the University? Of factors outside New Guinea like Indonesia or the United Nations? Are these seen as threatening and in what way?

(2) Identification of major lines of cleavage within the electorate. These can concern manifest issues or latent interests. Issues which might exist are (a) land shortage or differential access to land resources; (b) unemployment or lack of opportunities for career advancement; (c) presence of 'foreign natives'; (d) dispute over mineral or other royalties; (e) race relations or traditional rivalry between indigenous groups where such is currently being talked about. Each of these could also be a latent issue, together with ethnic blocs, different missions, cultists versus non-cultists, modernisers versus traditionals, and other group cleavages.

3. *The election proper*

This will be considered from three points of view: (1) that of the candidates; (2) that of the electors, and (3) that of the Administration. It should concentrate on the recruitment and socialisation functions, although there will be other aspects of importance.

(1) The candidates

(a) Social characteristics: Estimated age, social and occupational status, marital status; personal histories should include some account of traditional life, first contact with modernising influences and structures, formal education if any, status in traditional structures if any, membership of introduced structures, participation in economic activity, experience of founding or managing clubs, associations, and political structures, formal or informal; association with parties or other candidates; previous electoral career in terms of success. This information should be secured for all persons considered as candidates, whether or not they finally nominate, for it may well be relevant to the existence of a pre-selection process, and there may also be instances of people who did not stand, who some considered should have offered, which should be noted.

(b) Nomination and pre-selection: How did the candidates come to stand? Did they seek nomination on their own initiative or were they pressed or persuaded by others? How far was reluctance genuinely felt or considered appropriate to avoid charges of big-headedness? To whom did candidates turn for advice and support in seeking nomination? What was the role in nomination of parties, councils, missions, the Administration, other bodies? To what extent can one observe a pre-selection process? If candidates dropped out, at what stages and for what reasons? Who discouraged candidates from standing and why? How does the process in 1968 compare with what is remembered of 1964 and with the selection of other elective roles, especially councillors?

(c) Candidates' perception of the situation: What led particular candidates to stand? What benefits did they see accruing to themselves personally and to groups with which they were affiliated from candidacy and from membership in the House? In what way did they see themselves as fitting candidates, and/or their opponents as unfitted? In part this is their evaluation of the electoral situation and in part their life expectations.

The sitting Member (if any) deserves special attention in this context. What is his perception of his own role, and his performance as a Member? What was the degree to which he maintained channels of communication with his constituents? What were the issues with which he was personally associated in the House and in the electorate? What have been his relations with persons and groups outside the electorate, and within the electorate —with particular segments of the population, with Administration officers, missions, economic interests, local councils? Even where there is no sitting member standing, the electorate's experience of the previous member will be relevant to electors' perceptions and some factual account of the man will be needed.

What assessment do candidates make of their chances of success? What was the basis for that assessment, and how sound?

What were candidates' programs? How were these formulated if at all? Did they concentrate on policies or on personality?

(d) Mobilisation—the campaign: How far was the campaign conceived as an exercise in tactics? Competitive versus co-operative campaigning, and was this choice influenced by expatriates? What sort of campaign organisation was created? What use made of sophisticated techniques (radio, press, leaflets, posters, etc.) and how were these procured and financed? Generally where did candidates look for support in mounting the campaign in terms of manpower and money, and how far were these forthcoming? In what areas and among what groups were canvassing and campaigning conducted? Approaches to church organisations, councils, schools, traditional structures? What approach, if any, to particular sectors of the population and were certain areas or groups ignored and why? What was the relevance of kinship or other traditional forms of alliance in mobilisation? What was the relevance of new associations (e.g. mission circuits or non-traditional trade ties) to mobilisation?

Was there mutual assistance between candidates within an electorate or in adjoining electorates? Evidence of deals etc.? What guidance was offered on the distribution of preferences, and how far had the experience of 1964 of preferential voting shaped tactics here? Generally in the case of candidates who had stood previously, it would be instructive to discover how far they had learned anything from their previous experience, and to what changes of tactics this led.

What form did the appeal to the electorate take? Meetings, printed matter, mass media, campaign workers? What were the themes of speeches? Did they stress personal qualities, a programmatic approach, elements of cargo? Did the nature of the appeal change in the course of the campaign? Did it vary with the groups addressed and in what ways? Was there any feedback from the campaign? How far did linguistic problems affect the nature of the appeal, or other campaign communications? When candidates were endorsed by parties, how was the party connection presented to the electors and what influence, if any, did the party program and image have on the nature of the candidate's appeal? What allocation of resources between electorates resulted from party connections?

(2) The constituents

What were electors' preoccupations during the elections? Was there a high or low level of attention to elections? This will need some comparative basis (e.g. has the Administration undertaken any major campaign in the area recently?) Further, do electors consider themselves and their neighbours more or less interested in the 1968 elections than in the 1964, and if there is any change to what do they attribute it? How have the campaign and polling periods fitted into the cycle of ordinary social life?

What was the response to the techniques of campaigning? Attendance at meetings, participation in discussion, interest in the election and its issues expressed in continuing informal discussion? With whom did electors discuss elections informally? Spouse, expatriate, etc.?

What were their reactions and attitudes towards (i) candidates; (ii) candidates' activist supporters; (iii) parties (if any)? Was there any concept of a suitable or an ideal candidate in terms of local group or kinship allegiance, religious affiliation, party membership, personal qualities, past experience?

What were the reactions to the electoral process as a whole—the idea of representation, the responsibilities and privileges of an elected member? How far did they understand its mechanics: use of electoral terms (*resis,* polling booth, ballot box, vote, etc.), preferential voting, the counting of ballots, the neutrality of electoral officers? What voting patterns can be identified? Bloc voting by solidary groupings such as hamlets, villages, clans, phratries, etc.? What arrangements and arguments were made to achieve consensus voting? How far can one detect differences of electoral behaviour among different segments of the population: male/female, young/old, progressive/conservative, degree of modernisation? How far have these divisions in the community previously been activated by other issues?

What interest was there in announcement of results? How does this correlate with assessment of previous member? What is the response to the result: the acceptability of the winner to unsuccessful candidates and their supporters; the expectations aroused, if any, of what the election of the new member will bring? This should be assessed against the popular reaction to other changes (e.g. the introduction of local government); were people more aroused by that?

4. *Working of the electoral machinery*

What was the Returning Officer's conception of his own role? And the same for any other officers taking part in electoral activities in the area? What part did the Administration and its officers play: (i) in getting out the vote; (ii) assisting candidates with transport or anything else; (iii) stimulating or restricting the use of preferences; (iv) limiting the number of nominations?

How did the electoral education program work? Were there differences in the view of elections promulgated by the Administration, missions, expatriates, councillors, educated New Guineans, sitting members? How did the organisation and impact of the campaign compare (i) with 1964, and (ii) with comparable campaigns? Why, in the electors' minds, was the Administration going to all this trouble? What efforts were made to publicise the results of the elections?

5. *The results*

Scrutiny of the ballot papers:
Details to be finalised at Briefing Session in Lae.

6. *Regional electorates*

Is there any awareness of the Regional electorates, and how are they distinguished from the Opens? What is remembered about the Special electorates? Is the change from Special to Regional understood? What knowledge do candidates have of the requirements of candidates for Regional electorates and how do they value the requirements? Report the campaign for the local Regional seat as for the local Open, and specify any interaction between the campaign in the Regional and the Open.

7. *Political parties*

Whether or not political parties are contesting the election? What knowledge of and interest in parties is shown? Is support for and opposition to particular candidates connected with their party affiliation? Report any attempts to create a party or party-like organisation in the 12 months preceding the elections, identifying the individuals concerned in the attempt and giving some indication of their organisational and political background.

To what extent are the platforms of parties understood by constituents? What are the attitudes of candidates and constituents towards the degree of adherence to party principle needed for first preference votes? Come to think of it, to what extent are the platforms of parties understood by the candidates? Where parties are not offering, are they missed by anyone? How are parties regarded in relation to other organisations: councils, co-operatives, missions, business? Where a sitting member had any sort of organisation prior to the elections, how was this used and how was it perceived by electors?

APPENDIX III
SUMMARY OF CANDIDATES AND RESULTS
PAPUA AND NEW GUINEA HOUSE OF ASSEMBLY ELECTIONS
1964 and 1968

Race	1964 Open		1964 Special		1968 Open		1968 Regional	
	Candidates	Elected	Candidates	Elected	Candidates	Elected	Candidates	Elected
European	32	6	32	10	22	8	31	11
Mixed races	8	2	—	—	8	3	—	—
Asian	—	—	—	—	3	—	20	4
Indigenous	227	36	—	—	400	58	—	—
Total	267	44	32	10	433	69	51	15

SITTING MEMBERS OF OLD HOUSE

Total sitting elected members		Did not nominate	Nominated from	Nominated for	Elected	Defeated
Open	44	5	39	36 Open	20	16
Special	10	3	7	10 Regional	3	7
Total	54	8	46	46	23	23

Note: One sitting Official Member, J. K. McCarthy, nominated also.

APPENDIX IV

POLITICAL EDUCATION—SAMPLE LEAFLETS

GOVERNMENT IN PAPUA AND NEW GUINEA

No. 1. Majority Rule (No. 1)

In the Old Days

In olden days, when it was necessary for the clan or village people to decide something, the elders would have a meeting. They would all say what they thought should be done, and if all thought the same thing, they would do it. They would not do anything until everybody at the meeting agreed on the one thing. If only one elder did not agree they would not do anything but would talk about it some more to try and get everyone to think the same thing. In those days it took a long time to reach decisions. Often no decision was reached at all because everyone could not agree.

This did not matter very much in the old days, because village life did not change very much. It was not often necessary to make a new law, and there was plenty of time to sit and talk.

Today there are many new things and life is changing quickly. We must decide many new laws so we must decide them quickly. We cannot waste time waiting until everyone agrees on the same thing. We reach decisions quickly by doing what most people want. This is called majority rule.

Council Elections

When we elect someone to be a councillor, to represent our village or ward on the Local Government Council, we first tell people a way in which those who want to be councillors must say they want to. When someone does this he has nominated. When we know which people have nominated, each adult votes for one of these. This means he says which one of them he thinks would be the best councillor. The one who gets the most votes is the one who becomes councillor. This means that *most* people in the village think that he would be the best councillor. In other words, the *majority* of the people want him to be their councillor. Under our system of voting he becomes the councillor until the next election. This is *majority rule*.

House of Assembly Elections

When we elect a Member to the House of Assembly we find out who has nominated, then each adult votes for one of them. This means he says who he thinks would be the best person to represent him. The man or woman who the most, or majority, of people want becomes the Member for the next four years, when there will be another election. We choose our Members for the House of Assembly by majority vote, which is another form of majority rule.

How to Make a Law

Suppose there is something about which some people think it would be a good idea to have a new law. We think the best thing to do is to find out if most of the people want a law about it, and what kind of law. In your village, if some people want to move the village to another place the best thing to do is for all the people to talk about it and find out how many want to move. If only a few people want to move, then it is better to stay.

When a new law is to be made, the Members of the House of Assembly work the same way. They make laws which most of the Members want. This is done by taking a vote on all laws. If most members vote for the law it will be made. If most Members vote against it, it will not be made. This means that the House of Assembly makes its laws by majority rule.

Remember that every elected Member represents the majority of people in his electorate. So when the majority of elected Members of the House of Assembly vote for something they are speaking for the majority of the people in all of the electorates.

Democratic countries like Australia, England, America and Papua and New Guinea make their laws in this way.

Obeying The Law

Now you know how we do things by majority rule. We agree that we must do what most of the people want. When a new law is made, everyone must do as it says. We cannot have two different laws about one thing. There is only one law about each thing and everyone must do as it says, even those who think it is a bad law and who voted against it. This is because the majority, or most, of the people have decided it is a good law.

Minorities

When a law is passed we call the Members who vote for it the majority. We call the smaller number who vote against it the *minority*. When we say a minority do not like a law we mean that a small number do not like it. As we said, when a law is passed everyone in the country must obey it. Minority groups must obey it. However, people who do not like a law are free to say so, and to talk to others about it.

They can try to get other people to agree with them. If enough people agree with them they may be able to get the Members of the House of Assembly to change the law they do not like. If this happens the majority of the Members will vote for a different thing to what they wanted before. In this way, if a minority can get enough people to agree with them they become a majority. Majority rule is only good if minorities are allowed to speak out and tell people their ideas. In the kind of government which is growing up in Papua and New Guinea minority groups must have the right to say what they think.

GOVERNMENT IN PAPUA AND NEW GUINEA

No. 14. POLITICAL PARTIES

A political party is a group of like-minded people who aim at gaining effective power in the Government of a self-governing country. A political party is different from other associations because of the kinds of things it wants to do. It nominates its members to stand for election to the parliament, and works hard to get people to vote for them. The party tries to get so many of its members elected that it will have a majority in the parliament or House of Assembly. These members will be willing to vote for the things the party wants. In this way the party tries to ensure that the Government will do what the party thinks best for the country, and that the laws passed are the laws that the members of the political party want. To be successful, a political party must have enough members and supporters in most of the electorates to vote for the candidate it has chosen in each electorate.

Here is how a political party works in most democratic countries. First, people who recognize that they have common or similar interests, form the party. The people who belong to a political party are bound together by common ties. They may have the same political principles, or ideas about the way a country should be run. Some may have a common interest in keeping wages high. Others will have a common interest having things run so that their profits can be high. Some will be interested in getting social services, and help of all kinds, from the government. Farmers may join together to get themselves more help from the government, to make sure they get a good price for their crops, and a price which will not change too much. Common needs and ideas like these can lead to the rise of political parties. The different interest groups in the country speak in parliament through the different parties.

People may have a common interest in wanting certain things for their country, or in wanting to govern their country in a certain way. To be successful, a party usually needs to be able to get support from all over a country and not from just one or two parts of it.

Members decide what the party will do and what laws it will pass or change if it can get enough of its members elected to parliament, and thus influence the government to do the things it wants. This is usually written down and is called the party platform. Members then try to form branches of their party in as many electorates as possible, and by letters, by radio talks, through newspapers and at meetings, they tell voters about the party's platform, and the way it will work if it wins the election. In this way members try to persuade as many people as possible to join the party or to vote for its members in the elections.

At the time of the elections, the party endorses or marks candidates in as many electorates as possible and party workers and members do their best to get voters to vote for these party candidates. In return candidates must often promise to vote the way the party wants them to in the **parliament. This** work at election time costs money. This money has to be found from people who support the aims or the platform of the party and want to help party candidates to win in the elections.

After the elections, if a majority of the members elected to the parliament belong to one party, then in a fully self-governing country they can form a government. In a country which has not yet got self-government, they would form the strongest voice in the parliament to advise the government about how the people want things to be done. If a party has not got a majority of the members of the parliament, it might be able to make a majority by forming with other parties in what is called a "coalition". The parties in the coalition will agree about some things that they all want to do. We must remember that a party's aim is to influence the government to do what the party wants for the good of the country. A party formed on the basis of common interests can most easily organize the support it needs, and is best able to carry out its aims.

These days the party system allows changes to be made in the government peacefully and easily by the electors voting for the party they like. In the old days the government was changed in different ways. One common way was that an old ruler, when he died, was replaced by another member of his family according to a strict order. In some places old leaders were put out of power by force, and a group of rebels would take over the government. Such a government could only be changed by violence such as a revolution, or by trickery. In these kinds of governments there were no places for political parties.

Some countries have many political parties instead of two or three as in Australia, Britain, U.S.A. and others. This does not appear to work so well because perhaps four or five parties have to join together to get a majority. With many parties with different platforms in the coalition, there is usually a lot of argument about what should be done. Such coalitions often break down and the parliament has trouble in getting its work done.

Some other countries have only one political party. Many people think that this is dangerous to true democracy. They believe that in a democracy people should be able to choose between parties and their platforms as well as between candidates and that there must be an Opposition Party in the parliament to oppose and criticise and make sure that the people know what their leaders are doing.

When political parties are formed, each person can decide for himself whether he will join one or other of the parties or not. Before making up his mind, he may ask whether what the party wants is good for the Territory, for his electorate, for himself, and his family. He does not have to be a member of a party if he does not want to.

At election time he will need to decide if he likes the leaders of the party, and which of the candidates for election he prefers. It is for each individual to decide for himself how he will vote. He can vote for any candidate he likes whether or not the candidate is a member of a party.

In democracies such as we have been talking about in these papers, political parties work for peace and good order. They try to get the things they want by getting a majority of the people to agree that they are good things, and to vote for them. If a majority vote for another party then this is what the people want and the party that lost will not fight or cause trouble, but will obey all the laws. At the next election it will try again to see if a majority of people will agree with it. With this kind of government it has been found that economic development and standards of living can rise to a high level.

REFERENCES

This list includes sources cited in the text, and a small selection of the most relevant writings on New Guinea elections and comparable elections elsewhere.

Allen, Jerry and Hurd, Conrad (n.d.). *The Languages of the Bougainville District.* Port Moresby: Department of Information and Extension Services.
Apter, David. (1968). *Some Conceptual Approaches to the Study of Modernization.* Englewood Cliffs, N.J.: Prentice-Hall.
Bailey, F.G. (1963). *Politics and Social Change: Orissa in 1959.* Berkeley: University of California Press.
Beckett, Jeremy. (1967). Elections in a Small Melanesian Community. *Ethnology* 6.
Belshaw, C.S. (1955). In Search of Wealth. American Anthropological Association: *Memoirs,* vol. 57, Memoir No. 80.
Berndt, Ronald M. (1962). *Excess and Restraint.* Chicago: University of Chicago Press.
Bettison, D.G., Hughes, C.A., and van der Veur, Paul W. (eds.). (1965). *The Papua-New Guinea Elections 1964.* Canberra: Australian National University Press.
Bird, O.M. (1957). Administrative Problems of Elections in Developing Countries. *Journal of African Administration* 9.
Census. (1966). Territory of Papua and New Guinea. *Population Census, 1966: Preliminary Bulletin No. 23—Central District and Port Moresby.* Port Moresby: Government Printer.
C.E.O. (1968). Territory of Papua and New Guinea. *Report of the Chief Electoral Officer on the House of Assembly Election 1968.* Port Moresby: Government Printer.
Chowning, Ann. (1969). The Austronesian Languages of New Britain. *Papers in Linguistics of Melanesia,* No. 2. Canberra: Australian National University Press.
C.P.D. *Commonwealth Parliamentary Debates.* Canberra: Government Printer.
Dahl, Robert A. (1963). *Modern Political Analysis.* Englewood Cliffs, N.J.: Prentice-Hall.
Davenport, William and Coker, Gulbun. (1967). The Moro Movement of Guadalcanal, British Solomon Islands Protectorate. *Journal of the Polynesian Society* 76.

REFERENCES

D.D.A. (1967a). Memorandum, 'Political Education,' from Director, District Administration (previously Native Affairs) to all Field Staff. Konedobu, 8 February 1967.
—— (1967b). Memorandum, with enclosures on 'The 1967 Political Education Programme', from Director, District Administration to all Field Staff. Konedobu, 20 July 1967.
—— (1967c). Memorandum, with enclosures on 'The 1967 Political Education Programme', from Director, District Administration, to all Field Staff. Konedobu, 15 August 1967.
Distribution Committee. (1967). Territory of Papua and New Guinea. *Report to His Honour, the Administrator, by the Distribution Committee appointed for the purpose of Redistributing the Territory of Papua and New Guinea into Electorates.* Port Moresby: Government Printer.
Electoral Commission. (1970). Territory of Papua and New Guinea. *Report of the Electoral Commission of Inquiry into Electoral Procedures.* Port Moresby: Government Printer.
Epstein, A.L. (1958). *Politics in an Urban African Community.* Manchester: Manchester University Press.
—— (1969). *Matupit: Land, Politics, and Change Among the Tolai of New Britain.* Canberra: Australian National University Press.
Epstein, T.S. (1968). *Capitalism, Primitive and Modern: Some Aspects of Tolai Economic Growth.* Canberra: Australian National University Press.
Fink, Ruth. (1964). Esa'ala-Losuia Open Electorate: Campaigning with Lepani Watson. In New Guinea's First National Election, A Symposium. *Journal of the Polynesian Society* 73.
—— (1965). The Esa'ala-Losuia Open Electorate. In Bettison et al. (eds.). *The Papua-New Guinea Elections 1964.* Canberra: Australian National University Press.
Finney, Ruth. (1970). Would-be Entrepreneurs? A Study of Motivation in New Guinea. *New Guinea Research Bulletin No. 41.* Canberra: A.N.U. New Guinea Research Unit.
Friedrich, Carl J. (1961). Political Leadership and the Problem of the Charismatic Power. *Journal of Politics* 23.
Geertz, Clifford. (1963). The Integrative Revolution: Primordial Sentiments and Civil Politics in the New States. In Geertz, C. (ed.), *Old Societies and New States: The Quest for Modernity in Asia and Africa.* New York: The Free Press of Glencoe.
Gerth, H.H. and Mills, C. Wright (trans. and eds.). (1958). *From Max Weber: Essays in Sociology.* New York: Oxford University Press.
H.A.D. Territory of Papua and New Guinea. *House of Assembly Debates.* Port Moresby: Government Printer.
Harding, Thomas G. (1965). The Rai Coast Open Electorate. In Bettison et al. (eds.). *The Papua-New Guinea Elections 1964.* Canberra: Australian National University Press.

—— (1967a). *Voyagers of the Vitiaz Strait*. Seattle: University of Washington Press.
—— (1967b). A History of Cargoism in Sio, North-east New Guinea. *Oceania* 38.
Hasluck, P.M.C. (1960). *Papua and New Guinea: Some Recent Statements of Australian Policy on Political Advancement*. Issued by the Minister for Territories, Hon. Paul Hasluck, M.P. Canberra, n.d. [1960]
Hodgkin, Thomas. (1961). *African Political Parties*. Harmondsworth: Penguin Books.
Hogbin, H. Ian. (1958). *Social Change*. London: C.A. Watts and Co. Ltd.
Hughes, Colin A. and van der Veur, Paul W. (1965). The Elections: An Overview. In Bettison *et al.* (eds.). *The Papua-New Guinea Elections 1964*. Canberra: Australian National University Press.
Jinks, Brian. (1966). New Guinea Leadership: John Guise and After. *World Review* 5.
—— (1967). Electoral Education in New Guinea. *World Review* 6.
Kiki, Albert Maori. (1968). *Kiki: Ten Thousand Years in a Lifetime: A New Guinea Autobiography*. Melbourne: F.W. Cheshire; London: Pall Mall.
Lawrence, Peter. (1964). The Social and Cultural Background to the Election. In New Guinea's First National Election, A Symposium. *Journal of the Polynesian Society* 73.
—— (1964/67). *Road Belong Cargo*. Manchester: Manchester University Press; Melbourne: Melbourne University Press, 1964.
—— (1965). The Ngiang of the Rai Coast. In P. Lawrence and M.J. Meggitt (eds.), *Gods, Ghosts and Men in Melanesia*. Melbourne: Oxford University Press.
—— (1967). *Road Belong Cargo*. Melbourne: Melbourne University Press Paperback.
Long, Gavin. (1963). *The Final Campaigns: Australia in the War of 1939-45*. Canberra: Australian War Memorial.
Mackenzie, W.J.M. (1957). The Export of Electoral Systems. *Political Studies* 5.
—— and Robinson, Kenneth (eds.). (1960). *Five Elections in Africa: A Group of Electoral Studies*. Oxford: Clarendon Press.
Mair, Lucy. (1948). *Australia in New Guinea*. London: Christophers.
Malinowski, B. (1922). *Argonauts of the Western Pacific*. London: Routledge.
Meller, Norman. (1968). Papers on the Papua-New Guinea House of Assembly. *New Guinea Research Bulletin* No. 22. Canberra: A.N.U. New Guinea Research Unit.
—— and Anthony, James. (1968). *Fiji Goes to the Polls: the Crucial Legislative Council Elections of 1963*. Honolulu: East-West Center Press.
Milne, R.S. (1964-5). Elections in Developing Countries. *Parliamentary Affairs* 18.

Obara, George. (1968). The Journal of George Obara (student assistant to the Central District team). Unpublished.
Ogan, Eugene. (1965). An Election in Bougainville. *Ethnology* 4.
Oliver, Douglas L. (1955). *A Solomon Island Society*. Cambridge: Harvard University Press.
Parker, R.S. (1966). The Advance to Responsible Government. In E.K. Fisk (ed.), *New Guinea on the Threshold: Aspects of Social, Political and Economic Development*. Canberra: Australian National University Press.
—— (1967a). Problems in Administration—the Centre and the Perimeter. *New Guinea* 2. 2.
—— (1967b). Shaping Parties in New Guinea. *Dissent* No. 21.
Polansky, E.A. (1965). The Rabaul Open and West Gazelle Special Electorates. In Bettison *et al.* (eds.). *The Papua-New Guinea Elections 1964*. Canberra: Australian National University Press.
Read, K.E. (1955). Morality and the Concept of the Person Among the Gahuku-Gama. *Oceania* 25.
Reay, Marie. (1959a). Two Kinds of Ritual Conflict. *Oceania* 29.
—— (1959b). *The Kuma: Freedom and Conformity in the New Guinea Highlands*. Melbourne: Melbourne University Press.
—— (1964). Present-day Politics in the New Guinea Highlands. *American Anthropologist* 66. Special publication on *New Guinea, the Central Highlands*, Part 2.
—— (1965). The Minj Open Electorate. In Bettison *et al.* (eds.). *The Papua-New Guinea Elections 1964*. Canberra: Australian National University Press.
—— (1970). Roads and Bridges between Three Levels of Politics. In Ward (ed.). *The Politics of Melanesia*. University of Papua New Guinea and Australian National University.
Rowley, C.D. (1958). *The Australians in German New Guinea 1914-1921*. Melbourne: Melbourne University Press.
—— (1965). *The New Guinea Villager: A Retrospect from 1964*. New York: Praeger.
Rudolph, L. and S. (1967). *The Modernity of Tradition: Political Development in India*. Chicago: University of Chicago Press.
Rynkiewich, Michael A. (1968). A Speculative Analysis of North Bougainville. Typescript (unpublished).
Salisbury, R.F. (1962). *From Stone to Steel: Economic Consequences of a Technological Change in New Guinea*. Melbourne: Melbourne University Press.
Scott, D.J.R. (1958). Problems of West African Elections. In *What are the Problems of Parliamentary Government in West Africa?* London: Hansard Society.
Select Committee. (1967).Territory of Papua and New Guinea. House of Assembly. *Final Report from the Select Committee on Constitutional Development Together with Minutes of Proceedings*. Port Moresby: Government Printer.

Seligman, C.G. (1910). *The Melanesians of British New Guinea.* Cambridge: Cambridge University Press.
Smith, T.E. (1960). *Elections in Developing Countries: A Study of Electoral Procedures Used in Tropical Africa, South-East Asia and the British Caribbean.* London: Macmillan.
Strathern, Andrew. (1969). Finance and Production: Two Strategies in New Guinea Highlands Exchange Systems. *Oceania* 40.
—— (1970). To Choose a Strong Man: The House of Assembly Election in Mul-Dei. *Oceania* 41.
—— and Strathern, Marilyn. (1964). Minj Open Electorate: The Campaign in the Dei Council Area. In New Guinea's First National Election, A Symposium. *Journal of the Polynesian Society* 73.
Territories, Department of (External). *P.A.R. Territory of Papua, Annual Report.* Canberra: Government Printer.
—— *N.G.A.R. Territory of New Guinea, Annual Report.* Canberra: Government Printer.
Van der Veur, Paul W. (1966). The First 'National' Election in Papua-New Guinea in Retrospect. *Australian Quarterly* 38.
Visiting Mission. (1965). *Report of the United Nations Visiting Mission to the Trust Territories of Nauru and New Guinea: Report on New Guinea.* Document T/1635, 28 May 1965.
Ward, Marion M. (ed.) (1970). *The Politics of Melanesia.* Papers delivered at the Fourth Waigani Seminar. [Canberra] University of Papua and New Guinea, Port Moresby, and Research School of Pacific Studies, Australian National University.
Weber, Max. (1947). *The Theory of Social and Economic Organization.* Talcott Parsons (ed.). Glencoe: The Free Press.
White, Osmar. (1965). *Parliament of a Thousand Tribes.* London: Heinemann.
Wolfers, Edward P. (1966). The Special Electorates. *New Guinea* 1, 7.
—— (1967a). Politics and the House. *New Guinea* 2, 1.
—— (1967b). The Political Parties. *New Guinea* 2, 3.
—— (1967c). *Party Time Again.* Newsletter EPW-10. New York: Institute of Current World Affairs.
—— (1967d). The Elections—I. *New Guinea* 2, 4.
—— (1968a). *The 1968 Elections—III.* Newsletter EPW-14. New York: Institute of Current World Affairs.
—— (1968b). *The 1968 Elections—IV.* Newsletter EPW-15. New York: Institute of Current World Affairs.
—— (1968c). The Emergence of Political Parties in Papua and New Guinea. *Journal of Pacific History* 3.
—— (1968d). The Elections—II. *New Guinea* 3, 4.
Worsley, Peter. (1968). *The Trumpet Shall Sound: A Study of 'Cargo' Cultism in Melanesia.* Revised edition. New York: Schocken Books.

INDEX

Abal, Tei, *see* Tei Abal
Abel, Cecil, 32, 117, 118, 120, 127, 130, 330, 333, 350; alliances, 117, 125, 128; campaigning methods, 124-6; challenged by Elliott Elijah, 121-2, 125; missionary background, 119; Pangu Pati member, 32, 120, 124-5; political platform, 124, 125; polling results, 127, 130; reasons for standing, 120
Absentee voters, *see* Voters, absentee
Administration, the: attitude toward political parties, 337, 348-9; conduct of elections, 222, 271, 351-3; criticism of, 142, 150, 206, 351; dominant political force, 3, 25-7, 71-2, 221, 222, 240-1, 271, 331, 340; fragmented relations with people, 15, 49, 324; held responsible for political education, 30, 41-2, 49, 56, 143, 152, 171-2, 194, 197, 271, 353; influence on electoral behaviour (advice to candidates) 237-8, (advice to voters) 225, (attitude to candidates) 139, 222, 229, 234, 270, 272, 351, (enrolment) 197, (nominations) 59, 197, 242, 250; involvement in election, 221-2, 271, 350-1; policies on Gazelle Peninsula, 54; role in political development, 331, 350; voters' attitudes toward, 324-5
Administrative College of Papua and New Guinea, 278, 289
Administrator, the: constitutional powers, 20, 28, 39; High Commissioner as alternative, 32; opening of Luba Co-operative, 112
Administrator's Council, 20-1, 27, 38
Agriculture Reform Party, *see* New Guinea Agriculture Reform Party
Albaniel, Manuel, 287, 292, 309; polling results, 308, 313
All People's Party, 33-4, 172, 173, 175, 333-4; electoral alliances, 183
Alliances, *see* Electoral alliances

Alotau Open Electorate, 40, 91, 95; campaign, 95-8; candidates, 95; election results, 130
Ambenob Local Government Council, 176, 177, 187, 190
Amphlett Islands, 91, 93; people, 93
Anderson, 'Andy' (Frederic David), 289-90, 291, 305, 309, 331, 333; areas of support, 310; campaigning methods, 296, 298; experience, 290; political platform, 304; polling results, 309, 313
Andrew, Poate Henry, 101; campaigning methods, 101; political platform, 101; polling results, 130
Angmai Bilas, 176, 190, 196, 198, 200, 201, 316; campaigning methods, 185; electoral alliances, 187; gift-giving, 185; political platform, 176; polling results, 192-3, 216
Anti-European sentiment, *see* Expatriates
Ashton, O. I. (Roy), 50, 56, 67, 68; campaigning methods, 79-81; consultations with Tolai people, 80; polling results, 81, 89
Assistant Ministerial Members, 27
Associations, 326-9, 335-40; dearth of in New Guinea, 56, 326, 359
Astrolabe Bay Local Government Council, 181, 185, 193, 200n., 329
Australian aid, 14, 18-19, 52, 74
Australian Country Party, 229
Australian evacuation, 1942, 74, 135, 137, 324
Australian institutions, modification in New Guinea, 17, 351, 355, 357-8, 359
Australian policy in New Guinea politics, 348-53 *passim*; initiative in political change, 357-8
Australian political behaviour not a yardstick for New Guinea, 7, 67, 312-13, 354-5

381

Bailey, F. G., 9-10
Bainings area, New Britain, 54, 59, 67, 81; voter turn-out, 81
Bainings Local Government Council, 59
Bainings people, 54, 59; interests fostered by Roi Ashton, 81
Ballot, see Voting, 'Whisper' ballot
Ballot papers, 47, 190, 195-6, 233, 261, 263
Baloiloi, Enosi, 99-100, 102n., 103; campaigning methods, 100; polling results, 100, 130
Barrett, D., 50, 55-6, 68, 318, 353; campaigning methods, 79-81
Bato Bultin, 176, 177, 185, 186, 192, 196, 198, 333, 337; campaigning methods, 185; electoral alliances, 187, 188, 190; political platform, 177; polling results, 192-3, 216; suffers from 'Yali vote', 196
Beniona ToKarai, see ToKarai, Beniona
Bettison, D. G., 42
'Big men', 320, 337; Gazelle Peninsula, 87, 89n.; Western Highlands, 219-21, 238, 239
Birth control, 54, 70
Bisnis, 223-4
Bloc voting, see Denominational influence, Voting, bloc
Bogia Open Electorate, 171, 173; election results, 216; voter turnout, 194
Bondai Pita, 95, 96
Bougainville District, 132-9 *passim*; mining, 141-2, 144, 146, 147; missions, 133, 141-2, 149, (educational role of) 133-4; neglect by Administration, 137, 139, 150; plantations, 137-8; political future, 161; political unrest, 139, 358
Bougainville electorates, 7, 132-61 *passim*; election results, 155-9, 161; electoral alliances, 151, 152, 157, 158, 333; electoral redistribution, 132, 159; informal voting, 153-4, 156, 157, 159; role of missions, 149, 158-9; voter turn-out, 154, 156, 159
Bougainville North Open Electorate, 159
Bougainville people, 132; education, 133, 135; European contact, 133, 135, 137; Japanese occupation, 135; languages, 132-3; local government councils, 137, 139; opposition to planters, 138; resentment toward Europeans, 138, 139-40, 141, 142, 152, 153, 158; taxation issue, 137
Bougainville Regional Electorate, 323-4; campaigning methods and candidates, 149-51; election results, 156-8, 161; informal voting, 153-4, 156; non-voting, 157
Bougainville South Open Electorate, 132, 140, 147-9; campaigning methods, 148-9; candidates, 147-8; election results, 155-6, 161; voter turn-out, 156
British Solomon Islands Protectorate, 56, 132, 133, 153, 341
Bryant, R. R., 10; see also Chief Electoral Officer
Buaki Singery, 204, 209, 212; campaigning methods, 205, 215; polling results, 210, 211, 212, 217
Buckman, Leo, 292, 293, 299, 302
Buin people, 132, 133, 137, 138, 140, 147, 149, 152, 324

Campaign costs, 326
Campaign speeches, 305, 317, 344
Campaigning difficulties, 12-13, 194-5, 205, 284, 352
Campaigning methods, 46-7, 50-1, 61, 63, 326, 355; absence of personal contests, 249, 251, 298, 321, 322; Bougainville, 145, 147-51; campaign committees, 326; Central District, 292-9, 301-5; Gazelle Peninsula, 67-74, 76-81, 85-7; indigenous candidates, 230-2, 298; Madang District, 175, 178, 183-6, 214; Milne Bay, 96-107, 109-17, 122-7; Morobe District, 205-7, 214-15; personal recrimination avoided, 70-2, 102, 116, 184-6, 199, 213, 245, 248, 259, 298, 321-2; skills of candidates, 317-18; use of photographs, pamphlets and posters, 106, 124, 231; villagers' resistance to strangers, 295, 296, 298, 312; Western Highlands, 230-6, 243-52, 257-60
Candidates: absence of personal contests, 321, 322; attitudes toward political parties, 173, 179, 326, 336, 337, 339; avoid promises, 304; corporate sense, 322; divisive rivalries, 316; group relationships, 315-16; identification by photographs, 105, 106, 306, 310, 311, 318, 352, 354; little exploitation of political issues, 128, 158, 159-60,

INDEX

248, 329-32; motives in nominating, 227-8, 285-6, 291, 346-7; political skills and attributes, 76-7, 108, 110, 129, 198-9, 219, 221, 317-21, 338; provincial *v.* national concerns, 329-30; role in electoral education, 114, 172, 248, 251, 264, 304, 344; role in political education, 82, 105, 113-14, 147, 150, 172, 185, 343, 344; support from 'home area', 316; use of associations and organisations, 326-9; views on Administration's role, 351; views on self-government, 228, 330-1; *see also* European candidates, Indigenous candidates, Papuan candidates, Pre-selection, and names of individual electorates

Cargo beliefs, 168, 176, 177, 179-83, 194, 197, 199, 200, 201, 324, 354; aid to Paul Lapun's success, 139-40, 156; decline in influence, 186, 200, 213, 215, 323; importance to candidates, 316; influence on elections, 50-1, 181, 186, 199-201, 206, 322-3; influence in future, 201; influence on Yali Singina, 179-83; in Madang and Morobe, 170-1; leadership of Stoi Umut, 206, 209; main issue in Madang electorates, 186, 188-91 *passim*, 199-201, 213-15; on Bougainville, 139 and n., 145-6, 153, 154, 159; resentment toward Europeans, 181, 182

Cash crops: Madang and Morobe Districts, 168; Milne Bay District, 94; price as an election issue, 246; on Gazelle Peninsula, 53

Central District Electorates, 41, 278, 275-314 *passim*, 279-85, 311-14, 316; areas of support for candidates, 294-5; campaign committees, 292-4; campaigning methods, 304-5; candidates, 290-2, (European) 290-1, (Papuan) 291; commercial activities, 275; election results, 307-10, 313; political platforms, 294, 300-1; voter turn-out, 305, 306, 309, 311

Central Regional Electorate, 32, 283-5, 304, 306, 313; campaigning difficulties in, 284; campaigning methods, 296-7, 304; candidates, 288-90; election results, 309, 313; informal voting, 309; potential for sophisticated politics, 276, 278-9;

preferential voting, 310; voter turn-out, 305, 306, 311

Central Special Electorate, 285

Chatterton, Percy, 285, 286, 291, 300, 302; areas of support, 294-5, 307; campaign manager for, 292, 293, 299; campaigning methods, 292-3, 294-5, 298, 302; **electoral** battle with McCarthy, 298-9; experience, 290; political platform, 300; polling results, 306, 313; reasons for nominating, 291

Chief Electoral Officer, 10, 39, 45-7, 194n., 353

Chinese: campaign manager to ToLiman in 1964, 67; entrepreneurs (in South Bougainville) 138, (on Madang) 168-9; lack of interest in 1968 election, 73; planters on Gazelle Peninsula, 53; unpopular with Tolai, 58

Cleland, Sir Donald, 66

Cocoa growing: Bougainville, 137; Milne Bay, 94; raises demand for land, 53

Cocoa Project, Tolai, 52

Coffee growing, 201; Milne Bay, 94

Colman, John, 227, 228, 236, 260, 269; electoral alliance, 260; polling results, 262-5, 267, 268, 274

Colonial administration not politically neutral, 349-50

Communications: in Kabwum, 203; influence on electors, 194, 342, 359; on Bougainville, 143-4, 149; Radio Bougainville, 160

Contraception, 54, 70

Conzinc Riotinto of Australia Ltd, 29, 141-2, 144-7 *passim*, 340, 353; indigenous resentment of, 153, 323-4

Cooke, Gayne F., 150, 152; campaigning methods, 150; polling results, 157-8, 161

Co-operatives, 111, 112

Copper mining, 14, 29, 141-3, 144

Crawford, Sir John G., 11

Crocombe, R. G., 10

Crowhurst, John, 204, 213, 321; anti-mission stance, 205, 327; campaigning methods, 205, 215; election alliances, 207; polling results, 210, 211, 212, 217

Culture contact, 13-15, 358; Bougainville, 133, 135; Milne Bay, 93-4; New Britain, 48-52; north-east coast, 168

Dei Local Government Council, 219, 226, 253
Denominational influence in elections, 102, 110, 316, 320, 327; bloc voting, 62, 236, 249, (decline since 1964) 84-5; Bougainville electorates, 148, 151, 152-3, 157-8, 159; Kabwum Open Electorate, 204-5; Kula Open Electorate, 117; support for Elliott Elijah, 128; support for John Guise, 98
D'Entrecasteaux Islands, 91, 93, 94, 98, 99, 104, 105, 123; attitudes (toward elected members) 99, (toward independence) 123, (toward Pangu Pati) 104
Dependence, indigenous feelings of: economic, 18-19; political, 26, 30, 39, 89, 349, 356, 360
Deputy Chief Electoral Officer, 10, 46, 271
Dialogue, 142
Dickson, Merari, 95
Dickson, Osineru, 95, 96, 97; campaigning methods, 96; polling results, 98, 130
Dihm, W. (founder, Napro Party), 33, 287
Discussion Group, *see* Gazelle Discussion Group
Distribution Committee, 39-41, 91
Distribution of electorates, *see* Electoral redistribution
District Administration, Department of, 42, 45; Director of, 43, 328; view on Gazelle Council tax increase, 76-7
District Commissioner: East New Britain, 54; Western Highlands, *see* Ellis, T. W.
Dobu area, 99-101 *passim*
Downs, Ian F. G., 34, 226, 318; on political role of expatriates, 335
Dui (Yali's campaign manager), 181, 187, 188, 189, 191
Duke of York Islands, 50, 62, 82n.

East and West New Britain Regional Electorate, 48, 50, 56, 272; campaign, 78-81; election results, 81, 89; informal voting, 83; voter turn-out, 83
East New Britain Special Electorate, 63
East Papua Special Electorate, 118
East Sepik Regional Electorate, 325
Eastern Highlands District, 226
Economic development, 14-15, 18, 29, 51; as an election issue, 330, 347-8, (north-east coast) 199-201, 207, 208-9, 213, 215, (Western Highlands) 232, 273; Central District, 275, 276, 282-3; north-east coast, 168-9
Education, 15, 23, 52, 342; as an election issue, 101, 129; dropouts, 53-4; on Gazelle Peninsula, 53-4, 56
Education, Department of, 42, 53-4; sponsors increase in Gazelle Council tax, 76-7n.
El Rop, 254, 256, 257; campaigning methods, 258; polling results, 274
Election of 1964, 3, 5, 23, 41-3, 46-7, 55-6, 67, 162, 181, 332, 356; campaigns in, 70, 72; denominational influences, 84; informal voting, 23, 188; Minj Open, 219; preferential voting, 226; Rai Coast, 203, 204; results, 23, 140, 370; significance (Gazelle Peninsula) 86, (north-east coast) 171, 188, 214, (south Bougainville) 139-40; voter turn-out, 23, 194
Election of 1968: anxiety of Tolai voters, 54-5; importance of associations and organisations, 326-9; influence of cargo cults, 179-83; issues *v.* personalities, 75, 232, 234, 312, 318, 320, 329-32; issues, development of, 279, (in Madang Regional) 173, (in Western Highlands) 223-4, 229, 270; lack of voter interest, 73, 105, 250, 352-3; operation and procedure of, 270-1, 351-2; political development, 349, 356; political resources, 315-32; use of pamphlets and posters, 231; voter turn-out, 347, 352, 353
Election issues, 300-1, 329-31, 358; cash crops, cargo, 199-201, 330; economic development, 208-9, 213, 215, 330, 347-8; independence, 271, 300, 330; little development of, 270, 312, 329-32; provincial *v.* national, 329-30, 341
Election results, 1968, 370; Bougainville, 155-8, 161; Central District, 306-10 *passim*, 313; Kabwum Open, 209-12, 217; Madang District, 192, 216-17; Milne Bay, 127, 130-1; Morobe Regional, 212; New Britain, 81, 89-90; Western Highlands, 261-3, 265, 274
Election studies: methods used, 2, 3-6, 15-16, 73; value of, 1, 17-18

Elections: administrative difficulties, 12-13, 105; associated with imposition of local government councils, 50, 81-2, 347; electors' concepts of, 321; gift-giving by candidates, 116-17; issues v. personalities, 354; not understood by some people, 50, 51, 85-6, 105, 152, 342, 355; 'ritual' aspect, 86, 347; scepticism about, 50, 82, 214, 346-7; use of photographs, pamphlets and posters, 106, 124, 231

Electoral administration, 351-2; dealing with 'Yali vote', 189-90; polling procedures, 260-1, 266, 305; *see also* Ballot papers, Campaigning difficulties, Electoral education, Treating, Voting, 'Whisper' ballot

Electoral alliances, 321, 332-3, 359; Bougainville, 151, 152, 157, 158; Central, 294, 298; European role in, 184, 214, 259, 333; indigenous role in, 184, 259-60; lacking on Gazelle Peninsula, 72, 80n., 83; Madang, 183-4, 186-91, 196-7, 214; Milne Bay, 113, 117, 125-8 *passim*; Morobe, 205, 207, 214; New Britain, 80n.; Western Highlands, 257, 259-60

Electoral education, 42, 43, 45-7, 343-4; Bougainville, 147, 152; Madang, 172; New Britain, 56; role of local government councillors, 147, 172, 344; undertaken by candidates, 114, 171, 172, 185, 251, 304; Western Highlands, 236, 260-1, 263, 266

Electoral law, 21-3, 36-41; enrolment, 22; preferential voting, 22-3; qualifications of candidates and voters, 21, 37-8; 'reserved' seats, 21; rolls, compilation of, 22, 351; voting provisions, 22; 'whisper' ballot, 22

Electoral Ordinance 1963-67, 39-41, 46

Electoral redistribution, 39-41; Bougainville, 132, 159; criteria, 40; Hiri Open, 41, 279; Kabwum Open, 171, 202; Madang, 162-3, 171; Milne Bay, 91, 98; Moresby Open, 279; Morobe Regional, 162, 163, 171; Mul-Dei Open, 252-3; New Britain, 48, 55; north-east coast, 215; Wahgi Open, 238, 247; Western Highlands, 226

Electorates covered in this study, 5; *see* Open electorates, Regional electorates, Special electorates

Electors: apathy, 352, (Gazelle Peninsula) 73, (Esa'ala) 105, (Madang) 194, (Moresby Open) 305-6; attitudes toward (candidates) 128, 213, 321, (elections) 321, (European influence) 357, (House of Assembly) 29, 344-6, 348, (national politics) 279, (political parties) 173, 175, 326, (treating) 116-17; ignorance of House of Assembly, 29, 342; motives for voting, 347; views on (Administration's role) 324, 351, (candidates) 185, 186, (Parliamentary Under-Secretaries) 345, (representation) 325, (role of elected members) 30, 104, 152, 206, 222, 223, 224, 238, 239, 321; values and attitudes generally, 331-6; *see also* Voter turn-out, Voters, Voting

Elijah, Elliott, 32, 117, 118, 120, 125, 322, 325, 333; alliance with Lepani Watson, 127-8; campaigning methods, 123-4, 126-7; importance of indigenous leaders to, 126; Kula Open candidacy, 121; motives for standing, 120, 347; Pangu Pati member, 32, 120; political platform, 123; polling results, 127, 130; switch to Milne Bay Regional, 121-2

Ellis, T. W., 222, 224, 227, 232; criticisms of, 229-30; influence on election, 271, 273

Employment, indigenous, 14-15; opportunities in Madang, 169; shortage on Gazelle, 53

Epineri Titimur, 55, 58, 66, 76, 84, 89; campaigning methods, 68-9, 71, 87; spokesman for Tolai people, 66, 68-9, 74, 77, 324, 345; statements on independence, 74-5, 330; support by Catholic priests, 85

Esa'ala Open Electorate, 91; campaign, 98-107; candidates, 99-105 *passim*; election results, 130; lack of voter interest, 105; Pangu Pati contestants, 103; voter turn-out, 105

Esa'ala-Losuia Open Electorate, 91, 94, 107

European candidates: as representatives of expatriate political interest, 333-5; attitudes of voters

toward, 324-5; campaigning methods, 72, 298-9, 318; Central District, 290-1, 298; criticised by Elliott Elijah, 127; favoured in Esa'ala Open, 99, 100, 101, 107; rejected in Bougainville, 140, 150, 152-3, 158; role in electoral alliances, 184, 214, 259, 333; Western Highlands, 226, 227, 230-3, 260, 272
Evennett, Norman, 101, 102n., 106-7, 128, 130, 325, 326; campaigning methods, 101-2; ideal qualifications for members, 102; polling results, 100n., 106, 130
Expatriates: anti-European sentiment (Bougainville) 138, 142, 150, 152-3, 156, 158, 330, (Milne Bay) 127, (Western Highlands) 227, 234, 242; concentration around Port Moresby, 278; economic influence, 14-15, 51-3, 168, 224; lack of interest in election, 3, 73, 197, 305-6, 334-5; political influence (on candidates) 78, (on Highlanders) 228, (in House of Assembly) 3, 26, 28, (on political parties) 30, 32, (on views about self-government) 19; racial attitudes of, 138, 170; views on significance of election, 272, 334-5; *see also* Administration, the; European candidates

Finney, Ruth, 88n.
Fransing Ansuang, 204, 211; campaigning methods, 205; polling results, 209-10, 212
Freund, Roland, 226-7

Garrett, James J., 173-4, 185, 186, 187, 190, 192, 196, 198, 200, 201, 316, 325; campaigning methods, 185; electoral alliances, 187; gift-giving, 185; political platform, 173-4; polling results, 192, 216
Gavera Rea, 32, 289, 292, 309, 333; areas of support, 310; campaigning methods, 294, 297, 298, 303; electoral alliance, 294, 298, 333; Pangu Pati (association with) 297, (foundation member of) 289; political platform, 301; polling results, 309, 313
Gazelle Discussion Group, 67, 69, 74, 86n.
Gazelle Local Government Council, 52, 55, 57, 62, 66; leadership of ToBaining, 63; main political forum on Gazelle Peninsula, 57; offices, as a Tolai social centre, 80; relations with ToLiman, 68; tax issue in election, 70-1, 75, 76-7
Gazelle Open Electorate, 31, 55, 66; candidates, 58-61, 67; land as main issue, 77; predictability of results, 79; voter turn-out, 81
Gazelle Peninsula, 31, 48, 55, 324; attitude toward the Administration, 324; culture contact, 51-3; description, 51; economic development, 14, 51-2, 54-5; land alienation, 52-3; political parties in, 57-8, 336, 337; population explosion, 52-4, 87; strains and conflicts, 87, 358; teachers' salaries, 75; *see also* Tolai people
Geertz, Clifford, 359-60
Generation cleavage: complex on Gazelle Peninsula, 86-8; in Milne Bay District, 95
German rule in New Guinea, 51, 135, 168
Gerth, H. H., 140
Gift-giving, *see* Treating
Goilala Open Electorate, 41, 304; languages, 284; voter turn-out, 306
Goilala people, 41
Gold Coast (West Africa), 81
Goodenough Island, 93, 99, 106
Goroka, 169, 226
Grose, James, 140
Guava people: cargo cult, 145; copper mining dispute, 141, 142
Guise, John, 27, 32, 35, 95, 126, 327; campaigning methods, 97-8; denomination support for, 98; electioneering skills, 97; Pangu Pati candidate, 97, 337; polling results, 98, 130; popularity, 97, 98; sources of support, 98, 327

Hagai, Francis, 151, 159
Hagen Local Government Council, 219, 272
Hahalis Welfare Society, 145, 151, 154, 159
Hammersley, Tas, 227; campaigning methods, 230
Hanuabada, 286, 289, 302
Hasluck, Paul, 350
Hay, D. O., 112
Highland members of House of Assembly, 222-3; 'the government party', 225, 350

INDEX

Highland political attitudes, 19, 34-5, 223, 225, 272-3, 324, 334
Highlands Farmers' and Settlers' Association, 35, 226
Highlands Highway, 169, 245, 358
Highlands party sought, 224
Highlands Special Electorate, 226
Hiri Open Electorate, 41, 279, 281-3, 302-3; campaigning methods, 295-6, 302-4; candidates, 286-8; commercial activities, 282-3; election results, 306, 307-9, 313; electoral redistribution, 41, 279; enrolment, 282; local government councils in, 287; missions, 282; Motu and Koita electors in, 281-2; sources of support, 302-4; voter turn-out, 309, 311; voting patterns, 308-9
Hohola, 281
Holloway, B. B., 32
House of Assembly, 3, 5, 15, 17-18, 20-30, 36, 38-9, 142, 162, 223, 227, 291, 344-8; amends Mining Ordinance, 142-3; Australian veto, 20, 27-8; candidates' views of, 291; cargoists' views on, 182; constitution of, 20; elected members and role of, 23-30, 41, 50, 73, 222, 251, 344, 355, (ideal qualifications) 102; electors' expectations of, 194, 208, 321, 346, 359; interpretation service, 25; Leader of elected members, 26, 27, 32; official languages, 24-5; official members, 20, 23, 25-6; powers, 20; private members' Bills, 28; procedures, 25, 28; remote from village political issues, 270; Select Committees, 28; Speaker, 20, 23, 27; Standing Committees, 28; unfamiliar to people, 50, 73, 112, 143, 208, 342; Westminster as model, 26, 348, 349-50, 356, 360; women candidates, 102-03
How-to-vote cards, 232-3, 235, 352
Hughes, C. A., 11

Iaga Bakuk, 185, 187, 320, 324; political platform, 183; polling results, 193, 216
Iambakey, Okuk, 226-9 *passim*, 235, 236, 259, 271-3, 334, 341, 360; association with Pangu Pati, 234-5, 271, 273; campaigning methods, 231, 236; political platform, 234; polling results, 262, 264, 265, 268, 269, 274

Ideologies, little development, 330; *see also* Political parties
Independence, 119, 225, 341; associated with Australian departure, 74, 173, 347; candidates' views on, 61, 62, 64, 74, 79, 174, 175, 176, 177, 179; election issue, 271, 300, 330; Epineri's statements, 74-5; Evennett's views on, 102; prospects for, 9-10, 18-19, 34, 95; voters' views on, 73-5, 173, 271, 273, 347
India, comparison with New Guinea politics, 9-10
Indigenous candidates, 316, 325-6, 354; campaigning methods, 230-2, 298; political platforms, 232; role in electoral alliances, 184, 259-60; support for, 234, 312; youth of, 227
Indigenous politics, *see* 'Traditional' politics
Informal voting, *see* Voting, informal
Information and Extension Services, Department of, 42, 45
Inglis, K. S., 11
Interest-conflicts in the election, 331-2
Issues in 1968 election, 329-30
Iuri, Poio, 228

Japanese occupation, 135, 168
Jephcott, Bruce, 173, 174-5, 190, 192, 196n., 197, 198, 333; All People's Party candidate, 175, 337; campaigning methods, 184-5, 214; political platform, 175; polling results, 216
Jimi Open Electorate, 264
Jubilee, Ephraim, 75

Kabwum: communications in, 203; land demarcation, 203-4
Kabwum Local Government Council, 202, 204
Kabwum Open Electorate, 162n., 163, 202; campaigning methods, 205-6, 215; candidates, 204, 205, 213; decline of cargoism, 213; denominational influence, 204-5; election analysis, 213, 214-15; election results, 209-10, 211, 212; electoral alliances, 214; electoral redistribution, 171, 202; population, 202; voter turn-out, 210-11; voting pattern, 209

Kabwum people, 202-3; hostilities, 203, 204; languages, 203; literacy of, 203
Kaibelt Diria, 222, 224, 225, 237-8, 242, 254, 257, 263, 266, 273, 322, 333, 344; appeal to women constituents, 245; campaigning methods, 224, 245-7, 251, 252; challenged, 241-2; criticisms of, 239, 249; elected 1964, 226, 237; official support, 238, 240, 243; opposed to tax increase, 237; polling results, 252, 253, 263, 274; protégé of T. W. Ellis, 229, 351; southern opposition to, 240
Kaindi Open Electorate, 38, 206
Kairuku Local Government Council, 287
Kairuku Sub-District, 41, 282
Kaki Angi, 177, 178, 185, 186, 328, 333; campaigning methods, 178, 185; electoral alliances, 187; political platform, 178; polling results, 193, 217
Kalade, Francisco, 102n., 103-5, 318, 325; national election issues, 330; Pangu Pati allegiance, 103, 105; polling results, 130; views on members' role, 104
Kambia Mogul, 241-2
Kanaka: ToLiman's use of term offends Gazelle Council, 68n.
Kandep-Tambul Open Electorate, 264
Kandrian-Pomio Open Electorate, 48, 80n.; informal voting, 83; election results, 90
Kapena, Toua, 286-7, 298, 302, 305, 332; areas of support, 308-9; avoids electoral promises, 304-5; campaigning methods, 292, 293-4, 295-6, 298, 302-3; indigenous leader, 286-7; Motu candidate, 293; political platform, 301; polling results, 308, 309, 313
Karkar Island, 162, 163, 170, 186, 190, 193, 195n., 198, 200
Karkar Local Government Council, 178, 185, 190
Kaugere, 281, 285
Kaumi, S., 10; *see also* Deputy Chief Electoral Officer
Kieta Local Government Council, 137
Kiriwina Island, 94, 111-12, 115, 117
Kirke, Craig, 293
Koita people, 275, 276, 279, 280, 281-2, 288, 293, 297, 302

Koita villages, 281, 282, 295, 303, 309
Koke, 281, 295
Kokopo, 57, 61
Kokopo Open Electorate, 48, 53, 60; campaign in, 70, 72, 73, 87; candidates, 58, 61-4, 67; election results, 90; land as main issue, 77; voter turn-out, 81
Kombe people: long contact with Europeans, 49; one candidate 1968 election, 50
Komoro, Andrew, 140, 147-9, 327; campaigning methods, 148-9; election issues, 330; polling results, 155, 157, 159
Konedobu (Administration H.Q. at Port Moresby), 139, 286, 295, 299
Koriam Urekit, 61, 63, 80n., 82, 323
Koromira cargo activities, 145, 157
Kula Open Electorate, 40, 91, 95, 121, 129; campaign, 109-17; candidates, 107-9, 128, (Pangu Pati) 121; election results, 117, 131
Kula trading, 91
Kumaina, Robin, 73n.
Kwato, 96, 98, 119, 288; Extension Association, 94

Lae, 88, 169
Land: alienation (in Madang electorates) 199, (on Gazelle Peninsula) 52-3, (in Milne Bay) 93-4, (on north-east coast) 168, 178; demarcation (Kabwum) 203-4, (Madang) 169, 177; political significance, 53; problem, 334; shortage on Gazelle Peninsula, 53, 70, 82; ToLiman's policy, 68
Land Demarcation Committees, 54, 77, 177, 240
Languages, 279; English, 15, 23-4; in election campaigns, 69-70, 198, 230, 233; Kabwum Open, 202-3; Melanesian Pidgin, 15, 24; multiplicity, 13, 48; official, in House of Assembly, 23-4; Police Motu, 23-4; south Bougainville, 132-3
Lapun, Paul, 27, 32, 144-8 *passim*, 151-4 *passim*, 157, 160, 317, 333, 344; association with 'Matthew', 153; Bougainville mining, 142, 143, 144; campaigning methods, 145, 148; cargo cults and, 145-6, 156; charisma of, 139, 144-5, 148, 339; election victory 1964, 139; European attitude to, 145 and n., 148, 156; House of Assembly

record, 142, 143; Pangu Pati association, 145, 146, 148, 153; polling results, 155-6, 161; popularity, 139, 140, 144, 145, 148, 153, 156; Under-Secretary for Forests, 143
Latukefu, Ruth, 10
Leadership: courses in Gazelle Peninsula, 56; on Gazelle, 86-7; ToLiman's views on, 67; traditional, in Trobriands, 110-11
Leahy, John, 227
Lee, John Cairns, 149-50, 152, 159; campaigning methods, 150; political platform, 150; polling results, 157, 158, 161; raised election issues, 330
Legislative Council, 224, 226, 289, 290, 293, 335; Australian veto, 28; elections studied, 4; Electoral Ordinance, 21; ex-members, in House of Assembly, 24, 32, 38; Parliamentary Under-Secretary Ordinance, 27; ToBaining, election to, 63
Levy, Keith, 224, 226-30 *passim*, 235, 258, 259, 267, 269, 273, 344, 351; campaigning methods, 231, 235, 236; electoral alliance, 260; guides indigenous members in House of Assembly, 226; polling results, 262, 263, 265, 267, 268, 274; views on economic development, 232
Liwa (President, Ambenob Council), 187, 190, 196
lo, meaning of, 182n.
Local government council party proposed, 57, 328
Local government councillors: as potential candidates, 57, 238-9; future rulers? 273; in House of Assembly, 24; political role, 318, 329, 342-3, (Central District) 295-6, 298, (Milne Bay) 105-6, 123, 129-30, (north-east coast) 172, 181, 185, 190, 198, 200, (Western Highlands) 221, **230**, 232, 238, 240-1, 255, 257, 259; role in electoral education, 344, (Bougainville) 147, (north-east coast) 172, 197; role in political education, 343, (Milne Bay) 94-5, (north-east coast) 172, 194, 197; unofficial courts, 221
Local government councils, 4, 40; Bougainville, 137; Central District, 287; Gazelle Peninsula, 49-50, 52; Milne Bay, 94; north-east coast, 169, 202, 208; Western Highlands, 219, 221, (multi-racial) 226, 237, 324; political party proposed, 57, 328; political role, 316, 317, 328-9, (Central District) 295, 296, 297, 302, (Milne Bay) 91, 98 108-9, 117, 129-30, (north-east coast) 185, 190, 194, 197-8, (Western Highlands) 221, 230, 233, 252-3, 255, 270; resisted by some villagers, 50, 52, 137, 139, 194; role in electoral education, 46, 343, (Western Highlands) 230; role in political education, 343, (Bougainville) 143, (Milne Bay) 94-5, (Western Highlands) 270, 271
Louisiade Local Government Council, 109, 117, 129
Lue, Joseph, 151-4 *passim*, 160, 333; alliance with Paul Lapun, 151, 152, 157, 158; campaigning methods, 151; mission support, 159; polling results, 156-8, 159

Mabuso Open Electorate, 163, 173, 176-7, 197; candidates, 176-7; election results, 192-3, 216; influence of cargoism, 188-9; population, 171; voter turn-out, 194; 'Yali vote' in, 196, 197
McCarthy, J. D., 31
McCarthy, J. K., 285, 286, 291, 301-2; areas of support, 295, 307; campaign manager for, 293; campaigning methods, 292-5 *passim*, 302; charisma, 302; electoral battle with Chatterton, 298-9; experience, 290; political platform, 300; polling results, 306, 307, 313
Mackenzie, W. J. M., 1, 3-4, 6
McKinnon, James, 173, 176, 196n., 334; aids Niall and Tarosi, 207, 214
Madang: commercial decline in, 169; proposed roads to Highlands, 173, 175
Madang District, 162-3, 167-71 *passim*; cargo cults in, 170-1; cargoism as an election issue, 186; cash crops, 168; communication links, 169; economic development, 168; education, 169-70; European contact, 162, 168; geography of, 163; trade, 167-8; trade network, 198
Madang District people, 162, 163, 167, 169-70; attitudes toward

Europeans, 170; language differences, 167; socio-cultural systems, 167, 168, 198
Madang Open Electorate, 162, 171
Madang Regional Electorate, 7, 162 and n., 163, 171, 173-5; absentee voters, 194; campaign, 184; campaign failures, 194; candidates, 173-5; cargoism, 186; election issues, 173; election results, 192, 216; electoral alliances, 183, 184, 186-91, 196-7, 214, 333; electoral redistribution, 162, 163, 171; political education in, 171-2; voter turn-out, 194; Whitaker's police charge, effect of, 191, 199
Madang Workers' Association, 176, 197, 329
Maino, Charlie (Aukey), 288, 292; areas of support, 309; campaigning methods, 296, 303; political platform, 301; polling results, 308, 313
Mair, Lucy, 135
Maori Kiki, A., 34, 153
Mapai, George, 288, 292, 303-4, 317; polling results, 308, 313
Martin, Frank, 169, 325
Massim people, 93, 94
Matibri, Suguman, 169, 177, 178, 188
Matuakan, Philip, 225, 227-9 passim, 236, 269, 273; campaigning methods, 231; political platform, 234; polling results, 262, 265, 268, 274
Matupi people, 74, 76
Matupit Island, 65, 66, 71, 75, 76, 84
Mayer, H., 11
Meangarum, James, 32, 173, 328
Mek Gorop, 242
Mek Nugintz, 254-6, 259; campaigning methods, 257, 258, 260; electoral alliance, 260; polling results, 274
Meller, Norman, 24-5, 27-8
Members of House of Assembly: candidates' views on role, 102, 104, 227, 238-9, 326, 353-4; composition (first House) 23-4, (second House) 318-20; electors' dissatisfaction with, 73, 98-9, 206, 209, 227, 325, 345-6; electors' ignorance of role, 143; expectations from, 76, 152, 206, 344-6; failure to visit constituents, 342, 344, (Bougainville) 144-5,

(Gazelle Peninsula) 50, 61, 67, (Kabwum) 206, (Madang) 178, 185; future of, 160; Highland members' views on their role, 222-4; turn-over at 1968 election, 318-20
Middle Ramu Open Electorate, 171, 173; election results, 216; informal voting, 196 and n.; voter turn-out, 194
Middleton, John, 177, 178, 184, 185, 186, 198, 201; campaigning methods, 178, 185, 214; electoral alliances, 187; political platform, 178; polling results, 193, 217
Miklouho-Maclay, Baron, 168
Mills, C. Wright, 140
Milne Bay District, 91, 93-5 passim; cash crops, 94; commercial enterprise, 93, 94; European contact and settlement, 93-4; goldfields, 93; indigenous political leadership, 93; labour patterns, 94; local government councils, 91; missions, 93; subsistence economies, 93
Milne Bay District people, 91, 93; ethnic types and culture, 93; modes of life, 93
Milne Bay electorates, 7, 40, 91-131 passim; electoral redistribution, 91, 98
Milne Bay Local Government Council, 95, 96
Milne Bay Open Electorate, 91
Milne Bay Regional Electorate, 91, 117-27, 128; campaign, 122-7; candidates, 118-22, 128; difficulty in forecasting election result, 117-18; election results, 127, 130
Mining Ordinance, 141-2, 144, 156
Minister for Territories, 10, 38; appoints Public Service Commissioner, 32; by-passes House of Assembly, 28; on conditions of Australian aid, 18-19; on Papua New Guinea as seventh state of Australia, 31; on political parties, 30, 34, 337; on powers of Ministerial Members, 38
Ministerial Members, 27, 38-9, 76
Ministerial Membership, liability to candidates, 76, 78
Minj Open Electorate, 224
Mirau, Gaudi, 169
Misima Island, 108-10 passim, 113, 117, 121, 129
Missions, 13, 15, 357; Anglican (north-east coast) 168; Catholic

INDEX 391

(Bougainville) 133, 135, 141-2, 149, 157, 158-9, 327, (Central District) 282, 284, (New Britain) 55, 56, 85, (north-east coast) 168, 192-3, (Wewak) 31; conduct political education, 56, 329; London Missionary Society, 94, 98, 282, 284; Lutheran (north-east coast) 168, 204-5, 211, 327, (Western Highlands) 226, 236; Methodist (Bougainville) 133, 155, 157, (Kiriwina) 110, 327, (New Britain), 56; Milne Bay, 93; neutrality in elections, 85, 149, 151, 197, 236, 327; Papua Ekalesia (Central District) 282; role of, in elections, 133, 135, 148, 149, 155, 157-9, 197, 200, 204-5, 236, 317, 327, 340; Seventh Day Adventist (Bougainville) 133, 155, 159, (north-east coast) 168; spheres of influence, 85, 133; teachers' salaries, 75, 78n., 81; Yali and cargo movement, 180
Moral Rearmament Movement, 288
Morea, Sevese, 292, 309; areas of support, 310; campaigning methods, 297; member of Napro Party, 289; political platform, 301; polling results, 309, 313
Moresby Open Electorate, 32, 41, 272, 279-81, 301-2; campaigning methods, 301-2; candidates, 285-6; election issues, 299; election results, 305-6, 313; electors, 280, 281; electoral redistribution, 279; enrolment, 281n.; informal voting, 306; population, 280-1; voter turn-out, 305-6, 311; voting patterns, 306-7
Morobe District, 162-3, 167-71 passim; cargo cults, 170-1; economic development, 168; European contact, 162, 168; geography of, 163; trade, 167-8; trade network, 198
Morobe District people, 162, 163, 167; attitudes toward Europeans, 170; language differences, 167; socio-cultural systems, 167, 168, 198
Morobe Regional Electorate, 7, 162 and n., 202, 206; campaigning methods, 206-7; candidates, 206-7; economic development, 209; election issues, 208-9, 272; election results, 212, 214-15; electoral alliances, 214, 333; electoral re-

distribution, 162, 163, 171
Motu people, 41, 275, 276, 279, 280, 281-2, 287, 288, 293, 297, 302
Motu villages, 281, 282, 295, 303, 309, 310
Mount Hagen, 267
Mualat, William Tawanga, 58, 59, 351; polling results, 89
'Mud-slinging', 321; Wahgi Open, 243, 252
Mugap Baugum, 224, 238, 241, 242, 243, 246, 263, 266; attacks on, 243; campaigning methods, 248-50, 251, 252; drinking habits, 250; political platform, 224; polling results, 252, 253, 263, 274
Mul Local Government Council, 253, 255
Mul-Dei area, disputes in, 219
Mul-Dei Open Electorate, 219, 223, 252-60; campaigning methods, 257, 258-60; candidates, 254-9; election results, 274; electoral alliances, 257, 259; electoral redistribution, 252-3; hostilities between Mul and Dei, 252, 253-4; political platforms, 255

Nagovisi people, 132, 133, 137, 138, 151, 154, 157
Namasu Co-operative, 169
Nasioi people, 132, 133, 137, 139-47 passim, 152-4 passim, 159, 324; cargoist thinking, 145
National politics, 30, 35, 39, 67, 130, 300, 301, 332-48, 359
National Progress Party (Napro), 33, 303; candidates (Central Regional) 289, 294, (Hiri Open) 287; Osineru Dickson and the, 96; support for candidates, 338, 339
National unity, 75-6, 341-2, 359-60
Native Affairs, see District Administration
New Britain: description, 48-9; frontier for Tolai enterprise, 87
New Britain electorates, 48-90 passim; candidates, 55-72; election results, 89-90; informal voting, 83; voter turn-out, 81-3; voting patterns, 81-5
New Britain Special Electorate, 79
New Guinea Agriculture Reform Party, 31, 57-8, 60-1, 326, 336
New Guinea Planters' Association, 56
New Guinea Islands Special Electorate, 140

New Guinea Trust Territory, 2, 12; relations with Papua, 75-6, 208
New Guinea United National Party, 30, 225
Ngunts Gigma, 241
Nguu, Aisa, 287, 292, 303, 309; areas of support, 308, 309; campaigning methods, 294, 296, 298, 303; electoral alliance, 298; member of Pangu Pati, 287-8; political platform, 301, 303; polling results, 308, 313
Niall, H. L. R., 23, 169, 182, 205, 206, 207, 272, 318, 325, 333, 334, 338; campaigning methods, 207; electoral alliances, 205, 207, 214; polling results, 212
Nimagore, Joseph, 102n.; campaigning methods, 100-1; polling results, 130
Nombri, J. K., 32
Nopnop Tol, 237, 239-40, 250
North-east coast area: beachmen and bushmen, 167-8, 198, 203-4; culture contact, 168; description, 163; economic development, 168-9; education, 169-70; electoral redistribution, 162-3, 171, 214-15; languages, 167, 170; local government councils, 169; population, 163; trade network, 167-8, 170, 198-9, 204; traditional culture, 168
North-east coast electorates, 162-217 *passim*; campaign, 183-91; campaigning methods, 183-6; candidates, 173, 174, 185, 204-7; election issues, 186; election results, 191-202, 216-17; electoral alliances, 183-4, 186-7, 196-7; informal voting, 188-90, 193, 195-6, 196n.; local government councils, 197; members in first House of Assembly, 169; voter turn-out, 193, 194; voting determinants, 197-201; voting patterns, 191-201
Northern Regional Electorate, 37

Oala-Rarua, Oala, 31, 32, 34, 288-9, 291, 304, 309, 329, 332; avoids electoral promises, 304-5; campaigning methods, 292, 297; candidacy, reasons for, 291; criticised over National Party, 225; electoral education, 344; Motu candidate, 293-4; political platform, 301; polling results, 309, 313; public service, 288-9; sources of support, 304, 310-11; trade union leader, 289, 301, 311, 312, 329
Obara, George, 275n., 297, 303, 304
Open electorates, 5, 21-4, 625; belief that intended for indigenous candidates, 61, 78-9, 228, 304
Ovia, James T., 225, 273

Pacific Islands Regiment, 14, 63
Paliau Maloat, 25
Pangu Pati: 'anti-Administration', 271; associated with self-government and independence, 273, 300, 330, 337; attacked (by candidates) 102, 118, (by other expatriates) 225, 234, 271, 334, 337; candidates (Bougainville South) 145-6, 152, 153, 160, (Central District) 288, 289, 294, 297, 312, (East Sepik Regional) 325, (Kabwum Open) 204, (Madang District) 172-3, (Milne Bay District) 97, 103-5, 120-5 *passim*, 337, (Morobe Regional) 207, 209; electors' attitudes (East New Britain) 79, (Gazelle) 88, (Madang) 177, 337, (Milne Bay) 96, 125, 128; expels Oala-Rarua, 34; little organisation, 294, 339; misunderstood, 340-1; on economic development, 209; origins of, 32-4, 225; parliamentary wing, 32, 336; polling results, 311, 320, 337-8; Tolai leaders' association with, 57, 63, 88, 337
Papua, 2, 12, 91, 94; relations with New Guinea, 75-6, 341-2
Papua and New Guinea Act 1949-1968, 12, 20
Papua and New Guinea Workers' Association, 288-9
Papua New Guinea, 119; dependence on Australia, 102; description, 12-13; population, 2, 39; public revenues, 276; seventh state of Australia, 31-2, 177
Papuan candidates, 99, 100, 101, 127, 304, 312, 316; in Central District, 291, 312, 316, 320, 322; in Central Regional, 288, 289, 312; in Rai Coast Open, 179; reluctance to stand in Moresby Open, 285; villagers' resistance to strangers, 198, 295, 296, 298
Parliamentary Under-Secretaries, 27, 30, 32, 38, 78, 345
Parochial politics, 341
Patiliu, *see* ToPatiliu

INDEX 393

Patterson, Jack, 108-9, 110, 111, 112, 321, 328, 333; association with Cecil Abel, 117, 125, 128; with Taurega, 113, 126; campaigning methods, 112, 114-17; denominational support for, 117, 327; drinking habits, 115; personal traits, 115; political platform, 114, 115; polling results, 117, 131

Peruwa Kuri, 253, 254, 255, 256, 257; campaigning methods, 258-9; electoral alliances, 259-60; polling results, 263, 274

Pim Koropie, 254, 256, 257; campaigning methods, 258; polling results, 274

Pita, Bondai, 95; campaigning methods, 96-7; political platform, 97; polling results, 98, 130

Poe, John, 179, 190, 191, 193, 196, 198, 200, 201, 325; campaigning methods, 185; electoral alliances, 187; political platform, 179; polling results, 193, 216

Poio Iuri, 228

Polansky, E. A., 86

Police: actions in Gazelle Peninsula, 54; necessary on Bougainville, 141; *see also* Special Branch

Political change, 312, 356-60 *passim*; candidates' attitude to, 320

Political development, 341, 357-8, 359; begun on Gazelle Peninsula, 52; effect of European contact, 357; election of 1968, 322, 326, 349, 356; slowness of, 322

Political education, 104, 194, 197, 342; aim of program, 171, 350; as seen by elected members, 29; failure of official program, 41-2, 50, 56, 105, 172, 194, 342-4 *passim*, 353; for 1964 election, 41; for 1968 election, 42-5, 271; lack of, on Bougainville, 143 and n., 152; Madang electorates, 171-2; mission activity, 56; printed materials, 43-5; related to economic development policy, 271; sample leaflets, 371-5; *see also* Candidates, Local government councillors, Local government councils

Political institutions, 312-14 *passim*, 348, 349, 351, 355, 356; indigenes' understanding of, 320, 325; misunderstood by some electors, 342; modification of in New Guinea, 351, 355, 357-8, 359

Political leadership, 110, 129-30, 354, 359; *see also* 'Traditional' politics

Political parties: Administration attitudes to, 30, 34, 224-5, 349; associated with self-government and independence, 173, 224, 271, 273, 300, 330, 337, 339-40; Bougainville South, 145-6, 152, 153, 160; candidates, 346; Central District, 288, 289, 294, 297, 312; criticisms of, 88-9, 173, 225, 337; expatriate attacks on, 34-5, 118, 225, 271, 334, 337; expectations from, 57-8, 336-7; failure of, 326; Gazelle Peninsula, 57-8; hostility to, 96, 125, 128, 175, 177, 204, 224-5, 337-40; House of Assembly members in, 32, 336; Kabwum Open, 204; Madang District, 172-3; Milne Bay District, 97, 103-5, 120-5 *passim*, 337; Morobe Regional, 207, 209; motives for joining, 336; origins, 30-4; polling results, 311, 336-8; poorly organised, 34, 58, 96, 294, 326, 338-9; sign of political change, 359; Western Highlands, 224-5; *see also* All People's Party, Local government council party, National Progress Party (Napro), New Guinea Agriculture Reform Party, New Guinea United National Party, Pangu Pati, Territory Country Party, United (Christian) Democratic Party

Political resources, 315-32; candidates' political skills and attributes, 317-21; electors' values and attitudes, 321-6; group relationships, 315-16; issues and interests, 329-32; organisations and associations, 326-9

Population explosion, 169; *see also* Gazelle Peninsula

Port Moresby, 7, 25, 88, 222, 275; capital and administrative centre, 275, 276, 278; link with hinterland, 276, 285; political change in, 312, 314; population, 276, 280; 'squatter' settlements, 281; urbanisation in, 276; *see also* Konedobu, Moresby Open Electorate

Port Moresby Local Government Council, 287, 296, 302

Port Moresby people, 275, 276; attitude toward national politics, 278, 311-14; ethnic, social and religious

394 THE POLITICS OF DEPENDENCE

differences, 279; European contact, 278; indigenous economies, 275, 276; standard of living, 276, 278, 279; traditions, 275
Port Moresby Workers' Association, 31, 301, 329
Preferential voting, *see* Voting, preferential
Pre-selection of candidates: Esa'ala Open, 99-100; function of political parties, 57-8, 326, 336; Kabwum Open, 205; Milne Bay District, 121; Wahgi Open, 238-43; Western Highlands, 219-22
'Pressure Groups', *see* Associations, Local government councils, Missions, Political parties
Price, Albert, 31, 55-6, 58, 60-1, 86n., 87
Public service, 273, 330; Elliott Elijah's dissatisfaction with, 120; 'localisation', 29; salaries, 29, 32
Pung Nimp, 254-7 *passim*; campaigning methods, 258; electoral alliance, 260; polling results, 274

Rabaul: development of, 51; election meetings in, 69; stagnation of, 88
Rabaul Discussion Group, *see* Gazelle Discussion Group
Rabaul Open Electorate, 48, 53, 65, 85; campaign in, 70-2, 76-7; candidates, 58, 64-6, 82-3, 86, 87; comparison with 1964, 86-7; election results, 90; preferential voting, 83-4; voter turn-out, 81, 82-3
Rabaul Workers' Association, 66
Rabura, Allen, 287, 292, 303, 309; areas of support, 308; campaigning methods, 296; member of Napro Party, 287, 303; political platform, 300, 301; polling results, 308, 313
Racial issues, 324-5, 358-9; Bougainville, 138, 159; Milne Bay, 99, 127; North-east coast, 170; Western Highlands, 226, 235
Rai Coast, 169
Rai Coast Local Government Council, 179, 181, 185, 190, 193, 329
Rai Coast Open Electorate: (1964) 32, 162, 171, 203, (1968) 163, 171, 179, 182, 195; campaign failure, 194; candidates, 179-83; election results, 193, 216; influence of cargoism, 179-83; voter turn-out, 194 and n., 195
Raluana, 59, 62; land shortage, 82; low voter turn-out, 82
Raluana people, 60, 62
Ramu Open Electorate, 32
Ramu valley, 168-9, 200-1
Raniola Plantation dispute, 53, 54, 63, 70, 77-8, 80, 320
Rarupu, Eriko, 32, 297, 345
Rauke Gam, 204, 209, 210, 317; campaigning methods, 205; polling results, 209-10, 211, 212, 217; support by missions, 205, 211, 327
Reay, Marie, 5
Redistribution of electorates, *see* Distribution Committee, Electoral redistribution
Refugees, 119
Regional electorates, 5, 36-7, 152, 228; belief that intended for European candidates, 61, 78-9, 157-8, 228, 273; distinction from Open electorates not understood, 260
Returning Officers, 45-6
Rigo-Abau Open Electorate, 284; commercial activities, 285
Robinson, K. E., 4
Rossel Island, 91, 93, 109, 113
Rowley, C. D., 138
Rutledge, Noel, 227, 228, 230-3 *passim*, 235, 250, 333; campaigning methods, 232, 233; polling results, 262, 265, 268, 274

Saramuri Sinamaiba, 173, 176, 185, 196, 197; political platform, 176; polling results, 193, 197, 216
Schools, 231n.
Select Committee on Constitutional Development, 35-9, 57, 79, 182
Select Committee on Political Development, 21, 27, 36
Self-government, 225, 254, 334; associated with Australian departure, 273, 347; confusion with independence, 73-4; Chatterton's views on, 300; Epineri's initiative on, 75; Evennett's views on, 101-2; voters' views on, 173, 207, 271, 273, 330-1, 342, 347, 357
Seligman's Eastern Papuo-Melanesian, 93
Seminary of the Holy Spirit, Madang, 142, 144
Separatism, 341-2, 359-60
Sepik District, 31-2
Sepik people, labourers on Gazelle Peninsula, 54

INDEX 395

Settler politics, *see* Expatriates
Sio area, 162, 170, 202-3
Siwai Local Government Council, 146
Siwai people, 132, 133, 137, 138, 146-7, 152
Slaughter, Ron, 290, 291, 309, 311, 318; areas of support, 310-11; campaigning methods, 292, 297-8, 304; experience, 290; polling results, 309, 313
Somare, Michael, 325, 338
South Bougainville Open Electorate, *see* Bougainville South
South Pacific Post, 292, 299
Special Branch (of police), 30-1, 235, 271
Special electorates, 21, 36-7; in New Britain, 48, 50
Speeches, *see* Campaign speeches
Stoi Umut, 32, 169, 171, 204, 206, 213, 215, 325, 344, 351; cargoist activities, 206; charisma, 213; member of Pangu Pati, 204, 207, 338; no campaign, 206; polling results, 210-12; popularity declines, 209
Stuntz, John, 118, 121, 127, 129, 318, 334, 344; campaigning methods, 122-3; member of House of Assembly, 118; member of Legislative Council, 118; polling results, 129n., 130; views on political parties, 118
Sudest Island, 91, 93, 109, 113
Sumgilbar Local Government Council, 178, 185, 193, 328
Sumkar Open Electorate, 163, 177-9, 186, 196n.; candidates, 177-9; election results, 193, 216; population, 171; voter turn-out, 194
Swiss Evangelical Brotherhood, 249-50

Tabalu sub-clan (Trobriands), 116
Talasea Open Electorate, 48; election results, 90; informal voting in, 83
Talu Bor, 241
Tamberan, 182 and n., 183n., 189
Tamean, Bolton, 58, 59
Tammur, Oscar, 53, 55, 58, 60, 62, 63-4, 78, 82, 320, 334, 354, 360; campaigning methods, 70, 72, 73, 74, 87; first of new generation leaders on Gazelle, 86, 89; polling results, 90
Tarosi, Advent, 204, 205, 333, 334;

campaigning methods, 205; election alliances, 205, 207, 214; polling results, 210, 211, 212, 217; support by mission, 205
Taurega, Goweli, 107-8, 112, 115, 332, 347; campaigning methods, 112-14; drinking habits, 108, 113; opposition to Lepani Watson, 108, 113; political platform, 114; polling results, 131
Taylor, Andrew, 275n., 303
Teachers, distribution in Territory, 88n.
Tei Abal, 25-6, 221, 222, 223, 229, 273
Tei ritual exchange cycle, 269-70
Territory Country Party, 31, 153, 172
Timber rights (Tonolei), 142, 152
Titimur, Epineri, *see* Epineri Titimur
Tiut Turmarum, 58, 64, 65, 84
ToBaining, Vin, 33, 57, 58, 61, 62-3, 87, 88, 324; campaigning methods, 70; image as 'Establishment' man, 78, 324; Pangu Pati association, 33, 57, 63, 88, 337; polling results, 90
ToBunbun, Thomas, 33, 57, 58, 65-6, 76, 85, 88, 324, 325; campaigning methods, 69, 71, 87; failure to secure home base, 84; image as 'Establishment' man, 77; Pangu Pati association, 33, 57, 63, 88, 337; polling results, 90; unpopularity over council tax increases, 76-7
ToEnos, 62
Togop Siburia, 176, 177, 185, 197; political platform, 177; polling results, 193, 197, 216
ToKarai, Beniona, 58, 61-2
ToKau ToLogo, 58, 62, 82
ToKiala, Nason, 55, 59, 60
Tolai candidates: campaigning methods, 70-2; winners voice Tolai aspirations, 78
Tolai Cocoa Project, 52, 65
Tolai people, 325, 336, 345; anxiety about 1968 election, 54-5, 73-7, 89, 331; attitudes to local government councils, 49-50, 52, 81-2; educational advantages, 52, 56, 88n.; Epineri Titimur as spokesman, 66, 74-5; growing tensions, 87-9; lack of associational life, 56; land problems, 53-4, 77-8; long contact with outside cultures, 49, 51-2; new 'Westernised' class, 65,

86; reluctance to 'subsidise' Papua, 75-6, 88, 341-2; reticence about politics, 73; sense of group identity, 52; wealth, 49, 51-2, 75-6
ToLavutul, Lawrence, 58, 64, 83, 84
ToLiman, Matthias, 53, 54n., 55-61 *passim*, 63, 66, 82, 317, 334, 344, 351; campaigning methods, 67-8, 87; electors' criticisms of, 73; polling results, 89; reputation on Gazelle Peninsula, 77-8
ToLogo, ToKau, *see* ToKau ToLogo Toma, 61, 67
ToMarita, Stanley, 58, 59-60, 87
Tonolei dispute (Bougainville), 142, 152
ToPatiliu, Samson, 58, 65, 76, 84, 324; ambivalence about sharing Tolai wealth, 75-6; appeal to traditionalists, 87; campaigning methods, 71-2; image as 'Establishment' man, 77; polling results, 90
ToWalaka, Isimel, 58, 64-5
ToWartovo, 72
Trade unions, 301; influence on elections, 329
'Traditional' politics, 16-17, (north-east coast) 167, 203-4, (Western Highlands) 219; co-exist with introduced institutions, 358; decline of 'big man', 320; help to Paul Lapun, 152; influence on campaigning methods, 317, 321-2, 354-6, (Hiri Open) 302-3, (Kula Open) 116-17, (Western Highlands) 269-70; little influence on Madang results, 198; still strong in Central District, 314
Treating, 116-17, 185, 190, 252, 317
Trobriand Islands, 91, 98, 115; Kula Open, 109, 110, 113, 125; Milne Bay Regional, 125; people, 93, 94
Trusteeship Agreement, 12
Tumun Dubura, 224, 238, 240-1, 242, 245, 246, 263, 264, 266; campaigning methods, 247-9, 251, 252; drinking habits, 250; polling results, 252, 253, 263, 274

Under-Secretaries, *see* Parliamentary Under-Secretaries
United (Christian) Democratic Party, 31, 57, 148, 172, 225, 336
United Nations, 39, 234
United Nations Visiting Missions, 18, 66, 270-1, (1962) 27, 29, 139, (1965) 18-19, 25-6, 28, 29, 35, 41, (1968) 270-1

University of Papua and New Guinea, 10, 15, 107, 119, 170, 278, 289
Usino Local Government Council, 176

van der Veur, Paul W., 27
Voter turn-out, 246, 352; Bougainville electorates, 154, 156, 159; Central District, 305, 306, 309, 311; Duke of York Islands, 82n.; East and West New Britain Regional, 83; election of 1964, 23, 194; election of 1968, 347, 352, 353; expatriate, 335; Gazelle Peninsula, 81-2; Kabwum Open, 210-11; Milne Bay Electorates, 105; north-east coast, 193-5; Rabaul area, 83; Raluana census division, 82; Western Highlands, 267; women, 246, 306
Voters: absentee, 37, 194, 231, 311, 351-2; Chinese, 197; European, 197, 218, 307, 311, 335; motivation to vote, 194, 270, 347; Papuan, 307, 311, 312; views on independence and self-government, 347; women, 237, 246, 354, (turn-out) 246, 306; *see also* Electors
Voting, 344; abstention, 81, 153, 157, 194, 352, 355; aid of photographs, 105, 106, 306, 310, 311, 318, 352, 354; compulsory, 305, 352; secret ballot, 355; system, 22, 47, 270; *see also* 'Whisper' ballot
Voting, bloc, 269, 270, 295, 316, 317, 327, 328; decline since 1964, 84-5; denominational, *see* Denominational influence; for Advent Tarosi, 213; for Yali Singina, 198, 201
Voting determinants, 347-8; Bougainville, 155-9; Central District, 306-12; Milne Bay, 128-30; New Britain, 84-5; north-east coast, 197-201, 214-15; Western Highlands, 269-73
Voting, informal, 153, 156, 158, 195, 196, 309; Bougainville, 153-4, 156, 157, 159; Central District, 306, 309; correlation with literacy, 195, 352; election of 1964, 23, 188; New Britain, 83; north-east coast, 188-90, 193, 195-6, 196n.; Western Highlands, 261
Voting patterns: Bougainville, 159; Central Regional, 309-11; effect of electoral alliances (Bougainville)

158, (north-east coast) 196-7; Kabwum Open, 210-12; Hiri Open, 307-9; Mabuso Open, 192-3; Madang Regional, 191, 192; Moresby Open, 306-7; north-east coast, 186, 191-201; Rai Coast Open, 193; Sumkar Open, 193; Western Highlands, 262
Voting, preferential, 22, 105, 263, 264, 266, 310, 352; Bougainville experience, 158; Central District experience, 306, 310; confusion of, 226, 260-1; election of 1964, 226; Rabaul experience, 83-4; Western Highlands experience, 260, 263-6, 268-9
Voutas, Anthony C., 32, 38, 57, 182, 205, 206-7, 209, 213, 272, 325, 328, 330; campaigning methods, 205-7, 215; member of Pangu Pati, 207, 338; political platform, 207, 209; polling results, 212; suggestion for a local government council party, 57, 328
Vunamami Local Government Council, 62

Wabag Open Electorate, 229, 272-3
Wadau Marun, 177, 178, 185, 186, 196n.; campaigning methods, 185; influenced by Yali Singina, 179; polling results, 193, 216
Wahgi Open Electorate, 219, 224, 237-52, 273; campaigning methods, 243-52 *passim*; candidates, 221, 237-43 *passim*, (intimidation of) 243; challenge to unseat Kaibelt Diria, 241-2; council tax issue, 245-6, 251; electoral redistribution, 238, 247; election results, 253, 274; 'mud-slinging', 243-4, 252, 269, 354; voting patterns, 260-1
Waine, Paulus, 241
Wamell, Philip, 227, 228, 267, 269; campaigning methods, 231, 234, 236; mission assistance, 236; political platform, 234; polling results, 262, 264, 265, 268, 274
Wapurao, Nita, 227, 231, 236, 269; polling results, 262, 265, 268, 274
Warike Wema, 254-7 *passim*, 259; campaigning methods, 258; polling results, 263, 274
Waterhouse Memorial School, 64, 65, 86
Watson, Lepani, 98, 101, 107, 108, 115, 120, 122, 321, 325, 344; campaigning methods, 109-12, 113; election issues, 110-11, 330; electors' criticism, of, 98-9; gift-giving, 116; mission support for, 327; personal traits, 111; polling results, 117, 131; Under-Secretary for Trade and Industry, 107; Welfare Assistant, Department of Native Affairs, 107
Watts, John, 227, 228, 229, 249, 259, 269, 273, 326, 334; campaigning methods, 231, 232, 233, 235, 236; conservatism, 235; electoral alliance, 260; polling results, 262-8 *passim*, 274; views on economic development, 232
West Gazelle Special Electorate, 55, 60, 79
Western Highlands, 218; commercial activities, 218; economic development, 222; languages, 229, 232; local government councils, 219, 221
Western Highlands electorates, 218-74 *passim*; briefing session at Mt Hagen, 224-5, 339; campaigning methods, 230-6, 243-52, 257-60; candidates, 221-3, 225-30, (European *v.* indigenous) 226-7, 266, 267, 269, 271, 272, (views on electorates) 228, (discuss campaign prospects) 223; effect of traditional customs, 269; election analysis, 269-74; election issues, 223-4, 270-3; election results, 261-3, 265, 274; electoral alliances, 333; electoral redistribution, 226; expatriate political views, 272; political parties, 224-5; traditional politics, 269-70; voter turn-out, 267; voting patterns, 260-9
Western Highlands people: attitudes toward Europeans, 224; indigenous councils, 219; traditional hostilities, 219, 252, 253-4; tribal organisation, 219
Western Highlands Regional Electorate, 37, 218, 225, 228, 232; campaigning methods, 230-6; candidates, 226, 227, (European *v.* indigenous) 230-6, 273; communication difficulties, 230; election issues, 229, 232, 234, 235; election results, 262, 265-7, 274; European candidates' language handicap, 233; preferential voting, 263-6, 268-9; voting patterns, 260, 261

Westminster system, 349-50, 356
'Whisper' ballot, 22, 83n., 195 and n., 196, 306, 352
Whitaker, Edward J., 173, 175, 185, 186, 187, 190, 191, 192, 196, 197, 198; alliance with Yali Singina, 187-91 *passim*; campaigning methods, 175, 185; electoral alliances, 187; gift-giving, 185, 190; police charge, 191, 199; political platform, 175; polling results, 192, 216
White, Osmar, 135
Wilkinson, Jack, 103
Wilkinson, Jo, 102n.; campaigning methods, 103; polling results, 103, 130; woman candidate, 102
Wolfers, E. P., 11, 160, 194n., 320
Women voters, 246; turn-out, 246, 306
World Bank Report, 1964, 18, 29

Yali Singina, 170, 171, 178, 179-83, 193, 196, 197, 198, 199-200, 201, 215, 324, 342, 347, 355; campaigning methods, 185; candidate, Rai Coast Open, 179; cargoist political platform, 181-3, 188-91 *passim*; charisma, 179; electoral alliances, 187, (with Whitaker) 187-91 *passim*; informal votes for, 195, 196; leadership in cargo cult, 179-83; polling results, 193, 216; popularity, 186, 199-200
'Yali vote', 188-90, 195-201 *passim*
Yangalyo, Leme, 222, 227, 269, 354
Young, Dennis, 97, 118-19, 127, 128; campaigning methods, 123-4; member Milne Bay Local Government Council, 127; polling results, 130; views on political parties, 119; work for West Irianese refugees, 119

Designed by Richard Farmer
Text set in 9 pt Times Roman, 2 pt leaded
and printed on 85gsm Burnie MF
by Hogbin, Poole (Printers) Pty Ltd, Sydney

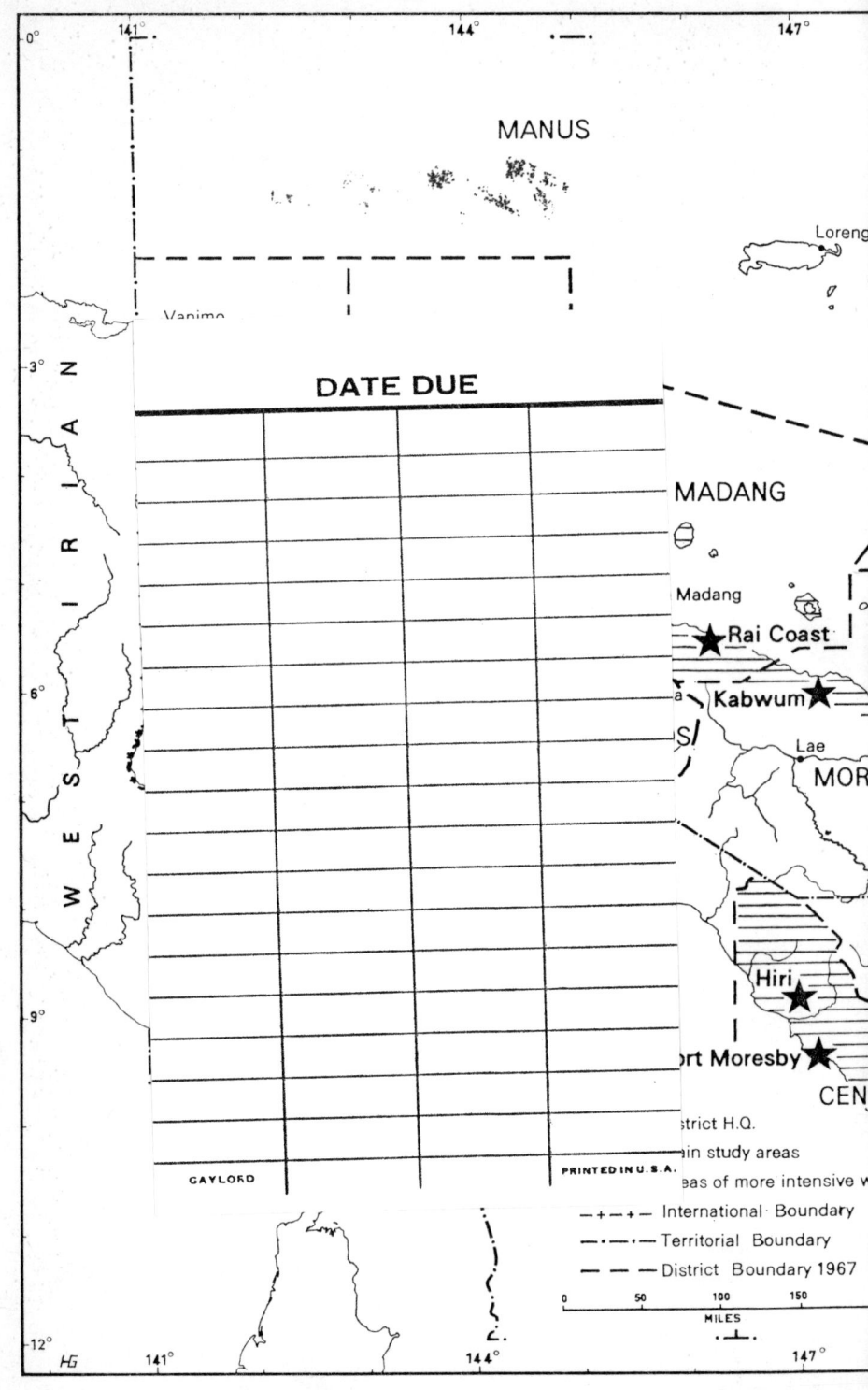